Study Guide

Principles of Macroeconomics

FIFTH EDITION

John B. Taylor

Stanford University

David H. Papell

University of Houston

Wm. Stewart Mounts, Jr.

Mercer University

John Solow

University of Iowa

Houghton Mifflin Company BOSTON NEW YORK

Publisher: *George Hoffman*
Senior Sponsoring Editor: *Ann West*
Development Editor: *Jessica Carlisle*
Editorial Assistant: *Alison McGonagle*
Editorial Assistant: *Brett Pasinella*
Manufacturing Coordinator: *Patricia Cadet*
Marketing Manager: *Mike Schenk*
Marketing Associate: *Kathleen Mellon*

Printed in the U.S.A.

ISBN13: 978-0-618-62323-5
ISBN10: 0-618-62323-X

123456789 – POO – 10 09 08 07 06

Contents

Preface

The chapters of this study guide follow those of John B. Taylor's *Principles of Macroeconomics, Fifth Edition*. Why use this study guide? The best reason is to help you learn the course content more efficiently. For each chapter of the book, this study guide highlights the major concepts, defines the most important terms, shows you how to work problems, and provides you numerous opportunities to test your understanding of the material.

What You'll Find Here

Each chapter begins with a *Chapter Overview*, which introduces the major topics covered in the text. This is followed by a *Chapter Review*, which defines and explains the key terms and concepts. Next comes a section called *Zeroing In*, which provides a more in-depth look at several of the chapter's most important topics. In this section, figures are often used to illustrate concepts.

The focus of the study guide chapter changes with the next section, called *Active Review*, which consists of a total of 40 to 50 fill-in, true/false, and short answer questions. You will find answers for all review questions, including explanations for the true/false and short answer questions, at the end of each chapter.

An important part of studying economics is learning how to solve problems, and the study guide provides you with extensive assistance in this area. The section called *Working it Out* begins by explaining how to use the techniques covered in the chapter. These may be analytical, graphical, numerical, or algebraic. Next comes several *Worked Problems*, for which complete answers are provided. These are followed by *Practice Problems*, for which the answers can be found at the end of each chapter.

Each chapter ends with a twenty-question, multiple choice *Chapter Test*. This test covers material from throughout the chapter and contains several graph-based and table-based questions. The answers to the *Chapter Test* can also be found at the end of the chapter.

This study guide also contains a multiple choice *Sample Test* at the end of each part—covering material from all the chapters in that part. There are four of these *Sample Tests* (and answers) in this volume.

How to Make the Best Use of this Book

Every student studies differently, and we do not presume to tell you how to study most effectively. Nevertheless, here are some suggestions. First, read the chapter in the text, but don't worry too much about understanding everything. Second, read the *Chapter Overview*, *Chapter Review*, and *Zeroing In* sections of the study guide. When you find a concept that you do not understand, look it up in the text. Third, answer the *Active Review* questions. Write down your answers and provide explanations for the true/false questions. When you miss a question, refer back to the text or study guide. Fourth, learn how to solve the problems in the *Working it Out* section. Study the *Worked Problems*, and answer the *Practice Problems*. Fifth, carefully read the chapters in the text to make sure that you understand it completely. Sixth, take the *Chapter Test* as if you were taking an exam. If you miss any questions, don't just find the correct answer at the end of the chapter, but go back to the appropriate sections of the text and study guide to make sure that you learn the material. Finally, when you reach the end of a part, take the *Sample Test*, again under exam conditions. You will be well prepared for the midterm and final. Good luck!

PART 1

Introduction to Economics

Scarcity exists because people's wants exceed their resources (or means). This forces them to make choices concerning the wants they will fill and the way they will use their resources. Economists investigate this behavior in order to explain facts and observations about the economy. Economists establish patterns by carefully organizing data and presenting this information in tables and graphs. They develop models of behavior and test them with data that have been collected. Chapters 1 through 4 address the fundamental questions of economics and the basics of "economic thinking."

Within a market economy, basic economic questions are answered by buyers (demand) and sellers (supply) interacting in markets and guided by prices. Demand and supply curves are graphical representations of the actions of individuals. Changes in demand and supply (seen as shifts in the demand and supply curves) introduce surpluses or shortages into the market and thereby change the market price. An actual market price moves toward the equilibrium price. In addition, the price elasticity of demand and supply quantifies the responsiveness of market participants to changes in prices. While governments can affect market processes by instituting price ceilings and price floors, free competition between buyers and sellers promotes economic efficiency, maximizes social welfare, and minimizes the deadweight loss.

CHAPTER 1

The Central Idea

CHAPTER OVERVIEW

Economic interactions involve scarcity and choice. Time and income are limited, and people choose among alternatives every day. In this chapter, we study the choices people make when faced with a scarcity of resources and the economic interactions among people when they make their choices. We begin by looking at scarcity, choice, and interaction for individuals. We study consumer and producer decisions, learn about the gains from trade, and see how the same principles that guide interactions between individuals can be used to study interactions between countries. We then look at scarcity and choice for the economy as a whole, and introduce the production possibilities curve. We conclude by studying two alternative economic systems, the market economy and the command economy, and focusing on the role of prices.

CHAPTER REVIEW

1. **Scarcity** is a situation in which people's wants exceed their resources. Scarcity is a fact of life; wants are unlimited, but resources are not. Because of scarcity, people must make a **choice**—to forgo, or give up, one thing in favor of another. **Economics** is the study of how people deal with scarcity. They make *purposeful choices* with *scarce resources* and *interact* with other people when they make their choices.

2. **Economic interaction** between people occurs when they trade or exchange goods and services with each other. Economic interactions occur in **markets**, arrangements where buyers and sellers can interact with each other, and within *organizations* such as families, firms, universities, and governments.

3. The **opportunity cost** of a choice is the value of the forgone alternative that was not chosen. In the examples below, the opportunity cost of football tickets is dinner, and the opportunity cost of studying economics is not doing as well in the physics test.

4. Economic interactions often involve **gains from trade**. Suppose that you can afford season tickets for either football or basketball, but not both, and that you would prefer attending half of the football games and half of the basketball games to attending all of either. If you could find someone with similar preferences to trade tickets with, you would both be better off. Gains from trade can occur in markets, such as a ticket agency, or in organizations, such as a family or a college dormitory.

5. Individual producers also face scarcity and choice; you cannot produce unlimited goods with limited time and resources. Gains from trade allow people to **specialize** in what they are good at. If a guitarist and a drummer form a rock group, **division of labor** allows each to concentrate on playing one instrument.

6. One person or group of people has a **comparative advantage** in producing one good relative to another good if they can produce with comparatively less time, effort, or resources than another person can produce that good. In the above example, production can be increased if the guitarist plays the guitar and the drummer plays the drums, rather than both trying to play both instruments. (There is one subtle aspect of the idea of comparative advantage: Even if the guitarist

plays both the guitar and the drums better than the drummer, the guitarist will be able to play one instrument, presumably the guitar, and the drummer will be able to play the other instrument, presumably the drums, *comparatively* better than the other musician.)

7. **International trade** occurs when individuals who live in different countries trade with each other. There are gains from international trade for the same reasons that there are gains from trade within a country: By trading, people can either better satisfy their preferences for goods or better utilize their comparative advantage.

8. **Production possibilities** represent the alternative choices of goods that the economy can produce. Consider an economy that produces two goods, steel and food. If it produces more of one, it must produce less of the other. The opportunity cost of producing more steel is the value of the forgone food. The idea of **increasing opportunity costs** is that as steel production rises, the value of the forgone food increases. The rate of decline in food production increases as we produce more steel.

ZEROING IN

1. The **production possibilities curve** is a graphical representation of the idea of production possibilities. We will see how to construct the production possibilities curve, what causes a movement along the curve, and what causes the curve to shift.

   a. Figure 1.1 depicts the production possibilities curve for steel and food. Steel is on the vertical axis, and food is on the horizontal axis. Both are measured in tons. If the economy devotes all of its resources to either steel or food production, it can produce the maximum amount of one and none of the other. The production possibilities curve slopes downward and is bowed out from the origin. The curve is bowed out because the opportunity cost of producing food increases as more food is produced. As more resources are shifted from steel to food production, each additional ton of food means a greater loss of steel produced.

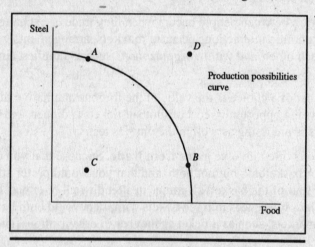

Figure 1.1

   b. The production possibilities curve shows three situations. Points on the curve are *efficient* because they represent the maximum amount that can be produced with available resources. Production of food can be raised only by lowering production of steel, such as by moving from point *A* to point *B*. Points inside the production possibilities curve, such as point *C*, are *inefficient*. Using the same resources, the economy could produce more steel, more food, or both. Points outside the production possibilities curve, such as point *D*, are *impossible*. The economy does not have the resources to produce those quantities of steel and food.

c.   It is important to understand the distinction between movements along a curve and shifts of the curve. A change in the production of one of the variables on the axes causes a movement along the production possibilities curve. For example, an increase in steel production is a movement from point *B* to point *A* in Figure 1.1. Economic growth causes an outward shift in the production possibilities curve. When there is economic growth, more resources are available, and more goods and services can be produced. The effects of economic growth are illustrated in Figure 1.2. The production possibilities curve shifts out from the curve labeled "Original" to the curve labeled "Growth."

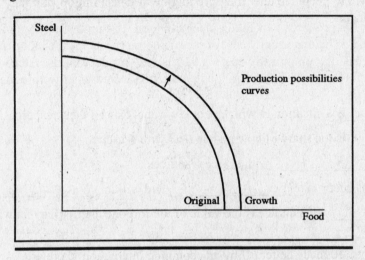

Figure 1.2

2.   Every economy focuses on three essential questions: *what* are the goods and services to be produced, *how* are these goods and services to be produced, and *for whom* are the goods and services to be produced? In a **market economy**, these decisions are made by consumers, firms, governments, and other organizations interacting in markets. In a **command economy**, these decisions are made through a central plan by those who control the government. A command economy is also called a centrally planned economy. One of the most important economic events of recent years has been the transition by the countries of Eastern Europe, the former Soviet Union, and China from command economies to market economies. China has been the most successful of the transitioning economies, with rapid economic growth in recent years.

3.   There are a number of important characteristics that distinguish market economies from command economies, and we consider some of these differences.

a.   **Freely determined prices**, set by individuals and firms, are an essential characteristic of a market economy. In a command economy, most prices are set by the government. **Property rights**, the legal authority to keep or sell property, provide **incentives** for invention and specialization and are another key element of a market economy. Competitive markets and freedom to trade at home and abroad also characterize market, but not command, economies.

b.   The role of government in a market economy is a subject of much debate among economists. It is generally agreed that the government should provide for defense, help establish property rights, and keep the overall price level stable, but modern governments do much more. **Market failure** is a situation in which the market economy does not provide good enough answers to the three questions posed above—what, how, and for whom—and in which there is a role for government in improving the market outcome. However, when the government, even in the case of market failure, does worse than the market would have done if left on its own, there is **government failure**.

c.   Many of the economic interactions in market economies take place within organizations, such as firms, households, and universities, instead of in markets. One important reason why organizations are created is that they reduce market *transaction costs*, the costs of buying and selling. These costs include the cost of finding a buyer or a seller and the cost of reaching agreement on a price.

d.   Prices play three important roles in a market economy. They serve as *signals* about what should be produced and consumed when there are changes in tastes or technology, they provide *incentives* to people to alter their production or consumption, and they affect the *distribution of* income.

ACTIVE REVIEW

Fill-In Questions

1.   _____ is a situation in which people's wants exceed their resources.

2.   _____ is the study of how people deal with scarcity.

3.   People make _____ with scarce resources.

4.   Economic interactions occur in _____ and within _____.

5.   The _____ of a choice is the value of the forgone alternative that was not chosen.

6.   When both participants are made better off by an economic interaction, there are _____.

7.   Specialization in production results in _____.

8.   One person or group of people has a(n) _____ in producing one good relative to another good when they can produce that good with comparatively less time, effort, or resources than another person can produce that good.

9.   _____ occurs when individuals who live in different countries trade with each other.

10.   _____ represent the alternative choices of goods that the economy can produce.

11.   The graphical depiction of production possibilities is called the _____.

12.   _____ causes an outward shift in the production possibilities curve.

13.   The two major types of economies are _____ economies and _____ economies.

14.   _____ are the legal authority to keep or sell property.

15.   In a market economy, prices serve as _____, provide _____, and affect the _____.

True-False Questions

1.   T   F   Economics is the study of how people can get anything they want.

2.   T   F   Scarcity is a characteristic of a command economy, but not of a market economy.

3.   T   F   An opportunity cost occurs every time there is a choice.

4.   T   F   Gains from trade occur only in markets.

5. T F   If Canada produces two goods with less resources than the United States, there can be no comparative advantage in those two goods.

6. T F   Trade takes place both within and between countries.

7. T F   Production possibilities represent the best choice of goods for the economy to produce.

8. T F   The production possibilities curve slopes downward.

9. T F   The production possibilities curve is linear.

10. T F   Points on the production possibilities curve are efficient.

11. T F   Points inside the production possibilities curve are inefficient.

12. T F   A market economy is also called a centrally planned economy.

13. T F   In recent years, Eastern Europe, the former Soviet Union, and China have moved away from central planning.

14. T F   Freely determined prices and property rights are characteristics of centrally planned economies.

15. T F   One reason why organizations are created is that they eliminate market failure.

16. T F   Applications to MBA programs rise during recessions. (Hint: See Economics in Action – Teaching Jobs and Graduate School Applications – Two Sides of the Same Coin.)

Short-Answer Questions

1. What must people do because of scarcity?

2. When do economic interactions between people occur?

3. Where do economic interactions occur?

4. What are opportunity costs?

5. What is comparative advantage?

6. Why are there gains from international trade?

7. Why are there increasing opportunity costs?

8. Why is the production possibilities curve bowed out?

9. What are the three situations defined by the production possibilities curve?

10. Why are points outside the production possibilities curve characterized as impossible?

11. How does economic growth affect the production possibilities curve?

12. What are the three essential questions faced by every economy?

13. Name four characteristics of market, but not command, economies.

14. What is the difference between market failure and government failure?

15. What are the three roles of prices in a market economy?

16. How has the Internet created new opportunities for gains from trade? (Hint: See Economics in Action—Gains from Trade on the Internet.)

17. Describe how opportunities for gains from trade can be created on the radio, a much older technology than the Internet. (Hint: See Reading the News About—Gains From Trade on the Radio.)

WORKING IT OUT

1. We have studied the idea of production possibilities and the production possibilities curve by using graphs. We will first consider the same two concepts using numerical examples and then see how we can combine graphs and numbers.

    a. Suppose that the production possibilities for steel and food are as follows:

Choice	Steel	Food
A	0	100
B	25	95
C	50	85
D	75	50
E	100	0

    Both steel and food are measured in tons. Increasing opportunity costs are illustrated by moving down the table. As we move from row to row, steel production increases by the same amount, 25 tons. The decline in food production, in contrast, gets larger, going from 5 tons between the first and second rows to 50 tons between the fourth and fifth rows. Each extra 25 tons of steel requires a loss of more and more food.

    b. The production possibilities curve for these numbers is depicted in Figure 1.3, with steel on the vertical axis and food on the horizontal axis. Both axes are measured in tons. The production possibilities curve is constructed by plotting pairs of points, labeled points *A* through *E*, for steel and food, and then connecting the dots. Since we do not know exactly how much food can be produced in between the 25-ton intervals for steel, we use straight lines to connect the dots.

Figure 1.3

2. We have learned that economic growth shifts out the production possibilities curve. We will illustrate this with a numerical example. Suppose that economic growth allows us to produce more goods, so that the new production possibilities for steel and food are as follows:

Choice	Steel	Food
A	0	125
B	25	120
C	50	110
D	75	90
E	100	50
F	125	0

The new production possibilities curve, labeled "Growth," is drawn with the original production possibilities curve in Figure 1.4. The new curve is farther away from the origin than the original curve at all points, indicating that more can be produced. For example, food production of 90 tons and steel production of 75 tons was impossible with the original production possibilities curve. After growth, that point is on the new production possibilities curve, and is therefore efficient.

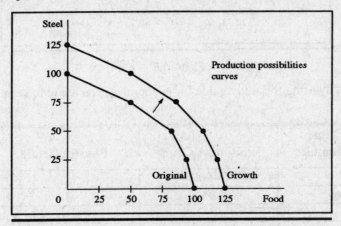

Figure 1.4

Worked Problems

1. Suppose that you must allocate your time between studying economics and studying physics. The percentage of time you spend studying economics and the grades you will get on the two exams are as follows:

Percent of Time Studying Economics	Economics Grade	Physics Grade
100	80	0
80	75	30
60	65	50
40	50	65
20	30	75
0	0	80

Draw the production possibilities curve. How does this example illustrate increasing opportunity costs?

Answer

The production possibilities curve is drawn in Figure 1.5. The example illustrates increasing opportunity costs because, as you move down the table or the curve, each additional point on your physics grade comes at a cost of more and more points on your economics grade.

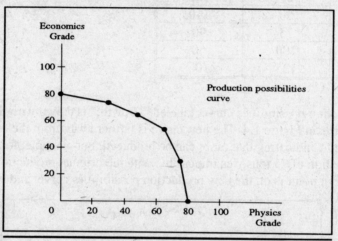

Figure 1.5

2.   Now suppose that, by using the study guide for economics, you are able to improve your choices as follows:

Percent of Time Studying Economics	Economics Grade	Physics Grade
100	100	0
80	95	30
60	85	50
40	70	65
20	40	75
0	0	80

a.   Draw the new production possibilities curve, and describe how the new curve is related to the old curve.

b.   Characterize an economics grade of 70 and a physics grade of 65 under the original and the new production possibilities curves.

Answer

a. The new production possibilities curve, labeled "Study Guide," and the original curve are depicted in Figure 1.6. Using this study guide raises your economics grade at each percent of time, above zero, spent studying economics, but it does not help your physics grade. Although the new curve is above the original curve, it tilts out rather than shifting out.

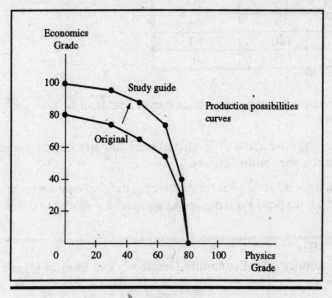

Figure 1.6

b. An economics grade of 70 and a physics grade of 65 were impossible to attain with the original production possibilities curve, but this combination is now efficient.

PRACTICE PROBLEMS

1. Suppose that the production possibilities for steel and food are as follows:

Choice	Steel	Food
A	0	100
B	25	90
C	50	70
D	75	40
E	100	0

Both steel and food are measured in tons. Draw the production possibilities curve. How does this example illustrate increasing opportunity costs?

2. Suppose that economic growth allows us to produce more goods, so that the new production possibilities for steel and food are as follows:

Choice	Steel	Food
A	0	120
B	25	115
C	50	105
D	75	90
E	100	60
F	125	0

a. Draw the new production possibilities curve, and describe how the new curve is related to the old curve.

b. Characterize the production of 75 tons of steel and 40 tons of food under the original and the new production possibilities curves.

3. Suppose that you must allocate your time between studying economics and studying physics. The percentage of time you spend studying economics and the grades you will get on the two exams are as follows:

Percent of Time Studying Economics	Economics Grade	Physics Grade
100	90	0
80	88	40
60	80	70
40	70	80
20	40	88
0	0	90

Draw the production possibilities curve. How does this example illustrate increasing opportunity costs?

4. Now suppose that, by using the study guide for economics, you are able to improve your choices as follows:

Percent of Time Studying Economics	Economics Grade	Physics Grade
100	100	0
80	96	40
60	90	70
40	80	80
20	50	88
0	0	90

a. Draw the new production possibilities curve, and describe how the new curve is related to the old curve.

b. Characterize an economics grade of 80 and a physics grade of 70 under the original and the new production possibilities curves.

CHAPTER TEST

1. A situation in which people's wants exceed their resources is called

    a. abundance.
    b. choice.
    c. scarcity.
    d. allocation.

2. Economists study how

    a. people make purposeful choices with scarce resources.
    b. people make purposeful choices with abundant resources.
    c. people make random choices with scarce resources.
    d. people make random choices with abundant resources.

3. An arrangement by which economic exchanges between people takes place is called

    a. a choice.
    b. a market.
    c. scarcity.
    d. gains from trade.

4. Which of the following represents the alternative choices of goods that the economy can produce?

    a. Opportunity costs
    b. Economic interactions
    c. Budget constraints
    d. Production possibilities

5. The value of the alternative that was not chosen is called the

    a. marginal cost of the choice.
    b. average cost of the choice.
    c. opportunity cost of the choice.
    d. gain from the choice.

6. Exchange of goods and services between people or firms in different nations is called

    a. intranational trade.
    b. international trade.
    c. gains from trade.
    d. comparative advantage.

7. When one person or group of people can produce one good relative to another good with comparatively less time, effort, or resources than another person can produce that good, this is called

    a.   comparative advantage.
    b.   specialization.
    c.   opportunity cost.
    d.   division of labor.

8. The production possibilities curve slopes

    a.   downward and is bowed out from the origin.
    b.   upward and is bowed out from the origin.
    c.   downward and is bowed in toward the origin.
    d.   upward and is bowed in toward the origin.

9. Points outside the production possibilities curve are

    a.   efficient.
    b.   inefficient.
    c.   impossible.
    d.   possible.

10. Economic growth causes a(n)

    a.   inward shift in the production possibilities curve.
    b.   outward shift in the production possibilities curve.
    c.   upward movement on the production possibilities curve.
    d.   downward movement on the production possibilities curve.

11. Which of the following is *not* one of the essential questions that an economy focuses on?

    a.   What are the goods and services to be produced?
    b.   When are the goods and services to be produced?
    c.   How are the goods and services to be produced?
    d.   For whom are the goods and services to be produced?

12. Which of the following is *not* one of the characteristics of a market economy?

    a.   Freely determined prices
    b.   Property rights
    c.   Competitive markets
    d.   Centrally planned production

13. The costs of buying and selling are called

    a.   transaction costs.
    b.   market costs.
    c.   opportunity costs.
    d.   incentive costs.

14. Which of the following is *not* one of the important roles of prices in a market economy?

    a.   They serve as signals.
    b.   They provide incentives.
    c.   They form preferences.
    d.   They affect the distribution of income.

Use the following table for questions 15 and 16.

Suppose that the production possibilities for guns and flowers are as follows:

Choice	Guns	Flowers
A	0	100
B	25	90
C	50	70
D	75	40
E	100	0

15. If all of the economy's resources were devoted to the production of flowers, the amount of guns that would be produced is

    a.   100.
    b.   75.
    c.   0.
    d.   50.

16. If the economy is currently producing 50 guns and 60 flowers, then

    a.   it is at an efficient level of production.
    b.   an efficient level of production can be achieved by producing 20 more flowers.
    c.   an efficient level of production can be achieved by producing less flowers and more guns.
    d.   an efficient level of production can be achieved by producing 10 more flowers.

Use Figure 1.7 for questions 17, 18, and 19.

Figure 1.7

17. If the economy devotes all of its resources to steel production, it will be producing at point

    a.   *A*.
    b.   *B*.
    c.   *H*.
    d.   G.

18.   Point *F* in Figure 1.7 represents
   a.   an efficient production level.
   b.   an inefficient production level.
   c.   an impossible production level.
   d.   a possible production level.

19.   If the economy is currently producing at point *E*, then
   a.   it is utilizing its resources efficiently.
   b.   it is utilizing its resources inefficiently.
   c.   it is on its production possibilities curve.
   d.   it is beyond its production possibilities curve.

Use Figure 1.8 for question 20.

Figure 1.8

20.   An economy experiences economic growth when it moves
   a.   from point *A* to point *B*.
   b.   from point *A* to point *C*.
   c.   from point *D* to point *C*.
   d.   from point D to point B.

ANSWERS TO THE REVIEW QUESTIONS

Fill-In Questions

1.   Scarcity

2.   Economics

3.   purposeful choices

4.   markets; organizations

5.   opportunity cost

6.   gains from trade

7.   division of labor

8.   comparative advantage

9.   International trade

10. Production possibilities

11. production possibilities curve

12. Economic growth

13. market, command

14. Property rights

15. signals; incentives; distribution of income

True-False Questions

1.   **False**. Economics is the study of how people deal with scarcity.

2.   **False**. Because wants are unlimited but resources are not, scarcity is a characteristic of all economies.

3.   **True**. The opportunity cost of a choice is the value of the forgone alternative that was not chosen.

4.   **False**. Gains from trade can also occur within organizations.

5.   **False**. The United States will still produce one of the goods with relatively less resources than Canada, leading to a comparative advantage in that good.

6.   **True**. International trade occurs when individuals who live in different countries trade with each other.

7.   **False**. Production possibilities represent the alternative choices of goods that the economy can produce.

8.   **True**. As more of one good is produced, less of the other can be produced.

9.   **False**. The production possibilities curve is bowed out.

10. **True**. They represent the maximum amount that can be produced with available resources.

11. **True**. Using the same resources, the economy could produce more of both goods.

12. **False**. A command economy is also called a centrally planned economy.

13. **True**. They are making the transition from command economies to market economies.

14. **False**. Freely determined prices and property rights are characteristics of market, not centrally planned, economies.

15. **False**. One reason why organizations are created is to reduce market transaction costs.

16. **True**. When unemployment rises during recessions, it becomes more difficult for students graduating from college to find jobs, and the available jobs often pay lower salaries. More students apply to MBA programs because the opportunity cost of getting an MBA, two years of foregone wages, has decreased.

Short-Answer Questions

1.   Because of scarcity, people must make choices to forgo one thing in favor of another.

2. Economic interactions between people occur when they trade or exchange goods or services with each other.

3. Economic interactions occur in markets and within organizations.

4. The opportunity cost of a choice is the value of the forgone alternative that was not chosen.

5. One person or group of people has a comparative advantage in producing one good relative to another good if they can produce that good with comparatively less time, effort, or resources than another person can produce that good.

6. There are gains from international trade because by trading, people can either better satisfy their preferences for goods or better utilize their comparative advantage.

7. There are increasing opportunity costs because as the production of one good increases, the value of the forgone good increases.

8. The production possibilities curve is bowed out because of increasing opportunity costs.

9. Points on the production possibility curve are efficient, those inside the curve are inefficient, and those outside the curve are impossible.

10. They are called impossible because the economy does not have the resources to produce outside the production possibilities curve.

11. Economic growth shifts out the production possibilities curve.

12. Every economy must determine what are the goods and services to be produced, how are these goods and services to be produced, and for whom are the goods and services to be produced.

13. Freely determined prices, property rights, competitive markets, and freedom to trade at home and abroad characterize market, but not command, economies.

14. Market failure is a situation in which there is a role for the government in improving the market outcome. Government failure occurs when the government, even in the case of market failure, does worse than the market would have done if left on its own.

15. Prices serve as signals about what should be produced and consumed when there are changes in tastes or technology, provide incentives to people to alter their production or consumption, and affect the distribution of income.

16. Internet auction sites like eBay create opportunities for gains from trade by providing a simple and easy-to-use way to allow millions of sellers to offer their goods for sale and millions of buyers a way to make bids on the sale items.

17. Tradio (pronounced TRADE-ee-o) is an on-the-air swap meet that creates opportunities for gains from trade among listeners. It has flourished in small-town radio stations for decades.

SOLUTIONS TO THE PRACTICE PROBLEMS

1. The production possibilities curve is drawn in Figure 1.9. The example illustrates increasing opportunity costs because, as you move down the table or up the curve, each additional 25 tons of steel comes at a higher cost in food production.

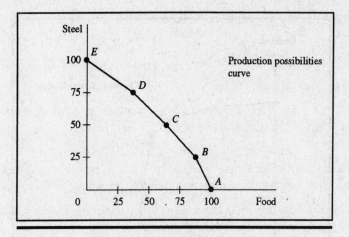

Figure 1.9

2. a. The new production possibilities curve, labeled "Growth," is drawn with the original production possibilities curve in Figure 1.10. The new curve shifts out from the old curve.

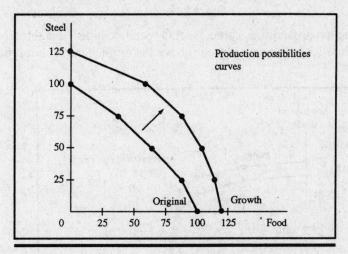

Figure 1.10

   b. Production of 75 tons of steel and 40 tons of food was efficient under the original production possibilities curve. It is inefficient under the new curve.

3. The production possibilities curve is drawn in Figure 1.11. Each additional point on your physics grade comes at a cost of more and more points on your economics grade.

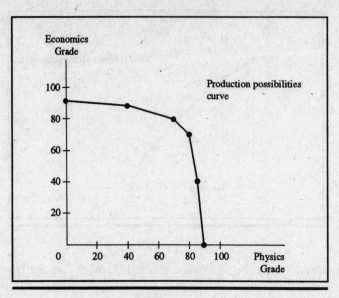

Figure 1.11

4. a. The new production possibilities curve, labeled "Study Guide," and the original curve are depicted in Figure 1.12. The new curve is above the original curve, but it tilts out rather than shifting out.

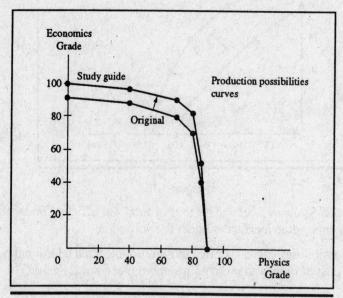

Figure 1.12

b. An economics grade of 80 and a physics grade of 70 were efficient with the original production possibilities curve, but this combination is now inefficient.

ANSWERS TO THE CHAPTER TEST

1. c

2. a

3. b

4. d

5.   c
6.   b
7.   a
8.   a
9.   c
10. b
11. b
12. d
13. a
14. c
15. c
16. d
17. a
18. c
19. b
20. b

CHAPTER 2

Observing and Explaining the Economy

CHAPTER OVERVIEW

What is economics? If you are tempted to answer "everything," you are at least partly correct. Economics is a way of thinking. It entails *describing* economic events, *explaining* why they occur, *predicting* whether they might occur in the future, and *recommending* appropriate courses of action to policymakers. When you listen to your professor in class, read the text, or work through the study guide, you should be learning to actively analyze economic events. This chapter introduces some of the tools of analysis. We consider the timely issue of health-care spending and see what economists attempt to explain and how to interpret what they find. We look at economic models and learn how economists abstract reality in order to make it manageable. We see how economics is used for public policy and consider some of its limitations. Finally, we introduce some tools that economists use in their analysis. Using both graphs and algebra, we begin to learn how to document and quantify observations about the economy.

CHAPTER REVIEW

1.   Economists divide people into broad categories. *Households* are either individuals or groups of individuals who share the same living quarters. *Organizations,* which include firms and governments, are producers of goods and services. *Firms* are private organizations that produce goods and services. *Governments* also produce goods and services, such as national defense and education. **A circular flow diagram** shows how funds flow through the economy from households to firms and back again.

2.   A *market* is an arrangement through which exchanges of goods or services between people take place. Households supply their *labor* to the firms that employ them. The resources used by firms to produce goods and services are called *capital.*

3.   An **economic model** is an explanation of how the economy or a part of the economy works. Economic models, like models in other sciences, are always simplifications of reality. Economic models can be described with words, with numbers, with graphs, or with algebra, and you will use all four as you work through the text and study guide.

4.   An **economic variable** is any economic measure that can vary over a range of values. *Correlation* means that two variables move together, either in the same direction or in opposite directions. There is a positive correlation, and the two variables are **positively related**, if the two variables move in the same direction: One increases when the other increases. There is a negative correlation, and the two variables are **negatively related**, if the two variables move in opposite directions: One decreases when the other increases. *Causation* means that the movements in one variable bring about, or cause, the movements in another variable. Correlation does not imply causation. Just because two variables move together does not mean that the movements of one caused the movements of the other.

5.   The assumption of ***ceteris paribus***, which means "all other things equal," is often used by economists for prediction. The idea of *ceteris paribus* is easiest to explain through an example. Suppose that you wanted to predict the effect of cold weather on football attendance. In making your prediction, you would want to hold other things, such as the team's won-lost record, equal.

6. Keeping other things equal is not easy in economics. In many sciences, such as physics, researchers perform **controlled experiments** to determine whether one event causes another. In economics, as in astronomy, controlled experiments are rare. If you want to study the causes of the Great Depression of the 1930s, you cannot ask the government to go back and change policy. In **experimental economics**, a new and growing area of economics, researchers have begun to conduct economic experiments in laboratory settings.

7. The two main branches of economics are microeconomics and macroeconomics. **Microeconomics** studies the behavior of individual firms, households, and markets. Questions such as how much milk consumption would fall if the price of milk rises or how much a college education increases an individual's lifetime earnings are part of microeconomics. **Macroeconomics** focuses on the whole national, or even world, economy. Questions such as what were the effects of lowering inflation in the early 1980s in the United States or what are the prospects for economic reform in the former Soviet Union are part of macroeconomics.

8. There are two basic types of economic systems: **capitalism**, an economic system based on a market economy in which capital is individually owned and production and employment decisions are decentralized, and **socialism**, an economic system in which the government owns and controls all the capital and makes decisions about prices and quantities as part of a central plan. In modern market economies, the government plays a large role, and such economies are sometimes called **mixed economies**.

9. Economics is an important part of public policy making. **Positive economics** describes or explains what happens in the economy. **Normative economics** makes recommendations about what the government should do. For example, interest rates in the United States were increased in the spring and summer of 1994. Positive economics describes the effects of the higher interest rates and explains why interest rates were raised. Normative economics is concerned with recommending whether they should be raised further. The work of the **Council of Economic Advisers**, which gives policy advice to the president, is an example of normative economics.

ZEROING IN

1. Health-care reform has been a major economic and political issue since the early 1990s. Health care provides a good introduction to thinking about economics.

    a. Two facts about health-care spending stand out. First, health-care spending grew more rapidly than the rest of the U.S. economy in the early-to-mid 1990s, slowed down relative to the rest of the economy in the late 1990s, and again grew more rapidly than the rest of the economy in early 2000s. Second, the price of health care has increased faster than most other prices. It is the task of economics to quantify, document, and explain these observations.

    b. Let's look at the first observation, that health-care spending has grown more rapidly than the rest of the U.S. economy. In order to evaluate this assertion, we need to measure both health-care spending and the economy as a whole. **Gross domestic product (GDP)** is the most comprehensive measure of the size of an economy. GDP for the United States is the total value of all goods and services made in the United States during a specified period of time, usually one year. In 2004, GDP for the United States was $11,735 billion.

    c. We can measure health-care spending the same way we measure GDP, by adding up what we spend on all categories of health care. That number was $1,392 billion in 2004. Health care is the largest industry in America, about three times as large as the entire automobile industry.

    d. Health-care spending as a *share* of GDP (in percentage terms) can be calculated by dividing health-care spending by GDP and multiplying by 100:

$$\text{Health-care spending as a share of GDP} = \frac{\text{Health-care spending}}{\text{GDP}} \times 100$$

In 2004, health-care spending as a share of GDP was $(1,392/11,735) \times 100 = 11.9$ percent. [If we did not multiply by 100, the share would have been .119 (out of 1) instead of 11.9 (out of 100). While we will usually represent shares in percentage terms, you should understand that the two numbers represent the same thing].

e. Now let's turn to prices. The health-care price is a measure of the price of all the items included in the measure of health-care spending. The relative price of health care can be calculated by dividing the health-care price by the average price of all goods and services:

$$\text{Relative price of health care} = \frac{\text{Health-care price}}{\text{Average price}}$$

f. Health-care spending and GDP for all years from 1990 to 2004 are reported in the text. Although both health-care spending and GDP have been rising, health-care spending has been increasing more quickly. The share of health-care spending as a percent of GDP has therefore been rising. The relative price of health care for the same years is also reported in the text. The relative price of health care has increased since 1990 because the price of health care has risen more rapidly than the average price level.

ACTIVE REVIEW

Fill-In Questions

1. _____ are individuals or groups of individuals who share the same living quarters.

2. Private organizations that produce goods and services are called _____.

3. A(n) _____ is an arrangement through which exchanges of goods or services between people take place.

4. Two factors of production are _____ and _____.

5. A(n) _____ is an explanation of how the economy or a part of the economy works.

6. Two variables are _____ if they move in the same direction.

7. The assumption of _____ means "all other things equal."

8. _____ is the branch of economics that studies the behavior of individual firms, households, and markets.

9. _____ is the branch of economics that focuses on the whole economy.

10. _____ economics is economic analysis that explains what happens in the economy.

11. _____ economics is economic analysis that makes recommendations about economic policy.

12. The most comprehensive measure of the size of an economy is _____.

13. The _____ is the price of a particular good compared to the average price level.

14. An _____ is any economic measure that can vary over a range of values.

15. The _____ gives policy advice to the president.

True-False Questions

1.   T   F   Governments produce goods and services.

2.   T   F   Money and capital are called factors of production.

3.   T   F   It is desirable to make economic models as realistic as possible.

4.   T   F   If two economic variables have a positive correlation, one must cause the other.

5.   T   F   The question of by how much a college education increases an individual's lifetime earnings is part of microeconomics.

6.   T   F   The question of what were the effects of lowering inflation in the early 1980s in the United States is part of macroeconomics.

7.   T   F   Gross domestic product (GDP) is measured for a specified time period.

8.   T   F   Health-care spending is over 10 percent of GDP in the United States.

9.   T   F   In the United States, we spend more for automobiles than for health care.

10. T   F   Health-care spending as a share of GDP has been rising during the last 15 years.

11. T   F   The relative price of health care has increased since 1990.

12. T   F   In experimental economics, researchers conduct economic experiments in uncontrolled environments.

13. T   F   Normative economics explains why interest rates were raised in 1994.

14. T   F   The two basic types of economic systems are microeconomics and macroeconomics.

15. T   F   A circular flow diagram shows how funds flow through the economy from households to the government.

16. T   F   It is possible for discrimination to exist even if men and women are being paid the same wage for equal work. (Hint: See Economics in Action—Science or Persuasion?)

Short-Answer Questions

1.   What is a market?

2.   What is the difference between labor and capital?

3.   What is the difference between correlation and causation?

4.   What does it mean for two variables to be negatively correlated?

5.   What is the assumption of *ceteris paribus*?

6.   What is experimental economics?

7.   In the context of public policymaking, what is the difference between positive and normative economics?

8.   What are two important facts about health-care spending during the last 15 years?

9.   How do economists calculate health-care spending as a share of GDP?

10. What is the average price level?

11. What is the difference between inflation and the inflation rate?

12. How do economists calculate the relative price of health care?

13. What is a circular flow diagram?

14. Define the four categories in which economists divide people.

15. How do economists study the economy?

WORKING IT OUT

1. We have studied how to calculate health-care spending as a share of GDP and how to compute the relative price of health care. These techniques are applicable to any category of spending. Let's consider housing spending for a fictional economy, starting in the year 2000.

    a. Suppose you are given the following data on GDP and housing spending:

Year	GDP	Housing Spending
2000	1,000	50
2010	2,000	20
2020	4,000	280
2030	8,000	640

    GDP and housing spending are in billions of dollars. You can calculate housing spending as a share of GDP (in percentage terms) by dividing housing spending by GDP and multiplying by 100.

Year	Housing Spending/GDP	Housing-Spending Share
2000	0.05	5 percent
2010	0.06	6 percent
2020	0.07	7 percent
2030	0.08	8 percent

    Housing spending as a share of GDP has increased from 5 percent to 8 percent over this 30 period.

    b. Now suppose you are given the following data for the same time period on the average price level and the price of housing:

Year	Average Price	Housing Price
2000	1.00	0.80
2010	1.10	0.99
2020	1.21	1.21
2030	1.33	1.46

You can calculate the relative price of housing by dividing the price of housing by the average price level.

Year	Relative Price of Housing
2000	0.80
2010	0.90
2020	1.00
2030	1.10

The relative price of housing has increased over this period.

2.   We can also use graphs to understand the relationship between housing spending as a share of GDP and the relative price of housing in the fictional economy described above.

a.   The movements in housing spending as a share of GDP and the relative price of housing can be shown by using time-series plots. In the first panel of Figure 2.1, the housing-spending share is on the vertical axis and time (the year) is on the horizontal axis. The curve is upward-sloping, indicating that housing spending as a share of GDP has increased over this period. The second panel of Figure 2.1 depicts the relative price of housing on the vertical axis and the year on the horizontal axis. This curve is also upward-sloping, indicating that the relative price of housing has also increased over this period.

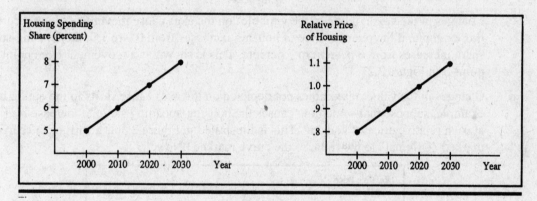

Figure 2.1

b. The relationship between the housing-spending share and the relative price of housing can be illustrated by using a scatter plot. In Figure 2.2, the relative price of housing is on the vertical axis and the housing-spending share is on the horizontal axis. Each dot represents a different year, and the curve, which has a positive slope, is drawn by connecting the dots. The housing-spending share and the relative price of housing are positively related; one increases when the other increases.

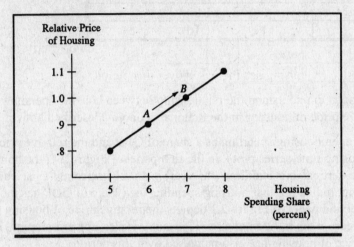

Figure 2.2

c. Changes in the value of one of the variables on the axes cause movement along a curve. In this example, if the relative price of housing increases from 0.9 to 1.0, the housing-spending share increases from 6 percent to 7 percent. This is shown as a movement from point *A* to point *B* in Figure 2.2.

d. Changes in the value of variables not depicted on the axes cause shifts in the curve. In this example, suppose that something causes the housing-spending share to increase by 1 percent at each relative price of housing. This is illustrated in Figure 2.3 as a shift of the curve marked "Original" to the right, to the curve marked "New."

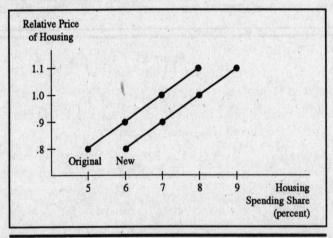

Figure 2.3

Worked Problems

1. Consider the following data for a fictional economy, starting in the year 2000:

Year	GDP	Food Spending	Average Price	Food Price
2000	1,000	100	1.00	1.00
2010	2,000	180	1.20	1.32
2020	4,000	320	1.40	1.68
2030	8,000	560	1.60	2.08

GDP and food spending are in billions of dollars.

a. Calculate food spending as a share of GDP (in percentage terms) and the relative price of food.

b. What has happened to the food-spending share and the relative price of food over this period?

Answer

a. Food spending as a share of GDP equals food spending divided by GDP multiplied by 100. The relative price of food equals the price of food divided by the average price level.

Year	Food-Spending Share	Relative Price of Food
2000	10 percent	1.00
2010	9 percent	1.10
2020	8 percent	1.20
2030	7 percent	1.30

b. The food-spending share has decreased, and the relative price of food has increased during this period.

2. Using the data for the economy in Worked Problem 1:

a. Draw a scatter plot to illustrate the relationship between food spending as a share of GDP and the relative price of food. Are the two variables positively or negatively related?

b. Suppose that the relative price of food rises from 1.1 to 1.2. Is this a movement along the curve or a shift of the curve? Illustrate your answer.

c. Suppose that something causes the food-spending share to decrease by 1 percent at each relative price of food. Is this a movement along the curve or a shift of the curve? Illustrate your answer.

Answer

a.   The scatter plot, with the relative price of food on the vertical axis and the food-spending share on the horizontal axis, is shown in Figure 2.4. The curve is downward-sloping, indicating that the two variables are negatively related.

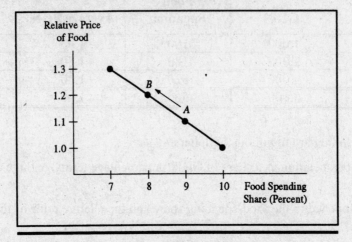

Figure 2.4

b.   The increase in the relative price of food is a movement along the curve; it is depicted by a movement from point A to point B in Figure 2.4. The food-spending share falls from 9 percent to 8 percent.

c.   The decrease in the food-spending share by 1 percent at each relative price of food is a shift of the curve; it is depicted in Figure 2.5 by a shift of the curve marked "Original" to the left, to the curve marked "New."

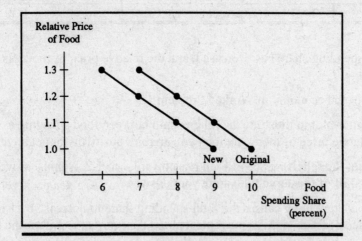

Figure 2.5

PRACTICE PROBLEMS

1. Consider the following data for a fictional economy, starting in the year 2000:

Year	GDP	Automobile Spending	Average Price	Automobile Price
2000	1,000	30	1.00	1.00
2010	2,000	70	1.20	1.10
2020	4,000	160	1.44	1.21
2030	8,000	360	1.73	1.33

GDP and automobile spending are in billions of dollars.

a. Calculate automobile spending as a share of GDP (in percentage terms) and the relative price of automobiles.

b. What has happened to the automobile-spending share and the relative price of automobiles over this period?

2. Consider the following data for a fictional economy, starting in the year 2000:

Year	GDP	Clothing Spending	Average Price	Clothing Price
2000	1,000	30	1.00	0.900
2010	2,000	70	1.10	1.045
2020	4,000	160	1.20	1.200
2030	8,000	360	1.30	1.365

GDP and clothing spending are in billions of dollars.

a. Calculate clothing spending as a share of GDP (in percentage terms) and the relative price of clothing.

b. What has happened to the clothing-spending share and the relative price of clothing over this period?

3. Using the data for the economy in Practice Problem 1:

a. Draw a scatter plot to illustrate the relationship between automobile spending as a share of GDP and the relative price of automobiles. Are the two variables positively or negatively related?

b. Suppose the relative price of automobiles falls from 0.92 to 0.84. Is this a movement along the curve or a shift of the curve? Illustrate your answer.

4. Using the data for the economy in Practice Problem 2:

a. Draw a scatter plot to illustrate the relationship between clothing spending as a share of GDP and the relative price of clothing. Are the two variables positively or negatively related?

b. Suppose that something causes the clothing-spending share to increase by 0.5 percent at each relative price of clothing. Is this a movement along the curve or a shift of the curve? Illustrate your answer.

CHAPTER TEST

1. Individuals or groups of individuals who share the same living quarters are called

    a. firms.
    b. households.
    c. governments.
    d. groups.

2. Private organizations that produce goods and services are called

    a. firms.
    b. households.
    c. governments.
    d. groups.

3. An arrangement through which exchanges of goods or services between people take place is called a(n)

    a. firm.
    b. industry.
    c. market.
    d. economic model.

4. When the movements in one variable bring about the movements in another variable, this is called

    a. causation.
    b. correlation.
    c. relationship.
    d. connection.

5. Two variables have a positive correlation if

    a. they move in opposite directions.
    b. they move in the same direction.
    c. one decreases when the other increases.
    d. one increases when the other decreases.

6. An economic model

    a. is any economic measure that can vary over a range of values.
    b. shows how funds flow through the economy from households to firms and back again.
    c. is an explanation of how the economy or a part of the economy works.
    d. is an arrangement through which exchanges of goods or services between people take place.

7. The assumption of "all other things equal" is called

    a. a market.
    b. a circular flow diagram.
    c. an economic variable.
    d. *ceteris paribus*.

8. Modern market economies in which the government plays a large role are called

    a. political economies.
    b. mixed economies.
    c. positive economies.
    d. normative economies.

9. Macroeconomics focuses on

    a. the whole national economy.
    b. the behavior of individual firms.
    c. the behavior of households.
    d. markets.

10. Which of the following is *most* likely to be studied by a microeconomist?

    a. Inflation of the general price level
    b. Unemployment in the economy
    c. Employment of labor in furniture production
    d. The growth rate of aggregate output

11. The work of the Council of Economic Advisers is an example of

    a. positive economics.
    b. negative economics.
    c. experimental economics.
    d. normative economics.

12. What was the relation between health-care spending and GDP in the early 2000s?

    a. Both health-care spending and GDP were rising, but GDP had been increasing more quickly.
    b. Both health-care spending and GDP were rising, but health-care spending had been increasing more quickly.
    c. Both health-care spending and GDP were falling, but GDP had been decreasing more quickly.
    d. Both health-care spending and GDP were falling, but health-care spending had been decreasing more quickly.

13. Positive economics

    a. describes or explains what happens in the economy.
    b. makes recommendations about what the government should do.
    c. studies the behavior of individual firms, households, and markets.
    d. focuses on the whole economy.

14. If a curve has a positive slope, then

    a. the two variables are negatively related.
    b. the two variables are positively related.
    c. one variable increases when the other decreases.
    d. the curve slopes down from left to right.

15. Health-care spending as a share of GDP is calculated by

    a. multiplying GDP by health-care spending.
    b. dividing GDP by health-care spending.
    c. multiplying health-care spending by GDP.
    d. dividing health-care spending by GDP.

16. The relative price of health care is calculated by

    a. multiplying the health-care price by the average price of all goods and services.
    b. multiplying the average price of all goods and services by the health-care price.
    c. dividing the health-care price by the average price of all goods and services.
    d. dividing the average price of all goods and services by the health-care price.

Use the following table for questions 17, 18, and 19.

Year	GDP	Food Spending	Average Price	Food Price
2000	2,000	120	1.00	1.00
2010	4,000	200	1.20	1.44
2020	8,000	340	1.40	1.70
2030	16,000	640	1.60	2.10

GDP and food spending are in billions of dollars.

17. What is food spending as a share of GDP (in percentage terms) in the year 2010?
    a. 3 percent
    b. 6 percent
    c. 10 percent
    d. 5 percent

18. What is food spending as a share of GDP (in percentage terms) in the year 2030?
    a. 4 percent
    b. 5 percent
    c. 10 percent
    d. 8 percent

19. What is the relative price of food in the year 2010?
    a. 1.00
    b. 1.10
    c. 1.20
    d. 1.30

Use Figure 2.6 for question 20.

Figure 2.6

20. Movement from point A to point B is a(n)
    a. upward movement along the curve.
    b. downward movement along the curve.
    c. upward shift of the curve.
    d. downward shift of the curve.

ANSWERS TO THE REVIEW QUESTIONS

Fill-In Questions

1. Households

2. firms

3. market

4. labor, capital

5. economic model

6. positively related

7. ceteris paribus

8. Microeconomics

9. Macroeconomics

10. Positive

11. Normative

12. gross domestic product

13. relative price

14. economic variable

15. Council of Economic Advisers

True-False Questions

1. **True**. They produce goods and services such as national defense and education.

2. **False**. Labor and capital are called factors of production.

3. **False**. Economic models are always simplifications of reality.

4. **False**. Correlation does not imply causation.

5. **False**. Microeconomics studies the behavior of individual firms, households, and markets.

6. **True**. Macroeconomics focuses on the whole national, or even world, economy.

7. **True**. GDP is usually specified for one year.

8. **True**. Health-care spending was 11.9 percent of the U.S. GDP in 2004.

9. **False**. Health-care spending is three times as large as spending on automobiles.

10. **True**. Although health-care spending and GDP have both been rising, health-care spending has been increasing more quickly than GDP.

11. **True**. The price of health care has risen more rapidly than the average price level.

12. **False**. In experimental economics, researchers conduct economic experiments in controlled laboratory settings.

13. **False**. Positive economics describes the effects of higher interest rates and explains why they were raised.

14. **False**. There are two basis types of economic systems: capitalism and socialism.

15. **False**. A circular flow diagram shows how funds flow through the economy from households to firms and back again.

16. **True**. In a recent case, the court ruled that a grocery store chain discriminated against female workers because they were regularly placed in jobs that paid less than jobs given to male coworkers with similar education and experience, even though there was little difference in the wages of male and female workers within each type of job.

Short-Answer Questions

1. A market is an arrangement through which exchange of goods and services between people takes place.

2. Households supply their labor to the firms that employ them. The resources used by firms to produce goods and services are called capital.

3. Correlation means that two variables move together, either in the same direction or in opposite directions. Causation means that the movements in one variable bring about, or cause, the movements in another variable.

4. When two variables are negatively correlated, it means they move in opposite directions.

5. The *ceteris paribus* assumption is that, when making a prediction of the effect of one variable on another, all other variables are unchanged.

6. Experimental economics is a new and growing branch of economics in which researchers conduct economic experiments in laboratory settings.

7. In the context of public policymaking, positive economics describes or explains what the government does. Normative economics makes recommendations about what the government should do.

8. Health-care spending has grown more rapidly than the rest of the U.S. economy, and the price of health care has increased more than most other prices.

9. Health-care spending as a share of GDP can be calculated by dividing health-care spending by GDP and multiplying by 100.

10. The average price level is a measure of the average price of all the goods and services in GDP.

11. Inflation is the general increase in prices over time. The inflation rate is the percentage increase in the average price level from one year to the next.

12. The relative price of health care is calculated by dividing the price of health care by the average price level.

13. A circular flow diagram shows how funds flow through the economy from households to firms and back again.

14. The four categories by which economists divide people are households, organizations, firms, and governments.

15. Economists study the economy by describing economic events, explaining why they occur, predicting whether they might occur in the future, and recommending appropriate courses of action to policymakers.

SOLUTIONS TO THE PRACTICE PROBLEMS

1. a. The automobile-spending share and the relative price of automobiles are as follows:

Year	Automobile-Spending Share	Relative Price of Automobiles
2000	3.0 percent	1.00
2010	3.5 percent	0.92
2020	4.0 percent	0.84
2030	4.5 percent	0.77

    b. The automobile-spending share has increased, and the relative price of automobiles has decreased over this period.

2. a. The clothing-spending share and the relative price of clothing are as follows:

Year	Clothing-Spending Share	Relative Price of Clothing
2000	3.0 percent	0.90
2010	3.5 percent	0.95
2020	4.0 percent	1.00
2030	4.5 percent	1.05

    b. The clothing-spending share and the relative price of clothing have both increased during this period.

3. a. The scatter plot is drawn in Figure 2.7. The curve is downward-sloping, indicating that the two variables are negatively related.

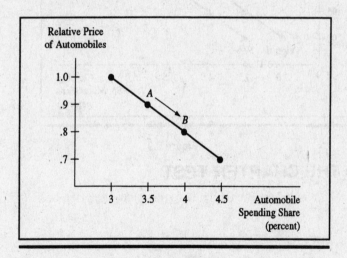

Figure 2.7

    b. This is a movement along the curve; it is depicted by a movement from point *A* to point *B* in Figure 2.7.

4. a. The scatter plot is drawn in Figure 2.8. The curve is upward-sloping, indicating that the two variables are positively related.

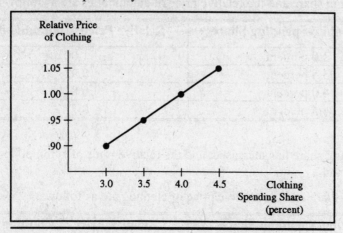

Figure 2.8

b. This is a shift of the curve; it is depicted in Figure 2.9 by a shift of the curve marked "Original" to the right, to the curve marked "New."

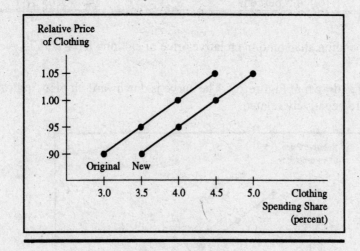

Figure 2.9

ANSWERS TO THE CHAPTER TEST

1. b
2. a
3. c
4. a
5. b
6. c
7. d
8. b
9. a

10. c
11. d
12. b
13. a
14. b
15. d
16. c
17. d
18. a
19. c
20. b

APPENDIX TO CHAPTER 2

Reading, Understanding, and Creating Graphs

OVERVIEW

Graphs and diagrams are used extensively in economics. They are useful both for uncovering correlations in economic variables and for understanding economic models.

REVIEW

1.

    a.   In a **Cartesian coordinate system**, pairs of observations on variables can be represented in a plane by designating one axis for one variable and the other axis for the other variable. Each point on the plane corresponds to a pair of observations. In economics, the axes are usually designated the vertical axis and the horizontal axis.

    b.   A **time-series graph** plots a series—several values of the variable—over time. Figure 2A.1 plots two variables, called x and y, over time. The value of the variable is depicted on the vertical axis, and time is on the horizontal axis. More than one variable can be plotted on the same graph. If the scales of measurement of the variables are very different, a **dual scale** can be used.

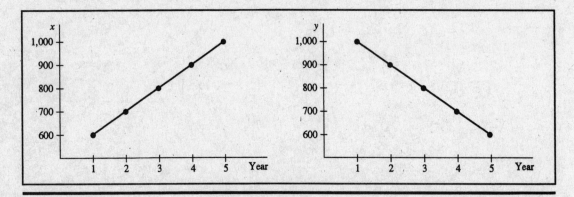

Figure 2A.1

    c.   Two variables can also be depicted with a **scatter plot**, where the vertical axis is used for one variable and the horizontal axis is used for the other variable. Figure 2A.2 shows a scatter plot for the variables x and y, with x on the horizontal axis and y on the vertical axis. Connecting the dots in the scatter plot creates a curve. If the curve is a straight line, as in Figure 2A.2, it is called *linear*. Economic relationships do not have to be linear.

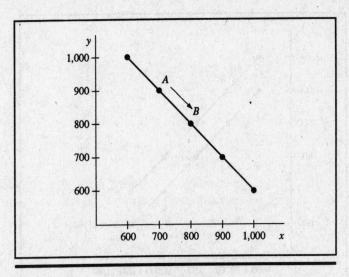

Figure 2A.2

d. The **slope** of the curve is the change in the variable on the vertical axis divided by the change in the variable on the horizontal axis. If the curve slopes up from left to right, it has a **positive slope** and the two variables are positively related. If the curve slopes down from left to right, it has a **negative slope** and the two variables are negatively related. In Figure 2A.2 the slope of the curve is negative because the curve slopes down from left to right and is constant along the curve because the curve is linear. Because y decreases by 100 for every increase of x by 100, the slope is $-100/100 = -1$.

e. When the value of one of the variables on the two axes changes, it causes a **movement along the curve**. For example, if x rises from 700 to 800 in Figure 2A.2, y falls from 900 to 800. This is a movement along the curve, and is shown by a movement from point A to point B. But suppose that the relationship between the variables x and y is affected by the value of a third variable, z. In Figure 2A.3, a change in the value of z causes a **shift of the curve**. We will consider movements along and shifts of curves many times in this course. It is important for you to understand that changes in the values of variables that are depicted on the axes cause movements along a curve, whereas changes in the values of other variables cause shifts of the curve.

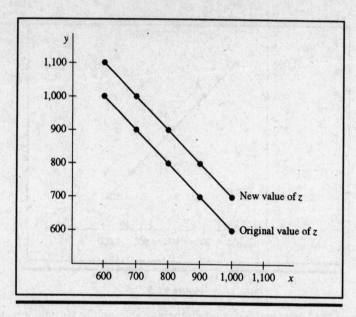

Figure 2A.3

ACTIVE REVIEW

Fill-In Questions

1. In a(n) _____, pairs of observations on variables can be represented in a plane by designating one axis for one variable and the other axis for the other variable.

2. A(n) _____ plots a series over time.

3. In a(n) _____, the vertical axis is used for one variable and the horizontal axis is used for the other variable.

True-False Questions

1. T   F   In a time-series graph, the value of the variable is depicted on the horizontal axis, and time is on the vertical axis.

2. T   F   If the curve depicting two variables in a scatter plot is linear, the two variables are negatively related.

3. T   F   When the value of one of the variables on the two axes changes, it causes a shift of the curve.

Short-Answer Questions

1. When is a dual scale used?

2. What is the relation between the slope of the curve in a scatter plot and the correlation between the variables on the axes?

3. What types of changes cause movements along a curve, and what types cause shifts of the curve?

ANSWERS TO THE REVIEW QUESTIONS

Fill-In Questions

1. Cartesian coordinate system

2. time-series graph

3. scatter plot

True-False Questions

1. **False**. The value of the variable is on the vertical axis, and time is on the horizontal axis.

2. **False**. Variables depicted by a linear relationship can be either positively or negatively related.

3. **False**. Changes in the value of one of the variables on the two axes cause a movement along the curve, not a shift of the curve.

Short-Answer Questions

1. A dual scale can be used when more than one variable is plotted on the same graph and the scales of measurement of the variables are very different.

2. The two variables are positively related if the slope is positive and negatively related if the slope is negative.

3. Changes in the values of variables that are depicted on the axes cause movements along a curve, whereas changes in the values of other variables cause shifts of the curve.

CHAPTER 3

The Supply and Demand Model

CHAPTER OVERVIEW

If people are left to choose for themselves what to consume and produce, what will society consume and produce? In this chapter, you will be introduced to the most important tool that economists have developed to answer this question. This is the market model of supply and demand. It starts with a description of buyers' behavior and a description of sellers' behavior and shows how their choices respond to changes in the economic environment. We will learn that neither buyers alone nor sellers alone, but both together, determine how much will be bought and sold and what the selling price will be. We will also see that when buyers and sellers respond to changes in the economic environment, the quantity bought and sold and the price are likely to change too. In this way, a price change signals to consumers *and* suppliers that something important has happened in the economy. This provides them with an incentive to make an adjustment to their new circumstances. Finally, we will see that interfering with the interaction of buyers and sellers in the marketplace, even with the best of intentions, can frequently make things worse.

CHAPTER REVIEW

1. Economics is concerned with explaining how people behave. To understand how buyers and sellers interact with each other, we need three things: a description of buyers' behavior, a description of sellers' behavior, and a description of how they deal with each other.

2. The term **demand** describes the relationship between the **price** of a particular good and the amount of that good that consumers want to buy, which is called **quantity demanded**. It is important to distinguish between these two concepts. Quantity demanded is an *amount*; it is measured in pounds, or gallons, or haircuts; and it is determined by price. Demand is a *relationship* (a function, in mathematical terms); it gives an amount for each possible price, not a single amount for a single price.

3. The demand relationship can be represented in several ways. One is in the form of a table of numbers that gives the amount that consumers want to buy (quantity demanded) at different prices; this presentation is called a **demand schedule**. Another is in the form of a graph of the amounts that consumers want to buy (quantity demanded) at different prices; this is called a **demand curve**. When graphing a demand curve, it is important to put the quantity demanded on the horizontal axis and the price on the vertical axis.

4. The **law of demand** says that the demand relationship is a negative relationship; that is, the amount of a good that people wish to buy (the quantity demanded) goes down as the price goes up, all other things being equal. More people will buy, and those who are buying will buy more, at lower prices because at the lower price the good looks more attractive compared to the alternatives than it did before. Remember the *ceteris paribus* condition, however. If other variables are changing at the same time that the price is falling, you can't tell what the relationship is between price and the amount that people want to buy.

5. Changes in other variables that affect the amount that people want to buy lead to a *shift in demand*. That is, they change the amount that people want to buy (quantity demanded) at each and every price. This is seen in the demand graph as a shift in the curve to the right or to the left and is

called a change in demand. Among the most important variables that can shift the demand for a product are *consumers' preferences, consumers' information, consumers' incomes, the number of consumers in the market, consumers' expectations of future prices,* and *the price of related goods.*

6. Changes in consumers' preferences can clearly change the amount that people want to buy. If consumers decide that a product is more or less desirable, they will obviously want to buy more or less of it at each price. Be careful to distinguish this effect from consumers' desire to buy more when the price falls. In that case, their tastes have not changed (and the demand curve has not shifted); instead, consumers now find it more affordable to indulge their tastes.

7. When people learn more about a good, they may change the amount that they want to buy at every price. Additional information about the benefits of a good will increase demand for it, and additional information about the harm from consuming a good will reduce demand for it.

8. When consumers' incomes increase, they can afford to buy more things, and demand for most goods will increase. Those goods are called **normal goods**. However, the demand for some goods will decrease when consumers become richer and can afford better; these are called **inferior goods**. For example, students with low incomes may buy a lot of ramen noodles, because they are a low-cost food. When these students graduate and start full-time jobs, they may buy less ramen and more pizza (or steak if they get a really good job). In that case, ramen is an inferior good, whereas pizza is a normal good.

9. Since demand is the relationship between the price of a good and the quantity demanded that *all* consumers want to buy, a change in the number of consumers is likely to change the amount that people want to buy at many prices. Therefore, the demand curve shifts when the number of consumers changes.

10. The demand for a good will shift when the price of a good that is a **substitute** for it changes. If the substitute becomes less expensive, it becomes relatively more attractive, and some consumers will switch. For example, if the price of crab falls and all other things remain equal, consumers as a group (although perhaps not every consumer) will want to buy less lobster. If the price of Corvettes increases and all other things remain equal, then consumers will want to buy more Camaros. Generally, demand for a good increases when the price of a substitute rises, and demand for a good decreases when the price of a substitute falls. The demand for a good is also shifted by changes in the price of a **complement,** a good that tends to be consumed together with another good. For example, if the price of playing a round of golf rises, the demand for golf carts will be reduced. If the price of coffee falls, the demand for coffee creamer increases. Generally, demand for a good decreases when the price of a complement rises, and demand for a good increases when the price of a complement falls.

11. Finally, demand will also respond to consumers' expectations of changes in the price of that good and of changes in other variables. For example, if consumers think they will be wealthier in the near future, they will start making additional purchases right now. Think about the graduating senior who just got that great job offer; isn't she already driving a new car? Similarly, if people believe that the price of something is going to change, their demand for it may change right away. For example, in December 1973, Johnny Carson's monologue joke on the *Tonight* show about the possibility of a toilet paper shortage led to such a large increase in the demand for toilet paper that in some places it really did become hard to find. (OK, so you probably don't know who Johnny Carson was. He was the Jay Leno of your parents' generation).

12. Changes in variables other than the price of the good in question *shift* the demand curve for that good. Changes in the price of the good in question, all other things being equal, result in consumers *moving along* the demand curve, but don't shift the demand curve. This is an important distinction to draw; don't confuse the two.

13. The term **supply** describes the relationship between the price of a good and the amount of that good that firms are willing to sell, which is called **quantity supplied**. As with demand, it is important to distinguish between these two concepts. Quantity supplied is an *amount*; it is measured in tons, or barrels, or shirts cleaned. Supply is a *relationship* or function; it gives an amount for each possible price, not a single amount.

14. Like the demand relationship, the supply relationship can be represented in several ways. One is in the form of a table of numbers that gives the amount that firms are willing and able to sell (quantity supplied) at different prices; this presentation is called a **supply schedule**. Another is in the form of a graph of the amount that firms are willing to sell (quantity supplied) at different prices; this is called a **supply curve**. When graphing a supply curve, it is important to put the quantity supplied on the horizontal axis and the price on the vertical axis.

15. The **law of supply** says that all other things being equal, the higher the price, the more firms will be willing to supply. Thus, the price and the quantity supplied are positively related. More firms will wish to sell and the firms that are selling will wish to sell more when the price rises because producing this product looks more profitable than the alternatives. Again, remember the *ceteris paribus* condition; if other variables that affect the amount that firms wish to sell are changing at the same time that the price is changing, the quantity supplied can either rise or fall.

16. When other variables that affect the amount that producers are willing and able to sell change, this leads to a *shift* in the supply curve. That is, those changes alter the amount that firms are willing to sell (quantity supplied) at each and every price. Among the most important variables that can shift the supply of a product are *technology, the price of goods used in production, the number of firms in the market, expectations of future prices,* and *government taxes, subsidies, and regulations.*

17. Technology refers to the ability to utilize other goods in order to produce the good or service. This can mean being able to utilize a chair, scissors, and someone's time and skill to produce a haircut, or being able to utilize complex equipment, silicon, and many people's time and skills to produce microchips. When knowledge improves in such a way that producers can produce the same amount of a good with fewer inputs, the cost of producing that good falls. Producing it becomes more attractive, all other things being equal, and the quantity supplied will increase at each and every price.

18. Similarly, if the price of the goods used in the production of a good falls, then the cost of producing that good falls. Again, producing that good becomes more profitable, all other things being equal, and firms will wish to sell more of it. This results in a rightward shift of the supply curve. Conversely, if the price of one or more inputs used in producing something rises, then firms will find it less profitable to produce that good and will be willing to sell less at each and every price, shifting the entire supply curve to the left.

19. Since the supply curve shows the amount that *all* of the producers together are willing to supply at different prices, an increase in the number of suppliers will increase that total and shift the supply curve to the right. Conversely, a decline in the number of sellers will reduce the total amount offered for sale at each and every price. This would lead to a leftward shift of the supply curve.

20. If firms expect that the price of their output is going to increase in the future, they will wish to delay selling their output until that price increase occurs. This results in less being offered for sale at any current price and a leftward shift of the supply curve. If the price of the goods that they sell is expected to fall in the future, sellers will want to sell more now; this increases supply and shifts the supply curve to the right.

21. Taxes imposed by the government raise firms' costs of production and, like increases in input prices, make selling the product less attractive. Subsidies to producers, on the other hand, lower the costs of production and make sales more attractive. Thus, taxes shift the supply curve to the

left (decreasing supply), and subsidies shift the supply curve to the right (increasing supply). Government regulations can also increase the costs of production—for example, by requiring the installation of pollution control equipment or additional safety testing of the product. These regulations will have the effect of decreasing supply.

22. As with the demand curve, it is important to distinguish *shifts* of the supply curve from *movements along* the supply curve. Changes in variables other than the price of the good in question shift the supply curve for that good. Changes in the price of the good in question, all other things being equal, result in a movement along the supply curve but do not shift the supply curve.

23. The demand curve describes how much consumers *want* to purchase at different prices, and the supply curve describes how much producers *want* to sell at different prices. In order to determine how much of a good actually gets bought (and sold), we need to understand how these two groups interact with each other. Economists believe that when consumers and producers get together, they will put pressure on the price that brings it to the level at which the amount that consumers want to purchase is just the amount that producers want to sell. This situation is called an *equilibrium*, because the quantity supplied and the quantity demanded are in balance. How much will be traded and the price at which those purchases take place can be determined from the numbers in the supply and demand schedules, or from a diagram that includes both the supply curve and the demand curve.

24. A **shortage** of a good occurs when, at the current price, consumers want to purchase more of the good than producers want to sell; the quantity demanded exceeds the quantity supplied at the current price in the market. In that case, we would expect some producers to take advantage of the situation by trying to get more from those who want to buy, and those consumers who are willing to pay more to try to outbid other consumers. This will cause the price to rise. Some consumers will decide that they are no longer willing to buy at the higher prices, and some producers will decide that they are willing to sell more at the higher prices. Eventually the price increases will bring the quantity supplied and the quantity demanded together, and there will be no further upward pressure on the price.

25. A **surplus** of a good, on the other hand, occurs when producers want to sell more units of the good than consumers want to purchase at the current price; the quantity supplied exceeds the quantity demanded. When there is a surplus, we would expect producers to start lowering the price to get their products sold. The surplus results in a falling price, which will cause some producers to decide that they no longer want to sell as much and some consumers to decide that they want to buy more. When the price falls to a level at which the quantity supplied equals the quantity demanded, there will be no further downward pressure on the price.

26. **Market equilibrium** is a situation with neither upward nor downward pressure on the price. This occurs when the quantity supplied equals the quantity demanded at the current price. We call this price the **equilibrium price**, and the quantity that gets bought and sold at that price the **equilibrium quantity**. If we have the supply and demand schedules for a good, we can find the equilibrium price by finding the price at which the quantity supplied equals the quantity demanded. If we have a supply and demand diagram that graphs the same information, we can find the equilibrium price and equilibrium quantity by finding where the supply curve and the demand curve cross. Look over to the vertical axis from the point at which the curves cross to find the equilibrium price, and look down to the horizontal axis from that point to find the equilibrium quantity.

27. Suppose a market is in equilibrium, and one or more of the variables that affect supply and demand change. As a result, either the demand curve or the supply curve or both will shift. At the original equilibrium price, there will now be either a shortage or a surplus (depending on which way the curves have shifted and by how much), and pressure on the price will lead to a new

equilibrium price and quantity. For example, if an increase in income leads to an increase (rightward shift) in demand, then there will be a shortage at the original equilibrium price, and the price will be forced up to a new equilibrium. A decrease in input prices leading to an increase (rightward shift) in supply will cause a surplus at the original equilibrium price, and the price will fall until a new equilibrium is reached. In this way, the equilibrium price and quantity respond to changes in variables that affect consumers' demand and producers' supply.

288. Governments often impose **price controls** in the form of **price ceilings** (maximum prices), to prevent prices from rising to levels that they feel are unfair to consumers, or **price floors** (minimum prices) to prevent prices from falling to levels that are viewed as unfair to suppliers. For example, **rent controls** are laws that put a ceiling on how high the price of rental housing can rise, while the **minimum wage** set by the federal government puts a floor below which wages (the price of labor inputs) cannot fall. When prices are prevented from rising or falling to their equilibrium levels, shortages or surpluses can persist, and other ways must be found to ration the goods. These often have undesirable features: People waste valuable time waiting in lines to make their purchases or take their chances on an illegal black market.

ZEROING IN

1.

   a.   The key to understanding and being able to use demand and supply diagrams is being able to distinguish between *shifts* of the demand and supply curves and *movements along* them. To see the difference, imagine yourself riding a bicycle on a flat road and think about the relationship between how fast your pedals turn and how fast the bike goes. This is a positive relationship; turning the pedals slowly (say, once every second) makes the bike go slowly, and turning the pedals quickly (say, three times a second) makes the bike go faster. If you were to draw a graph showing how fast the pedals turn on the vertical axis and the speed of the bike on the horizontal axis, the graph would slope upward, something like Figure 3.1.

Figure 3.1

   b.   Now suppose you shift the gears on the bicycle to a higher gear. The relationship between how fast you turn the pedals and how fast the bicycle goes is still a positive one: The faster you turn the pedals, the faster the bike goes. But turning the pedals at the once-per-second low speed now makes the bike go faster than it did in low gear, and turning the pedals at the three-times-per-second high speed also makes the bike go faster than it did in low gear. If you were to graph the relationship between how fast you turn the pedals and how fast the bike goes in the higher gear, you would get a new upward-sloping line to the right of the first line, as in Figure 3.2. For a ten-speed bicycle, there would be ten different lines, one for each gear.

Figure 3.2

c. Whatever gear you are in, you move *along* the line corresponding to that gear by turning the pedals faster or more slowly, or changing the value on the vertical axis. When you shift gears, you *shift* to a different line, and how fast you go on that line depends on how fast you choose to turn the pedals. The same is true of supply and demand curves. For a given set of levels of the other things that affect the supply of or demand for a good, you move *along* the curves when the price of that good (which is on the vertical axis) changes. When one of the other variables that affect supply or demand changes, you *shift* to a new supply or demand curve, and what quantity will be supplied or demanded on that curve depends on what price is chosen.

2.

a. The next most important issue is being able to separate the things that shift the demand curve from the things that shift the supply curve. Since households demand goods and services, the variables that shift demand curves are generally things that affect households: their income, their preferences or tastes, their beliefs or expectations, and their number. Also remember that a demand curve shows how much of *one particular* product consumers wish to buy at different prices for that product. Since the answer to that question is likely to depend on whatever else consumers are buying, the prices of *other* products affect buyers' decisions and hence shift the demand curve.

b. Firms supply goods and services, and so the variables that shift supply curves are generally things that affect firms: the prices they pay for inputs, including any taxes they pay or subsidies they receive from the government, their knowledge about how to produce (i.e., technology), their beliefs about profitability, and their number.

3.

a. It is also important to remember that supply and demand curves shift *left* (decrease) or *right* (increase), not down or up. The reason for this is that quantity is always on the horizontal axis and price is always on the vertical axis. When consumers' income rises, the quantity that consumers wish to buy increases (if the good in question is a normal good) no matter what the price is, and an increase in quantity is shown as a movement to the *right*, as in Figure 3.3.

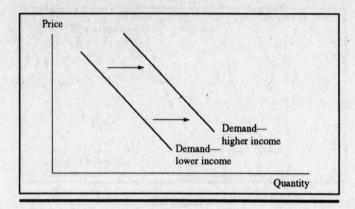

Figure 3.3

b.   This point doesn't seem very important when you look at shifts in demand curves, since a leftward shift looks like an upward shift (although the right answer is still that demand curves shift right for increases and left for decreases). But if you don't keep this straight when thinking about increasing or decreasing supply, you will get things wrong. An increase in supply because input prices fall moves the supply curve to the *right*, which looks like a shift downward, as in Figure 3.4. This is still an increase because at each and every price, the amount that firms wish to sell has increased.

Figure 3.4

4.   It is worth remembering how the market adjusts from an initial equilibrium to a new equilibrium when something changes that shifts either supply or demand or both. Recall that an actual price adjusts toward equilibrium as the market responds to surpluses and shortages. It's not merely that one or both of the curves move and there is a new point at which they cross. The supply and demand analysis is intended to capture the behavior of real people. Suppose that the market for small cars is initially in equilibrium and that because of rising gas prices consumers now want to buy more small cars. Car dealers find their inventory of small cars on the lot declining; they also find that they can charge a higher price for small cars without hurting sales. Thus, small car prices start to rise. This means more profits for firms that sell small cars, and they respond by increasing the number of small cars that they produce for sale. Thus, the quantity supplied rises. At the same time, the rising price of small cars deters some buyers who wanted a new small car at the initial price but are not so excited about the prospect at a higher price. The price continues to rise until the dealers find that further price increases hurt business by driving too many customers away. At that point, the new equilibrium has been established; the new equilibrium price is higher, and the quantity bought and sold at that price is higher as well.

ACTIVE REVIEW

Fill-In Questions

1.   Demand is the relationship between _____ and the _____ of a good.

2.   A demand schedule is a table of numbers showing _____ and _____. When these numbers are graphed, the resulting line is called a(n) _____.

3.   The law of demand states that as the _____ falls (*ceteris paribus*), the quantity demanded will _____. Therefore, demand curves slope _____.

4.   Changes in the price of a good, all other things being equal, lead to _____ the demand curve for that good.

5.   Shifts in the demand curve for a good are caused by changes in anything that affects the amount consumers want to buy *except* the _____ of that good.

6.   Demand reflects, among other things, consumers' preferences. When consumers' tastes increase, the demand curve _____ to the _____.

7.   Inferior goods are goods whose demand _____ as consumer _____ rises.

8.   When the price of a complement for a good falls, the demand for that good _____; as a result, the demand curve for that good shifts to the _____. When the price of a substitute falls, on the other hand, demand for the good in question _____, and the demand curve shifts to the _____.

9.   If consumers expect that the price of a good will fall in the future, they will wish to buy _____ of it today. This results in a(n) _____ in demand.

10.   The relationship between the _____ of a good and the quantity that producers are willing to sell is known as _____. The amount that producers wish to sell is called _____.

11.   The _____ is a graph of the _____ of a good and the _____.

12.   The _____ states that as the price of a good rises (all else remaining equal), firms will wish to sell _____ of that good. As a result, _____ slope upward.

13.   Movements along the supply curve are caused by changes in _____, while shifts of the supply curve are caused by changes in _____.

14.   The ability to produce goods and services is known as _____. When improvements in this ability lead to savings in the amounts of inputs required to produce a given amount of output, the _____ shifts to the right.

15.   When the prices of inputs rise, production becomes more _____. Firms will wish to sell _____ of the good, and the supply curve will shift to the _____. The same thing happens when government imposes _____ or _____ that raise the cost of production.

16.   Exit by new firms means that _____ will be offered for sale at every price. This causes a(n) _____ shift of the _____.

17. A market is said to be in _____ when the amount that _____ want to buy at the current price just equals the amount that _____ wish to _____.

18. Surpluses occur in a market when the _____ exceeds the _____. At these prices, _____ is greater than _____.

19. Conversely, if the price is below the _____ price, the quantity _____ will be less than the quantity _____ and a(n) _____ will occur. In this case, the price can be expected to _____.

20. Government restrictions on prices, such as _____, which prevent prices from rising to their equilibrium levels, or _____, which prevent prices from falling, lead to _____ or surpluses.

True-False Questions

1. T F   Price is determined by the interaction of households and firms.

2. T F   When beans cost 69 cents a can, consumers in Oskaloosa wish to purchase 357 cans per month, so we would say that at this price, demand is 357 cans per month.

3. T F   The law of demand states that, all other things being equal, as price rises demand falls.

4. T F   When T-shirts cost $17.50 apiece, consumers bought 336 T-shirts. After the price rose to $20.00, consumers purchased 286 of them. We would say that quantity demand fell by 50 units.

5. T F   The law of demand implies that demand curves slope downward.

6. T F   Charcoal and lighter fluid are complementary goods.

7. T F   Inferior goods refers to poor-quality, low-cost products.

8. T F   When incomes rise, the demand for inferior goods increases.

9. T F   Supply shows how much firms wish to sell at different prices.

10. T F   As the quantity supplied rises, price rises, according to the law of supply.

11. T F   When the price of computer chips falls, lowering the cost of producing computers, the supply of computers can be expected to increase.

12. T F   The equilibrium price in a market is the price that equates supply and demand.

13. T F   A shortage occurs when supply is greater than demand.

14. T F   A rising price will eliminate a shortage by increasing quantity supplied and reducing quantity demanded.

15. T F   If supply increases and demand remains unchanged, the equilibrium quantity will increase and the equilibrium price will rise.

16. T F   Price ceilings keep prices from falling to equilibrium.

Short-Answer Questions

1. Why do consumers wish to buy less when prices increase? How is this reflected in the demand curve?

2. What is the difference between supply and quantity supplied?

3. Why does the demand for a good rise when the price of a substitute rises?

4. List four things that cause demand curves to shift, and explain how changes in them affect demand. What is the only thing that causes movement along the demand curve?

5. Why do firms wish to supply less at lower prices? How is this reflected in the supply curve?

6. Why does the supply of a good increase when the expected future price of the good falls?

7. List four things that cause supply curves to shift, and explain how changes in them affect supply. What is the only thing that causes movement along the supply curve?

8. Explain how a decrease in price eliminates a surplus.

9. Explain why people's behavior should cause the price to settle at the equilibrium price.

10. What happens to the equilibrium price and quantity if demand and supply both increase at the same time? Illustrate your answer with a diagram, and explain.

11. What is the purpose of a price floor? What does a floor say about the level of the equilibrium price?

WORKING IT OUT

1. Remember that changes in the *price* of a good do not shift its demand or supply curve but represent different points on the supply or demand curve. When price changes, you move *along* the demand or supply curve. Figure 3.5 shows the demand curve for Swiss cheese. When the price falls from $1.50 per pound to $1.25 per pound, and all other things remain the same, the demand curve does not change, but the amount that consumers want to buy increases from 1,250 pounds per day to 1,575 pounds per day. The arrow in Figure 3.5 shows the movement along the demand curve.

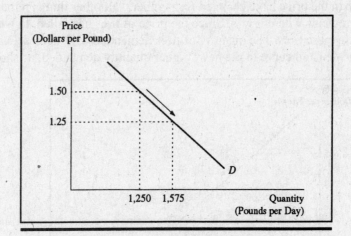

Figure 3.5

2. Changes in *anything else* that affects how much consumers want to buy or firms want to sell shift the demand and supply curves. To know which curve shifts, you need to know what other variable is changing. Is it something that affects consumers' well-being? Then it shifts the demand curve. Is it something that affects producers' profits? Then it shifts the supply curve.

3. The other thing that is central to understanding the supply and demand model is knowing how to combine supply and demand shifts to predict changes in the equilibrium price and quantity. Remember that supply and demand show the amounts that producers *want* to sell and consumers *want* to buy at different prices. The model also predicts that the price will eventually settle down

at the equilibrium level, where the amount consumers want to buy just equals the amount that producers want to sell. When something changes either the supply or the demand, price will adjust to a new equilibrium level.

Worked Problems

1. Figure 3.6 shows the demand curve for whitewall tires. Currently the price of tires is $45 per tire. If the price of tires falls to $40 per tire (and all other things remain the same), what happens to the demand for tires and the quantity of tires demanded?

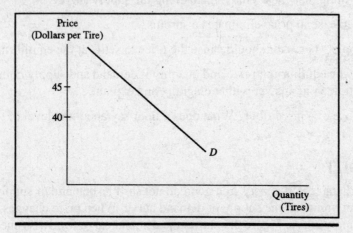

Figure 3.6

Answer

Nothing happens to the demand for tires. None of the variables that affect how much consumers want to buy other than the price have changed (remember, "all other things remain the same"). The demand curve remains where it was. Since the price of tires has fallen, however, consumers will wish to purchase more tires. The quantity of tires demanded will increase, and we move downward along the demand curve to the new, higher quantity demanded, as shown in Figure 3.7.

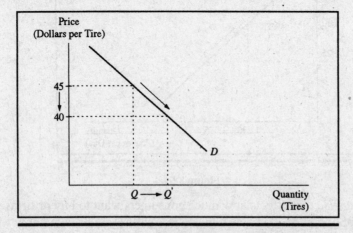

Figure 3.7

2. Suppose the demand curve for whitewall tires is still the one shown in Figure 3.6, but now the price of *blackwall* tires rises from $35 per tire to $40 per tire. What happens to the demand for whitewall tires?

Answer

It seems believable that at least some people who are currently buying blackwall tires view whitewall tires as substitutes. When the price of blackwall tires rises, those consumers will find the blackwall tires a less attractive purchase just because they're more expensive and will switch from blackwalls to whitewalls. This will happen no matter what the price of whitewalls is currently; the demand for whitewalls will increase at each and every possible price. The increase in the price of a substitute (blackwalls) increases the demand for this good (whitewalls), and the demand curve shifts to the right (not up), as in Figure 3.8.

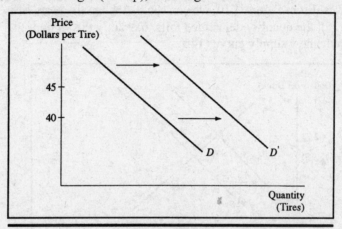

Figure 3.8

3.   Figure 3.9 shows the market for peach daiquiris in Greenwich. At first, the market is in equilibrium, with the price of peach daiquiris at $2.50 per drink and 175 drinks being purchased each week. Now suppose that, because of bad weather in Georgia, the price of peaches rises sharply. What happens to the supply and demand for peach daiquiris, and what happens to the equilibrium price and quantity?

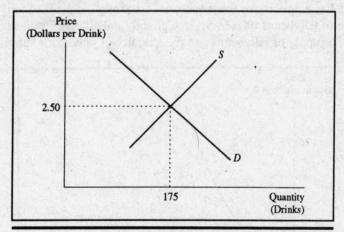

Figure 3.9

Answer

First, we need to know what happens to the supply and demand for peach daiquiris. Nothing happens to the demand; none of the variables that affect the amount that consumers want to buy have changed. However, peaches are an important ingredient in peach daiquiris, and an increase in their price increases the cost of making the drink. Producers will find it less profitable to sell peach daiquiris, and some will choose to stop selling them. The increase in the price of an input decreases the supply of the good and shifts the supply curve to the left, as shown in Figure 3.10.

At the original equilibrium price of $2.50, consumers still want to purchase 175 drinks each week, but producers now want to sell fewer drinks. There is a shortage of peach daiquiris at this price, and there will be upward pressure on the price. Producers will find that they can still sell all the drinks that they want to sell at $2.50 even if they increase the price; in fact, at the higher price, producers want to sell somewhat more drinks, and they find that they can. At that price, some consumers find that peach daiquiris are not worth the extra outlay, and they switch to strawberry margaritas. Thus, while the demand for peach daiquiris hasn't changed, the quantity demanded falls as the price rises. From Figure 3.10, we can see that when the price rises to the new equilibrium (at $2.75), the quantity demanded falls to exactly the amount that producers want to sell at that price on the new supply curve (145).

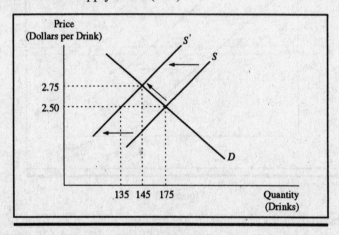

Figure 3.10

PRACTICE PROBLEMS

1. Figure 3.11 shows the supply curve for jellybeans. Currently the price of jellybeans is $1.00 a pound. If the price of jellybeans rises to $1.25 a pound (and all other things remain the same), what happens to the supply of jellybeans and the quantity of jellybeans supplied?

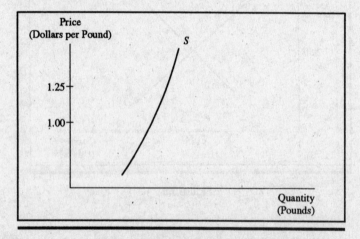

Figure 3.11

2. Figure 3.12 shows the demand for denim skirts. If the price of denim skirts rises from $27 to $32, what happens to the demand for denim skirts and the quantity of denim skirts demanded?

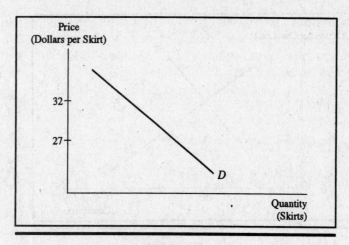

Figure 3.12

3. Suppose the demand for whitewall tires is as shown in Figure 3.6, and suppose that, because of rumors of increasing instability in the Middle East, consumers believe that the price of gasoline is going to increase dramatically and remain at that higher level for a long time. What happens to the demand for whitewall tires?

4. Suppose the supply of jellybeans is as shown in Figure 3.11, and suppose the price of sugar, which is a major ingredient in jellybeans, rises from $1.50 per pound to $1.78 per pound. What happens to the supply of jellybeans?

5. Figure 3.13 shows the supply and demand curves for the market for running suits in Portland. The market is initially in equilibrium at a price of $75 and 1,750 suits sold per year. Suppose that, because of an improving local economy, incomes in Portland rise significantly. What happens to the supply and demand for running suits and the equilibrium price and quantity?

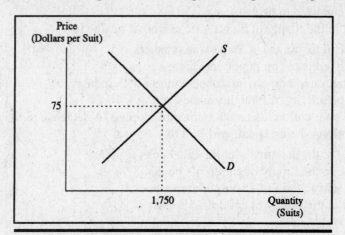

Figure 3.13

6. Figure 3.14 shows the supply and demand curves for the market for tofu in San Leandro, California. The market is initially in equilibrium at a price of $1.50 per container, and 450 containers are consumed per month. Suppose that, simultaneously, consumers become concerned about soybean pesticide residue in tofu and the state government eases regulations on the disposal of soybean wastes, which lowers the cost of producing tofu. What happens to the supply and demand for tofu and the equilibrium price and quantity?

Figure 3.14

CHAPTER TEST

1. Potatoes would be classified as a normal good if

   a. people at all levels of income consumed them.
   b. other food was more nutritious.
   c. more were consumed as incomes rose.
   d. fewer were consumed when the price of bread fell.

2. The demand curve for pizza is downward-sloping. Suddenly the price of pizza rises from $8 per pizza to $10 per pizza. This will cause

   a. the demand curve to shift to the left.
   b. the demand curve to shift to the right.
   c. quantity demanded to increase.
   d. quantity demanded to decrease.

3. A leftward shift in the supply of Swiss watches might be due to

   a. an increase in the wages of Swiss watchmakers.
   b. an increase in the tax on imported watches.
   c. the introduction of cost-saving robots in the watch industry.
   d. increased popularity of foreign watches.

4. The supply curve for children's books is upward-sloping. A decrease in the price of children's books, all other things being equal, will lead to

   a. an increase in the quantity of children's books supplied.
   b. an increase in the supply of children's books.
   c. producers wishing to sell fewer children's books.
   d. a decrease in the supply of children's books.

Use Figure 3.15 to answer the next three questions. The diagram refers to the demand for and supply of baseball caps. The baseball cap market is initially in equilibrium at point *C*. Assume that baseball caps are a normal good.

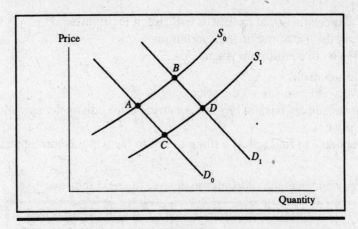

Figure 3.15

5. The baseball cap market moves from point *C* to a new equilibrium at point *A*. There has been a(n)
    a. decrease in demand and a decrease in supply.
    b. decrease in demand and a decrease in quantity supplied.
    c. increase in quantity demanded and an increase in quantity supplied.
    d. decrease in quantity demanded and a decrease in quantity supplied.
6. A movement from point *C* to point *D* might have been caused by

    a. a tightening of worker safety regulations in the production of baseball caps.
    b. a decrease in the price of cowboy hats (a substitute for baseball caps).
    c. a decrease in the cost of the cloth used in the baseball cap industry.
    d. increased income.
7. The discovery that wearing a hat reduces skin cancer would be likely to move the market from point *A* to

    a. point *B*.
    b. point *C*.
    c. point *D*.
    d. None of the above.
8. Which of the following is likely to cause a decrease in the demand for gasoline?

    a. An increase in the price of cars
    b. A decrease in the price of gasoline
    c. An increase in subway and bus fares
    d. A decrease in the price of crude oil
9. You observe that the price of houses and the number of houses purchased both rise over the course of a year. You conclude that

    a. the demand for houses has increased.
    b. the demand curve for houses must be upward-sloping.
    c. the supply of houses has increased.
    d. housing construction costs must be decreasing.
10. An increase in the quantity supplied is shown by

    a. shifting the supply curve up.
    b. shifting the supply curve to the left.
    c. shifting the supply curve to the right.
    d. moving upward along the supply curve.
11. An increase in the price of cars could be explained by all of the following *except*

    a. stricter auto emission standards.
    b. a fall in the price of gasoline.

    c.   producers' expectations that car prices will rise in the future.

    d.   an increase in the use of public transportation.

12.   A market is said to be in equilibrium when

    a.   supply equals demand.

    b.   there is downward pressure on the price.

    c.   the amount consumers wish to buy at the current price equals the amount producers wish to sell at that price.

    d.   all buyers are able to find sellers willing to sell to them at the current price.

Use the following supply and demand schedules to answer the next four questions.

Price	Quantity Supplied	Quantity Demanded
$3	30	75
$4	40	70
$5	50	65
$6	60	60
$7	70	55
$8	80	50

13.   When the price is $4, this market has a

    a.   shortage of 30 units.

    b.   shortage of 10 units.

    c.   surplus of 30 units.

    d.   surplus of 15 units.

14.   There is a surplus of 30 units when the price equals

    a. $4.

    b. $5.

    c. $6.

    d. $8.

15.   This market is in equilibrium when the price equals

    a. $5.

    b. $6.

    c. $7.

    d. $8.

16.   Suppose that the demand for this product shifts so that 15 fewer units are demanded at each price. The new equilibrium price will be

    a. $5.

    b. $6.

    c. $7.

    d. $8.

17.   If wine and cheese are complements, then an increase in the price of wine will cause

    a.   an increase in the price of cheese.

    b.   a decrease in the demand for wine.

    c.   less cheese to be demanded at each price.

    d.   a rightward shift in the demand curve.

18. If both supply and demand increase simultaneously, the equilibrium
    a.   price must rise and the equilibrium quantity must fall.
    b.   price must rise and the equilibrium quantity may either rise or fall.
    c.   quantity must rise and the equilibrium price may either rise or fall.
    d.   price must fall and the equilibrium quantity may either rise or fall.
19. Which of the following would *not* eliminate a shortage of a good?
    a.   A fall in the number of consumers
    b.   A fall in the price of a substitute for the good
    c.   A fall in the price of a complement for the good
    d.   An increase in the price of the good
20. Supply for a product could increase for all of the following reasons *except*
    a.   an improvement in technology.
    b.   a rise in the price of the product.
    c.   an expected decrease in the price of the product in the future.
    d.   an increase in the price of an important input.

ANSWERS TO THE REVIEW QUESTIONS

Fill-In Questions

1.   price; quantity demanded

2.   price; quantity demanded; demand curve

3.   price; rise; downward

4.   movement along

5.   price

6.   shifts; right

7.   decreases; income

8.   rises; right; falls; left

9.   less; decrease

10. price; supply; quantity supplied

11. supply curve; price; quantity supplied

12. law of supply; more; supply curve

13. price; technology, input prices, number of firms, expectations or government policies

14. technology; supply curve

15. costly; less; left; taxes; regulations

16. less; left; supply curve

17. equilibrium; consumers; producers; sell

18. price; equilibrium price; quantity supplied; quantity demanded

19. equilibrium; supplied; demanded; shortage; increase

20. price ceilings; price floors; shortages

True-False Questions

1. **True**. Household behavior (demand) and producer behavior (supply) determine price.

2. **False**. Quantity demanded is 357 cans per month. Demand is not an amount.

3. **False**. When price rises, quantity demanded falls, not demand.

4. **True**. When the price of a good changes, quantity demanded changes.

5. **True**. Since the law of demand says that quantity demanded is inversely related to price, it implies that demand curves slope downward.

6. **True**. When the price of charcoal rises, people will cook outside less often. This reduces the demand for lighter fluid; less lighter fluid will be purchased no matter what its price is.

7. **False**. Inferior goods are goods that consumers want to buy less of when their incomes rise. They may be perfectly well made products.

8. **True**. This is the definition of a normal good, not an inferior good. Demand will fall when income rises.

9. **True**. This is the definition of supply.

10. **False**. Quantity supply is determined by price, not the other way around.

11. **True**. Computer chips are an input into the production of computers. When their price falls, producing computers becomes less costly and hence more profitable; firms will increase the amount they wish to sell, no matter what the current price is. Thus, supply increases.

12. **False**. The equilibrium price equates quantity supplied and quantity demanded.

13. **False**. A shortage occurs when quantity supplied is less than the quantity demanded.

14. **True**. A shortage occurs when quantity supplied is less than quantity demanded at the current price. As the price rises, the amount consumers wish to purchase (quantity demanded) will fall, and the amount firms wish to sell (quantity supplied) will rise. This eliminates the shortage.

15. **False**. If supply increases and demand remains unchanged, the equilibrium quantity will increase, but the price will fall as consumers move downward along the demand curve.

16. **False**. Price ceilings keep prices from rising to equilibrium.

Short-Answer Questions

1. When the price of a good rises (all other things being equal), the good becomes a less desirable alternative than other products. More has to be given up in order to consume the product than before, and consumers will generally wish to consume less of it. This inverse relationship between the price and the quantity demanded is reflected in the negative (downward) slope of the demand curve.

2. Quantity supplied is the amount that producers wish to produce. It is measured in units of product (pounds, gallons, haircuts, etc.). The amount that producers wish to sell depends on many things. Supply is the relationship between one of those things (the price of the good) and the quantity supplied.

3. When the substitute becomes more expensive, people will look for alternatives to buy.

4. Changes in any of the following will cause a shift in the demand curve: consumers' preferences, consumers' information, consumers' income, consumers' expectations of future prices, the

number of consumers in the population, and the price of closely related goods. A change in the price of the good is the only thing that leads to movement along the demand curve.

5. Fewer firms will wish to sell, and the firms that are selling will wish to sell less, when the price falls because producing this product looks less profitable than the alternatives. This direct relationship between the price and the quantity supplied is reflected in the positive (upward) slope of the supply curve.

6. If the expected future price of a good falls, firms will want to supply more now while the price is relatively high. This shifts the supply curve to the right.

7. Changes in any of the following will cause a shift in the supply curve: technology, the price of goods used in production, the number of firms in the market, expectations of future prices, and government taxes, subsidies, and regulations. A change in the price of the good is the only thing that leads to movement along the supply curve.

8. When there is a surplus, quantity supplied is greater than quantity demanded at the current price. As the price falls, quantity demanded rises as we move downward along the demand curve, whereas quantity supplied falls as we move back down along the supply curve. If the price continues to falls, eventually quantity demanded and quantity supplied are equal, and the surplus has been eliminated.

9. When there are either shortages or surpluses, there will be pressure on the price to move in the direction that eliminates the shortage or surplus. In the event of a shortage, producers find that they can raise the price and still sell everything they wish to sell. Consumers who are unable to find the product they want to buy will start offering a higher price for it. The increase in price will induce suppliers to offer more and will also reduce the amount that buyers wish to purchase. In the event of a surplus, producers will find themselves unable to sell everything they wish to sell and will lower the price to sell their output. Consumers will find that they can negotiate discounts successfully. The decrease in price will lead buyers to purchase more and will lead suppliers to wish to sell less. In this way, shortages and surpluses are eliminated, and the price moves toward the equilibrium level.

10. When both supply and demand increase (shift rightward) at the same time, the equilibrium quantity will increase. The equilibrium price can either rise or fall, depending on whether the shift of supply or demand is greater. For example, in the first panel of Figure 3.16, while both supply and demand increase, the shift of demand is greater and the new equilibrium price is higher. In the second panel of Figure 3.16, the shift of supply is greater and the new equilibrium price is lower. In both cases, the new equilibrium quantity is larger.

Figure 3.16

11.   Price floors are attempts to keep prices from falling. They are based on the perspective that the equilibrium price for the product is too low.

SOLUTIONS TO THE PRACTICE PROBLEMS

1.   The *supply* of jellybeans is unchanged. None of the variables that affect how much producers want to sell other than the price have changed (remember, "all other things remain the same"). The supply curve remains where it was. Since the price of jellybeans has risen, however, producers wish to sell more of them. The quantity of jellybeans supplied increases, and we move upward along the supply curve to the new, higher quantity supplied, as shown in Figure 3.17.

Figure 3.17

2.   Nothing happens to the *demand* for denim skirts. The price of denim skirts has changed, but none of the other variables that affect how many skirts consumers wish to buy have changed. Since the price has risen, consumers will wish to buy fewer denim skirts, and the quantity demanded falls. We move upward along the demand curve, as shown in Figure 3.18.

Figure 3.18

3.   Tires and gasoline are complements; the more you drive, the more gasoline you purchase and the more tires you purchase. If consumers expect that gasoline is going to be much more expensive in the future, they will probably expect to be doing less driving in the future. In that case, there will be reduced demand for new tires; the old tires will last longer if they aren't going to be driven on as much. The increase in the price of a complement (gasoline) decreases the demand for this good (whitewall tires), and the demand curve shifts to the left (not down), as in Figure 3.19.

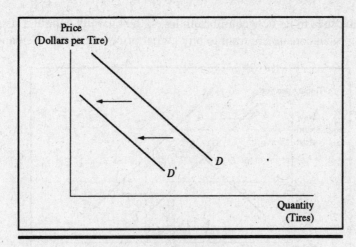

Figure 3.19

4.   The increase in the price of sugar raises the cost of producing jellybeans and makes producing them less profitable. Some producers find that they can no longer continue to make a living selling jellybeans, and they stop producing them. This will happen no matter what the price of jellybeans is currently; the supply of jellybeans will decrease at each and every possible price. The increase in the price of an input (sugar) decreases the supply of this good (jellybeans), and the supply curve shifts to the *left* (not down), as in Figure 3.20.

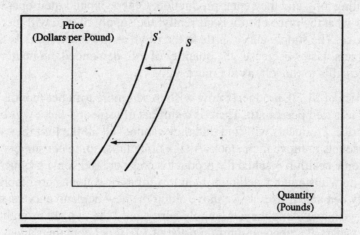

Figure 3.20

5.   First, what happens to the supply and demand for running suits? Since none of the (nonprice) variables that affect the amount that producers want to sell have changed, nothing happens to the supply. It is likely, however, that running suits are a normal good; when people's incomes rise, they do more of their running in track suits and less in old sweats. At any price of running suits, the increase in income will result in consumers wanting to buy more of them. Demand increases, and the demand curve shifts to the right, as shown in Figure 3.21.

At the original equilibrium price of $75, consumers now want to purchase more running suits per year, but producers still want to sell 1,750 per year. There is a shortage of running suits at this price, and there will be upward pressure on the price. Producers will find that they can still sell 1,750 suits per year if they raise the price; in fact, at higher prices, producers want to sell more suits, and they find that they can. At that price, some consumers find that running suits are not worth the extra outlay, and they stick to their old sweatshirts. Thus, while the supply of running suits has not changed, the quantity supplied rises as the price rises. From Figure 3.21, we can see that when the price rises to its new equilibrium level, the quantity supplied rises to a level that is exactly the amount that consumers want to buy at that price on the new demand curve.

Figure 3.21

6.   First, what happens to the supply and demand for tofu? The decreased regulation lowers the cost of producing tofu and makes producing it more profitable. Some producers find that they can now make a living selling tofu, and they enter production. Others expand their operations. This will happen no matter what the price of tofu is currently; the supply of tofu will increase at each and every possible price. The supply curve shifts to the right, as in Figure 3.22. At the same time, the change in consumers' tastes decreases the quantity of tofu demanded, no matter what the price; the demand curve shifts to the left, as in Figure 3.22.

At the original price of $1.50, producers now wish to sell more tofu per month, but consumers now wish to buy less tofu per month. There is a surplus of tofu, and there will be downward pressure on the price. Producers will find that they cannot sell all the tofu they wish to, and will start offering discounts to move their stock. As the price falls, some consumers will decide that it is worth taking some health risk when the product is cheaper, and some producers will find that, eased regulation notwithstanding, selling tofu at lower prices is not as profitable as they thought. Thus, the quantity demanded rises as we move along the new demand curve and the quantity supplied falls as we move along the new supply curve, until the two are brought into balance. In Figure 3.22, this occurs at a new equilibrium price of $1.10 per container and a new equilibrium quantity of 500 containers per month. Notice, however, that if the increase in supply had been smaller and the decrease in demand had been larger, the new equilibrium quantity could have been smaller than the initial equilibrium quantity. When demand decreases and supply increases, all you can say for certain is that the equilibrium price will fall.

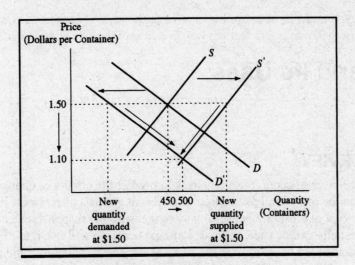

Figure 3.22

ANSWERS TO THE CHAPTER TEST

1. c
2. d
3. a
4. c
5. d
6. d
7. a
8. a
9. a
10. d
11. d
12. c
13. a
14. d
15. b
16. a
17. c
18. c
19. c
20. b

CHAPTER 4

Elasticity and Its Uses

CHAPTER OVERVIEW

One of the most practical uses of economic analysis is to predict the effects of changes in underlying conditions or policies on the prices and production of different goods and services. In this chapter, you will learn about the concept of elasticity, a useful way to measure the responsiveness of one economic variable to another. Elasticity can be used in many settings; here, we will use it to explore the sensitivity of quantity demanded to changes in the price of the good, in income, and in the prices of other closely related goods. We will also use elasticity to explore the sensitivity of quantity supplied to price. Finally, we will see how useful the concept is in answering different questions through supply and demand analysis.

CHAPTER REVIEW

1. *Elasticity* is a very general concept. It refers to a measure of the sensitivity of one economic variable to changes in another economic variable in percentage terms. There are many different pairs of variables between which we can calculate an elasticity. Here, we will focus on some of the elasticities that are most useful in economics.

2. The **price elasticity of demand,** sometimes referred to as the *elasticity of demand* or even just the *elasticity* when the meaning is clear from the context, measures the responsiveness of quantity demanded to changes in price. It answers the question "By what percentage will quantity demanded change for every 1 percent that price changes, holding all else equal?" The price elasticity of demand is defined as the percentage change in quantity demanded divided by the percentage change in price, or

    $$\text{Price elasticity of demand} = \frac{\text{Percentage change of quantity demanded}}{\text{Percentage change in price}}$$

    This tells us by what percentage quantity demanded changed for each percentage point change in price. So, for example, if the price elasticity of demand for a good is 3, each 1 percent increase in its price leads to a 3 percent decrease in its quantity demanded.

3. Remember that to calculate the elasticity of demand, you need to know two points on the *same* demand curve. Price elasticity measures the responsiveness of quantity demanded to a change in price, *holding all else equal*.

4. To calculate the percentage change in quantity demanded, we take the number of units by which the quantity changed and divide by the initial quantity. Similarly, we take the number of dollars by which the price changed and divide by the initial price to calculate the percentage change in price.

    So, using symbols,

    $$e_d = \frac{\Delta Q_d}{Q_d} \div \frac{\Delta p}{p}$$

    where e_d represents the price elasticity of demand and Δ means "change in."

5.   Since the demand curve slopes downward, an increase in the price causes a decrease in the quantity demanded. Thus, the elasticity of demand is a negative number; when $\Delta P/P$ is positive, $\Delta Q_d/Q_d$ is negative. It is common practice to multiply the number by a negative 1 and then just talk about the absolute value of the price elasticity of demand.

6.   Since elasticities measure changes in percentage terms, you get the same answer no matter what units quantity and price are measured in—elasticity is a **unit-free measure.** The advantage of this is that you can easily compare the responsiveness of quantity demanded to price for different goods. It also means that the elasticity will not change if you use different units of measurement—say, six-packs instead of bottles. A 10-six-pack increase in consumption is not the same as a 10-bottle increase, but a 10 percent increase in the number of six-packs is also a 10 percent increase in the number of bottles.

7.   The elasticity of demand is not the same thing as the *slope* of the demand curve. The slope of the demand curve is the change in price divided by the change in quantity demanded, or $\Delta P/\Delta Q$, and it depends on the units chosen to measure price and quantity. Changing the units that quantity is measured in, for example, will change the slope of the demand curve. If a 25-cent increase in the price of soft drinks causes a 6,000-bottle reduction in the quantity of soft drink demanded, it causes only a 1,000-six-pack reduction. But if consumption was originally 60,000 bottles (or 10,000 six-packs), the price increase causes a 10 percent reduction either way you measure soft drinks.

8.   Goods for which the price elasticity of demand is greater than 1 are said to have an **elastic demand.** That is, a 1 percent change in the price causes a more than 1 percent change in quantity demanded. Goods for which the price elasticity of demand is less than 1, so that a 1 percent change in the price causes a *less* than 1 percent change in quantity demanded, are said to have an **inelastic demand.** Goods with a price elasticity of demand of exactly 1 are called **unit elastic.**

9.   When the quantity demanded is completely unresponsive to the price, the demand curve is a vertical line, and we say that the demand is **perfectly inelastic.** When the demand curve is a horizontal line, consumers are not willing to buy any of the good if the price rises even a little bit above that price. In this case, even the smallest change in price would cause a total reduction in quantity demanded, and we say that the demand is **perfectly elastic.**

10.   When calculating percentage changes in price and quantity, we need to divide the absolute change in price or quantity by the level of price or quantity. However, if the change in price or quantity is big enough, we will get different answers depending on whether we divide by the starting price or quantity, or by the ending price or quantity. For example, when the price rises from $1.00 to $1.50, that's a 50 percent increase based on the $1.00 starting price, but only a 33 percent increase based on the $1.50 ending price. Neither of these is "right" or "wrong." What is needed is some standard way of doing things to avoid confusion. The economists' convention is to use the *average*, or *midpoint*, of the starting price (or quantity) and the ending price (or quantity) for calculating percentage changes. Using that convention, the price increase from $1.00 to $1.50 is a 40 percent increase, because 50 cents is 40 percent of $1.25, the average of $1.00 and $1.50.

11.   When the price elasticity of demand is calculated using the average of the starting and ending prices and quantities, the *midpoint formula* is used. To calculate elasticity using the midpoint formula, you need to know two points on the demand curve: the old price and quantity (P_{old} and Q_{old}) and the new price and quantity (P_{new} and Q_{new}). The elasticity of demand is given by

$$\text{Price elasticity of demand} = \frac{Q_{new} - Q_{old}}{(Q_{new} - Q_{old})/2} \div \frac{P_{new} - P_{old}}{(P_{new} - P_{old})/2}$$

12. Revenue is the total amount of money that consumers pay and producers receive when some amount of a good is sold at some price. If Q units are sold at a price of P per unit, then revenue is the product of price and quantity, or $P \times Q$.

13. When the price rises, the quantity demanded falls, and so revenue can change as well. But it's not obvious which way revenue will change when the price rises. Two things are occurring at the same time: Each unit that is sold is selling for more, which increases revenue; but fewer units get sold, which decreases revenue. The price elasticity of demand tells us which of these two effects is stronger, and therefore tells us whether revenue will rise or fall when the price rises. When demand is inelastic (elasticity of demand is less than 1), the percentage decrease in quantity will be less than the percentage increase in price, and so revenue will rise as the price rises. When demand is elastic (elasticity of demand is greater than 1), the percentage decrease in quantity will be larger than the percentage increase in price, and so revenue will fall as the price rises. And when demand is unit elastic (elasticity of demand is equal to 1), the percentage decrease in quantity is exactly equal to the percentage increase in price, and revenue will not change when price rises. This explains why grain farmers are worse off when they all share a bumper crop; since the demand for grain is inelastic, the increased quantity sold is more than offset by falling prices.

14. Several variables determine whether the elasticity of demand for a good is large or small. The most important of these is whether there are good substitutes for the product. If there are, changes in price will cause consumers to switch to the substitutes, and the quantity demanded will fall dramatically; in this case, the elasticity of demand will be high. If, on the other hand, good substitutes are not available, consumers will continue to buy as the price rises, and demand will have a lower elasticity.

15. The price elasticity of demand will be higher for goods on which people spend a large fraction of their income. Changes in the price of something that you spend a lot on have big effects on your buying power, necessitating big adjustments. Changes in the price of something that represents only a small part of your income have little effect on what you can buy, and so only small changes in the amount you buy are needed.

16. People will respond more to price changes that are expected to be temporary than to long-lasting price changes, and so the price elasticity of a temporary change will tend to be high. If a price decrease is going to last a long time, there is no hurry to take advantage of the low price. Similarly, if a price increase is expected to persist, you might as well go on buying now, because the good will still be more expensive later on.

17. If a price changes permanently, the price elasticity of demand is likely to be lower immediately after the price change than after some time has passed. In the *short run*, people have only limited opportunities to adjust their consumption, but in the *long run*, more adjustments are possible. For example, when the price of home heating oil rises, in the short run people with oil heat can turn down their thermostats and wear sweaters, but they still have to heat their houses. In the long run, however, more new homes will be built with electric or natural gas heating, and the change in the quantity of oil demanded will be larger.

18. So far, we have been thinking about the price elasticity of demand. Price certainly is an important determinant of quantity demanded, but remember that there are other variables that also affect the amount that consumers want to buy. When those variables change, the demand curve shifts. We can also use the concept of elasticity to measure the responsiveness of quantity demanded to these changes.

19. One of the most important variables (other than price) that affects consumer demand is consumer income. The **income elasticity of demand** is the percentage change in quantity demanded divided by percentage change in income, holding all else (including the price) constant. That is,

$$\text{Income elasticity of demand} = \frac{\text{Percentage change in quantity demanded}}{\text{Percentage change in income}}$$

20. Likewise, the cross-price elasticity of demand tells us how responsive the quantity demanded of one good is to changes in the price of another good. It is the percentage change in quantity demanded of one good divided by percentage change in the price of the other good, holding all else (including the good's own price) constant. That is,

$$\text{Income elasticity of demand} = \frac{\text{Percentage change in quantity demanded}}{\text{Percentage change in income}}$$

Recall that the quantity demanded of a good rises when the price of its substitutes rises, and falls when the prices of complementary goods rise. Therefore, if two goods are substitutes, their cross-price elasticity of demand will be positive, and if they are complements, it will be negative.

21. We can also apply the elasticity concept to the responsiveness of quantity supplied to price. Recall from Chapter 3 that the **price elasticity of supply** measures this. It is defined as the percentage change in the quantity supplied divided by the percentage change in the price, or

$$\text{Price elasticity of supply} = \frac{\text{Percentage change in quantity supplied}}{\text{Percentage change in price}}$$

22. A vertical supply curve is **perfectly inelastic** because any change in price will lead to no response in the quantity supplied, and the elasticity of supply is therefore zero. A horizontal supply curve is **perfectly elastic.** The slightest decrease in price reduces the supply to zero.

ZEROING IN

1. From the applications in the chapter, you can see that the elasticity concept is quite general. We can talk about the parking fine elasticity of parking tickets, or the tax rate elasticity of cigarette sales. Remember that elasticity just means responsiveness of one variable to changes in another, in percentage terms.

2. The main formula to learn in this chapter is the midpoint formula. In the section above, this was given for the price elasticity of demand. It also applies when calculating other elasticities, such as the price elasticity of supply. To calculate that elasticity using the midpoint formula, you need to know two points on the supply curve: the old price and quantity (P_{old} and Q_{old}) and the new price and quantity (P_{new} and Q_{new}). The price elasticity of supply is given by

$$\text{Price elasticity of supply} = \frac{\text{Change in quantity supplied}}{\text{Average of old and new quantity}} \div \frac{\text{Change in price}}{\text{Average of old and new price}}$$

$$= \frac{Q_{new} - Q_{old}}{(Q_{new} + Q_{old})/2} \div \frac{P_{new} - P_{old}}{(P_{new} + P_{old})/2}$$

So, if firms wish to supply 560 units when the price is $13 per unit, and are willing to supply 640 units if the price rises to $17 per unit, then if we call the first price and quantity the old point on the supply curve and the second price and quantity the new point, we have

$$\text{Price elasticity of supply} = \frac{\text{Change in quantity supplied}}{\text{Average of old and new quantity}} \div \frac{\text{Change in price}}{\text{Average of old and new price}}$$

$$= \frac{640\text{-}560}{(640+560)/2} \Big/ \frac{17\text{-}13}{(17+13)/2} = \frac{80}{600} \Big/ \frac{4}{15} = \frac{1}{2}$$

3. It's common to think that a demand curve has *a* price elasticity of demand, the way an object has *a* weight. This isn't right, however; the same demand curve can have different elasticities of demand depending on from which prices and quantities you start and finish. To see this, look at the following demand schedule, which is graphed as a demand curve in Figure 4.1.

Price	Quantity Demanded
10	0
8	40
6	80
4	120
2	160
0	200

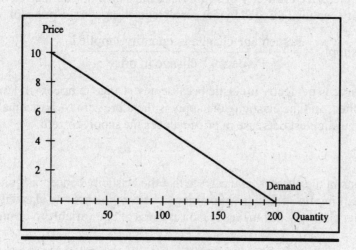

Figure 4.1

If we calculate the elasticity of demand using 10 as the starting price (and 0 as the starting quantity) and 8 as the ending price (and 40 as the ending quantity), we get

$$\text{Price elasticity of demand} = \frac{\text{Change in quantity demanded}}{\text{Average of old and new quantity}} \div \frac{\text{Change in price}}{\text{Average of old and new price}}$$

$$= \frac{40\text{-}0}{(40+0)/2} \Big/ \frac{8\text{-}10}{(8+10)/2} = \frac{40}{20} \Big/ \frac{(\text{-}2)}{9} = 9 \, \textit{(ignoring the minus sign)}$$

But if we calculate the elasticity of demand using 4 as the starting price (and 120 as the starting quantity) and 2 as the ending price (and 160 as the ending quantity), we get

$$\text{Price elasticity of demand} = \frac{\text{Change in quantity demanded}}{\text{Average of old and new quantity}} \div \frac{\text{Change in price}}{\text{Average of old and new price}}$$

$$= \frac{160\text{-}120}{(160\text{-}120)/2} / \frac{2\text{-}4}{(2+4)/2} = \frac{40}{140} / \frac{(\text{-}2)}{3} = \frac{3}{7}$$

In each case, the price falls by $2 and the quantity demanded rises by 40 units, so why does the elasticity come out differently? The key is remembering that elasticity uses *percentage* changes. In the first case, the price fell from 10 to 8, which is only a 22 percent change (based on the average price of 9), whereas in the second case, the price fell from 4 to 2, which is a 67 percent change (based on the average price of 3). Similarly, in the first case, quantity demanded rose from 0 to 40, which is a 200 percent increase (based on the average of 20), whereas in the second case, quantity demanded rose from 120 to 160, which is only a 29 percent increase (based on the average of 140). So in the first case, a small percentage change in price led to a large percentage change in quantity demanded, whereas in the second case, a larger percentage change in price led to a smaller percentage change in quantity demanded. In percentage terms, quantity demanded is much more responsive to price in the first case than in the second, and the elasticity of demand shows this.

4. When you read about how elasticities are used in economic analysis, you will see that often the main issue is whether revenue will rise or fall with an increase in the price, which in turn hinges on whether demand is elastic or inelastic. Remember that revenue is simply $P \times Q$. When P rises, Q falls; the question is, how fast? Elasticity gives you the answer; when demand is elastic, the percentage fall in quantity is greater than the percentage rise in price. When demand is inelastic, the percentage fall in quantity is less than the percentage increase in price. You can remember how this affects revenue by the following:

- Elastic demand: $P\uparrow$ means $Q\downarrow$, so $P \times Q \downarrow$

- Inelastic demand: $P\uparrow$ means $Q\downarrow$, so $P \times Q \uparrow$

ACTIVE REVIEW

Fill-In Questions

1. _____ is the general concept of measuring the responsiveness of one economic variable to another in _____ terms.

2. The price elasticity of demand measures how _____ changes in response to a change in _____ .

3. To calculate the price elasticity of demand, you need to know _____ points on a _____ demand curve.

4. Since the demand curve slopes _____, the elasticity of demand has a(n) _____ sign. Economists, however, multiply elasticity by a_____ to make it_____ .

5. When you calculate elasticities, you will get the same answer no matter what _____ the prices and quantities are measured in; this means that elasticities for different goods can be compared. It is important to remember that elasticity is not the same as the _____ of the demand curve.

6. Demand is said to be _____ when the elasticity of demand is less than _____ .

7.   Since elasticities are _____, we can compare the elasticities of demand for _____ different goods. For example, if the elasticity of demand for peas were 2.5 and the elasticity of demand for carrots were 3.1, we would say that the demand for peas was _____ compared to the demand for carrots. However, we would still say that both of these goods had _____ demands.

8.   When the elasticity of demand is zero, demand is said to be _____. In this case, the demand curve is a _____ line.

9.   When the demand curve is horizontal, a tiny price increase will lead to a very large percentage change in quantity demanded. We say that such a demand curve is _____.

10.   The midpoint formula uses the _____ of the starting and ending _____ and quantities to calculate the _____ changes used in the elasticity formula.

11.   When demand is elastic, price and revenue move in _____ direction(s); that is, an increase in price leads to a(n) _____ in revenue. On the other hand, when demand is inelastic, price and revenue move in _____ direction(s).

12.   The elasticity of demand for a product will be larger if many good _____ for that good exist, if consumers spend a(n) _____ of their income on it, or if changes in price are expected to be _____.

13.   The _____ elasticity of demand measures the responsiveness of _____ to changes in consumer income, holding all else equal.

14.   _____ have positive income elasticities, whereas _____ will have _____ income elasticities.

15.   The elasticity of supply measures how _____ changes in response to a change in _____.

True-False Questions

1.   T   F   The concept of elasticity has only limited applicability, since it refers only to the responsiveness of quantity demanded to price.

2.   T   F   The price elasticity of demand is the same as the slope of the demand curve.

3.   T   F   Elasticity of demand is the change in quantity demanded divided by the change in price.

4.   T   F   The steeper the demand curve, the less elastic the demand.

5.   T   F   Elasticity of demand is generally discussed as a negative number.

6.   T   F   It makes no sense to compare elasticities for different goods, because that is like comparing apples and oranges.

7.   T   F   If the percentage change in quantity demanded is more than the percentage change in price that caused it, demand is inelastic.

8.   T   F   If a 5 percent increase in the price of tea causes a 10 percent decrease in the quantity of tea demanded in Indianapolis, we would say that the demand for tea in Indianapolis is elastic.

9.   T   F   When the demand for a product is perfectly inelastic, its demand curve is a horizontal line.

10.   T   F   A rise in the price of a good will always result in a decrease in the amount spent on that good.

11.   T   F   If the income elasticity of demand for fast-food cheeseburgers is negative, we know that cheeseburgers must have many close substitutes.

12.   T   F   The elasticity of demand will be lower if the change in price is only temporary, since no one pays much attention to temporary things.

13.   T   F   If the income elasticity of demand for pizza is 0.75, pizza must be a normal good.

14.   T   F   The elasticity of supply is the ratio of the percentage change in quantity supplied to the percentage change in price, all else being equal.

15.   T   F   Perfectly elastic supply is represented by a vertical supply curve.

Short-Answer Questions

1.   How would you calculate the rainfall elasticity of umbrella sales? What information would you need to know?

2.   How do you calculate the price elasticity of demand using the midpoint formula?

3.   What is the difference between elastic demand and inelastic demand?

4.   If the demand curve has unit elastic demand, what happens to quantity demanded when price rises 5 percent?

5.   The City Council proposes raising parking fees in order to provide additional funds for the city bus system. What must the council be assuming about the elasticity of demand for parking?

6.   List three things that tend to make the demand for a good more elastic.

7.   Why is the long-run elasticity of demand for gasoline likely to be greater than the short-run elasticity of demand?

8.   Explain the difference between the price elasticity of demand and the income elasticity of demand.

9.   What is the sign of the income elasticity of demand for inferior goods? Explain.

10.   Why is the elasticity of supply low if firms' production decisions are based on their expectations of future prices?

11.   What is price elasticity of supply?

12.   How do you interpret a supply curve that is perfectly inelastic?

13.   How does time relate to price elasticity of supply?

WORKING IT OUT

1.   It is important to be able to use the midpoint formula correctly to calculate elasticities. To calculate an elasticity of demand, you need to know the quantity demanded at two different prices, when all else remains equal. To calculate an income elasticity of demand, you need to know the quantity demanded at two income levels, with all else equal. Then you need to apply the midpoint formula correctly.

2.   It is actually very easy to find the revenue that is collected by sellers of a good (which is also the expenditure on that good by consumers) by looking at the demand curve. For each price, the demand curve tells us how much will be bought—for every P, the demand curve gives us a Q.

Look at Figure 4.2; suppose the price is P_1 dollars per unit, and the resulting quantity is therefore Q_1 units. Revenue (in dollars) is the number of units sold times the number of dollars for which each one sells, or $P_1 \times Q_1$. This is the area of the rectangle in Figure 4.2 that has P_1 as its height and Q_1 as its base (since the area of a rectangle is the base times the height).

Figure 4.2

Worked Problems

1. Using the data from Table 4.1 on the demand for burgers and pizzas, calculate the price elasticity of demand for burgers.

TABLE 4.1				
Quantity of Burgers	**Quantity of Pizzas**	**Price of Burgers**	**Price of Pizzas**	**Weekly Income**
750	300	$2.50	$8.00	$150
900	150	$2.00	$9.00	$170
850	250	$2.50	$10.00	$150
800	300	$2.00	$9.00	$190
550	200	$3.00	$8.00	$150

Answer

First, you need to find two points on the same demand curve for burgers. The first row and the fifth row give you this: The price of pizza (a closely related good) and income are the same in these two rows. The only things that are different are the price and quantity of burgers (and the quantity of pizza, but that's not part of the demand curve for burgers). So if we let P_{old} be $2.50 and Q_{old} be 750, and let P_{new} be $3.00 and Q_{new} be 550, then the midpoint formula says that

$$\text{Price elasticity of demand} = \frac{\text{Change in quantity demanded}}{\text{Average of old and new quantity}} \div \frac{\text{Change in price}}{\text{Average of old and new price}}$$

$$= \frac{550\text{-}750}{(550+750)/2} / \frac{3.00\text{-}2.50}{(3.00+2.50)/2} = \frac{-200}{650} / \frac{0.50}{2.75} = \frac{22}{13}$$

2. Using Figure 4.3, what is the revenue when the price is $6 per unit? What area in Figure 4.3 corresponds to this revenue? What happens to revenue if the price falls to $5 per unit? Is the demand curve elastic or inelastic at $6 per unit?

Figure 4.3

Answer

At $6 per unit, 30 units are demanded, so the revenue would be $6 per unit × 30 units, or $180. The area that gives this revenue is the area of the rectangle whose corners are $6–A–30–0. If the price falls to $5 per unit, the quantity demanded rises to 42 units, and revenue rises to $210. Since the price decrease leads to a revenue increase, we know that the demand curve must be elastic at this price.

PRACTICE PROBLEMS

1. Using the data from Table 4.1, find the price elasticity of demand for pizza.

2. Using the data from Table 4.1, find the income elasticity of demand for burgers.

3. Using the data from Table 4.1, find the cross-price elasticity of demand for burgers with respect to the price of pizza.

4. Using Figure 4.3, what is the revenue when the price is $3 per unit? What area on Figure 4.3 corresponds to this revenue? What happens to revenue if the price rises to $4 per unit? Is the demand curve elastic or inelastic at $3 per unit?

5. Calculate the price elasticity of demand (using the midpoint formula) as the price rises from $3 per unit to $4 per unit in Figure 4.3, and verify your answer to the last part of question 4.

CHAPTER TEST

1. The price elasticity of demand shows us
   a. the steepness of the demand curve.
   b. how fast demand responds to price.
   c. how much demand shifts when income changes.
   d. the responsiveness of quantity demanded to price changes.

2. In order to calculate the price elasticity of demand, you need to know
   a. two prices and two quantities demanded as the demand curve shifts.
   b. the slope of the demand curve.
   c. the equilibrium price and quantity in the market.
   d. the quantity demanded at two different prices, *ceteris paribus*.

3.   Price elasticities are measured in percentage terms because

    a.   it makes students' lives more complicated.
    b.   the resulting measure is unit-free.
    c.   it gives a more accurate answer.
    d.   the answer is always negative that way.

4.   The price elasticity of demand is given by the formula

    a. $e_d = \dfrac{\Delta Q_d}{Q_d} \div \dfrac{\Delta P}{P}$

    b. $e_d = \dfrac{\Delta Q_d}{Q_d}$

    c. $e_d = \dfrac{\Delta Q_d}{Q_d} \times \dfrac{\Delta P}{P}$

    d. $e_d = \dfrac{\Delta P}{P} \div \dfrac{\Delta Q_d}{Q_d}$

5.   Demand is elastic when the elasticity of demand is

    a.   greater than 0.
    b.   greater than 1.
    c.   less than 1.
    d.   less than 0.

6.   If the price of gasoline rises 10 percent, the quantity of gasoline purchased falls by 10 percent. The demand for gasoline in this case is

    a.   perfectly elastic.
    b.   unit elastic.
    c.   elastic.
    d.   inelastic.

7.   The quantity demanded of heart transplants does not respond to changes in the price of the operation. This means that the demand for heart transplants is

    a.   perfectly elastic.
    b.   perfectly inelastic.
    c.   inelastic, but not perfectly inelastic.
    d.   elastic, but not perfectly elastic.

8.   The elasticity of demand for salt is 0.5. We can say that the demand for salt is

    a.   inelastic.
    b.   elastic.
    c.   unit elastic.
    d.   horizontal.

9.   Each month, 300 pairs of shoelaces are purchased at a price of $1.30 per pair. When the price rises to $1.50 per pair, the quantity demanded falls to 250 pairs per month. Using the midpoint formula, the elasticity of demand for shoelaces is

    a.   14/11.
    b.   2/77.
    c.   11/14.
    d.   2/11.

10.   The Campus Cinema discovered that when it charged $3 for the afternoon matinee, it took in $360 per showing, but when it lowered the price to $2, it took in $480 per showing. This implies that the elasticity of demand for afternoon matinee movies is

    a.   3/5.

    b.   5/3.

    c.   5/2.

    d.   12/18.

11. We know that the demand for a product is elastic if

    a.   when price rises, revenue rises.

    b.   when price rises, revenue falls.

    c.   when price rises, quantity demanded rises.

    d.   when price falls, quantity demanded rises.

12. If a product has an inelastic demand, then

    a.   we are probably thinking about the long-run demand curve.

    b.   it has many close substitutes.

    c.   an increase in the price leads to an increase in revenue.

    d.   it probably represents a large proportion of consumer expenditures.

13. Which of the following products is likely to have the *most* elastic demand?

    a.   The latest CD for a popular singer

    b.   Compact disks for all singers

    c.   Musical entertainment in general

    d.   The demand for hearing aids

14. Which of the following goods is likely to have the *least* elastic demand?

    a.   Meals at restaurants

    b.   Vacation travel around the world

    c.   Bubblegum

    d.   College educations

15. When the price of gasoline rises, people immediately cut back on unnecessary trips. If the price of gasoline stays high, people eventually replace their cars with more fuel-efficient models. As a result, the

    a.   long-run demand for gasoline falls.

    b.   short-run demand for gasoline is less elastic than the long-run demand.

    c.   short-run demand for gasoline is more elastic than the long-run demand.

    d.   price of gasoline is forced down to its original level.

16. If scissors manufacturers cannot quickly and easily increase their output when the price of scissors rises, it is likely that

    a.   scissors are a normal good.

    b.   the supply of scissors is perfectly elastic.

    c.   the supply of scissors is elastic.

    d.   the supply of scissors is inelastic.

17. If the income elasticity of demand for boots is 0.4, a 10 percent decrease in consumer income will lead to a

    a.   40 percent increase in the demand for boots.

    b.   40 percent decrease in the demand for boots.

    c.   4 percent decrease in the demand for boots.

    d.   0.4 percent decrease in the demand for boots.

18. John Taylor, a movie star, makes two movies each year, for which he is paid $1 million each. John tells his agent, Slippery Slim, that if he were paid $2 million per movie, he'd be willing to make an additional movie each year. John's elasticity of movie supply is

    a.   2/3.

    b.   2/5.

    c.   3/5.

    d.   4/15.

19. Because the fish that are caught each day go bad very quickly, the daily catch will be offered for sale no matter what price it brings. As a result, we know that the daily supply curve for fish

    a.   slopes upward.
    b.   is perfectly inelastic.
    c.   is perfectly elastic.
    d.   is a horizontal line at today's price.

20. The size of the price elasticity of demand depends on

    a.   the availability of substitutes for the item.
    b.   whether the item represents a large fraction of income.
    c.   whether the price change is permanent or temporary.
    d.   all the above factors.

ANSWERS TO THE REVIEW QUESTIONS

Fill-In Questions

1.   Elasticity; percentage

2.   quantity demanded; price

3.   two; nonshifting

4.   downward; negative; 1; positive

5.   units; slope

6.   .inelastic; 1

7.   unit-free; relatively; inelastic; elastic

8.   perfectly inelastic; vertical

9.   perfectly elastic

10.   average; prices; percentage

11.   opposite; decrease; the same

12.   substitutes; large fraction; temporary

13.   income; quantity demanded

14.   Normal goods; inferior goods; negative

15.   quantity supplied; price

True-False Questions

1.   **False.** Elasticity can be used to measure the responsiveness of the relationship between any two economic variables.

2.   **True.** First, slope is unit-free while elasticity is not. Second, the formula for calculating elasticity and slope are different.

3.   **False.** The elasticity of demand is the percent change in quantity demanded divided by the percent change in price.

4.   **False.** Slope and elasticity are not the same thing.

5.   **False.** Although price elasticities of demand are technically negative numbers, economists often ignore the minus sign and discuss them in positive terms.

6. **False.** Since elasticities are unit-free, they can be compared across goods.

7. **False.** If the percentage change in quantity demanded is more than the percentage change in price, then the former divided by the latter is greater than 1, and demand is elastic.

8. **True.** Demand is elastic if the percentage change in quantity demanded is greater than the percentage change in price.

9. **False.** When the demand for something is perfectly inelastic, its demand curve is a vertical line.

10. **False.** Revenue, which is the amount spent on the good, will rise only when the price rises if the demand is inelastic.

11. **False.** The income elasticity of demand doesn't tell us about substitutes; it tells us whether goods are normal goods or inferior goods.

12. **False.** When price changes are expected to be temporary, consumers will respond more quickly in order to take advantage of the limited opportunity to save or to avoid the limited extra cost.

13. **True.** When income rises 1 percent, demand for pizza rises 0.75 percent. Since demand increases when income increases, this is a normal good.

14. **True.** This is the definition of the price elasticity of supply.

15. **False.** The vertical supply curve is inelastic; a higher price cannot bring about a higher quantity supplied.

Short-Answer Questions

1. To calculate the rainfall elasticity of umbrella sales, you would need to know how many umbrellas were sold on two days when the only thing that was different was the amount of rainfall. You would then calculate the percentage change in the sales of umbrellas (based on the average) and the percentage change in rainfall, and divide the former by the latter to find out what percentage change in umbrella sales you get for each percentage point change in rainfall.

2. To calculate the price elasticity of demand using the midpoint formula, you need to know two points on the demand curve: the old price and quantity (P_{old} and Q_{old}) and the new price and quantity (P_{new} and Q_{new}). The elasticity of demand is given by:

$$\text{Price elasticity of demand} = \frac{\text{Change in quantity demanded}}{\text{Average of old and new quantity}} \div \frac{\text{Change in price}}{\text{Average of old and new price}}$$

$$= \frac{Q_{new} - Q_{old}}{(Q_{new} + Q_{old})/2} \div \frac{P_{new} - P_{old}}{(P_{new} + P_{old})/2}$$

3. Elastic demand refers to a demand curve with an elasticity greater than 1; a 1 percent change in price causes a more than 1 percent change in quantity demanded. Inelastic demand refers to a demand curve with an elasticity less than 1; a 1 percent change in price causes a less than 1 percent change in quantity demanded.

4. When the demand curve has unit elastic demand (elasticity equal to 1), quantity demanded falls by the same percentage (in this case 5 percent) as the price rises.

5. The City Council must think that the demand for parking is inelastic; if it is not, the increase in parking fees will lead to such a large decrease in the amount of parking that revenue will fall and there will be less funds for the bus system.

6. Any three of the following: there are many good substitutes; the good represents a large fraction of consumers' spending; price changes are expected to be temporary; and consumers have lots of time to adjust to the price changes.

7. In the short run, people can respond to an increase in the price of gasoline by taking fewer trips, carpooling, riding the bus more often, and so forth. In the long run, they can do all those things *plus* buy a more fuel-efficient car the next time they buy a car, move closer to town to shorten their commute, and so on. In the long run, people have additional opportunities to adjust their consumption, and so the long-run elasticity will be greater than the short-run elasticity.

8. The price elasticity of demand measures the responsiveness of the quantity of a good that is demanded to a change in that good's price, holding all else equal. The income elasticity of demand measures the responsiveness of the quantity of a good that is demanded to changes in consumer income, holding all else equal.

9. The sign of the income elasticity of demand for an inferior good is negative. When a good is an inferior good, an increase in consumer incomes will decrease the quantity demanded of that good. Thus, the percent change in quantity demanded that accompanies an increase in consumer income is a negative number.

10. If firms' production decisions are based on their expectations of future prices, they will not want to supply more or less if the current price changes. They will respond only to changes in what they think the future price will be.

11. Price elasticity of supply tells you about the responsiveness of quantity supplied to changes in price, *ceteris paribus*. It is calculated by the percentage change in the quantity supplied divided by the percentage change in price.

12. This would be interpreted as the same quantity supplied regardless of the price. Seats in a movie theater would be an example of this type of supply curve.

13. With time, more and more inputs become variable. As such, producers can change output to a greater degree for a given change in price. Therefore, as the period of time increases, the supply curve will become more elastic.

SOLUTIONS TO THE PRACTICE PROBLEMS

1. In this case, you need to find two points on the same demand curve for pizza. The first row and the third row give you this: The price of burgers and income are the same in these two rows. The only things that are different are the price and quantity of pizzas (and the quantity of burgers, but that's not part of the demand curve for pizzas). So if we let P_{old} be \$8.00 and Q_{old} be 300, and let P_{new} be \$10.00 and Q_{new} be 250, then the midpoint formula says that

$$\text{Price elasticity of demand} = \frac{\text{Change in quantity demanded}}{\text{Average of old and new quantity}} \div \frac{\text{Change in price}}{\text{Average of old and new price}}$$

$$= \frac{250-300}{(250+300)/2} \div \frac{10.00-8.00}{(10.00+8.00)/2} = \frac{-50}{275} \div \frac{2.00}{9.00} = \frac{9}{11} \left(\text{ignoring the minus sign}\right)$$

2. In this case, you need to find two points where the only things that have changed are income and the quantity of burgers (and possibly the quantity of pizzas). The second row and the fourth row give you this; the prices of burgers and pizzas are the same in these two rows. So if we let I_{old} be \$170 and Q_{old} be 900, and let I_{new} be \$190 and Q_{new} be 800, then the midpoint formula says that

$$\text{Income elasticity of demand} = \frac{\text{Change in quantity demanded}}{\text{Average of old and new quantity}} \div \frac{\text{Change in income}}{\text{Average of old and new income}}$$

$$= \frac{800-900}{(800+900)/2} \div \frac{190-170}{(190+170)/2} = \frac{-100}{850} \div \frac{20}{180} = \frac{-18}{17}$$

Here we can't ignore the minus sign; it tells us that burgers are an inferior good. When income rises, the quantity of burgers demanded falls.

3. In this case, we want to find out how the quantity of burgers responds to a change in the price of pizzas, all else equal, so we return to the first and third rows, where the only things that are different are the price of pizza and the quantities of pizzas and burgers. Let P_{old} be $8.00 and Q_{old} be 750, and let P_{new} be $10.00 and Q_{new} be 850; then the midpoint formula says that

$$\text{Cross-price elasticity of demand} = \frac{\text{Change in burgers demanded}}{\text{Average of old and new quantity}} \div \frac{\text{Change in pizza price}}{\text{Average of old and new price}}$$

$$= \frac{850-750}{(850+750)/2} \div \frac{10.00-8.00}{(10.00+8.00)/2} = \frac{100}{800} \div \frac{2.00}{9.00} = \frac{9}{16}$$

Here, the sign of the cross-price elasticity is positive, which tells us that burgers and pizzas are substitutes. An increase in the price of pizzas leads to an increase in the demand for burgers.

4. At $3 per unit, 66 units are demanded, so the revenue would be $3 per unit × 66 units, or $198. The area that gives this revenue is the area of the rectangle whose corners are $3–D–66–0. If the price rises to $4 per unit, the quantity demanded falls to 54 units, and revenue rises to $216. Since the price increase leads to a revenue increase, we know that demand must be inelastic at this price.

5. Using the midpoint formula,

$$\text{Price elasticity of demand} = \frac{\text{Change in burgers demanded}}{\text{Average of old and new quantity}} \div \frac{\text{Change in pizza price}}{\text{Average of old and new price}}$$

$$= \frac{54-66}{(54+66)/2} \div \frac{4-3}{(4+3)/2} = \frac{-12}{60} \div \frac{1}{3.50} = \frac{7}{10} \text{ (ignoring the minus sign)}$$

Since the elasticity is less than 1, we have verified that demand is indeed inelastic at $3 per unit.

ANSWERS TO THE CHAPTER TEST

1. d
2. d
3. b
4. a
5. b
6. b
7. b
8. a
9. a

10. b
11. b
12. c
13. a
14. c
15. b
16. d
17. c
18. c
19. b
20. d

PART 1

Sample Test (Chapters 1–4): Introduction to Economics

SAMPLE TEST QUESTIONS

1. The problem of scarcity is

    a. a problem only for poor countries.
    b. faced by all economies.
    c. not faced by free market economies.
    d. eliminated as the economy grows.

2. When an economy is operating on its production possibilities curve, more production of one good means less production of another because

    a. resources are limited.
    b. resources are unlimited.
    c. wants are limited.
    d. wants are unlimited.

3. The value of the alternative that was *not* chosen is called the

    a. marginal cost of the choice.
    b. average cost of the choice.
    c. opportunity cost of the choice.
    d. gain from the choice.

4. An essential characteristic of the market economy is

    a. freely determined prices.
    b. an absence of property rights.
    c. prices set by the government.
    d. lack of competition.

5. In an economic interaction between two people, there are gains from trade if

    a. the two people trade involuntarily.
    b. neither person has any incentive to trade.
    c. reallocation makes at least one of the two people better off.
    d. the trade reallocates goods between the two people in a way that they both prefer.

6. An important reason for international trade is

    a. market failure.
    b. government failure.
    c. comparative advantage.
    d. opportunity costs.

7. A situation in which the market does *not* lead to an efficient economic outcome and in which there is a potential role for government is referred to as

    a. government failure.
    b. market failure.
    c. a competitive market.
    d. economic growth.

8.   The term *household* refers to

   a.   housing developments.
   b.   private organizations that produce goods and services.
   c.   public organizations that produce goods and services.
   d.   individuals or groups of individuals who share the same living quarters.

9.   Economic analysis that explains what happens in the economy and why and that makes policy recommendations is called

   a.   market economics.
   b.   normative economics.
   c.   positive economics.
   d.   subjective economics.

10.   Economic models

   a.   need to be the same as the phenomena they describe.
   b.   require either algebra or graphs.
   c.   are complicated, since human behavior is complicated.
   d.   are simplifications of the phenomena they attempt to explain.

11.   The law of demand states that

   a.   there is a direct relationship between price and quantity supplied.
   b.   as price increases, quantity demanded increases.
   c.   there is an inverse relationship between price and quantity demanded.
   d.   there is an inverse relationship between price and quantity supplied.
   e.   as price decreases, demand increases.

12.   The law of supply states that

   a.   price and quantity supplied are positively related.
   b.   the higher the price, the smaller the quantity that will be sold.
   c.   price and quantity supplied are inversely related.
   d.   price and quantity demanded are inversely related.
   e.   price and supply are positively related.

13.   When both supply and demand shift at the same time,

   a.   the change in equilibrium price cannot be predicted, but the change in equilibrium quantity can be predicted.
   b.   the change in equilibrium price can be predicted, but the change in equilibrium quantity cannot be predicted.
   c.   neither the change in equilibrium price nor the change in equilibrium quantity can be predicted.
   d.   both the change in equilibrium price and the change in equilibrium quantity can be predicted.
   e.   if the change in equilibrium quantity cannot be predicted, the change in equilibrium price cannot be predicted.

14.   A substitute is a good

   a.   that provides some of the same uses or enjoyment as another good.
   b.   for which demand increases when income rises and decreases when income falls.
   c.   that tends to be consumed together with another good.
   d.   for which demand decreases when income rises and increases when income falls.

15.   Which of the following is an example of two goods that are complements of each other?

   a.   Bicycles and kayaks
   b.   Rollerblades and knee pads
   c.   Baseball hats and ski caps
   d.   Cobblestones and brick paving

16. What would be the probable effect of the minimum wage if the equilibrium wage were above the minimum wage?

   a. There would be no effect on employment.
   b. It could cause increased unemployment.
   c. It could cause decreased unemployment.
   d. Unemployment would rise only for workers whose wages were already above the minimum.

17. Elasticity is a measure of

   a. how quickly a particular market reaches equilibrium.
   b. the change in income associated with increased education.
   c. the responsiveness of one variable to a change in another variable.
   d. the effect of an increase in the number of consumers in a particular market.
   e. how quickly expansion can take place in an economy.

18. For demand to be *elastic*,

   a. the percentage change in quantity demanded must be greater than the associated percentage change in price.
   b. the percentage change in quantity demanded must be less than the associated percentage change in price.
   c. the percentage change in quantity demanded must be equal to the associated percentage change in price.
   d. quantity demanded must change with a change in price.
   e. demand must change with a change in price.

19. If a good represents a small portion of consumers' income, then the price elasticity of demand will be

   a. low.
   b. high.
   c. the same as when it represents a small portion of people's income.
   d. inelastic.

20. Because the price elasticity of demand for agricultural products is very low,

   a. increases and decreases in supply result in large price changes.
   b. increases and decreases in supply result in small price changes.
   c. increases in supply result in large price changes, whereas decreases in supply result in small price changes.
   d. increases in supply result in small price changes, whereas decreases in supply result in large price changes.
   e. increases and decreases in supply do not result in price changes.

ANSWERS TO THE SAMPLE TEST

1. b
2. a
3. c
4. a
5. d
6. c
7. b
8. d
9. b
10. d
11. c
12. a
13. e
14. a
15. b
16. a
17. c
18. a
19. a
20. a

PART 2

Principles of Macroeconomics

Macroeconomics is the study of long-term economic growth and short-term economic fluctuations. Chapter 5 provides an overview of macroeconomics and introduced the elements that comprise economic growth theory and economic fluctuations theory. Important concepts such as gross domestic product (GDP), inflation, unemployment, and the interest rate are also discussed. Chapter 6 examines how production of goods and services in the whole economy is measured, focusing on the spending, income, and production approaches to measuring GDP. A second important topic covered in the chapter involves measuring the price level and the inflation rate.

Chapter 7 reinforces important GDP concepts with its discussion of how investment, consumption, and net exports are determined in the long run. Chapter 8 focuses on unemployment and employment, considering why unemployment in normal times is so high.

Economic growth holds the key to economic well being, and increasing labor productivity is the key to increasing economic growth. Chapter 9 introduces the growth accounting formula and demonstrates how technology has been a key factor in the recent productivity growth rebound in the United States.

Chapter 10 describes the monetary system. The first part of the chapter introduces the functions of money, how it is defined, and the role of banks in creating money. Later, the quantity equation, the relationship between money growth and inflation, the Philips curve, the relationship between inflation and unemployment, and the effects of inflation on productivity growth are explained.

CHAPTER 5

Macroeconomics: The Big Picture

CHAPTER OVERVIEW

Macroeconomics is the study of the whole market economy, including economic growth and fluctuations—how the economy grows and changes over time. The topics of macroeconomics—inflation, unemployment, interest rates, and exchange rates—are the subject of newspaper headlines and television stories. The study of macroeconomics entails understanding how they all relate to one another. This chapter provides a preview of this enterprise. We introduce the two basic concepts of macroeconomics, long-term economic growth and short-term economic fluctuations. We study unemployment, inflation, and interest rates, and see how they are related to growth and fluctuations. We consider how the government can use macroeconomic policies to promote economic growth and smooth economic fluctuations. Remember that this chapter is only a preview. It introduces a number of concepts and a lot of terminology, and you should not expect to master it all just yet. Try to see the big picture here; details and more complete understanding will come later.

CHAPTER REVIEW

1. **Real gross domestic product (real GDP)** is the total value of all goods and services produced in the economy during a specified period of time, usually a year or a quarter. It is called *real* because the measure of production is adjusted for the increase in prices over the same time period. Real GDP is also called *output* or *production*. Real GDP divided by the population is called *real GDP per capita*; it measures average production per person.

2. **Economic growth** describes increases in real GDP. It is measured by the annual *economic growth rate*, the percentage increase in real GDP each year. For countries with a growing population, real GDP per capita grows more slowly than real GDP. Over the past two centuries, growth in real GDP per capita has greatly increased living standards. In the United States, real GDP per capita doubled during the last 40 years.

3. **Economic fluctuations**, also called *business cycles*, are short-run movements around an economy's long-run economic growth path. A **recession** is a fall in real GDP that lasts for 6 months or more. There have been 16 recessions in the United States since the 1920s, the last occurring in 2001. A *peak* is the highest point in the business cycle before the start of a recession, and a *trough* is the lowest point at the end of a recession. An *expansion* is the period between recessions, from the trough to the next peak. The start of an expansion, when the economy is emerging from the recession, is called a *recovery*.

4. A **depression** is an extremely large recession. The period 1929–1932, when real GDP fell by one-third, is called the *Great Depression*. The recent recessions of the mid-1970s, early 1980s, early 1990s, and 2001 are not comparable in severity to the Great Depression.

5. The **labor force** consists of those people who are either working or looking for work. If you are out of work and looking for work, you are unemployed, and the **unemployment rate** is the number of unemployed people as a percentage of the labor force. The unemployment rate rises during recessions and falls during expansions. The labor force is not constant. The *labor force participation rate*, the number of people in the labor force as a percentage of the working-age population, falls in recessions and rises in recoveries.

6. The **inflation rate** is the increase in the general price of goods and services in the economy, measured as a percentage per year. The consumer price index is the most widely used measure of inflation. A decline in inflation is called *disinflation*, while negative inflation, a fall in the price level, is called *deflation*.

7. Inflation is also characterized by long-term trends and short-term fluctuations. First, inflation in the United States has been positive during every year since 1955. Second, inflation fluctuates; U.S. inflation rose from 3 to 4 percent per year in the mid-1960s to double digits, 10 percent per year or higher, in 1980, then returned to 3 to 4 percent per year in the mid-1980s, and has averaged around 2 to 3 percent in the 1990s and early 2000s. The rise of inflation in the late 1970s is called the *Great Inflation*. Third, inflation is closely related to the business cycle. Inflation has increased prior to every recession in the United States in the past 40 years and then decreased during and after each recession.

8. The **interest rate** is the amount charged to borrow money, expressed as a percent of the amount borrowed. There are many different interest rates, such as the *mortgage interest rate*, the *Treasury bill interest rate*, and the *savings deposit interest rate*. The *federal funds rate* is the interest rate that banks charge each other on overnight loans. The **real interest rate** is the interest rate minus the *expected rate of inflation*, the rate of inflation that people expect to occur. The term **nominal interest rate** is sometimes used to refer to an interest rate that is not adjusted for inflation.

9. **Potential GDP** is the average or normal level of real GDP. Despite the use of the word *potential*, it is not the maximum attainable level of real GDP. Real GDP fluctuates above and below potential GDP. The growth rate of potential GDP represents the long-run growth rate for the economy.

10. **Aggregate supply** is the total of all goods and services produced in the economy. Aggregate supply is determined by **labor**, the total number of hours workers are available to work; **capital**, the total available amount of factories, land, and machines; and **technology**, the available knowledge, which can be combined to produce real GDP. Potential GDP is, in turn, determined by aggregate supply.

11. **Aggregate demand** is the total demand for goods and services in the economy. Demand in the whole economy can be divided into demand by four groups—consumers, business firms, government, and foreigners—and aggregate demand is the sum of these four demands.

ZEROING IN

1. *Macroeconomic theory* consists of economic growth theory and economic fluctuations theory. Later in the text, we will develop each theory in a greater detail. Here, in the spirit of a preview, we will illustrate each theory with one diagram.

   a. The goal of *economic growth theory* is to explain the long-term upward rise of real GDP over time. Figure 5.1 presents a very stylized picture of economic growth for the United States during the past 50 years. The line represents potential GDP, therefore recessions and expansions have been smoothed out. The figure is drawn using a *ratio scale* so that constant growth of potential GDP is depicted as a straight line. The potential GDP line is steeper from 1955 to 1973 than it is from 1973 to 2005, indicating that economic growth was higher during the first 20 years than during the second 30 years.

Figure 5.1

b. *Economic fluctuations theory* attempts to explain short-run movements around the long-run growth path. Figure 5.2 depicts a stylized picture of economic fluctuations for the United States. The economy was in an expansion until 2000, a recession during 2001, and a recovery through 2004. The cycle of expansion, peak, recession, trough, and recovery is an important feature of economic fluctuations.

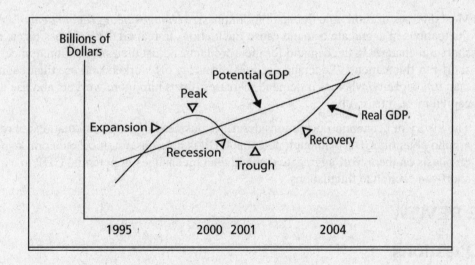

FIGURE 5.2

2. Economic growth is an important part of macroeconomics. Understanding economic growth involves learning about both economic growth theory and how macroeconomic policies can affect growth.

a. The **production function** is the heart of economic growth theory. According to the production function, real GDP is a function of labor, capital, and technology. In symbols, the production function is written as:

$$Y = F(L,K,T)$$

where Y is real GDP, L is labor, K is capital, and T is technology. The symbol F represents a function and means that Y is determined by L, K, and T. How does this relate to growth theory? If real GDP is determined by labor, capital, and technology, then real GDP growth must be determined by the growth of labor, the growth of capital, and the growth of technology. In other words, the slowdown in real GDP growth in the 1970s must have been caused by a slowdown in the growth of labor, capital, or technology.

b. *Supply side policies* are government policies that attempt to increase long-term economic growth. These policies focus on increasing the available supply of labor, capital, and technology. Supply side policies can affect growth by changing the *incentives* for business firms to invest in capital or to hire more workers, for workers to work harder or to enter the labor force, and for researchers to invent new technologies. Providing funds for education is another important policy by which the government aims to increase productivity and growth.

c. *Fiscal policy* is government policy concerning spending, taxing, and borrowing. Fiscal policy affects long-term economic growth by affecting the incentives of workers and firms. *Monetary policy* is government policy concerning the money supply and control of inflation. Monetary policy affects long-term economic growth because the inflation rate in the long run depends on the growth rate of the money supply. In the long run, countries with low and stable inflation have higher economic growth than countries with high and variable inflation.

3. As with economic growth, understanding economic fluctuations, the focus of Part 3 of the text, involves learning about both economic fluctuations theory and how macroeconomic policies affect business cycles.

a. Most theories of economic fluctuations emphasize *changes in aggregate demand*. Why do fluctuations in aggregate demand cause fluctuations in real GDP? Business firms, faced with short-run changes in the demand for their products, adjust their production to meet these short-run fluctuations. If demand declines, firms lay off workers and use their capital at less than full capacity, whereas if demand increases, firms hire more workers and use their capital more intensively.

b. The theory of economic fluctuations describes business cycles as fluctuations of real GDP around potential GDP. Although potential GDP is not constant, most economists place more emphasis on the role of aggregate demand than on changes in potential GDP to explain short-run economic fluctuations.

ACTIVE REVIEW

Fill-In Questions

1. Real _____ is the total of all goods and services produced in the economy during a specified period of time.

2. Real GDP divided by the population is called _____.

3. The _____ is the percentage increase in real GDP each year.

4. _____ or _____ are short-run movements around an economy's long-run economic growth path.

5.   A(n) _____ is a fall in real GDP that lasts for six months or more.

6.   A(n) _____ is the highest point in the business cycle before the start of a recession.

7.   A(n) _____ is an extremely large recession.

8.   The _____ is the number of unemployed people as a percentage of the labor force.

9.   _____ is the increase in the general price of goods and services in the economy.

10. The _____ is the amount charged to borrow money, expressed as a percent.

11. _____ GDP is the average or normal level of real GDP.

12. The total supply of all goods and services in the economy is called _____.

13. According to the production function, real GDP is a function of _____, _____, and _____.

14. Fiscal policy is government policy concerning _____, _____, and _____.

15. Monetary policy is government policy concerning the _____.

True-False Questions

1.   T F   Real GDP per capita in the United States has not increased since World War II.

2.   T F   The growth rate of real GDP equals the growth rate of real GDP per capita.

3.   T F   A recession is a decrease in the economic growth rate.

4.   T F   The recession of 2001 was so severe that it can be characterized as a depression.

5.   T F   In recent years, inflation in the United States has been greater than zero.

6.   T F   The federal funds rate is the interest rate on Treasury bills.

7.   T F   Potential GDP is not the maximum attainable level of real GDP.

8.   T F   Aggregate demand is determined by labor, capital, and technology.

9.   T F   One goal of economic fluctuations theory is to explain the economic growth slowdown.

10. T F   The production function is important for understanding economic growth theory.

11. T F   Supply side economic policies are government policies that attempt to smooth out short-run economic fluctuations.

12. T F   In the long run, economic growth is unrelated to inflation.

13. T F   According to economic fluctuations theory, potential GDP fluctuates around real GDP.

14. T F   Economic fluctuations are caused by changes in aggregate demand.

15. T F   Fiscal and monetary policies have little effect on economic fluctuations.

Short-Answer Questions

1.   What are two other names for real gross domestic product (GDP)?

2.   Describe the phases of a business cycle.

3.   What happens to the labor force participation rate over the business cycle?

4.   What is the difference between disinflation and deflation?

5.   What is the Great Inflation?

6.   What happens to inflation during the business cycle?

7.   What is the real interest rate?

8.   Describe the relationship between real GDP and potential GDP.

9.   According to the production function, what caused the slowdown in real GDP growth in the 1970s?

10. How can supply side policies affect growth?

11. How can fiscal policy affect long-run economic growth?

12. How can monetary policy affect long-term economic growth?

13. What is the relationship between inflation and economic growth in the long run?

14. Why do fluctuations in aggregate demand cause fluctuations in real GDP?

15. How do business firms increase their production in response to an increase in demand?

16. Did the terrorist attacks of September 11, 2001, have a substantial long-term economic impact on the U.S. economy? (Hint: See *Economics in Action—The Economic Impact of September 11.*)

WORKING IT OUT

1.   The unemployment rate is one of the most discussed economic statistics. Plotting the unemployment rate over time lets you see how the economy experiences fluctuations. The following data are for the United States in the 1980s.

Year	Unemployment Rate (percent)
1979	5.8
1980	7.0
1981	7.5
1982	9.5
1983	9.5
1984	7.4
1985	7.1
1986	6.9
1987	6.1

Plotting the unemployment rate on the vertical axis and the year on the horizontal axis produces the following picture.

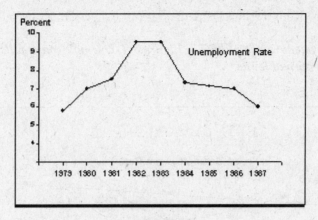

Figure 5.3

Unemployment rose from 1979 to 1983 and then declined to more normal levels by 1987.

2. The relation between the real interest rate and the nominal interest rate is an important topic for you to understand.

    a. The real interest rate is the nominal interest rate minus the expected rate of inflation. For example, if the nominal interest rate is 6 percent and expected inflation is 2 percent, the real interest rate is 4 percent $(6-2=4)$.

    b. You can also use the formula to calculate the nominal interest rate, which equals the real interest rate plus the expected rate of inflation. Using the same numbers, if the real interest rate is 4 percent and expected inflation is 2 percent, the nominal interest rate is 6 percent $(4+2=6)$.

    c. Finally, you can use the formula to calculate the expected inflation rate, which equals the nominal interest rate minus the real interest rate. Again using the same numbers, if the nominal interest rate is 6 percent and the real interest rate is 4 percent, expected inflation is 2 percent $(6-4=2)$.

Worked Problems

1. The following data are for the United States in the late 1990s and early 2000s.

Year	Unemployment Rate (percent)
1996	5.4
1997	4.9
1998	4.5
1999	4.2
2000	4.0
2001	4.7
2002	5.8
2003	6.0
2004	5.5

Plot the unemployment rate on the vertical axis and the year on the horizontal axis. What is depicted by the figure?

Answer

The unemployment rate is plotted in Figure 5.4. Unemployment falls until 2000 and then rises to more normal levels.

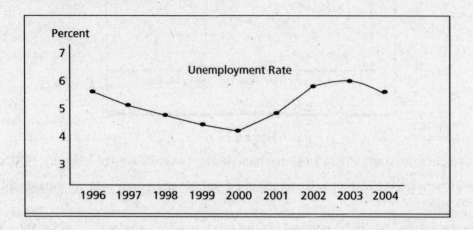

Figure 5.4

2.

a.   If the nominal interest rate is 5 percent and expected inflation is 3 percent, what is the real interest rate?

b.   If the real interest rate is 2 percent and expected inflation is 3 percent, what is the nominal interest rate?

c.   If the nominal interest rate is 5 percent and the real interest rate is 2 percent, what is expected inflation?

Answer

a.   *The real interest rate is the nominal interest rate minus expected inflation. The real interest rate is 2 percent* $(5-3=2)$.

b.   *The nominal interest rate is the real interest rate plus expected inflation. The nominal interest rate is 5 percent* $(2+3=5)$.

c.   *Expected inflation is the nominal interest rate minus the real interest rate. Expected inflation is 3 percent* $(5-2=3)$.

PRACTICE PROBLEMS

1. The following data are for the United Kingdom in the 1980s.

Year	Unemployment Rate (percent)
1980	6.4
1981	9.8
1982	11.3
1983	12.5
1984	11.7
1985	11.2
1986	11.1
1987	10.2
1988	8.3
1989	6.9

Plot the unemployment rate on the vertical axis and the year on the horizontal axis. What is depicted by the figure?

2. The following data are for the United States in the 1960s.

Year	Unemployment Rate (percent)
1963	5.5
1964	5.0
1965	4.4
1966	3.6
1967	3.7
1968	3.5
1969	3.4
1970	4.8

Plot the unemployment rate on the vertical axis and the year on the horizontal axis. What is depicted by the figure?

3.

a. If the nominal interest rate is 4 percent and expected inflation is 1 percent, what is the real interest rate?

b. If the real interest rate is 3 percent and expected inflation is 1 percent, what is the nominal interest rate?

c. If the nominal interest rate is 4 percent and the real interest rate is 3 percent, what is expected inflation?

4.

a. If the nominal interest rate is 7 percent and expected inflation is 6 percent, what is the real interest rate?

b. If the real interest rate is 1 percent and expected inflation is 6 percent, what is the nominal interest rate?

c. If the nominal interest rate is 7 percent and the real interest rate is 1 percent, what is expected inflation?

CHAPTER TEST

1. The growth in real GDP per capita

   a. is slower than the growth in real GDP for countries with a growing population.
   b. is faster than the growth in real GDP for countries with a growing population.
   c. is about the same as the growth in real GDP for countries with a growing population.
   d. has greatly decreased living standards over the past two centuries.

2. Economic growth describes increases in

   a. the labor force.
   b. real GDP.
   c. inflation.
   d. interest rates.

3. A fall in real GDP that lasts 6 months or more is called a(n)

   a. expansion.
   b. peak.
   c. economic growth slowdown.
   d. recession.

4. The highest point in the business cycle before the start of a recession is called a(n)

   a. trough.
   b. peak.
   c. recovery.
   d. expansion.

5. Which of the following groups of people are *not* considered part of the labor force?

   a. People who are unemployed
   b. People who are working
   c. People who are not working and are looking for work
   d. People who are not working and are not looking for work

6. The unemployment rate

   a. is always rising.
   b. is always falling.
   c. rises during recessions and falls during expansions.
   d. falls during recessions and rises during expansions.

7. The labor force participation rate is the number of people

   a. unemployed as a percentage of the labor force.
   b. unemployed as a percentage of the working-age population.
   c. employed as a percentage of the labor force.
   d. in the labor force as a percentage of the working-age population.

8. A fall in the price level is called

   a. a growth slowdown.
   b. deflation.
   c. disinflation.
   d. inflation.

9. Inflation

   a. increases prior to recessions and decreases during and after recessions.
   b. decreases prior to recessions and increases during and after recessions.
   c. increases prior to recessions and increases during and after recessions.
   d. decreases prior to recessions and decreases during and after recessions.

10. The real interest rate is the interest rate minus the
    a. federal funds rate.
    b. Treasury bill interest rate.
    c. mortgage interest rate.
    d. expected inflation rate.

11. Real GDP is the
    a. normal, or average, level of production for an economy.
    b. maximum attainable level of production for an economy.
    c. total of all goods and services produced in an economy during a specified period of time.
    d. total of all goods and services produced in an economy during a specified period of time divided by the population.

12. The goal of economic growth theory is to explain
    a. short-run movements around the long-run growth path.
    b. the short-term upward rise of real GDP over time.
    c. the long-term upward rise of real GDP over time.
    d. the long-term downward fall of real GDP over time.

13. Government policies that focus on increasing the available supply of labor, capital, and technology are
    a. supply side economic policies.
    b. fiscal policies.
    c. monetary policies.
    d. demand side economic policies.

14. Fiscal policy
    a. is government policy concerning the money supply.
    b. is government policy concerning money demand.
    c. is government policy concerning spending, taxing, and borrowing.
    d. affects long-term economic growth because inflation in the long run depends on the growth rate of the money supply.

15. Theories of economic fluctuations emphasize
    a. the inflation rate.
    b. the interest rate.
    c. aggregate supply.
    d. aggregate demand.

16. Economic fluctuations theory
    a. postulates that business cycles are due to changes in potential GDP.
    b. postulates that business cycles are due to changes in inflation.
    c. describes business cycles as fluctuations of real GDP around potential GDP.
    d. describes business cycles as fluctuations of potential GDP around real GDP.

17. Suppose that an economy with per capita GDP of $4,000 grows at a rate of 5 percent per year. What is the per capita GDP after 2 years?
    a. $4,200
    b. $4,400
    c. $4,410
    d. $4,500

Use Figure 5.5 for question 18.

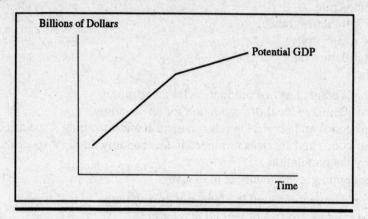

Figure 5.5

18. Figure 5.5 illustrates a(n)

 a. recession.
 b. recovery.
 c. expansion.
 d. economic growth slowdown.

Use Figure 5.6 for questions 19 and 20.

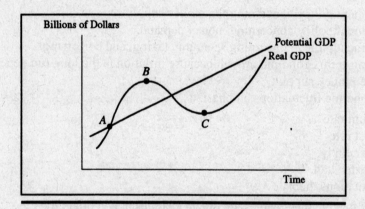

Figure 5.6

19. Point *C* on Figure 5.6 illustrates a(n)

 a. expansion.
 b. trough.
 c. peak.
 d. recovery.

20. Movement from point *A* to point *B* on Figure 5.6 illustrates a(n)

 a. expansion.
 b. trough.
 c. peak.
 d. recovery.

ANSWERS TO THE REVIEW QUESTIONS

Fill-In Questions

1. gross domestic product (GDP)
2. real GDP per capita
3. economic growth rate
4. Economic fluctuations; business cycles
5. recession
6. peak
7. depression
8. unemployment rate
9. Inflation
10. interest rate
11. Potential
12. aggregate supply
13. labor; capital; technology
14. spending; taxing; borrowing
15. money supply and the control of inflation

True-False Questions

1. **False**. Real GDP per capita has doubled during the last 40 years.
2. **False**. For countries with a growing population, real GDP per capita grows more slowly than real GDP.
3. **False**. A recession is a fall in the level, not just the growth rate, of real GDP.
4. **False**. The recession of 2001 was not comparable in severity to the Great Depression.
5. **True**. Inflation in the United States has been positive during every year since 1955.
6. **False**. The federal funds rate is the interest rate on overnight loans between banks.
7. **True**. Potential GDP is the average or normal level of real GDP.
8. **False**. Labor, capital, and technology determine aggregate supply.
9. **False**. Economic fluctuations theory attempts to explain short-run movements around the long-run growth path. The economic growth slowdown is a long-term decrease in the economic growth rate.
10. **True**. The production function is the heart of economic growth theory.
11. **False**. Supply side economic policies attempt to increase long-run economic growth.
12. **False**. Countries with low inflation have higher long-run economic growth than countries with high inflation.
13. **False.** Real GDP fluctuates around potential GDP.

14.   **True.** Changes in aggregate demand cause economic fluctuations.

15.   **False.** Macroeconomic policies have large effects on economic fluctuations.

Short-Answer Questions

1.   Real GDP is also called output or production.

2.   Starting with an expansion, the economy attains its peak. Then real GDP falls, initiating a recession. Once the economy reaches bottom, at the trough, a recovery occurs.

3.   The labor force participation rate falls in recessions and rises in recoveries.

4.   Disinflation is a decline in the inflation rate. Deflation, or negative inflation, is a fall in the price level.

5.   The Great Inflation is the rise of inflation in the United States in the late 1970s.

6.   Inflation increases prior to recessions and then decreases during and after recessions.

7.   The real interest rate is the interest rate minus the expected rate of inflation.

8.   Real GDP fluctuates above and below potential GDP.

9.   The economic growth slowdown was caused by a slowdown in the growth of labor, capital, or technology.

10.   Supply side policies can affect growth by changing the *incentives* for business firms to invest in capital or to hire more workers, for workers to work harder or to enter the labor force, and for researchers to invent new technologies.

11.   Fiscal policy can affect growth by changing the incentives for firms and workers.

12.   Monetary policy can affect growth by keeping inflation low and stable.

13.   In the long run, countries with low and stable inflation have higher economic growth than countries with high and variable inflation.

14.   In response to fluctuations in aggregate demand, business firms adjust their production, causing fluctuations in real GDP.

15.   If demand increases, firms hire more workers and use their capital more intensively.

16.   The terrorist attacks of September 11, did not have a substantial long-term economic impact on the U.S. economy. While there was a large short-term impact, the Federal Reserve cut interest rates, aid was provided to New York City and to the airline industry, and the economy has recovered in the ensuing years.

SOLUTIONS TO THE PRACTICE PROBLEMS

1.   The unemployment rate is plotted in Figure 5.7. Unemployment rises until 1983 and then slowly falls to more normal levels.

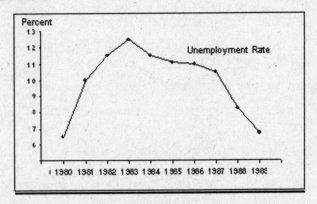

Figure 5.7

2.   The unemployment rate is plotted in Figure 5.8. Unemployment falls until 1966, stays low through 1969, and then rises to more normal levels.

Figure 5.8

3.   a.   The real interest rate is 3 percent.

    b.   The nominal interest rate is 4 percent.

    c.   Expected inflation is 1 percent.

4.   a.   The real interest rate is 1 percent.

    b.   The nominal interest rate is 7 percent.

    c.   Expected inflation is 6 percent.

ANSWERS TO THE CHAPTER TEST

1. a
2. b
3. d
4. b
5. d
6. c
7. d
8. b
9. a
10. d
11. c
12. c
13. a
14. c
15. d
16. c
17. c
18. d
19. b
20. a

APPENDIX TO CHAPTER 5

The Miracle of Compound Growth

OVERVIEW

Compound growth explains why seemingly small differences in growth rates result in huge differences in real GDP over time.

REVIEW

1. If real GDP grows by 10 percent per year, how long does it take for it to double? Your first thought might be 10 years, since adding 10 percent per year would add up to 100 percent. But you would be wrong; compound growth makes the process faster.

    a. Suppose the real GDP of a country that initially has real GDP of $100 billion grows by 10 percent per year. In year 1, real GDP is $110 (we will suppress the "billion"). In year 2, adding 10 percent to $110 gives $121. In year 3, it is $133.1; in year 4, $146.4; in year 5, $161.1; in year 6, $177.2; in year 7, $194.9; in year 8, $214.4; in year 9, $235.8; and in year 10, $259.4. Because of compounding, it takes between 7 and 8 years, instead of 10, for real GDP to double. Another way to look at this is to see that, after 10 years, real GDP increases by 160 percent, not 100 percent.

    b. The formula for compound growth is:

    $$(\text{Initial level}) \times (1 + g)^n = \text{Level at end of n years} ,$$

    where g is the annual growth rate stated as a fraction. In the above example, the 10 percent growth rate stated as a fraction is 0.1, so that:

    $$\$100 \times (1.1)^{10} = \$100 \times 2.594 = \$259.40$$

    You need a hand calculator with a key that calculates y^x to do this calculation.

    c. The compound growth formula can be inverted to calculate growth rates from initial and final income levels:

    In the above example, since growth is constant, we can calculate the growth rate using any year. Choosing year 7,

    $$g = (1.94.9/100)^{1/7} - 1 = (1.949)^{1/7} = 1.10 - 1 = 0.1 .$$

    As above, you need a hand calculator with a key that calculates y^x.

    d. Calculating growth rates after one year is much easier.

    In the above example,

    $$g = (110/100) - 1 = 1.1 - 1 = 0.1 .$$

2. Plotting growing variables involves a few subtleties. Let's consider real GDP in problem 1, which we know is growing at 10 percent per year:

Year	Real GDP (billions)
0	$100.0
1	$110.0
2	$121.0
3	$133.1
4	$146.4
5	$161.1
6	$177.2
7	$194.9
8	$214.4
9	$235.8
10	$259.4

In Figure 5A.1, these data are plotted on a ratio or logarithmic scale, where equal percentage changes in the variable have the same vertical distance. On a ratio scale, a variable that grows at a constant rate is depicted as a straight line. Ratio scales are very useful for plotting growing variables.

Figure 5A.1

WORKED PROBLEMS

1. Suppose that an economy with per capita GDP of $2,000 grows at a rate of 2 percent per year.

    a. What is per capita GDP after 1 year?

    b. What is per capita GDP after 10 years?

    c. What is per capita GDP after 100 years?

Answer

a. Although you don't need the formula for compound growth to solve this part, using it is good practice. The formula for compound growth is:

(Initial level) × (1 + g)ⁿ = Level at end of n years

With 2 percent stated as a fraction = 0.02 and n=1,

$\$2,000 \times (1.02) = \$2,040$

b. Using the compound growth formula, after 10 years:

$\$2,000 \times (1.02)^{10} = \$2,000 \times 1.219 = \$2,438$

c. Again using the compound growth formula, after 100 years:

$\$2,000 \times (1.02)^{100} = \$2,000 \times 7.245 = \$14,490$

2. Suppose that real GDP for an economy is as follows:

Year	Real GDP (billions)
0	$5,000
1	$5,250
2	$5,510
3	$5,680
4	$5,630
5	$5,560
6	$5,730
7	$6,020
8	$6,330

a. What is the growth rate of potential GDP?

b. Using a ratio scale, plot real GDP and potential GDP.

c. Identify the expansion, peak, recession, trough, and recovery.

Answer

a. The growth rate of potential GDP is the long-run growth rate of the economy. To determine the long-run growth rate g, use the compound growth formula between the initial (year 0) and final (year 8) levels. Using the formula:

The growth rate of potential GDP is 3 percent per year.

b. With a ratio scale, the constant growth of potential GDP is depicted as a straight line. Figure 5A.2 illustrates this and also shows the fluctuations of real GDP around potential GDP.

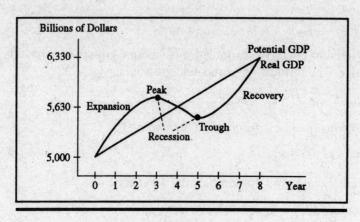

Figure 5A.2

c. The economy starts in an expansion that peaks in year 3. A recession occurs as real GDP falls, with a trough in year 5. The recovery begins in year 6 and continues through year 8.

PRACTICE PROBLEMS

1. Suppose that an economy with real GDP of $300 billion per year grows at a rate of 4 percent per year.

   a. What is real GDP after 1 year?

   b. What is real GDP after 5 years?

   c. What is real GDP after 10 years?

2. Suppose that an economy with per capita GDP of $1,000 grows at a rate of 3 percent per year.

   a. What is per capita GDP after 1 year?

   b. What is per capita GDP after 10 years?

   c. What is per capita GDP after 50 years?

3.   Suppose that real GDP for an economy is as follows:

Year	Real GDP (billions)
0	$6,000
1	$6,300
2	$6,610
3	$6,550
4	$6,420
5	$6,480
6	$6,610
7	$6,810
8	$7,030

a.   What is the growth rate of potential GDP?

b.   Using a ratio scale, plot real GDP and potential GDP.

c.   Identify the expansion, peak, recession, trough, and recovery.

4.   Suppose that real GDP for an economy is as follows:

Year	Real GDP (billions)
0	$5,000
1	$4,900
2	$5,050
3	$5,350
4	$5,780
5	$6,240
6	$6,610
7	$6,910
8	$6,840

a.   What is the growth rate of potential GDP?

b.   Using a ratio scale, plot real GDP and potential GDP.

c.   Identify the expansion, peak, recession, trough, and recovery.

SOLUTIONS TO THE PRACTICE PROBLEMS

1. a.   Real GDP $= \$300 \times (1.04) = \$312$ billion.

    b.   Real GDP $= \$300 \times (1.04)^5 = \$365$ billion.

    c.   Real GDP $= \$300 \times (1.04)^{10} = \$440$ billion.

2. a.   Per capita GDP $= \$1,000 \times (1.03) = \$1,030$.

    b.   Per capita GDP $= \$1,000 \times (1.03)^{10} = \$1,344$.

    c.   Per capita GDP $= \$1,000 \times (1.03)^{50} = \$4,384$.

3. a.   Using the compound growth formula:

$$g = (7,030/6,000)^{1/8} - 1 = (1.172)^{1/8} - 1 = 1.02 - 1 = 0.02 .$$

The growth rate of potential GDP is 2 percent per year.

    b.   Using a ratio scale, Figure 5A.3 shows potential GDP as a straight line and the fluctuations of real GDP around potential GDP.

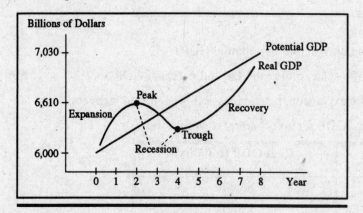

Figure 5A.3

    c.   The economy starts in an expansion that peaks in year 2. A recession occurs as real GDP falls, with a trough in year 4. The recovery begins in year 5 and continues through year 8.

4. a.   Using the compound growth formula:

$$g = (6,840/5,000)^{1/8} - 1 = (1.368)^{1/8} - 1 = 1.04 - 1 = 0.04 .$$

The growth rate of potential GDP is 4 percent per year.

    b.   Using a ratio scale, Figure 5A.4 shows potential GDP as a straight line and the fluctuations of real GDP around potential GDP.

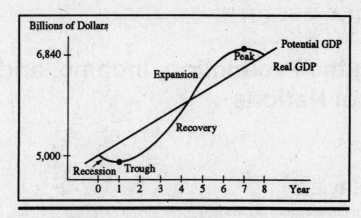

Figure 5A.4

c.   The economy starts in a recession that ends with a trough in year 1. A recovery occurs as real GDP rises, with an expansion culminating in a peak in year 7. Another recession begins in year 8.

CHAPTER 6

Measuring the Production, Income, and Spending of Nations

CHAPTER OVERVIEW

Accurate measurement of growth and fluctuations is essential for making economic decisions. Although we looked at how the economy grows and fluctuates over time in Chapter 4, it is not enough to be able to say that the economy has entered a growth slowdown or is in a recession; we want to know how much growth has fallen or how bad the recession is. In this chapter, we learn how to measure the macroeconomy. We study gross domestic product (GDP) in detail and learn about the spending, income, and production approaches to its measurement. We then consider a country's saving, investment, and net exports, and see how they are related. We learn about the difference between real and nominal GDP and see how to measure inflation. Measurement of GDP is not perfect, and we consider some of the problems. Finally, we look at international comparisons of GDP and see how fluctuating exchange rates make cross-country comparisons difficult.

CHAPTER REVIEW

1. *Gross domestic product (GDP)* is a measure of all the goods and services newly produced in a country during some period of time. The definition contains a number of important concepts. First, both goods—such as automobiles and computers—and services—such as health care and legal services—are included. Second, GDP includes only newly produced goods and services. Sales of used cars, for example, are not included. Also excluded are **intermediate foods**, which are goods that undergo further processing before being sold to consumers; intermediate foods are part of **final goods**; which are counted as part of GDP. Third, only goods and services produced within the borders of a country are included. The location of the production, not the ownership, is what matters. Fourth, GDP is always measured during a specified period of time, usually one year.

2. There are three ways to measure GDP; all reported in the national income and product accounts. The *spending* approach measures the total amount that people spend on goods and services made in America. The *income* approach measures the total income that is earned by all workers and businesses. The *production* approach measures the total of all the goods and services as they are produced. We consider each of the three approaches in turn.

3. The *spending* approach to measuring GDP divides spending into four categories: consumption, investment, government purchases, and net exports. GDP is the total of spending on the four categories.

    a. **Consumption** consists of purchases of final goods and services, ranging from automobiles to college tuition, by individuals. Consumption is the largest category of GDP—it accounts for 69 percent of GDP in the United States.

    b. **Investment** includes three types of spending. *Business fixed investment* is the purchase of final goods by business firms, including building a new factory or purchasing a new computer. *Residential investment* is the purchase of new houses and apartment buildings. Even though most new houses are purchased by consumers, they are still counted as part of investment because they provide long-term services. *Inventory investment* is the change in inventories, goods that have been produced but not yet sold.

c.   **Government purchases** consist of spending by federal, state, and local governments on new goods and services. Government outlays also include *transfer payments*, such as social security and unemployment benefits, and interest on the debt; these are not included in GDP.

d.   **Net exports** are **exports**, what Americans sell to foreigners, minus **imports**, what Americans buy from foreigners. Net exports are also called the **trade balance**. Exports are included separately in GDP because they are produced in the United States but are not part of consumption, investment, or government purchases. Imports are subtracted to get GDP because they are part of consumption and investment spending but, not being produced in the United States, should not be included in GDP.

4.   The income approach to measuring GDP adds up the income received by workers and businesses for producing the goods that make up GDP. This includes labor income, capital income, depreciation, indirect business taxes, net income of foreigners, and the statistical discrepancy.

a.   **Labor income**, which consists of wages, salaries, and fringe benefits, is the largest component of income. **Capital income**—profits, rental payments, and interest payments—is the next largest.

b.   **Depreciation** is the amount by which factories and machines wear out each year. Much of investment spending goes to replace worn-out factories and equipment, and that spending is included in GDP. Investment, which is sometimes called *gross investment*, minus depreciation equals *net investment*. Spending to replace depreciated factories and machines is not included in capital income, however, because firms subtract depreciation to compute profits. Since depreciation is included in GDP but not in capital income, it must be added as a separate category.

c.   *Indirect business taxes* consist mainly of sales taxes. Like depreciation, they are included in GDP but not in firms' profits and need to be added as a separate category. *Net income of foreigners* equals income earned by foreigners in the United States minus income earned by Americans abroad. This is also part of GDP, but it is not included in labor and capital income, and so it is added as another category. Finally, because data on income and spending are collected in different ways, the *statistical discrepancy* is added to produce a measure of *aggregate income* that equals GDP.

5.   The production approach to measuring GDP adds up the production of each firm or industry in the economy. When using this method, it is important to avoid double counting goods, such as automobile tires, which are final goods for one firm but intermediate goods for another. **Value added** is the value of a firm's output less the value of the intermediate goods used in production. Measuring GDP by production involves counting the value added, not the final sales, at each level of production, which avoids double counting.

6.   It is important to understand the difference between *stocks*, the amount of goods at a particular date, and *flows*, the change in the amount of goods between two dates. For example, if your campus bookstore has 100 copies of this textbook when it opens on the morning of September 1, the stock of inventory is 100 books. If it sells 10 copies of the book during that day, the stock of inventory decreases to 90 books and the flow of inventory investment equals minus 10 books.

7.   For an individual, saving equals income less consumption. For a country, government purchases must also be accounted for. **National saving**, the sum of all saving in the economy, equals income less consumption less government purchases. At any time, some people, whose income is greater than their consumption, are saving, while others, who consume more than their income, are

dissaving. Middle-aged people generally save, while the young and the old either save very little or dissave.

8. The budget surplus is the difference between the government's receipts from taxes and its expenditures. When expenditures exceed receipts, as has been the case for the United States in recent years, there is a budget deficit. When there is a budget surplus, the government saves, and when there is a budget deficit, the government dissaves.

9. Gross domestic product (GDP) measures goods and services at their current prices. When there is inflation and prices increase, GDP rises even if the quantity of goods and services produced is unchanged. **Real GDP** is a measure of production that corrects for inflation. It measures what GDP would have been if prices were constant. GDP is sometimes called **nominal GDP**. If there is inflation, as there has been in the United States over the last 40 years, nominal GDP grows faster than real GDP.

10. The **GDP deflator** is the measure of the **price level** that is used to compute real GDP. More precisely, the GDP deflator equals nominal GDP divided by real GDP. The GDP deflator is a measure of the price of all goods and services in GDP: consumption, investment, government purchases, and net exports. The **consumer price index (CPI)** is another measure of the price level. It is the price of a fixed collection of consumer goods and services in a given year divided by the price of the same collection in some base year. The *chain-weighted price index* is a third measure of prices. Unlike the CPI, it is not based on a fixed quantity of goods and services in some base year. The quantities in the index change each year, and the percentage changes in the index are "chained" together.

11. The use of fixed weights is an important reason why economists believe that the CPI overstates inflation. By not allowing quantities to change when prices change, the CPI puts too much weight on items with rising prices and too little weight on items with falling prices. The result is that measured inflation is greater than actual inflation.

ZEROING IN

1. How can you tell what is counted, and what is not counted, as part of GDP? The first step is to remember the definition. GDP is a measure of all the goods and services newly produced in a country during some period of time.

    a. *Goods and services*. GDP is not just a measure of tangible goods like dishwashers and televisions. Services such as banking and tourism are a very important part of GDP.

    b. *Newly produced*. When an automobile is manufactured, it is counted as part of GDP. Whether it remains with the original owner until it falls apart or is sold ten times in the next five years does not affect GDP; only newly produced goods are counted.

    c. *In a country*. The location of the production is what matters for GDP, not the ownership. Honda Accords produced in Ohio count toward U.S., not Japanese, GDP. Similarly, IBM computers manufactured in Malaysia do not add to the GDP of the United States; they count toward the GDP of Malaysia.

    d. *Measure*. GDP can include only what can be measured. Child care by parents and relatives does not count toward GDP, but daycare does. Illegal activities do not count toward GDP.

2. One of the most confusing parts of this chapter is the meaning of investment. Economists define *investment* as the purchase of new factories, houses, or equipment. To everybody else, investment is putting away money for the future, perhaps in the stock market. This doesn't mean that economists are right and everybody else is wrong; it simply means that you need to be careful with your use of language.

3. Although GDP is the most comprehensive measure of economic activity, it is not perfect. We discuss some of its shortcomings:

    a. Collection of data on GDP is a big job, and it takes time. *Revisions in GDP* are the changes in GDP as new data become available. Some of these revisions are quite large and can change our perception of how the economy is performing.

    b. There are a number of important *omissions from GDP*. Home production is not included in GDP because the transactions are not recorded in markets. Illegal activity, also called the *underground economy*, is omitted for the same reason. Improvements in the quality of goods and services are difficult to measure. A $3,000 personal computer in 1995 is a vastly different good from a $3,000 personal computer in 1985, yet they count exactly the same toward GDP. Finally, leisure activity is not included in GDP.

    c. GDP is not a complete measure of the well being of individuals. Life expectancy, infant mortality, and environmental quality, among others, also measure how a country is performing over time.

ACTIVE REVIEW

Fill-In Questions

1. _____ is a measure of the value of all the goods and services newly produced in a country during some period of time.

2. GDP can be measured by the _____, _____, and _____ approaches.

3. The spending approach divides spending into _____, _____, _____, and _____.

4. _____ is the largest category of GDP.

5. The three types of investment spending are _____, _____, and _____.

6. _____ consist of spending by federal, state, and local governments on new goods and services.

7. Net exports are _____ minus _____.

8. The two largest components of income are _____ and _____.

9. Gross investment minus _____ equals net investment.

10. _____ is the value of a firm's output minus the value of the intermediate goods used in production.

11. National saving equals _____ minus _____ minus _____.

12. When the government's expenditures exceed its receipts, there is a(n) _____.

13. _____ is a measure of production that corrects for inflation.

14. Three measures of the price level are the _____, the _____, and the _____.

15. The difference between the CPI and the chain-weighted price index is that the CPI uses a _____ quantity of goods and services.

True-False Questions

1.   T   F   Haircuts are not included in GDP.

2.   T   F   Sales of used textbooks are not part of GDP.

3.   T   F   When General Motors builds a truck in Brazil, this adds to U.S. GDP.

4.   T   F   If a woman marries her nanny, who becomes a stay-at-home husband, GDP falls.

5.   T   F   Legalization of marijuana would increase GDP.

6.   T   F   All government outlays are part of GDP.

7.   T   F   Capital income (profits, rental payments, and interest payments) is the largest component of income.

8.   T   F   GDP can be measured by counting final sales at each level of production.

9.   T   F   The spending, income, and production approaches to GDP all add up to the same value.

10.   T   F   The change in the flow of inventories between two dates is the stock of inventory investment.

11.   T   F   People usually save throughout their lifetimes.

12.   T   F   Government saving is always positive.

13.   T   F   Nominal GDP always grows faster than real GDP.

14.   T   F   Investing in the stock market adds to GDP.

15.   T   F   Much of the data that make up GDP is not quickly available in its final form.

16.   T   F   GDP is a complete measure of the well-being of a country.

Short-Answer Questions

1. What determines GDP—the location or the ownership of the production?

2. What is the spending approach to measuring GDP?

3. Why is residential investment counted as part of investment instead of consumption?

4. Why does GDP include net exports instead of simply exports?

5. How is GDP calculated by the income approach?

6. What is the difference between gross and net investment?

7. What is the production approach to measuring GDP?

8. With the production approach, why is value added counted instead of final sales?

9. How can GDP increase if production of goods and services is constant?

10. What is the difference between nominal and real GDP?

11. What is the GDP deflator?

12. What is the difference between the chain-weighted price index and the CPI?

13. Why do economists believe that the CPI overstates inflation?

14. Why are home production and illegal activities omitted from GDP?

15. Why do personal computers cause difficulties in measuring GDP?

16. Was the U.S economy stagnant during the fourth quarter of 2004? (Hint: See Reading the News About—GDP Each Month.)

WORKING IT OUT

1. The spending approach to measuring GDP can be illustrated using algebra. It is important that you familiarize yourself with these terms and equations now, because they will be used a great deal later.

   a. According to the spending approach, GDP is the sum of consumption, investment, government purchases, and net exports. Let Y stand for GDP, C for consumption, I for investment, G for government purchases, and X for net exports. In symbols:

   $$Y = C + I + G + X.$$

   GDP is computed by adding up consumption, investment, government purchases, and net exports.

   b. We earlier defined national saving as income minus consumption minus government purchases. Since GDP can be measured by income as well as by spending or production, we let Y stand for income too. Call national saving S and use, as above, C for consumption and G for government purchases. In symbols:

   $$S = Y - C - G.$$

   c. *Private saving* is defined as income minus consumption minus taxes. *Government saving* is defined as taxes minus government purchases. In symbols:

   Private saving $= Y - C - T$.

   Government saving $= T - G$.

   d. Combining the equations, we can see that private saving plus government saving equals national saving:

   $$(Y - C - T) + (T - G) = (Y - C - G).$$

2. The relationship among real GDP, nominal GDP, and the GDP deflator can also be illustrated using algebra.

   a. The GDP deflator was defined to equal nominal GDP divided by real GDP. Written as an equation:

   GDP deflator = Nominal GDP/Real GDP.

   This expression can be manipulated to provide a formula for real GDP:

   Real GDP = Nominal GDP/GDP deflator.

   Alternatively, nominal GDP can be written:

   Nominal GDP = GDP deflator × Real GDP.

   b. Inflation is positive when the price level is increasing. Since the GDP deflator is a measure of the price level, inflation means that the GDP deflator is growing over time. From the formula for the GDP deflator, it can be growing only if the numerator, nominal GDP, is rising faster than the denominator, real GDP. This is another way of showing that when there is inflation nominal GDP grows faster than real GDP.

Worked Problems

1. Suppose you are given the following information about the economy, with the values in billions of dollars:

Consumption	$5,000
Investment	$2,000
Government purchases	$1,000
Net exports	$1,000
Taxes	$1,500

   a. What is GDP?

   b. What is private saving?

   c. What is government saving?

   d. What is national saving?

Answer

   a. Using the spending approach, GDP equals consumption plus investment plus government purchases plus net exports. In equation form:

   $Y = C+I+G+X$.

   Substituting the values:

   $Y = \$5,000+\$2,000+\$1,000+\$1,000=\$9,000$ billion .

   b. Private saving equals income minus consumption minus taxes. Written as a formula:

   $\text{Private saving} = Y - C - G$.

   Substituting the values, including the value of income (GDP) calculated above:

   $\text{Private saving} = \$9,000 - \$5,000 - \$1,500 = \$2,500$ billion .

   c. Government saving equals taxes minus government purchases. Written as a formula:

   $\text{Government saving} = T - G$.

   Substituting the values, Government saving equals $\$1,500 - \$1,000 = \$500$ billion ..

   d. National saving equals income minus consumption minus government purchases. Written as a formula:

   $S = Y - C - G$,

   Substituting the values, including the value of income (GDP) calculated above:

   $S = \$9,000 - \$5,000 - \$1,000 = \$3,000$ billion .

   National saving also equals private saving plus government saving.

   Substituting the values calculated above:

$S = \$2,500 + \$500 = \$3,000$ billion.

2. Suppose that the economy is characterized by the following information, with values in billions of dollars:

Year	Nominal GDP	Real GDP
2000	$5,000	$5,000
2001	$6,000	$5,455
2002	$7,200	$6,000

   a.   What is the GDP deflator for the three years?

   b.   Which is growing faster, nominal or real GDP?

Answer

   a.   The GDP deflator equals nominal GDP divided by real GDP. For the year 2000, the GDP deflator $= \$5,000/\$5,000 = 1.00$. For the year 2001, the GDP deflator $= \$6,000/\$5,455 = 1.10$. For the year 2002, the GDP deflator $= \$7,200/\$6,000 = 1.20$.

   b.   Since the GDP deflator is increasing over time, there is inflation. When there is inflation, nominal GDP grows faster than real GDP.

PRACTICE PROBLEMS

1. Suppose you are given the following information about the economy, with the values in billions of dollars:

Consumption	$6,000
Investment	$2,000
Government purchases	$1,000
Net exports	−$1,000

   a.   What is GDP?

   b.   What is national saving?

2. Suppose you are given the following information about the economy, with the values in billions of dollars:

Income	$9,000
Consumption	$6,000
Government purchases	$2,000
Taxes	$1,000

   a. .   What is private saving

   b.   What is government saving?

3.   Suppose that the economy is characterized by the following information, with values for real GDP in billions of dollars:

Year	GDP Deflator	Real GDP
2000	0.90	$6,000
2001	1.00	$6,000
2002	1.10	$6,000

What is nominal GDP for the three years? What is happening in the economy?

4.   Suppose that the economy is characterized by the following information, with values for nominal GDP in billions of dollars:

Year	GDP Deflator	Nominal GDP
2000	1.25	$8,000
2001	1.25	$8,500
2002	1.25	$9,000

What is real GDP for the three years? What is happening in the economy?

CHAPTER TEST

1.   Which of the following would *not* be included in the measurement of gross domestic product (GDP) for the United States?

   a.   New Honda Accords produced in the United States
   b.   Used Ford Broncos sold in the United States
   c.   Health care and legal services
   d.   Computers and software products

2.   When calculating GDP, what matters is

   a.   the location of production only.
   b.   the ownership of production only.
   c.   both the location and the ownership of production.
   d.   neither the location nor the ownership of production.

3.   The production approach to calculating GDP measures the total

   a.   amount people spend on goods and services made in the United States.
   b.   amount people spend on goods and services made in the United States and abroad.
   c.   income that is earned by workers and businesses.
   d.   of all goods and services produced.

4.   The income approach to calculating GDP measures the total

   a.   amount people spend on goods and services made in the United States.
   b.   amount people spend on goods and services made in the United States and abroad.
   c.   income that is earned by workers and businesses.
   d.   of all goods and services produced.

5. The spending approach to calculating GDP divides spending into four categories:

    a. income, production, investment, and consumption.
    b. consumption, income, production, and net imports.
    c. consumption, investment, imports, and exports.
    d. consumption, investment, government purchases, and net exports.

6. Which of the following accounts for the largest portion of GDP?

    a. Investment
    b. Net exports
    c. Consumption
    d. Government expenditures

7. Net investment equals

    a. gross investment plus depreciation.
    b. gross investment minus depreciation.
    c. net business fixed investment plus residential investment plus inventory investment.
    d. net business fixed investment plus residential investment plus financial investment.

8. Which of the following is *not* a component of income?

    a. Labor income
    b. Depreciation
    c. Transfer payments
    d. Indirect business taxes

9. The largest component of income is

    a. capital income.
    b. labor income.
    c. depreciation.
    d. transfer payments.

10. Value added is

    a. used to measure GDP under the spending approach.
    b. the final sales value of a firm's output.
    c. the value of a firm's output plus the value of intermediate goods used in production.
    d. the value of a firm's output minus the value of intermediate goods used in production.

11. National saving equals income

    a. minus consumption.
    b. plus consumption.
    c. minus consumption minus government purchases.
    d. plus consumption plus government purchases.

12. When the government's expenditures exceed the government's receipts from taxes,

    a. there is a budget deficit.
    b. there is a budget surplus.
    c. there is a balanced budget.
    d. the government saves.

13. If there is inflation,
    a.   nominal GDP grows faster than real GDP.
    b.   nominal GDP grows faster than the GDP deflator.
    c.   real GDP grows faster than nominal GDP.
    d.   real GDP grows faster than the GDP deflator.

14. The GDP deflator equals
    a.   real GDP divided by nominal GDP.
    b.   nominal GDP divided by real GDP.
    c.   nominal GDP plus real GDP.
    d.   nominal GDP minus real GDP.

15. The measure of the price level that is the price of a fixed collection of consumer goods and services in a given year divided by the price of the same collection in some base year is
    a.   the GDP deflator.
    b.   the chain weighted price index.
    c.   nominal GDP.
    d.   the consumer price index.

16. National saving equals
    a. $I - X$.
    b. $I + X$.
    c. $X - I$.
    d. $I + C$.

17. When saving is less than investment,
    a.   net exports are positive, and there is a trade deficit.
    b.   net exports are positive, and there is a trade surplus.
    c.   net exports are negative, and there is a trade deficit.
    d.   net exports are negative, and there is a trade surplus.

18. Which of the following is *not* omitted from GDP?
    a.   Home production
    b.   Illegal activities
    c.   Leisure activities
    d.   Legal services

Use the following table for questions 19 and 20.

Suppose you are given the following information about the economy (values in billions of dollars).

Consumption	$6,000
Investment	$2,000
Government purchases	$1,000
Net exports	$2,000

19. What is GDP?
    a. $11,000 billion
    b. $9,000 billion
    c. $7,000 billion

    d. $5,000 billion
20. What is national saving?

    a. $2,000 billion
    b. $3,000 billion
    c. $4,000 billion
    d. $5,000 billion

ANSWERS TO THE REVIEW QUESTIONS

Fill-In Questions

1.   Gross domestic product (GDP)

2.   spending; income; production

3.   consumption; investment; government purchases; net exports

4.   Consumption

5.   business fixed investment; residential investment; inventory investment

6.   Government purchases

7.   exports; imports

8.   labor income; capital income

9.   depreciation

10. Value added

11. income; consumption; government purchases

12. budget deficit

13. Real GDP

14. GDP deflator; consumer price index; chain weighted price index

15. fixed

True-False Questions

1.   **False**. Haircuts are a service and are part of GDP.

2.   **True**. The textbook was included in GDP when it was new; it is not counted again.

3.   **False**. Building a truck in Brazil adds to Brazilian GDP. It does not matter who owns the truck.

4.   **True**. Child care counts toward GDP only when it is a market activity.

5.   **True**. Illegal activities are not included in GDP.

6.   **False**. A large part of government outlays is for transfer payments, which are not included in GDP.

7.   **False**. Labor income (wages, salaries, and fringe benefits) is the largest component of income.

8.   **False**. GDP is measured by counting value added, not final sales.

9.   **True**. GDP is the same however it is measured.

10. **False**. The change in the stock of inventories between two dates is the flow of inventory investment.

11. **False**. Most saving is done by the middle-aged. The young and the old either save very little or dissave.

12. **False**. When there is a budget deficit, as has often been the case for the United States, the government dissaves.

13. **False**. Nominal GDP grows faster than real GDP if there is inflation.

14. **False**. Buying stocks is not a form of investment, and therefore is not part of GDP.

15. **True**. Revisions to GDP can be quite large.

16. **False**. Many other factors, such as life expectancy, infant mortality, and environmental quality, measure how a country is performing over time.

Short-Answer Questions

1. The location determines GDP. The ownership is irrelevant.

2. The spending approach measures the total amount that people spend on goods and services.

3. Residential investment provides long-term services, and so it is counted with investment rather than consumption.

4. Imports need to be subtracted when computing GDP because they are included in consumption and investment spending, but they are not produced in the United States.

5. In the income approach, the income received by workers and businesses for producing the goods that make up GDP is added up.

6. Net investment equals gross investment minus depreciation.

7. In the production approach, the production of each firm or industry in the economy is added up.

8. Counting value added avoids double counting goods that are final goods for one firm but intermediate goods for another.

9. When there is inflation, GDP increases even if production is unchanged.

10. Real GDP adjusts nominal GDP for changing prices.

11. The GDP deflator, the measure of the price level that is used to compute real GDP, equals nominal GDP divided by real GDP.

12. Unlike the CPI, the chain-weighted price index is not based on a fixed quantity of goods and services. Its quantities change each year, and the percentage changes in the index are "chained" together.

13. By using fixed weights that do not allow quantities to change when prices change, the CPI puts too much weight on items with rising prices and too little weight on items with falling prices.

14. Home production and illegal activities are not recorded in markets, and so they cannot be counted as part of GDP.

15. Goods whose quality is improving rapidly over time, such as personal computers, cause problems in measuring GDP.

16. The U.S. economy was not stagnant. GDP grew at an annual rate of 3.8 percent during the fourth quarter of 2004.

SOLUTIONS TO THE PRACTICE PROBLEMS

1. a. The formula for GDP is $Y = C + I + G + X$. Using the values:

   $$Y = \$6,000 + \$2,000 + \$1,000 + (-\$1,000) = \$8,000 \text{ billion}$$

   b. The formula for national saving is $S = Y - C - G$. Using the values:

   $$S = \$8,000 - \$6,000 - \$1,000 = \$1,000 \text{ billion}.$$

2. a. Private saving = income − consumption − taxes. Using the values:

   $$\text{Private saving} = \$9,000 - \$6,000 - \$1,000 = \$2,000 \text{ billion}.$$

   b. Government saving = taxes − government purchases. Using the values:

   $$\text{Government saving} = \$1,000 - \$2,000 = -\$1,000 \text{ billion}.$$

3. Nominal GDP = GDP deflator × Real GDP. Using the values, nominal GDP = $5,400 in the year 2000, $6,000 in the year 2001, and $6,600 in the year 2002. Because of inflation, nominal GDP is growing even though real GDP is constant.

4. Real GDP = Nominal GDP/GDP deflator. Using the values, real GDP = $6,400 in the year 2000, $6,800 in the year 2001, and $7,200 in the year 2002. With constant prices, there is no inflation. Real and nominal GDP grow at the same rate.

ANSWERS TO THE CHAPTER TEST

1. b
2. a
3. d
4. c
5. d
6. c
7. b
8. c
9. b
10. d
11. c
12. a
13. a
14. b
15. d
16. b
17. c

18. d
19. a
20. c

CHAPTER 7

The Spending Allocation Model

CHAPTER OVERVIEW

The *spending allocation model* determines how GDP is allocated among the four components of spending: consumption, investment, net exports, and government purchases. We first learn how the interest rate affects each of these components of spending. We then learn how to determine the equilibrium interest rate and see how changes in government purchases affect consumption, investment, and net exports and how shifts in consumption affect investment and not exports.

CHAPTER REVIEW

1. The **consumption share** of GDP is consumption C divided by GDP, or C/Y. It is the proportion of GDP that is used for consumption. The consumption share is negatively related to the interest rate. A higher interest rate encourages saving, decreasing consumption.

2. The **investment share** of GDP is investment I divided by GDP, or I/Y. It is the proportion of GDP that is used for investment. The investment share is also negatively related to the interest rate. A higher interest rate increases the cost of borrowing, making it more expensive for a firm to build a new factory or buy a new computer. When mortgage interest rates rise, it becomes more expensive to purchase new houses, and so the residential component of investment falls. The investment share is more sensitive to interest rates than the consumption share.

3. The **net exports share** of GDP is net exports X divided by GDP, or X/Y. It is the proportion of GDP that is used for net exports. The net exports share is also negatively related to the interest rate. A higher interest rate in the United States raises the exchange rate because it makes dollar-denominated assets more attractive than foreign assets. The higher exchange rate makes domestic goods more expensive and foreign goods cheaper, reducing exports and increasing imports. With lower exports and higher imports, net exports, which are exports minus imports, decline. Thus a higher interest rate decreases net exports. Conversely, a lower interest rate in the United States lowers the exchange rate, increasing net exports. The net exports share is also more sensitive to interest rates than the consumption share. The net exports share can be positive, zero, or negative. When the net exports share is positive, there is a trade surplus. When the net exports share is negative, there is a trade deficit.

4. The **government purchases share** of GDP is government purchases G divided by GDP, or G/Y. It is the proportion of GDP that is used for government purchases. Since government purchases are not affected by the interest rate, the government purchases share is not related to the interest rate.

5. The *nongovernment share* of GDP is the sum of the consumption, investment, and net exports shares. The nongovernment share is negatively related to the interest rate because each of its components, the consumption, investment, and net exports shares, is negatively related to the interest rate. The interest rate adjusts to ensure that the government and nongovernment shares add up to 100 percent of GDP. Equivalently, the interest rate adjusts to ensure that the sum of the consumption, investment, government purchases, and net exports shares equals 1.

6. The *real interest rate* is the nominal interest rate, the interest rate on loans, minus the expected inflation rate. It is the real interest rate, not the nominal interest rate that determines how real GDP

is divided among consumption, investment, government purchases, and net exports. In addition, it is important to remember that it takes time for consumers and firms to completely respond to a change in the interest rate. The division of real GDP into shares is applicable to the long run, three years or more, not to short-run fluctuations.

7.   When the government purchases share of GDP increases, the nongovernment share decreases by the same amount. Since the nongovernment share is negatively related to the interest rate, the interest rate must rise. Furthermore, since each component of the nongovernment share is negatively related to the interest rate, the consumption, investment, and net exports shares all fall. The decline in investment resulting from an increase in government purchases is called **crowding out**. The process is reversed when the government purchases share of GDP decreases. The interest rate falls, and the consumption, investment, and net exports shares rise.

ZEROING IN

1.   The division of real GDP between government and nongovernment shares and the determination of the **equilibrium interest rate** are two of the most important topics in this chapter. We now focus on using graphs to further our understanding.

   a.   The consumption, investment, and net exports shares are depicted in Figure 7.1. The real interest rate is on the vertical axis, and the shares, as a percent of GDP, are on the horizontal axis. Although all three are negatively related to the interest rate, the fact that consumption is less sensitive to the interest rate than investment and net exports is shown by the steeper slope of the consumption share line. Note that the consumption and investment shares are always positive, whereas the net exports share can be positive or negative.

Figure 7.1

   b.   The nongovernment share, which is determined by adding up the consumption, investment, and net exports shares, is illustrated in Figure 7.2. The nongovernment share depends negatively on the interest rate. Because the shares are expressed as a percent of GDP, the government purchases share, which is not shown, is 100 minus the nongovernment share. If the shares were expressed as fractions, the government purchases share would be 1 minus the nongovernment share.

Figure 7.2

c.   The equilibrium interest rate is determined by the division of GDP into the government purchases share and the nongovernment share. In Figure 7.2, a non-government share of 80 percent of GDP produces a real interest rate of 3 percent. Looking back at Figure 7.1, the 3 percent interest rate divides the nongovernment share into consumption, investment, and net exports shares.

2.   What happens when the share of government purchases increases? As shown in Figure 7.3, an increase in the government purchases share of GDP from 20 to 25 percent lowers the nongovernment share from 80 to 75 percent. The smaller nongovernment share raises the real interest rate from 3 to 4 percent, reducing the consumption, investment, and net exports shares.

Figure 7.3

3.   The saving investment approach is an alternative method of determining the equilibrium interest rate. The interest rate determined using the saving investment approach is exactly the same as that obtained by dividing GDP into shares.

    a.   *National saving* is defined as aggregate income minus consumption minus government purchases, or

$$S = Y - C - G$$

    The **national saving rate**, the ratio of national saving to GDP, is obtained by dividing both sides by Y,

$$S/Y = 1 - C/Y - G/Y$$

    The national saving rate equals 1 minus the consumption share minus the government purchases share. When the interest rate rises, the national saving rate increases because the consumption share falls. Thus the national saving rate is positively related to the interest rate.

    b.   From the identity $Y = C + I + G + X$, we can show that national saving equals investment plus net exports. Subtract consumption and government purchases from both sides of the identity.

$$Y - C - G = I + X$$

    From the definition of national saving,

$$S = I + X$$

    An alternative expression for the national saving rate is obtained by dividing both sides by Y,

$$S/Y = I/Y + X/Y$$

    The national saving rate equals the investment share plus the net exports share.

    c.   The determination of the equilibrium interest rate is shown in Figure 7.4. The real interest rate is on the vertical axis, and the share of GDP (in percent) is on the horizontal axis. The line S/Y is upward-sloping because the national saving rate is positively related to the interest rate. The line $I/Y+X/Y$ is downward sloping because both the investment share and the net exports share are negatively related to the interest rate. The intersection of the two lines, where the national saving rate equals the investment share plus the net exports share, determines the equilibrium interest rate.

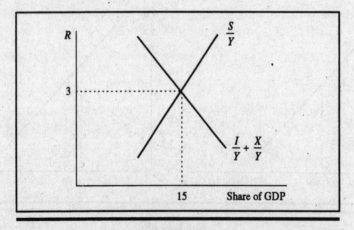

Figure 7.4

ACTIVE REVIEW

Fill-In Questions

1. The _____ of GDP is consumption divided by GDP.

2. The investment share of GDP is _____ related to the interest rate.

3. The net exports share of GDP can be _____, _____, or _____.

4. The _____ of GDP is the proportion of GDP that is used for government purchases.

5. An increase in any of the shares must entail a _____ in one of the other shares.

6. The nongovernment share of GDP is the sum of the _____, _____, and _____ shares.

7. The sum of all four spending shares must equal _____.

8. The relative price of consuming today relative to the price of consuming tomorrow is the _____.

9. If the interest rate rises, the consumption share will _____.

10. When a factor other than the interest rate causes a change in the consumption share, we say there is a _____ in the consumption share line.

11. The _____ is the nominal interest rate minus the expected inflation rate.

12. The decline in investment caused by an increase in government purchases is called _____.

13. The _____ is the sum of the investment and net exports shares of GDP.

14. The national saving rate is _____ related to the interest rate.

15. The _____ interest rate makes the sum of the consumption, investment, and net export shares equal to the share of GDP available.

True-False Questions

1. T F The consumption share of GDP is negatively related to the interest rate.

2. T F A decrease in consumption due to an increase in taxes on consumption would represent a movement along the consumption share line.

3. T F The investment share of GDP is negatively related to the interest rate.

4. T F The net exports share of GDP is negatively related to the interest rate.

5. T F All spending shares must be positive.

6. T F The government purchases share of GDP is negatively related to the interest rate.

7. T F The nongovernment share of GDP is negatively related to the interest rate.

8. T F The nominal interest rate determines how real GDP is divided into shares.

9. T F A higher dollar exchange rate tends to make imported goods more attractive.

10. T F Consumers and firms fully adjust their spending to changes in the real interest rate very quickly.

11.   T   F   A nominal interest rate of 50 percent means that the real interest rate must be very high.

12.   T   F   When the government purchases share of GDP rises, the nongovernment share falls by the same amount.

13.   T   F   The decline in consumption resulting from an increase in government purchases is called crowding out.

14.   T   F   National saving equals income minus consumption.

15.   T   F   The national saving rate is positively related to the interest rate.

Short-Answer Questions

1.   Why is the consumption share of GDP less sensitive to interest rates than the investment and net exports shares?

2.   What is the relationship between interest rates and consumption?

3.   Why does investment fall when interest rates rise?

4.   Why does a higher interest rate in the United States raise the exchange rate?

5.   How do exchange rates affect the amount of goods imported?

6.   Why do economists use *real* instead of *nominal* interest rates to determine how real GDP is divided in to shares?

7.   What mechanism ensures that the sum of the consumption, investment, government purchases, and net exports shares of GDP equals 1?

8.   What is the relationship between the real interest rate and the nominal interest rate?

9.   Why do the consumption, investment, and net exports shares all fall when the government purchases share of GDP increases?

10.   What happens to the real interest rate when the government purchases share of GDP decreases?

11.   What happens to the consumption, investment, and net exports shares when the government purchases share of GDP increases?

12.   How is the equilibrium interest rate determined?

13.   What are the two expressions for the national saving rate?

14.   According to the saving investment approach, how is the equilibrium interest rate determined?

15.   What is the relationship between the interest rate determined by dividing GDP into shares and the interest rate determined by the saving investment approach?

WORKING IT OUT

1.   Suppose that you are given data on consumption, investment, government purchases, and net exports. From the identity

$$Y = C + I + G + X.$$

you can determine GDP. In order to determine the shares of GDP, divide both sides by Y:

$$1 = C/Y + I/Y + G/Y + X/Y.$$

The sum of the consumption, investment, government purchases, and net export shares must equal 1. If any one of the shares increases, the sum of the other three must decline by the same amount. The nongovernment share can be calculated by adding the consumption, investment, and net exports shares. The national saving rate is determined by adding the investment and net export shares.

2. We have analyzed the effects of an increase in the government purchases share of GDP and seen how the interest rate rises and the consumption, investment, and net exports shares decline. The same technique can be used to consider the effects of shifts in consumption, investment, and net exports. We will focus on investment.

    a. Suppose that the desire to invest rises at every interest rate, perhaps as a result of a change in the tax law designed to stimulate investment. This is shown in Figure 7.5 as a shift of the investment share line to the right. Because the nongovernment share is the sum of the consumption, investment, and net exports shares, the nongovernment share line also shifts to the right. Now comes the subtle part. Even though the *nongovernment share line* shifts to the right, the *nongovernment share* of GDP does not change. Government purchases are not affected by the increased desire to invest. With long-run GDP unchanged, the government purchases share is also not changed. Since the government purchases share does not change, the nongovernment purchases share does not change.

Figure 7.5

b. Since the nongovernment share line shifts to the right, but the nongovernment share is unchanged, the interest rate must rise, as shown in Figure 7.5. The higher interest rate decreases the consumption share and the net exports share. The investment share rises. Thus an increase in the desire to invest increases the interest rate, raises the investment share, and lowers the consumption and net export shares.

Worked Problems

1. Suppose that consumption = 3,400, investment = 800, government purchases = 700, and net exports = 100.

   a. Calculate GDP. What are the consumption, investment, government purchases, and net exports shares of GDP?

   b. What are the nongovernment share of GDP and the national saving rate?

   c. Suppose that government purchases decrease to 600 and GDP does not change. What are the new government purchases and nongovernment shares of GDP?

Answer

   a. To calculate GDP, use the identity

   $Y = C + I + C + G = 3,400 + 800 + 700 + 100 = 5,000$

   To determine the shares, divide the values for consumption, investment, government purchases, and net exports by the value for GDP:

   Consumption share = $C/Y = 3,400/5,000 = 0.68$

   Investment share = $I/Y = 800/5,000 = 0.16$

   Government purchases share = $G/Y = 700/5,000 = 0.14$

   Net exports share = $X/Y = 100/5,000 = 0.02$

   Note that the sum of the four shares = $0.68 + 0.16 + 0.14 + 0.02 = 1$

   b. The nongovernment share is the sum of the consumption, investment, and net exports shares, $0.68 + 0.16 + 0.02 = 0.86$. The nongovernment share can also be calculated as 1 minus the government purchases share, $1 - 0.14 = 0.86$. The national saving rate equals the investment share plus the net exports share, $0.16 + 0.02 = 0.18$.

   c. If government purchases decrease to 600 and GDP does not change, the new government purchases share equals $600/5,000 = 0.12$. The nongovernment share is $1 - 0.12 = 0.88$.

2. Suppose that the government purchases share of GDP decreases. Using diagrams, illustrate what happens to the consumption, investment, and net exports shares of GDP.

Answer

The lower government purchases share of GDP raises the nongovernment share of GDP, illustrated by a movement along the nongovernment share line in Figure 7.6. The interest rate falls. The consumption, investment, and net exports shares all rise.

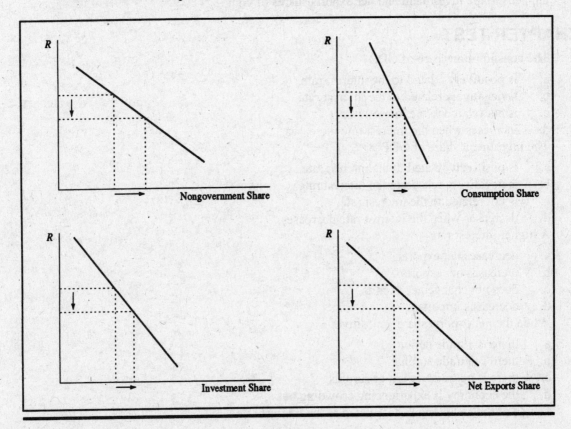

Figure 7.6

PRACTICE PROBLEMS

1. Suppose that consumption = 2,800, investment = 600, government purchases = 800, and net exports = −200.

   a. Calculate GDP. What are the consumption, investment, government purchases, and net exports shares of GDP?

   b. What are the nongovernment shares of GDP and the national saving rate?

   c. Suppose that government purchases increase to 1,000 and GDP does not change. What are the new government purchases and nongovernment shares of GDP?

2. Suppose that consumption = 7,200, investment = 900, government purchases = 1,600, and net exports = 300.

   a. Calculate GDP. What are the consumption, investment, government purchases, and net exports shares of GDP?

   b. What are the nongovernment shares of GDP and the national saving rate?

   c. Suppose that government purchases decrease to 1,200 and GDP does not change. What are the new government purchases and nongovernment purchases shares of GDP?

3. Suppose that net exports rise at every level of the interest rate, perhaps caused by an increase in foreign demand for U.S. automobiles. Using diagrams, show what happens to the consumption and investment shares of GDP.

4. Suppose that consumption falls at every level of the interest rate. Using diagrams, show what happens to the investment and net exports shares of GDP.

CHAPTER TEST

1. The consumption share of GDP

   a. is positively related to the interest rate.
   b. is negatively related to the interest rate.
   c. is not related to the interest rate.
   d. increases when the interest rate increases.

2. The investment share of GDP

   a. is positively related to the interest rate.
   b. is negatively related to the interest rate.
   c. is not related to the interest rate.
   d. decreases when the interest rate decreases.

3. A higher interest rate

   a. decreases net exports.
   b. increases net exports.
   c. does not change net exports.
   d. decreases imports.

4. When the net exports share is positive,

   a. there is a trade deficit.
   b. there is a trade surplus.
   c. there is no trade deficit or surplus.
   d. the economy is experiencing crowding out.

5. Which of the following is *not* related to the interest rate?

   a. The consumption share of GDP
   b. The investment share of GDP
   c. The net exports share of GDP
   d. The government purchases share of GDP

6. Which of the following would cause a movement along the consumption share line?

   a. National sales tax
   b. A fall in the real interest rate
   c. A decrease in taxes on consumption
   d. A trade deficit

7. The nongovernment share of GDP is the

   a. proportion of GDP that is used for government purchases.
   b. sum of the consumption, investment, and net exports shares.
   c. investment share minus the consumption share.
   d. investment share minus the net exports share.

8. Which of the following is the *least* sensitive to interest rates?

   a. The investment share of GDP
   b. The net exports share of GDP
   c. The consumption share of GDP
   d. The nongovernment share of GDP

9. The nominal interest rate minus the expected inflation rate is called the

    a. real interest rate.
    b. expected interest rate.
    c. interest rate on loans.
    d. real inflation rate.

10. Net exports may be

    a. positive.
    b. zero.
    c. negative.
    d. All of the these.

11. The sum of the consumption, investment, government purchases, and net exports shares equals

    a. zero.
    b. one.
    c. one-half.
    d. one-fourth.

12. Which of the following determines how real GDP is divided among consumption, investment, government purchases, and net exports?

    a. The nominal interest rate
    b. The real interest rate
    c. The real inflation rate
    d. The expected inflation rate

13. An economy experiences crowding out when

    a. consumption declines because of an increase in government purchases.
    b. net exports decline because of an increase in government purchases.
    c. investment declines because of an increase in government purchases.
    d. imports decline because of an increase in government purchases.

14. A downward shift in the national saving rate is equivalent to an upward shift in the

    a. investment share.
    b. consumption share.
    c. government share.
    d. net export share.

15. Which of the following is national saving?

    a. Investment minus consumption
    b. Investment minus government purchases
    c. Investment plus government purchases
    d. Investment plus net exports

16. The national saving rate is the ratio of national saving to

    a. consumption.
    b. investment.
    c. GDP.
    d. government purchases.

17. The national saving rate is

    a. negatively related to the interest rate.
    b. positively related to the interest rate.
    c. not related to the interest rate.
    d. negatively related to investment.

Use Figure 7.7 for question 18.

Figure 7.7

18.   What is the government purchases share of GDP when the interest rate is 4 percent?

  a. 25 percent
  b. 15 percent
  c. 35 percent
  d. 20 percent

Use Figure 7.8 for question 19.

Figure 7.8

19.   What is the equilibrium interest rate when the government purchases share of GDP is 30 percent?

  a. 1 percent
  b. 2 percent
  c. 3 percent
  d. 4 percent

Use Figure 7.9 for question 20.

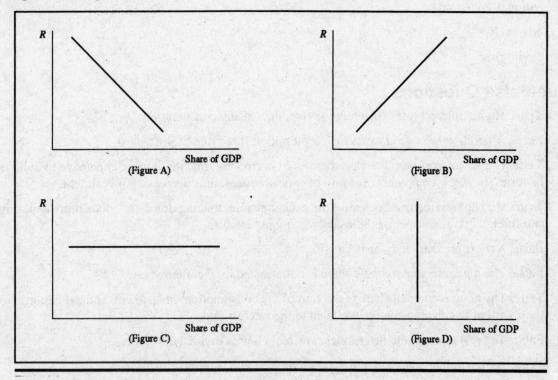

Figure 7.9

20. Which of the above figures appropriately represents the national saving rate line?
    a. Figure A
    b. Figure B
    c. Figure C
    d. Figure D

ANSWERS TO THE REVIEW QUESTIONS

Fill-In Questions

1. consumption share

2. negatively

3. positive; zero; negative

4. government purchases share

5. reduction

6. consumption; investment; net exports

7. one

8. interest rate

9. fall

10. shift

11. real interest rate

12. crowding out

13. national saving rate

14. positively

15. equilibrium

True-False Questions

1. **True**. Higher interest rates encourage saving, decreasing consumption.

2. **False**. A tax increase would cause the consumption share line to shift.

3. **True**. Higher interest rates increase the cost of borrowing, making it more expensive to build new factories, buy new equipment, and purchase new houses, thus decreasing investment.

4. **True**. Higher U.S. interest rates raise the exchange rate, making domestic goods more expensive and foreign goods cheaper, and thus decreasing net exports.

5. **False**. Net export share may be negative.

6. **False**. The government purchases share is not affected by the interest rate.

7. **True**. The nongovernment share is the sum of the consumption, investment, and net exports shares, all of which are negatively related to the interest rate.

8. **False**. The real interest rate determines how real GDP is divided into shares.

9. **True**. A high dollar exchange rate makes imported goods relatively cheaper.

10. **False**. The division of real GDP into shares is applicable to the long run, three years or more, not to short-run fluctuations.

11. **False**. For example, if the expected rate of inflation were 48 percent, the real rate would be only 2 percent.

12. **True**. The government purchases and nongovernment shares of GDP must sum to 1.

13. **False**. Crowding out is the decline in investment, not consumption, caused by an increase in government purchases.

14. **False**. National saving equals income minus consumption minus government purchases.

15. **True**. When the interest rate rises, the national saving rate increases because the consumption share falls.

Short-Answer Questions

1. Changes in the interest rate, either through the cost of borrowing or through the exchange rate, have a strong effect on investment and net exports. The effects of interest rates on consumption, through encouraging or discouraging saving, are much weaker.

2. The relationship is negative since a higher interest rate raises the relative price of consuming today as compared to consuming in the future. Thus, the higher the interest rate the less likely one is to consume today.

3. Interest rates are the price the firm pays for the investment good. Therefore, as the price of the investment good rises, the amount purchased will fall. Likewise, homeowners view the interest rate (mortgage rate) as part of the price of purchasing a new home. As interest rates rise, fewer new homes will be sold.

4. A higher interest rate in the United States raises the exchange rate because it makes dollar-denominated assets more attractive than foreign assets.

5. Exchange rates indicate the relative price of domestic to foreign goods. As the exchange rate rises, the price of the foreign good falls, making imports more attractive.

6. Economists use real instead of nominal interest rates to determine how real GDP is divided in to shares because firms and consumers use real rates to make consumption, investment, export, and import decisions.

7. The interest rate adjusts to ensure that the sum of the four shares equals 1.

8. The real interest rate is the nominal interest rate minus the expected inflation rate.

9. The higher government purchases share lowers the nongovernment share, raising the interest rate. Since each component of the nongovernment share is negatively related to the interest rate, the consumption, investment, and net exports shares all fall.

10. The real interest rate falls when the government purchases share of GDP rises.

11. The consumption, investment, and net exports shares all rise when the government purchases share of GDP falls.

12. The equilibrium interest rate is determined by the division of GDP into the government purchases share and the nongovernment share.

13. The national saving rate equals 1 minus the consumption share minus the government purchases share, which is equivalent to the sum of the investment share plus the net exports share.

14. According to the saving investment approach, the equilibrium interest rate is the rate at which the national saving rate equals the investment share plus the net exports share of GDP.

15. The two methods determine the same interest rate.

SOLUTIONS TO THE PRACTICE PROBLEMS

1. a. $GDP = 2,800 + 600 + 800 - 200 = 4,000$. The consumption share $= 2,800/4,000 - 0.70$, the investment share $= 600/4,000 = 0.15$, the government purchases share $= 800/4,000 = 0.20$, and the net exports share $= -200/4,000 = -0.05$.

    b. The nongovernment share $= 0.70 + 0.15 - 0.05 = 0.80$. The national saving rate $= 0.15 - 0.05 = 0.10$.

    c. The new government purchases share $= 1,000/4,000 = 0.25$ The nongovernment share $= 1 - 0.25 = 0.75$.

2. a. $GDP = 7,200 + 900 + 1,600 + 300 = 10,000$. The consumption share $= 7,200/10,000 = 0.72$, the investment share $900/10,000 = 0.09$, the government purchases share $1,600/10,000 = 0.16$, and the net exports share $300/10,000 = 0.03$.

    b. The nongovernment share $= 0.72 + 0.09 + 0.03 = 0.84$. The national saving rate $= 0.09 + 0.03 = 0.12$.

    c. The new government purchases share $= 1,200/10,000 = 0.12$. The nongovernment share $= 1 - 0.12 = 0.88$.

3. The net exports share line shifts to the right, causing the same shift in the nongovernment share line. With unchanged government purchases and constant GDP, the nongovernment share does

not change, raising the interest rate. The consumption and investment shares fall. These effects are illustrated in Figure 7.10.

Figure 7.10

4.   The consumption share line shifts to the left, causing the same shift in the nongovernment share line. With unchanged government purchases and constant GDP, the nongovernment share does not change, lowering the interest rate. The investment and net exports shares rise. These effects are illustrated in Figure 7.11.

Figure 7.11

ANSWERS TO THE CHAPTER TEST

1. b
2. b
3. a
4. b
5. d
6. b
7. b
8. c
9. a
10. d
11. b
12. b
13. c
14. b
15. d
16. c

17. b
18. a
19. c
20. b

CHAPTER 8

Unemployment and Employment

CHAPTER OVERVIEW

In normal times, when the economy is neither in a boom nor in a recession, the unemployment rate is about 5 percent. Why are over 5 million workers unemployed on any given day in the United States? This chapter examines the causes of unemployment and explains why the natural unemployment rate, unemployment in normal times, seems so high. We first study measures and trends in employment and unemployment, how the two concepts are defined, and how patterns of employment and unemployment are evolving over time. We then focus on the nature of unemployment—who becomes unemployed and for how long. You will then learn about the determination of employment and unemployment, how economic theory can explain unemployment, and why the unemployment rate is always greater than zero. The experience of Europe, where the long-term unemployment rate is over 10 percent, is contrasted with that of the United States. We focus on the determinants of the natural unemployment rate in this chapter and consider unemployment resulting from recessions when we study economic fluctuations.

CHAPTER REVIEW

1. The **natural unemployment rate** is the rate of unemployment when the economy is in normal times, neither in a recession nor in a boom, and real GDP is equal to potential GDP. The natural unemployment rate is not a constant, and economists do not know its precise value. For the United States, it is now somewhere near 5 percent, about the level found in the 1950s and early 1960s and down from about 6 percent in the 1970s and 1980s. For some European countries, the natural unemployment rate is now about 10 percent or even higher. Unemployment above the natural rate during and immediately following recessions, such as occurred in the United States during 2002, is called **cyclical unemployment**.

2. There are two aspects of unemployment in normal times. **Frictional unemployment** occurs as workers either change jobs or enter the labor force and are unemployed for a time until they find work. Most frictional unemployment is short term. In contrast, **structural unemployment** occurs when workers are unemployed for a long time, six months or more, either because they have insufficient skills or because shifts in tastes or technology cause their skills to no longer be in demand.

3. Understanding how to measure unemployment requires learning a few definitions. The **working-age population** consists of those people age 16 and above (and not in jail or in a hospital). Out of the working-age population, you are *employed* if you have a job and *unemployed* if you do not have a job and are looking for work. You are in the **labor force** if you are either employed or unemployed. You are *not in the labor force* if you do not have a job and are not looking for work. In the United States, employment and unemployment are measured by the *Current Population Survey*.

4. Some of these definitions can get tricky. You are counted as employed if you have a job outside the home or a paid job inside the home, but not if you have an unpaid job inside the home. You are also counted as employed if you are a *part-time worker*, working as little as 1 hour per week. On the other hand, *discouraged workers*, who have stopped looking for work because they cannot

find a job, are out of the labor force and are not counted as unemployed. Full-time college students, who are not employed and are not looking for work, are also neither employed nor unemployed; they are out of the labor force.

5. The **unemployment rate** is the ratio of unemployed workers to the labor force. Although the natural unemployment rate has been fairly steady for the United States, the unemployment rate has fluctuated, reaching a post-World War II high of about 10 percent in 1982 following the 1981–1982 recession. The **labor force participation rate** is the ratio of people in the labor force to the working-age population. It is now about 66 percent. The **employment-to-population ratio** is the ratio of employed workers to the working-age population. It is now about 62 percent. Both the labor force participation rate and the employment-to-population ratio have increased since the 1970s, mainly because of more women entering the labor force.

6. **Aggregate hours**, the total number of hours worked by all workers, is the most comprehensive measure of labor input to the production of real GDP. Aggregate hours are the number of hours worked per employed worker times the number of employed workers. When the total number of hours worked is measured, rather than the total number of employed workers, part-time workers do not count as much as full-time workers. Aggregate hours grew by slightly more than 1 percent per year in the 1990s and early 2000s.

7. Why do people become unemployed? The many reasons can be divided into three broad categories. *Job losers* are people who have lost their previous job, *job leavers* are those who have quit their previous job, and *new entrants and re-entrants* have either just entered the labor force or are re-entering the labor force and are looking for work. *Seasonal unemployment* is the increase in unemployment each June, when students graduate and enter the labor force, as well as the decrease in unemployment around the holiday season, when many employers hire extra workers.

8. **Job vacancies** are the jobs that firms are trying to fill. Unemployment and job vacancies can exist simultaneously because the available jobs may require different skills, be at a different location, or pay lower wages than the former jobs of the unemployed workers.

9. When we think about unemployment, we view long-term structural unemployment very differently from the short-term unemployment associated with changing jobs. About 50 percent of unemployment is very short term, less than five weeks. Another 35 percent of unemployed workers have been unemployed for between five weeks and six months, and the remaining 15 percent have been unemployed for more than six months—the truly long-term unemployed.

10. Unemployment rates are very different for different groups of people in the United States. Unemployment is lowest for adult men and women and is very high for teenagers. In 2004, with the overall unemployment rate equal to 5.4 percent, the unemployment rate for adult men and women was 4.8 percent and the unemployment rate for teenagers was 17.6 percent.

ZEROING IN

1. What determines employment and unemployment? A good starting point is to look at the demand for labor and the supply of labor. In Figure 8.1, the **real wage** (the price of labor) is on the vertical axis and the quantity of labor (measured by employment) is on the horizontal axis. The **labor supply curve** describes the behavior of workers; it is upward sloping because workers are willing to supply more labor if the real wage (what they receive for working) is higher. The **labor demand curve** describes the behavior of firms; it is downward sloping because firms are willing to hire more workers if the real wage (the cost of labor) is lower. The intersection of the labor supply curve and the labor demand curve determines the equilibrium real wage that equates the quantity of labor supplied with the quantity of labor demanded.

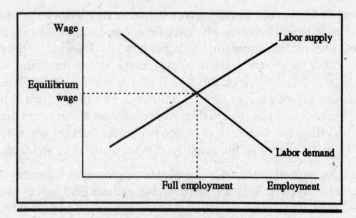

Figure 8.1

2. What is wrong with Figure 8.1? The intersection of the labor supply curve and the labor demand curve determines employment, but what about unemployment? According to the figure, there should be no unemployment, a prediction contrary to the facts. There are several explanations for why the unemployment rate is always greater than zero.

    a. **Job rationing** is a situation in which workers are willing to take jobs at the wage that firms are paying, but there are not enough jobs available at that wage. Job rationing is illustrated in Figure 8.2. Suppose that the wage is higher than the wage that would equate the quantity of labor supplied with the quantity of labor demanded. At this wage, the number of workers demanded by firms, at *A*, is smaller than the number of workers willing to supply their labor, at *B*, and there is unemployment. The amount of unemployment is measured by the horizontal distance between the labor supply curve and the labor demand curve at the given wage, shown by the distance between *A* and *B*.

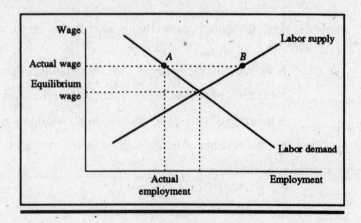

Figure 8.2

    b. The job-rationing story raises several questions. Why is the wage always too high to produce zero unemployment? Moreover, why doesn't the wage fall when there is unemployment? In most markets, a situation of excess supply causes the price to fall. Since the wage is the price of labor, and there is an excess supply of labor, why doesn't the wage fall by enough to equate the quantity of labor supplied with the quantity of labor demanded? Economists have proposed several explanations for why the wage might always be above the wage at the intersection of the labor supply curve and the labor demand curve.

    c. The *minimum wage* is the lowest possible wage that employers can legally pay their employees. If the minimum wage is too high, it could price unskilled workers, such as many teenagers, out of the market, causing unemployment. **Insiders** versus **outsiders** is the theory that sometimes groups of workers who have jobs—the insiders—can prevent the wage from declining and thus prevent firms from hiring unemployed workers—the outsiders—at a lower wage. Labor unions and legislation preventing firms from firing workers without significant legal costs could create this situation. The theory of an **efficiency wage** is that firms will choose to pay workers an extra amount to encourage them to be more productive or efficient. Turnover will be lower when workers are paid more, and there will be less shirking. With efficiency wages, workers are paid more than the wage that equates the quantity of labor supplied with the quantity of labor demanded, and there is unemployment.

d. **Job search** is the second explanation for why unemployment is greater than zero. The labor market is never characterized by the static supply and demand curves in Figure 8.1. There is constant job creation and job destruction, and the curves are always shifting. In such a situation, some people will always be searching for a job. It is not necessarily to their advantage to take the first job that comes along, and they may turn down offers in the hope of finding a higher-paying job. While they are searching for a job, they are unemployed.

ACTIVE REVIEW

Fill-In Questions

1. The _____ is the rate of unemployment when the economy is in normal times.

2. Unemployment above the natural rate is called _____ unemployment.

3. Unemployment in normal times can be divided into _____ and _____ unemployment.

4. If you are part of the working-age population, you are classified as either _____, _____, or _____.

5. People who have stopped looking for work because they cannot find a job are called _____ workers.

6. The _____ is the ratio of unemployed workers to the labor force.

7. The _____ is the ratio of people in the labor force to the working-age population.

8. The _____ is the ratio of employed workers to the working-age population.

9. _____ are the total number of hours worked by all workers.

10. People who become unemployed are either _____, _____, or _____.

11. _____ are the jobs that firms are trying to fill.

12. The _____ is the price of labor.

13. Two explanations for why the unemployment rate is always greater than zero are _____ and _____.

14. The _____ is the lowest possible wage that employers can pay their employees.

15. The theory of _____ is that firms will choose to pay workers an extra amount to encourage them to be more productive.

True-False Questions

1. T F In normal times, the unemployment rate for the United States is about 5 percent.

2. T F Frictional and structural unemployment both occur during normal times.

3. T F If you are of working age, you are classified as either employed or unemployed.

4. T F If you are working part-time but looking for a full-time job, you are classified as unemployed.

5. T F The unemployment rate fluctuates more than the natural unemployment rate.

6. T F Aggregate hours have been falling since 1980.

7. T F When a new college graduate begins to look for a job, she is counted as unemployed until she finds work.

8. T F Most unemployed workers stay unemployed for more than one year.

9. T F Since long-term unemployment represents only about 15 percent of unemployment, it is not a matter of concern for policymakers.

10. T F Unemployment rates are similar for different groups of people in the United States.

11. T F The natural unemployment rate is higher for most European countries than for the United States.

12. T F The intersection of the labor supply curve and the labor demand curve provides a good explanation of unemployment.

13. T F With job rationing, workers are unwilling to accept jobs at the prevailing wage.

14. T F The minimum wage is the wage paid to the lowest-paid worker in the firm.

15. T F Unemployment can be caused by job rationing or job search, but not both.

Short-Answer Questions

1. The unemployment rate for the United States in 1994 was about 5 percent. What was cyclical unemployment?

2. What is the difference between frictional and structural unemployment?

3. What is the difference between being unemployed and not being in the labor force?

4. Why are discouraged workers not counted as unemployed?

5. Why have the labor force participation rate and the employment-to-population ratio increased from the mid-1970s to today?

6. Why are aggregate hours a better measure of labor input to the production of real GDP than employment?

7. What is the difference between job losers and job leavers?

8. How can there be unemployment and job vacancies at the same time?

9. How is unemployment divided among short-term, medium-term, and long-term unemployment?

10. Describe the overall unemployment rate, the unemployment rate for adult men and women, and the unemployment rate for teenagers in 2004.

11. What is job rationing?

12. According to the job-rationing story, why is the wage rate always above the wage at the intersection of the labor supply curve and the labor demand curve?

13. What is the insiders versus outsiders explanation for why wages don't fall when there is unemployment?

14. If workers are paid efficiency wages, why is there unemployment?

15. According to the job search explanation, why is there unemployment?

16. In February 2005, employment increased and the unemployment rate rose. How is this possible? (Hint: See Reading the News About—Unemployment Each Month.)

WORKING IT OUT

1. We have defined aggregate hours to be:

   Aggregate hours = (Hours per employed worker) × (Employment) .

   Since employment, the number of employed workers, can be written as:

   Employment = (Employment-to-population ratio) × (Working-age population) ,

   we can rewrite our definition of aggregate hours:

   Aggregate hours = (Hours per employed worker) × (Employment-to-population ratio)

   × (Working-age population).

   We can use data on these three variables to compute aggregate hours and employment, and see how they change over time. If hours per employed worker are constant, aggregate hours will grow at the same rate as employment. If hours per employed worker are increasing, aggregate hours will grow faster than employment. If hours per employed worker are decreasing, aggregate hours will grow more slowly than employment.

2. The job rationing explanation for unemployment can be illustrated by using numbers and graphs. Suppose you are given the following data on the labor demand curve and the labor supply curve:

Labor Demand Curve		Labor Supply Curve	
Wage	Employment	Wage	Employment
10	180	10	220
9	190	9	210
8	200	8	200
7	210	7	190
6	220	6	180

where wages are in dollars per hour and employment is in millions of workers.

a. The first step is to determine the equilibrium wage and the level of full employment. As shown in Figure 8.3, the labor demand curve is downward sloping and the labor supply curve is upward sloping. The equilibrium wage, determined by the intersection of the labor demand curve and the labor supply curve, is the wage that equates the quantity of labor supplied and the quantity of labor demanded, or the wage at which employment is equal on the two curves. At the intersection of the two curves, the wage is $8 per hour and full employment is 200 million.

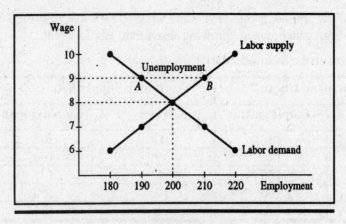

Figure 8.3

b. Now suppose that the actual wage is $9 per hour. This wage, as shown in Figure 8.3, is too high to produce full employment. The actual level of employment is the quantity of labor demanded, which is determined by the labor demand curve and is 190 million. The quantity of labor supplied, determined by the labor supply curve, is 210 million. Unemployment is the difference between the quantity of labor supplied and the quantity of labor demanded. It is the horizontal distance between *A* and *B* and equals 20 million. Note that unemployment is the difference between the quantity of labor supplied and the quantity of labor demanded at the given wage, not the difference between the quantity of labor demanded at the given wage and the level of full employment at the equilibrium wage.

Worked Problems

1. Suppose you are given the following data:

Year	Hours per Employed Worker	Employment-to-Population Ratio	Working-Age Population
2000	1,700	0.60	200
2010	1,800	0.70	210

where hours per employed worker are for the year and the working-age population is in millions.

a. Calculate employment and aggregate hours for the years 2000 and 2010.

b. Calculate the growth rate of aggregate hours and employment. Are aggregate hours growing faster than, slower than, or at the same rate as employment?

Answer

a. Employment = (Employment-to-population ratio) × (Working-age population) . In the year 2000, employment = (0.60) x (200) = 120 million. In 2010, employment = (0.70) x (210) = 147 million. Aggregate hours = (Hours per employed worker) × (Employment) . In the year 2000, aggregate hours = (1,700) x (120) = 204,000 million, or 204 billion. In 2010, aggregate hours = (1,800) x (147) = 264,600 million, or 264.6 billion.

b. The growth rate of aggregate hours for the decade between 2000 and 2010 is (264.6 - 204)/204 = 0.297, or 29.7 percent. The growth rate of employment is $(147 - 120)/120 = 0.225$, or 22.5 percent. Because hours per employed worker are increasing, aggregate hours are growing faster than employment.

2. Suppose you are given the following data:

Labor Demand Curve		Labor Supply Curve	
Wage	Employment	Wage	Employment
10	130	10	205
9	140	9	190
8	150	8	175
7	160	7	160
6	170	6	145

where wages are in dollars per hour and employment is in millions of workers. Graph the labor demand curve and the labor supply curve. What are the equilibrium wage and the level of full employment? If the actual wage equals $9 per hour, what is the level of unemployment?

Answer

The labor demand curve and the labor supply curve are graphed in Figure 8.4, with the labor demand curve downward sloping and the labor supply curve upward sloping. The equilibrium wage, determined at the intersection of the labor demand curve and the labor supply curve, is $7 per hour, and full employment is 160 million workers. If the actual wage equals $9 per hour, unemployment is the difference between the quantity of labor supplied and the quantity of labor demanded, and it equals 50 million workers.

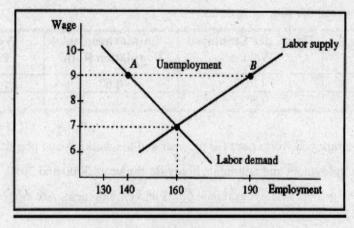

Figure 8.4

PRACTICE PROBLEMS

1. Suppose you are given the following data:

Year	Hours per Employed Worker	Employment-to-Population Ratio	Working-Age Population
2000	1,500	0.50	120
2010	1,400	0.60	140

    where hours per employed worker are for the year and the working-age population is in millions.

    a.   Calculate employment and aggregate hours for the years 2000 and 2010.

    b.   Calculate the growth rate of aggregate hours and employment. Are aggregate hours growing faster than, slower than, or at the same rate as employment?

2. Suppose you are given the following data:

Year	Hours per Employed Worker	Employment-to-Population Ratio	Working-Age Population
2000	1,900	0.55	170
2010	1,900	0.65	180

    where hours per employed worker are for the year and the working-age population is in millions.

    a.   Calculate employment and aggregate hours for the years 2000 and 2010.

    b.   Calculate the growth rate of aggregate hours and employment. Are aggregate hours growing faster, slower, or at the same rate as employment?

3. Suppose you are given the following data:

Labor Demand Curve		Labor Supply Curve	
Wage	Employment	Wage	Employment
10	125	10	150
9	140	9	140
8	155	8	130
7	170	7	120
6	185	6	110

    where wages are in dollars per hour and employment is in millions of workers. Graph the labor demand curve and the labor supply curve.

    a.   What are the equilibrium wage and the level of full employment?

    b.   If the actual wage equals $10 per hour, what is the level of unemployment?

4.   Suppose you are given the following data:

Labor Demand Curve		Labor Supply Curve	
Wage	Employment	Wage	Employment
10	210	10	270
9	220	9	260
8	230	8	250
7	240	7	240
6	250	6	230

where wages are in dollars per hour and employment is in millions of workers.

a.   Graph the labor demand curve and the labor supply curve. What are the equilibrium wage and the level of full employment?

b.   If the actual wage equals $7 per hour, what is the level of unemployment?

CHAPTER TEST

1.   The natural rate of unemployment for the United States is about

    a.   0 percent.
    b.   4 percent.
    c.   5 percent.
    d.   10 percent.

2.   The natural rate of unemployment is the rate of unemployment when the economy is

    a.   in a recession.
    b.   in a boom.
    c.   in either a recession or a boom.
    d.   in neither a recession nor a boom.

3.   Unemployment that occurs during and immediately following a recession is called

    a.   natural unemployment.
    b.   cyclical unemployment.
    c.   frictional unemployment.
    d.   structural unemployment.

4.   What are the two types of unemployment that occur in normal times?

    a.   Frictional and structural unemployment
    b.   Frictional and cyclical unemployment
    c.   Structural and cyclical unemployment
    d.   Cyclical and seasonal unemployment

5.   Unemployment that occurs when workers either change jobs or enter the labor force is called

    a.   structural unemployment.
    b.   frictional unemployment.
    c.   seasonal unemployment.
    d.   cyclical unemployment.

6.   Unemployment that occurs when workers have insufficient skills or their skills are no longer in demand is called

    a.   structural unemployment.
    b.   frictional unemployment.
    c.   seasonal unemployment.

    d.   cyclical unemployment.

7. Which of the following are considered part of the working-age population?

    a.   People in jail
    b.   People in the hospital
    c.   People over the age of 16, but in school
    d.   People under the age of 16

8. If an individual does not have a job but is looking for work, then he or she is considered

    a.   a discouraged worker.
    b.   not in the labor force.
    c.   unemployed.
    d.   employed.

9. An individual who has stopped looking for work because he or she cannot find a job is considered

    a.   a discouraged worker.
    b.   in the labor force.
    c.   unemployed.
    d.   employed.

10. The unemployment rate is the number of

    a.   unemployed workers divided by the number of people in the working-age population.
    b.   unemployed workers divided by the number of people in the labor force.
    c.   people in the labor force divided by the number of people in the working-age population.
    d.   people in the working-age population divided by the number of people in the labor force.

11. The labor force participation rate is the number of

    a.   unemployed workers divided by the number of people in the working-age population.
    b.   unemployed workers divided by the number of people in the labor force.
    c.   people in the labor force divided by the number of people in the working-age population.
    d.   people in the working-age population divided by the number of people in the labor force.

12. What percentage of unemployment is long-term unemployment?

    a.   15 percent
    b.   25 percent
    c.   35 percent
    d.   50 percent

13. The unemployment rate for teenagers in the United States is

    a.   about the same as the unemployment rate for adults.
    b.   lower than the unemployment rate for adults.
    c.   about 6 percent.
    d.   about 20 percent.

14. The labor supply curve
    a. describes the behavior of firms.
    b. describes the behavior of workers.
    c. is downward-sloping.
    d. is horizontal.

15. Which of the following is *not* an explanation for why the actual wage rate may always be above the equilibrium wage rate?
    a. The minimum wage
    b. Job vacancies
    c. The insiders versus outsiders theory
    d. The efficiency wages theory

Use the following table for questions 16 and 17.

Suppose you are given the following data:

Year	Hours per Employed Worker	Employment-to-Population Ratio	Working-Age Population
2000	1,000	0.50	100
2010	1,200	0.60	120

where hours per employed worker are for the year and the working-age population is in millions.

16. What is employment in the year 2000?
    a. 50 million
    b. 72 million
    c. 500 million
    d. 720 million

17. What are the aggregate hours in the year 2010?
    a. 50 billion
    b. 60 billion
    c. 72 billion
    d. 86.4 billion

Use Figure 8.5 for questions 18 to 20.

Figure 8.5

18.   What is the equilibrium wage rate?

    a. $4 per hour

    b. $5 per hour

    c. $6 per hour

    d. $7 per hour

19.   What is the level of full employment?

    a.   100 million

    b.   105 million

    c.   110 million

    d.   115 million

20.   If the actual wage equals $7, what is the level of unemployment?

    a.   0 million

    b.   5 million

    c.   10 million

    d.   15 million

ANSWERS TO THE REVIEW QUESTIONS

Fill-In Questions

1.   natural unemployment rate

2.   cyclical

3.   frictional; structural

4.   employed; unemployed; not in the labor force

5.   discouraged

6.   unemployment rate

7.   labor force participation rate

8.   employment-to-population ratio

9.   Aggregate hours

10. job losers; job leavers; new entrants and re-entrants

11. Job vacancies

12. real wage

13. job rationing; job search

14. minimum wage

15. efficiency wages

True-False Questions

1. **True**. The natural unemployment rate for the United States is 6 percent.

2. **True**. They are the two parts of the natural unemployment rate.

3. **False**. You can also be classified as not in the labor force

4. **False.** You are counted as employed if you are working, whether part- or full-time.

5. **True.** Although the natural unemployment rate is fairly steady, the unemployment rate fluctuates over the business cycle.

6. **False**. Aggregate hours grew at about 1 percent per year in the 1980s, and that growth rate is expected to continue in the 1990s.

7. **True**. She would be a new entrant and would be classified as unemployed.

8. **False**. About 85 percent of unemployment is for six months or less.

9. **False**. When 15 percent of 7 million workers are unemployed for more than six months, it is a matter of great concern for policymakers.

10. **False**. Unemployment is lowest for adult men and women and is very high for teenagers.

11. **True**. The natural unemployment rate is over 10 percent for most European countries, compared with 6 percent for the United States.

12. **False**. At the intersection of the labor supply and labor demand curves, there is no unemployment, a prediction that is contrary to the facts.

13. **False**. Under job rationing, workers are willing to accept jobs at the prevailing wage, but not enough are available.

14. **False**. The minimum wage is the lowest possible wage that employers can legally pay their employees.

15. **False**. The job rationing and job search explanations are complementary. Unemployment can be caused by either or both.

Short-Answer Questions

1. Since the natural unemployment rate for the United States is also about 5 percent, cyclical unemployment was zero in 1994.

2. Frictional unemployment occurs when workers either change jobs or enter the labor force. Structural unemployment occurs when workers are unemployed for a long time.

3. You are unemployed if you do not have a job and are looking for work. You are not in the labor force if you do not have a job and are not looking for work.

4. Discouraged workers have stopped looking for work, and so they are not in the labor force.

5. The increase in both statistics is mainly due to more women entering the labor force.

6. In computing aggregate hours, unlike employment, part-time workers do not count as much as full-time workers.

7. Job losers are people who have lost their previous job; job leavers are people who have quit their previous job.

8. Unemployment and job vacancies can exist simultaneously because the available jobs may require different skills, be at a different location, or pay lower wages than the former jobs of the unemployed workers.

9. About 50 percent of unemployment is for less than 5 weeks, another 35 percent is for between 5 weeks and 6 months, and the remaining 15 percent is for more than 6 months.

10. The overall unemployment rate was 5.4 percent, the unemployment rate for adult men and women was 4.8 percent, and the unemployment rate for teenagers was 17.6 percent in 2004.

11. Job rationing is a situation in which workers are willing to take jobs at the wage that firms are paying, but there are not enough jobs available at that wage.

12. Minimum wage laws, insiders versus outsiders, and efficiency wages are several explanations of why wages are too high to produce zero unemployment.

13. The insiders versus outsiders explanation is that sometimes groups of workers who have jobs—the insiders—can prevent the wage from declining and thus prevent firms from hiring unemployed workers—the outsiders—at a lower wage.

14. With efficiency wages, workers are paid more than the wage that equates the quantity of labor supplied with the quantity of labor demanded, and so there is unemployment.

15. With constant job creation and job destruction, there will always be people searching for jobs, and they are counted as unemployed while they are looking.

16. When more people enter the labor force, some find jobs (employed) and some are still looking for jobs (unemployed). Therefore, if the labor force increases, it is possible for both employment and the unemployment rate to increase.

SOLUTIONS TO THE PRACTICE PROBLEMS

1. a. In the year 2000, employment $= (0.50) \times (120) = 60$ million. In 2010, employment $= (0.60) \times (140) = 84$ million. Aggregate hours in the year 2000 $= (1,500) \times (60) = 90,000$ million, or 90 billion. In 2010, aggregate hours $= (1,400) \times (84) = 117,600$ million, or 117.6 billion.

    b. The growth rate of aggregate hours = 30.6 percent. The growth rate of employment = 40 percent. Because hours per employed worker are decreasing, aggregate hours are growing more slowly than employment.

2. a. In the year 2000, employment $= (0.55) \times (170) = 93.5$ million. In 2010, employment $= (0.65) \times (180) = 117$ million. Aggregate hours in the year 2000 $= (1,900) \times (93.5) = 177,650$ million, or 177.65 billion. In 2010, aggregate hours $= (1,900) \times (117) = 222,300$ million, or 222.3 billion.

    b. The growth rate of both aggregate hours and employment = 25.1 percent. Because hours per employed worker are constant, aggregate hours are growing at the same rate as employment.

3. a. The labor demand curve and the labor supply curve are graphed in Figure 8.6. The equilibrium wage is $9 per hour, and full employment is 140 million workers. If the actual wage equals $10 per hour, unemployment equals 25 million workers.

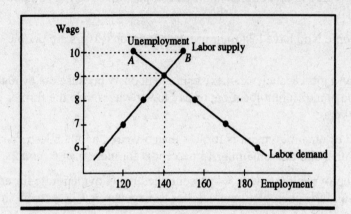

Figure 8.6

b. The labor demand curve and the labor supply curve are graphed in Figure 8.7. The equilibrium wage is $7 per hour, and full employment is 240 million workers. If the actual wage also equals $7 per hour, there is zero unemployment.

Figure 8.7

ANSWERS TO THE CHAPTER TEST

1. c
2. d
3. b
4. a
5. b
6. a
7. c
8. c
9. a

10. b
11. c
12. a
13. d
14. b
15. b
16. a
17. d
18. c
19. b
20. c

CHAPTER 9

Productivity and Economic Growth

CHAPTER OVERVIEW

What caused the dramatic increase in economic growth over the last 200 years? Why did economic growth slow down in the 1970s and 1980s, only to rise again starting in the mid-1990s? In this chapter, we study technology, the key to understanding the growth process. We first demonstrate that labor alone, or even labor and capital, cannot explain the miracle of economic growth during the past two centuries. We then show how to combine labor, capital, and technology to create the modern theory of economic growth and learn about the aggregate production function and the growth accounting formula. We apply the growth accounting formula to understand such diverse topics as the 1970s productivity slowdown in the United States, the 1990s rebound and the new economy, and the demise of the former Soviet Union. Finally, we study policies to improve technological progress and see how they might increase productivity growth in the United States.

CHAPTER REVIEW

1. **Productivity** is output per hour of work. *Productivity growth* is the percentage increase in productivity from one year to the next.

2. **Technology** is anything that raises the amount of real GDP that can be produced with a given amount of capital and labor. *Technological progress* is an improvement in technology between two dates. **Technological change** is simply the change in the existing technology, but since technology is usually increasing, this term is often used synonymously with technological progress. *Labor-saving technological change* means that fewer workers are needed to produce the same amount of output. *Capital-saving technological change* means that fewer machines are needed to produce the same amount of output.

3. Technological change occurs when new ideas are developed into new products that increase production. This process has several stages: **invention** is the discovery of new knowledge or a new principle; **innovation** is when the invention is brought into application with a new product; and **diffusion** is the spreading of the innovation throughout the economy.

4. The organization of a firm is also part of technology, for the organization helps determine how much the firm produces from its labor and capital. Specialization of workers, called *division of labor*, adds to productivity. **Learning by doing**, the process by which workers become more proficient with experience, is part of the reason why specialization increases productivity.

5. Two special qualities of technology help us understand how much technology will be produced. *Nonrivalry* means that one person's use of the technology does not reduce the amount that another person can use. The author's use of computer software to write this study guide does not affect your use of the same software to write a term paper. *Nonexcludability* means that the owner of the technology cannot prevent other people from using it. Continuing with the example, the software that the author used contains many features originally developed by other programs. *Intellectual property laws* provide for patents, copyrights, and trademarks, which determine in part the degree of nonexcludability.

6.   The **growth accounting formula** enables economists to estimate the relative contributions of capital and technology to economic growth. The formula states that the growth rate of real GDP per hour of work equals 1/3 times the growth rate of capital per hour of work plus the growth rate of technology. The growth of capital per hour is multiplied by 1/3 because capital income plus depreciation for the U.S. economy as a whole is about 1/3 of aggregate income.

   a.   The1970s *productivity slowdown* in the United States can be analyzed by the growth accounting formula. The 1970s slowdown in the growth of real GDP per hour of work was largely attributable to a slowdown in the growth rate of technology. Although the growth rate of capital per hour of work also slowed down, this was of secondary importance.

   b.   The former Soviet Union experienced high rates of growth in the 1970s and early 1980s. Most of that was due to increases in capital per worker, not to technological change, and it could not be sustained.

   c.   The 1990s *productivity rebound* in the United States can be analyzed by the growth accounting formula. The **new economy** conveys the idea that new technology, especially more powerful computers and the Internet, has raised productivity growth since the mid-1990s.

7.   If economic policy is to help maintain the higher productivity growth since the mid-1990s, it must provide incentives for technological progress. There have been a number of proposals for technology policy.

   a.   The education and training of workers is called **human capital**. If education can be improved, more human capital can improve the production of technology. Proposals to reform education, especially in mathematics and science at the primary and secondary levels, are designed to raise human capital and increase productivity growth.

   b.   Increased funding for *research and development* (R&D) would positively affect technological progress. There is controversy, however, over whether the government should directly support research in certain industries at the expense of others. A *tax credit for research* would be another way to increase research and development. Intellectual property laws could be improved to give inventors a more certain claim to the property rights from their inventions.

8.   Although the growth accounting formula separates the effects of capital and technology on productivity growth, it is not always possible to separate them in practice. It may be necessary to invest in new capital in order to take advantage of a new technology. *Embodied technological change* requires new capital, whereas *disembodied technological change* does not require new capital in order to be implemented.

ZEROING IN

1.   Why is technological progress necessary in order to explain economic growth? The first step is to show that labor alone cannot produce economic growth. This theory was originally proposed by the eighteenth-century British economist Thomas Malthus, and its predictions were so pessimistic that they gave economics the name the "dismal science."

a.   Consider an economy with fixed capital and fixed technology, such as a farm with fixed acreage and equipment, so that labor is the only variable input to production. The production function for such an economy is shown in Figure 9.1, with output on the vertical axis and labor input on the horizontal axis. The curvature of the production function illustrates **diminishing returns** to labor—the greater the number of workers used in producing output, the less the additional output that comes from each additional worker.

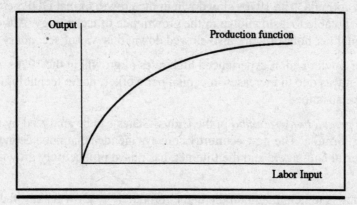

Figure 9.1

b.   As more workers are added to the economy, output increases, but at a decreasing rate. Labor alone cannot explain increases in GDP per worker.

2.   The next step is to add capital to the economy. But this will only be part of the story. Although growth of capital can produce economic growth, it cannot account for the sustained growth over the last 200 years.

a.   The production function with variable capital is illustrated in Figure 9.2. As in Figure 9.1, output is on the vertical axis and labor input is on the horizontal axis. With more capital, the production function shifts up. More output can be produced at every level of labor input.

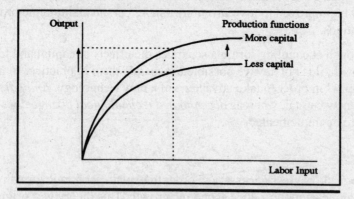

Figure 9.2

b.   In an economy with positive net investment, capital is continually growing, and so the predictions of this model are not as dismal as the Malthusian predictions. But there are also *diminishing returns to capital*; each additional amount of capital results in a smaller addition to output. If we keep adding equal increments of capital, the production function shifts up at a decreasing rate, limiting productivity growth.

3.   We have shown that a model that allows only for labor growth cannot produce economic growth and that adding capital growth is not sufficient to explain the growth explosion of the last 200 years. Our final step is to include technological progress.

a.   We need to develop a different, although related, diagram. Figure 9.3 shows the *productivity curve*, with productivity (Y/L) on the vertical axis and capital per hour of work (K/L) on the horizontal axis. The productivity curve illustrates diminishing returns to capital; each additional amount of capital per hour of work causes a smaller increase in productivity.

Figure 9.3

b.   An increase in capital per hour of work, as shown in Figure 9.4, causes a movement along the productivity curve and an increase in productivity. Because of diminishing returns to capital, however, productivity does not rise by as much as capital per hours of work increases.

Figure 9.4

c. Technological change, as shown in Figure 9.5, shifts the productivity curve up. Even with a constant level of capital per hour of work, productivity increases. With continual technological progress, as in the last two centuries, the productivity curve always shifts up. Sustained economic growth can be achieved.

Figure 9.5

d. Technological change plus increases in capital per hour of work, as shown in Figure 9.6, causes both a shift in the productivity curve and a movement along the productivity curve. Productivity increases for both reasons.

Figure 9.6

ACTIVE REVIEW

Fill-In Questions

1. _____ is output per hour of work.

2. _____ is anything that raises the amount of real GDP that can be produced with a given amount of capital and labor.

3. Technological _____ or _____ is an improvement in technology between two dates.

4. _____ means that fewer workers are needed to produce the same amount of output.

5. The three stages of technological change are _____, _____, and _____.

6. The process by which workers become more proficient with experience is called _____.

7. Two special features of technology are _____ and _____.

8. Intellectual property laws provide for _____, _____, and _____.

9. The _____ estimates the relative contributions of capital and technology to economic growth.

10. The education and training of workers is called _____.

11. _____ technological change requires new capital in order to be implemented.

12. With _____, each additional amount of labor results in a smaller addition to output.

13. With _____, each additional amount of capital results in a smaller addition to output.

14. The _____ conveys the idea that new technology, especially more powerful computers and the Internet, has raised productivity growth since the mid-1990s.

15. The _____ depicts the relation between productivity and capital per hour of work.

True-False Questions

1. T F   In the process of technological change, innovation precedes diffusion.

2. T F   The organization of a firm is part of technology.

3. T F   Specialization of workers is called division of capital.

4. T F   Intellectual property laws affect the degree of nonrivalry of technology.

5. T F   The growth accounting formula enables economists to estimate the relative contributions of labor and capital to economic growth.

6. T F   The productivity slowdown is a slowdown in the growth of real GDP per hour of work.

7. T F   The high rates of growth in the former Soviet Union during the 1970s were due to technological progress.

8. T F   The new economy conveys the idea that lower unemployment has raised productivity growth since the mid-1990s.

9. T F   The effects of capital and technology on economic growth cannot always be separated in practice.

10. T F   In an economy with fixed capital and fixed technology, the production function will exhibit diminishing returns to labor.

11. T F   Labor alone cannot produce economic growth.

12. T F   Unlike labor, capital is not subject to diminishing returns.

13. T F   Capital growth is not sufficient to fully explain economic growth.

14. T F   The productivity curve illustrates diminishing returns to capital.

15. T F   Technological change raises productivity.

16.   T   F   Productivity growth between 1995 and 2000 was about the same as productivity growth in the 1970s and the 1980s. (Hint: See Reading the News About—The Productivity Growth Rebound.)

Short-Answer Questions

1.   What is the difference between labor-saving and capital-saving technological change?

2.   What is meant by nonrivalry?

3.   What is meant by nonexcludability?

4.   What is the growth accounting formula?

5.   What has caused the productivity slowdown in the United States since the mid-1970s?

6.   How can economic policy help maintain the higher productivity growth since the mid-1990s?

7.   Why is improving education important for technological progress?

8.   Name three proposals for increasing research and development.

9.   What is the difference between embodied and disembodied technological change?

10.   What is the new economy?

11.   Why is economics sometimes called the "dismal science"?

12.   Why is labor growth incapable of accounting for sustained productivity growth?

13.   Why is capital growth incapable of accounting for sustained productivity growth?

14.   What is the effect on the productivity curve of technological change plus increases in capital per hour of work?

15.   How does technological change allow the economy to achieve sustained economic growth?

16.   Compare and contrast the change in productivity in the United States between 1955 and 1995 with the change in productivity between 1975 and 1995. (Hint: See Economics in Action—A Formula Goes to Washington.)

WORKING IT OUT

1.   The growth accounting formula is one of the most important topics in this chapter. It is also very simple.

a.   The formula can be written as follows:

(Growth rate of real GDP per hour of work) = 1/3(Growth rate of capital per hour of work) +(Growth rate of technology)

For example, if the growth rate of capital per hour of work is 3 percent per year and the growth rate of technology is 2 percent per year, then the growth rate of real GDP per hour of work is $[\frac{1}{3}\times3]+2=1+2=3$ percent per year.

b.   The formula can be rewritten to determine the growth rate of technology from productivity growth and the growth rate of capital:

(Growth rate of technology) = (Growth rate of real GDP per hour of work) −1/3(Growth rate of capital per hour of work)

Continuing with the same example, if the growth rate of real GDP per hour of work is 3 percent per year and the growth rate of capital per hour of work is 3 percent per year, the growth rate of technology is $3-[\frac{1}{3}\times3]=3-1=2$ percent per year.

2. The economy is always undergoing technological progress, and so the productivity line is always shifting up. So what is meant by the productivity slowdown? Even though there has been technology growth in the United States during the past 20 years, technology has grown more slowly than between the end of World War II and the mid-1970s. The productivity function, while still shifting up, is shifting up at a slower rate than before, causing productivity, while growing, to grow at a slower rate. In other words, productivity growth is slowing down.

Worked Problems

1.

   a. Suppose that the growth rate of capital per hour of work is 1.5 percent per year and the growth rate of technology is 2 percent per year. What is the growth rate of real GDP per hour of work?

   b. Suppose that technology growth falls to 1 percent per year. How large is the productivity slowdown?

Answer

   a. According to the growth accounting formula, the growth rate of real GDP per hour of work
   $=[\frac{1}{3}\times1.5]+2=0.5+2=2.5$ percent per year.

   b. If technology growth falls to 1 percent per year, the growth rate of real GDP per hour of work $=[\frac{1}{3}\times1.5]+2=0.5+2=2.5$ $=[\frac{1}{3}\times1.5]+1=0.5+1=1.5$ percent per year. Productivity falls by 1 percent per year.

PRACTICE PROBLEMS

1.

   a. Suppose that the growth rate of capital per hour of work is 2.7 percent per year and the growth rate of technology is 1 percent per year. What is the growth rate of real GDP per hour of work?

   b. Suppose that technology growth rises to 1.5 percent per year. How large is the increase in productivity?

2.

   a. Suppose that the growth rate of real GDP per hour of work is 2 percent per year and the growth rate of capital per hour of work is 3 percent per year. What is the growth rate of technology?

   b. If the growth rate of capital per hour of work rises to 4.5 percent per year and the growth rate of real GDP per hour of work is unchanged, what is the new growth rate of technology?

CHAPTER TEST

1. Anything that raises the amount of real GDP that can be produced with a given amount of capital and labor is called

    a. innovation.
    b. technology.
    c. invention.
    d. diffusion.

2. The discovery of new knowledge or a new principle is called

    a. innovation.
    b. technology.
    c. invention.
    d. diffusion.

3. An improvement in technology between two dates is called

    a. innovation.
    b. technology.
    c. invention.
    d. technological progress.

4. Spreading of an innovation throughout the economy is called

    a. diffusion.
    b. technological change.
    c. invention.
    d. technological progress.

5. When the owner of the technology cannot prevent other people from using it, it is called

    a. nonrivalry.
    b. learning by doing.
    c. nonexcludability.
    d. diffusion.

6. Which of the following is *not* one of the stages of technological change?

    a. Invention
    b. Innovation
    c. Diffusion
    d. Learning by doing

7. Which of the following enables economists to estimate the relative contributions of capital and technology to economic growth?

    a. The growth accounting formula
    b. Intellectual property laws
    c. Nonexcludability
    d. Productivity slowdown

8.   Which of the following is *not* a way of increasing research and development?

    a.   A tax credit for research
    b.   Eliminating patents, copyrights, and trademarks
    c.   Increased funding
    d.   Improving intellectual property laws

9.   The process by which workers become more proficient is called

    a.   learning by doing.
    b.   increasing returns to labor.
    c.   nonrivalry.
    d.   decreasing returns to labor.

10.   The high rates of growth in the 1970s and early 1980s in the former Soviet Union were mostly due to

    a.   technological change.
    b.   technological progress.
    c.   increases in capital per worker.
    d.   an industrial policy.

11.   Each additional amount of labor results in a smaller addition to output; this is called

    a.   increasing returns to capital.
    b.   diminishing returns to capital.
    c.   increasing returns to labor.
    d.   diminishing returns to labor.

12.   The education and training of workers is called

    a.   technological change.
    b.   technological progress.
    c.   human capital.
    d.   increasing returns to labor.

13.   Labor and capital alone cannot produced sustained growth because of

    a.   diminishing returns to labor and increasing returns to capital.
    b.   increasing returns to labor and diminishing returns to capital.
    c.   diminishing returns to labor and capital.
    d.   increasing returns to labor and capital

14.   Economic growth can be explained by

    a.   adding nonrivalry to labor and capital.
    b.   adding technology to labor and capital.
    c.   adding nonrivalry to labor and productivity.
    d.   adding technology to labor and productivity.

15.   Suppose that the growth rate of capital per hour of work is 1.8 percent per year and the growth rate of technology is 2.5 percent per year. What is the growth rate of real GDP per hour of work?

    a.   2.5 percent
    b.   2.3 percent
    c.   1.9 percent
    d.   3.1 percent

16.   Suppose that the growth rate of real GDP per hour of work is 3 percent per year and the growth rate of capital per hour of work is 1.5 percent per year. What is the growth rate of technology?

    a.   2.0 percent
    b.   2.5 percent
    c.   3.0 percent
    d.   3.5 percent

Use the following table for questions 17 and 18.

Capital per Hour of Work (K/L)	Output per Hour of Work (Y/L)
5	18
10	22
15	26
20	30

Consider an economy in which the productivity curve is given by the data above, where capital per hour of work and output per hour of work are measured in dollars, and the original equilibrium is with $K/L = 10$ and $Y/L = 22$.

17. Suppose that technological progress shifts the productivity curve up by $4 at each level of capital per hour of work and raises the level of capital per hour of work (K/L) to 15. What is the new equilibrium?

    a. $K/L = 10$ and $Y/L = 22$
    b. $K/L = 10$ and $Y/L = 26$
    c. $K/L = 15$ and $Y/L = 26$
    d. $K/L = 15$ and $Y/L = 30$

18. Suppose that negative technological change shifts the productivity curve down by $4 at each level of capital per hour of work. What is the new equilibrium if capital per hour of work (K/L) is constant?

    a. $K/L = 5$ and $Y/L = 14$
    b. $K/L = 10$ and $Y/L = 18$
    c. $K/L = 15$ and $Y/L = 22$
    d. $K/L = 20$ and $Y/L = 26$

Use Figure 9.7 for question 19.

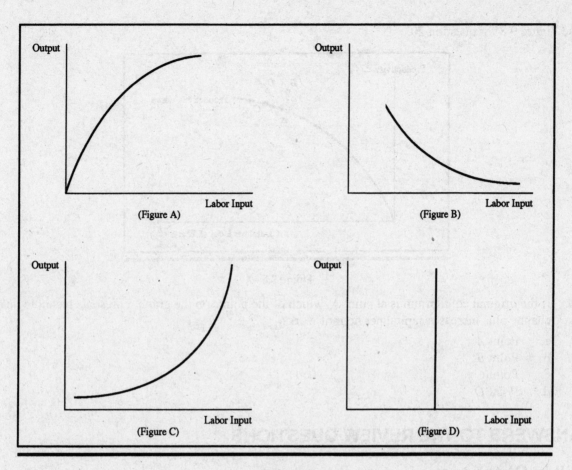

Figure 9.7

19. Which of the figures above appropriately represents a production function?
    a. Figure A
    b. Figure B
    c. Figure C
    d. Figure D

Use Figure 9.8 for question 20.

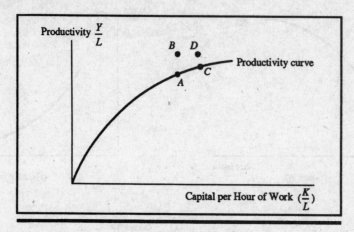

Figure 9.8

20. If the original equilibrium is at point A, which of the points on the graph represents technological change plus increases capital per hour of work?

   a. Point A
   b. Point B
   c. Point C
   d. Point D

ANSWERS TO THE REVIEW QUESTIONS

Fill-In Questions

1. Productivity

2. Technology

3. change or progress

4. Labor-saving technological change

5. invention; innovation; diffusion

6. learning by doing

7. nonrivalry; nonexcludability

8. patents; copyrights; trademarks

9. growth accounting formula

10. human capita

11. Embodied

12. diminishing returns to labor

13. diminishing returns to capital

14. new economy

15. productivity curve

True-False Questions

1. **True.** Innovation, bringing an invention into application with a new product, comes before diffusion, the spreading of the innovation throughout the economy.

2. **True.** The organization helps determine how much a firm produces from its capital and labor.

3. **False.** Specialization of workers is called division of labor.

4. **False.** Intellectual property laws affect the degree of nonexcludability of technology. They do not affect nonrivalry.

5. **False.** The growth accounting formula measures the contributions of capital and technology to economic growth.

6. **True.** Productivity is output per hour of work, and so productivity growth is the growth of real GDP per hour of work.

7. **False.** Most of the growth in the former Soviet Union during the 1970s was due to increases in capital per worker.

8. **False.** Technology growth is the foundation behind the new economy.

9. **True.** Although the growth accounting formula separates the effects of capital and technology on productivity growth, it is not always possible to separate them in practice.

10. **True.** If labor is the only variable input to production, each additional amount of labor will result in a smaller addition to output.

11. **True.** With fixed capital and fixed technology, labor growth will not produce economic growth.

12. **False.** With fixed labor and fixed technology, each additional amount of capital results in a smaller addition to output.

13. **True.** Although growth of capital can produce economic growth, it cannot account for the sustained growth over the last 200 years.

14. **True.** Each additional amount of capital per hour of work causes a smaller increase in productivity.

15. **True.** Technological change shifts the productivity curve up, increasing productivity even with a constant level of capital per hour of work.

16. **False.** Productivity grew at an average annual rate of about 2.6 percent between 1995 and 2000, much higher than productivity growth during the 1970s and 1980s.

Short-Answer Questions

1. With labor-saving technological change, fewer workers are needed to produce the same amount of output. Capital-saving technological change means that fewer machines are needed to produce the same amount of output.

2. Nonrivalry means that one person's use of technology does not reduce the amount that another person can use.

3. Nonexcludability means that the owner of technology cannot prevent other people from using it.

4. The growth accounting formula states that the growth rate of real GDP per hour of work equals 1/3 times the growth rate of capital per hour of work plus the growth rate of technology.

5. The productivity slowdown is largely attributable to a slowdown in the growth rate of technology.

6. Economic policy can help maintain the higher productivity growth since the mid-1990s by providing incentives for technological progress.

7. If education can be improved, more human capital can improve the production of technology.

8. Government support, a tax credit for research, and improving intellectual property laws are three proposals for increasing research and development.

9. Embodied technological change requires new capital in order to be implemented, whereas disembodied technological change does not require new capital.

10. The new economy is the idea that new technology has raised productivity growth since the mid-1990s.

11. The Malthusian predictions were so pessimistic that they gave economics the name the "dismal science."

12. Because of diminishing returns to labor, adding equal increments of labor causes the production function to shift up at a decreasing rate, limiting productivity growth.

13. Because of diminishing returns to capital, adding equal increments of capital causes the production function to shift up at a decreasing rate, limiting productivity growth.

14. Technological change plus increased capital per hour of work causes both a shift in the productivity curve and a movement along the productivity curve.

15. With continual technological change, the productivity curve always shifts up, and sustained economic growth can be achieved.

16. Productivity in the United States increased by a much smaller percentage between 1975 and 1995 than it did between 1955 and 1975.

SOLUTIONS TO THE PRACTICE PROBLEMS

1. a. The growth rate of real GDP per hour of work $=[\frac{1}{3} \times 2.7]+1=0.9+1=1.9$ percent per year.

    b. The new growth rate of real GDP per hour of work $=[\frac{1}{3} \times 2.7]+1.5=0.9+1.5=2.4$ percent per year. Productivity increases by 1/2 percent per year.

2. a. The growth rate of technology $=2-[\frac{1}{3} \times 3]=2-1=1$ percent per year.

    b. The new growth rate of technology $=2-[\frac{1}{3} \times 4.5]=2-1.5=0.5$ percent per year.

ANSWERS TO THE CHAPTER TEST

1. b
2. c
3. d
4. a
5. c
6. d
7. a

8.   b
9.   a
10. c
11. d
12. c
13. c
14. b
15. d
16. b
17. d
18. b
19. a
20. d

APPENDIX TO CHAPTER 9

Deriving the Growth Accounting Formula

OVERVIEW

In Chapter 9, we developed the productivity curve and showed how both technological change and increases in capital per hour of work raise productivity. In this advanced topic, we use the productivity curve to derive the growth accounting formula.

REVIEW

1. The *productivity curve* is depicted in Figure 9A.1. Productivity (Y/L) is on the vertical axis and capital per hour of work (K/L) is on the horizontal axis. The productivity curve illustrates diminishing returns to capital; each additional amount of capital per hour of work causes a smaller increase in productivity.

2. Using the productivity curve, we can show the effects of technological change and increases in capital per hour of work on productivity. Figure 9A.1 depicts the economy's original equilibrium at point A, the point on the productivity curve (original) consistent with the amount of capital per hour of work. Technological change shifts up the productivity curve. The new equilibrium is at point B. Technological change plus increases in capital per hour of work causes both a shift up and a movement along the productivity curve. The new equilibrium is at point C.

3. The growth accounting formula is derived by dividing an increase in productivity into a shift in the productivity curve (due to more technology) and a movement along the productivity curve (due to more capital per worker).

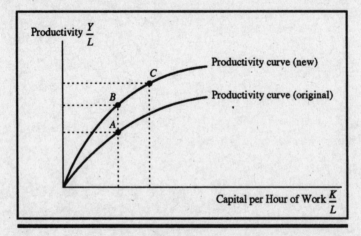

Figure 9A.1

ACTIVE REVIEW

Fill-In Questions

1. The _____ depicts a relation with productivity (Y/L) on the vertical axis and capital per hour of work (K/L) on the horizontal axis.

2. The productivity curve illustrates _____ returns to capital.

3. Technological change _____ the productivity curve.

True-False Questions

1. T F   The productivity curve is the same as the production function.

2. T F   The productivity curve illustrates diminishing returns to capital.

3. T F   The productivity curve shows how both increases in labor and capital raise productivity.

Short-Answer Questions

1. What is the effect of technological change on the productivity curve?

2. What is the effect of technological change plus increases in capital per hour of work on the productivity curve?

3. How is the growth accounting formula derived?

WORKED PROBLEMS

1. Consider an economy in which the productivity curve is given by the following data:

Capital per Hour of Work (K/L)	Output per Hour of Work (Y/L)
10	13
20	21
30	27
40	31
50	33

Capital per hour of work and output per hour of work are measured in dollars.

a. Plot the productivity curve. What is the equilibrium if capital per hour of work $(K/L) = 30$?

b. Suppose that technological change shifts the productivity curve up by $5 at each level of capital per hour of work and the level of capital per hour of work (K/L) increases to 40. Plot the new productivity curve. What is the new equilibrium?

Answer

a. The productivity curve (original) is plotted in Figure 9A.2, with output per hour of work (Y/L) on the vertical axis and capital per hour of work (K/L) on the horizontal axis. The equilibrium is determined at point A, with output per hour of work $(Y/L) = 27$ and capital per hour of work $(K/L) = 30$.

Figure 9A.2

b.   The new productivity curve is also plotted in Figure 9A.2. The new equilibrium is at point B, with output per hour of work $(Y/L) = 36$ and capital per hour of work $(K/L) = 40$.

PRACTICE PROBLEMS

1.   Consider an economy in which the productivity curve is given by the following data:

Capital per Hour of Work (K/L)	Output per Hour of Work (Y/L)
10	14
20	22
30	28
40	32
50	34

Capital per hour of work and output per hour of work are measured in dollars.

a.   Plot the productivity curve. What is the equilibrium if capital per hour of work (K/L) = 40?

b.   Suppose that negative technological change shifts the productivity curve down by $4 at each level of capital per hour of work. Plot the new productivity curve. What is the new equilibrium if capital per hour of work (K/L) is constant?

2.   Consider an economy in which the productivity curve is given by the following data:

Capital per Hour of Work (K/L)	Output per Hour of Work (Y/L)
10	20
20	26
30	30
40	32
50	33

Capital per hour of work and output per hour of work are measured in dollars.

a. Plot the productivity curve. What is equilibrium if capital per hour of work $(K/L) = 30$?

b. Suppose that the level of capital per hour of work (K/L) increases to 40. What is the new equilibrium?

ANSWERS TO THE REVIEW QUESTIONS

Fill-In Questions

1. productivity curve

2. diminishing

3. shifts up

True-False Questions

1. **False**. The production function has output on the vertical axis and labor input on the horizontal axis. The productivity curve has productivity on the vertical axis and capital per hour of work on the horizontal axis.

2. **True**. Along the productivity curve, each additional amount of capital per hour of work causes a smaller increase in productivity.

3. **False**. The productivity curve shows how both technological change and increases in capital per hour of work raise productivity.

Short-Answer Questions

1. Technological change shifts up the productivity curve.

2. Technological change plus increases in capital per hour of work causes both a shift up and a movement along the productivity curve.

3. The growth accounting formula is derived by dividing an increase in productivity into a shift in the productivity curve and a movement along the productivity curve.

SOLUTIONS TO THE PRACTICE PROBLEMS

1. a. The productivity curve (original) is plotted in Figure 9A.3. The equilibrium is at point A, with output per hour of work $(Y/L) = 32$ and capital per hour of work $(K/L) = 40$.

   b. The new productivity curve is also plotted in Figure 9A.3. The new equilibrium is at point B, with output per hour of work $(Y/L) = 28$ and capital per hour of work $(K/L) = 40$.

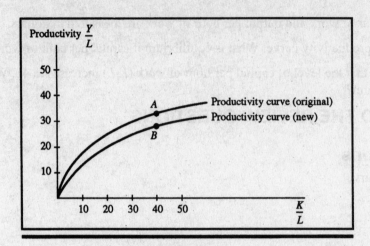

Figure 9A.3

2. a.   The productivity curve (original) is plotted in Figure 9A.4. The equilibrium is at point A, with output per hour of work $(Y/L) = 30$ and capital per hour of work $(K/L) = 30$.

Figure 9A.4

b.   The new equilibrium is at point B, with output per hour of work $(Y/L) = 32$ and capital per hour of work $(K/L) = 40$.

CHAPTER 10

Money and Inflation

CHAPTER OVERVIEW

Money is a vital component of economic activity. Without money, buyers and sellers would not make transactions unless they wanted each other's goods. This is almost impossible to imagine, and the economic system as we know it would cease to exist. In this chapter, we study the monetary system, the arrangement through which people carry out transactions with one another. We first learn about the functions of money and how it is defined. Then we examine the role of banks in creating money and learn about the money multiplier. Two important topics of this chapter are the relationship between money growth and inflation and the quantity equation.

CHAPTER REVIEW

1. **Money** is the part of a person's wealth that can be readily used for transactions. Money is not the same as wealth. Although the dollar bills in your wallet can be used to buy groceries, the equity in your house cannot. Money is therefore defined as the sum of **currency** (coin and paper money) and deposits at banks.

2. Should all deposits at banks be counted as money? **Checking deposits**, which can easily be used to make payments, obviously count because they can be readily used for transactions. The narrowest measure of the **money supply**, called *M1*, consists mainly of currency plus checking deposits. What about *time deposits* and *savings deposits*? Although you can't write a check on these accounts, you can withdraw the funds, so the answer is ambiguous. A broader measure of the money supply, called *M2*, is defined as M1 plus time and savings deposits. Most of money is held as deposits. Only about one-third of M1, and one-tenth of M2, consists of currency.

3. Money has three functions. One of its functions is as a **medium of exchange**, an item that people are willing to accept as payment for the goods they are selling. Money also serves as a **store of value** from one period to another. If you receive money as payment for your goods today, you will be able to use the money in the future to make purchases. Finally, money also serves as a **unit of account** because prices of goods are usually stated in units of money. You say that an apple costs 25 cents, not that an apple costs 8 grapes.

4. A *barter* system, in which goods are exchanged only for other goods, does not have a single medium of exchange. The advantage of a monetary system over a barter system is that a barter system requires a *coincidence of wants*; the person who wants to buy what you want to sell needs to have exactly what you want to buy in order to make a transaction.

5. Many items have been used for money, including cigarettes and large stones. Although *commodity money* describes any monetary system in which money is linked to an item, or commodity, gold and silver are the most common forms of commodity money. The *gold standard* is a monetary system in which the price of gold in terms of money is fixed by the government. The United States was on the gold standard from 1879 until World War I.

6. The *central bank* is the part of the government that supplies currency. In the United States, the central bank is called the **Federal Reserve System**, or "Fed." The **Federal Open Market Committee (FOMC)** makes decisions about the supply of currency and deposits.

7. **Banks** are firms that channel funds from savers to investors by accepting deposits and making loans. They play an important role in the monetary system. Banks are sometimes called *commercial banks* to distinguish them from other *financial intermediaries*, a more general name for firms that "intermediate" between savers and investors. The **assets** of a bank are the **reserves** that commercial banks hold at the Fed, the *loans* that are made by banks to individual or firms, and the *bonds* that the banks hold. The **liabilities** of a bank are the deposits that individuals or firms have made.

8. Banks serve as creators of money. By law, commercial banks are required to hold a fraction of their deposits as reserves at the Fed; that fraction is called the **required reserve ratio**. Since reserves do not pay interest, banks have incentives to make loans or buy bonds with as much of their deposits as possible. Suppose a bank receives a deposit of $1 million. If the reserve ratio is 10 percent, it would deposit $100,000 at the Fed as reserves and make loans or buy bonds with the remaining $900,000. The people who receive the loans or sell the bonds will then deposit the $900,000 in their banks, which will in turn deposit 10 percent, or $90,000, as reserves and make loans or buy bonds with the remaining $810,000. These rounds of lending continue, and so deposits, and thus money, expand by much more than the initial $1 million.

9. The **monetary base** consists of currency plus reserves. When the Fed buys and sells bonds, it changes the amount of bank reserves. When the Fed buys bonds, reserves and loans rise. Through the rounds of lending described above, deposits expand. The **money multiplier** describes by how much a change in the monetary base changes the money supply.

10. Inflation is the rate of growth of the price level. In the long run, inflation is closely related to money growth. When money growth increases, inflation rises, and when money growth decreases, inflation falls. Countries with higher money growth have higher long-run inflation than countries with lower money growth.

11. *Hyperinflation* is extremely high inflation. The most common reason for hyperinflation is that governments run very large budget deficits and finance them by printing money. The resultant very high money growth causes very high inflation.

ZEROING IN

1. We have defined the money multiplier as the number that describes by how much a change in the monetary base changes the money supply. Let's look at that process in more detail.

   a. We need to review some definitions. Money is defined as currency plus deposits. If CU is currency and D is deposits, then $M = CU + D$. The monetary base is currency plus reserves. If MB is the monetary base and BR is the reserves that commercial banks hold at the Fed, then $MB = CU + BR$.

   b. The *reserve ratio* is the fraction of commercial bank deposits that the banks hold in the form of reserves at the Fed. If rr is the reserve ratio, then reserves equal the reserve ratio times deposits, or $BR = rrD$. At any time, people hold both currency and deposits. We define the **currency to deposit ratio**, denoted by k, to be the amount of currency divided by the amount of deposits; $k = CU / D$. Remember that currency is a fraction of deposits, so that k is less than 1. Multiplying both sides of the definition by deposits, $CU = kD$.

c. We now derive the money multiplier, the link between the monetary base MB and money M. Start with the definition of money, $M = CU + D$, and substitute the equation for currency, $CU = kD$; you get $M = kD + D$ or $M = (k+1)D$. Now take the definition of the monetary base, $MB = CU + BR$, and substitute the equation for currency, $CU = kD$, and the equation for reserves, $BR = rrD$; you get $MB = kD + rrD$ or $MB = (k + rr)D$. Finally, divide the expression for money by the expression for the monetary base:

$$\frac{1}{MB} = \frac{(k+1)D}{(k+rr)D} = \frac{(k+1)}{(k+rr)}$$

The ratio $(k+1)/(k+rr)$ is the money multiplier, which is greater than 1 because the reserve ratio rr is less than 1.

2. The relationship between money growth and inflation is one of the most important topics in this chapter. We will use the quantity equation of money to understand the relationship.

a. The **quantity equation of money** describes the relationship between money and nominal GDP. Remember that nominal GDP is the price level times real GDP. The quantity equation is written: Money × Velocity = Price level × Real GDP. **Velocity** is simply the term by which money is multiplied to get nominal GDP. Using growth rates, Money growth + Velocity growth = Inflation + Real GDP growth.

b. The quantity equation is the key to understanding the long-run relationship between money growth and inflation. Along a long-run growth path, where real GDP growth equals potential GDP growth, an increase in money growth will increase inflation by the same amount (in percentage points) unless there is a change in velocity growth. In other words, higher money growth leads to higher inflation in the long run.

ACTIVE REVIEW

Fill-In Questions

1. _____ is the part of a person's wealth that can readily be used for transactions.

2. Money is the sum of _____ and _____.

3. The three functions of money are as a(n) _____, a(n) _____, and a(n) _____.

4. In a(n) _____, goods are exchanged only for other goods.

5. A(n) _____ is required in order to make transactions in a barter system.

6. The _____ is a monetary system in which the price of gold in terms of paper money is fixed by the government.

7. The _____ makes decisions about the supply of currency and deposits.

8. The assets of a commercial bank are _____, _____, and _____.

9. _____ are firms that channel funds from savers to investors.

10. The fraction of deposits that commercial banks are required to hold as reserves at the Fed is called the _____.

11. The _____ equals currency plus reserves.

12. The _____ describes by how much the change in the monetary base changes the money supply.

13. _____ is extremely high inflation.

14. The _____ ratio measures the amount of currency divided by the amount of deposits.

15. _____ is the term by which money is multiplied to get nominal GDP in the quantity equation.

True-False Questions

1. T F   Money is not the same as wealth.

2. T F   Over 50 percent of money consists of currency.

3. T F   Unlike a monetary system, a barter system does not have a single medium of exchange.

4. T F   Currency in the United States is an example of commodity money.

5. T F   When a bank receives a deposit, it cannot use that entire deposit to buy bonds or make loans.

6. T F   Banks attempt to hold as much reserves as possible.

7. T F   The money multiplier describes by how much a change in M1 changes M2.

8. T F   Money growth and inflation are not related in the long run.

9. T F   Inflation and unemployment are not related in the long run.

10. T F   The United States experienced hyperinflation in the late 1970s.

11. T F   Inflation appears to be negatively correlated with economic growth.

12. T F   Inflation in the United States in the early 1990s was high and variable.

13. T F   If the reserve ratio falls, the money multiplier rises.

14. T F   If the currency to deposit ratio falls, the money multiplier rises.

15. T F   The quantity equation of money describes the relationship between money and real GDP.

Short-Answer Questions

1. What is the difference between money and the monetary base?

2. What is the difference between M1 and M2?

3. What is the major disadvantage of a barter system?

4. During what period was the United States on the gold standard?

5. What is the central bank of the United States?

6. What are the assets and liabilities of commercial banks?

7. Define the currency to deposit ratio.

8. Along a long-run growth path, where real GDP growth equals potential GDP growth, what is the effect of an increase in money growth on inflation?

9. What is the role of the Federal Open Market Committee?

10. What is a financial intermediary?

11. What is the required reserve ratio?

12. What is the monetary base?

13. What is the money multiplier?

14. According to the quantity equation of money, what is the relationship between money growth and inflation along a long-run growth path?

15. What is velocity of money?

16. Who is Alan Greenspan, and why is he often considered to be the second most powerful person in America? (Hint: See Economics in Action – The Second (?) Most Powerful Person in America).

WORKING IT OUT

1. The money multiplier is a number that indicates by how much a change in the monetary base changes the money supply. The formula for the money multiplier, derived above, is

$$\frac{(k+1)}{(k+rr)}$$

where k is the currency to deposit ratio and rr is the reserve ratio.

a. Suppose that all money is held as deposits, so that the currency to deposit ratio k equals zero, and the reserve ratio rr equals 10 percent. The money multiplier is $1/0.1 = 10$.

b. Now suppose that the currency to deposit ratio is 20 percent, while the reserve ratio is still 10 percent. The money multiplier is $(0.2+1)/(0.2+0.1) = 1.2/0.3 = 4$.

2. The quantity equation of money can be used both in levels, to describe the relationship between money and nominal GDP, and in growth rates, to describe the relationship between money growth and inflation.

a. According to the quantity equation, money times velocity equals real GDP times the price level. Suppose you are given the following information:

Year	Money	Velocity	Real GDP	Price Level
2000	1,000		4,000	1.00

By the quantity equation,

$1,000 \times \text{velocity} = (4,000) \times (1.00)$

$\text{Velocity} = 4,000/1,000 = 4$

You can use the same technique to solve for any of the variables if you are given values for the other three variables.

b. Now consider data for two years:

Year	Money	Velocity	Real GDP	Price Level
2000	1,000	4	4,000	1.00
2010	1,100	4	4,200	

The inflation rate between the years 2000 and 2010 can be calculated in two ways. Using the quantity equation in levels for the year 2010,

$$Money \times Velocity = Real\ GDP \times Price\ level$$

$$(1,100)(4) = 4,200 \times Price\ level$$

$$Price\ level = 4,400/4,200 = 1.05$$

$$Inflation = (1.05 - 1.00)/1.00 = 0.05\ (5\ percent)$$

Using the quantity equation in growth rates, Money growth + Velocity growth = Real GDP growth + Inflation. Money growth is 10 percent, velocity growth is zero, and real GDP growth is 5 percent. By the quantity equation, 10 percent + 0 percent = 5 percent + Inflation. Therefore, inflation is 5 percent.

Worked Problems

1. Suppose that the currency to deposit ratio k is 40 percent and the reserve ratio rr is 10 percent.

   a. What is the money multiplier?

   b. Suppose that the reserve ratio increases to 12 percent. What is the new money multiplier?

Answer

   a. The money multiplier is $(0.4+1)/(0.4+0.1) = 1.4/0.5 = 2.8$.

   b. When the reserve ratio rises, the money multiplier falls. The new money multiplier is $(0.4+1)(0.4+0.12) = 1.4/0.52 = 2.69$.

2. Consider an economy described by the following information:

Year	Money	Velocity	Real GDP	Price Level
2000	1,000	4.00		1.00
2010	1,100	4.40	4,200	
2020	1,210	4.40	4,410	

   a. What is real GDP in the year 2000?

   b. What is inflation for the decades between 2000 and 2010 and between 2010 and 2020?

Answer

   a. You need to use the quantity equation in levels to determine real GDP for the year 2000. By the quantity equation, $1,000 \times 4.00 = Real\ GDP \times 1.00$. Therefore, Real GDP = 4,000.

   b. Although you can solve for inflation by first using the quantity equation in levels to compute the price level and then computing the inflation rates, it is easier to work in growth rates. Calculating growth rates:

Decade	Money	Velocity	Real GDP	Inflation
2000 to 2010	10%	10%	5%	?
2010 to 2020	10%	0%	5%	?

The quantity equation in growth rates is Money growth + Velocity growth = Real GDP growth + Inflation. For the first decade, 10 percent + 10 percent = 5 percent + Inflation. Therefore, inflation is 15 percent. For the second decade, 10 percent + 0 percent = 5 percent + Inflation. Therefore, inflation is 5 percent.

PRACTICE PROBLEMS

1. Suppose that the currency to deposit ratio k is 30 percent and the reserve ratio rr is 10 percent.

   a. What is the money multiplier?

   b. Suppose that the currency to deposit ratio decreases to 25 percent. What is the new money multiplier?

2. Suppose that the currency to deposit ratio k is 15 percent and the reserve ratio rr is 10 percent.

   a. What is the money multiplier?

   b. Suppose that the reserve ratio decreases to 8 percent. What is the new money multiplier?

3. Consider an economy described by the following information:

Year	Money	Velocity	Real GDP	Price Level
2000	4,000		8,000	1.00
2010	4,400	2.00		1.10
2020	5,280	2.00		1.32

   a. What is velocity in the year 2000?

   b. What is real GDP growth for the decades between 2000 and 2010 and between 2010 and 2020?

4. Consider an economy described by the following information:

Year	Money	Velocity	Real GDP	Price Level
2000		3.00	6,000	2.00
2100	6,000	3.30	7,800	
2200	9,000	3.96	9,360	

   a. What is money in the year 2000?

   b. What is inflation for the twenty-first and twenty-second centuries?

CHAPTER TEST

1. M1 is
   a. the broadest measure of money.
   b. currency plus time and savings deposits.
   c. currency plus checking, time, and savings deposits.

    d.   currency plus checking deposits.

2.   M2 is

    a.   the narrowest measure of money.
    b.   currency plus time and savings deposits.
    c.   currency plus checking, time, and savings deposits.
    d.   currency plus checking deposits.

3.   About what percentage of M1 consists of currency?

    a.   One-tenth
    b.   One-third
    c.   One-half
    d.   Two-thirds

4.   Which of the following is *not* a function of money?

    a.   A medium of exchange
    b.   A store of value from one period to the next
    c.   A means of facilitating a barter system
    d.   A unit of account

5.   Which of the following is *not* considered part of the assets of a bank?

    a.   Reserves held at the Fed
    b.   Loans made to individuals and firms
    c.   Bonds held by the bank
    d.   Deposits made by individuals and firms

6.   The monetary base consists of

    a.   currency plus reserves.
    b.   currency plus loans.
    c.   currency plus bonds.
    d.   reserves plus loans.

7.   The money multiplier describes how much a change in

    a.   loans changes bank assets.
    b.   money growth changes inflation.
    c.   money supply changes the monetary base.
    d.   the monetary base changes the money supply.

8.   If money growth decreases, in the long run

    a.   inflation increases.
    b.   inflation increases, but at a decreasing rate.
    c.   inflation decreases.
    d.   inflation remains unchanged.

9.   Hyperinflation is

    a.   money growth and inflation.
    b.   a decrease in the inflation rate.
    c.   extremely high inflation.
    d.   extremely low inflation.

10. In the long run, inflation is closely related to

    a.   velocity of money.
    b.   money growth.
    c.   declining GDP.
    d.   budget deficits.

11. Inflation is

    a.   positively correlated with economic growth.

b.   negatively correlated with economic growth.

c.   uncorrelated with economic growth.

d.   either positively or negatively correlated with economic growth, depending on other factors.

12.   The reserve ratio is the fraction of commercial bank

   a.   deposits held in reserve at the Fed.

   b.   deposits held in reserve at a commercial bank.

   c.   assets held in reserve at the Fed.

   d.   assets held in reserve at a commercial bank.

13.   The expression for the money multiplier is

   a. $\dfrac{(k+r)}{(k+1)}$.

   b. $\dfrac{(k+1)}{(k+r)}$.

   c. $\dfrac{(k-1)}{(k+r)}$.

   d. $\dfrac{(k+r)}{(k-1)}$.

14.   The money multiplier is

   a.   less than 0.

   b.   between 0 and 1.

   c.   equal to 1.

   d.   greater than 1.

15.   The money multiplier rises if the

   a.   currency to deposit ratio rises.

   b.   currency to deposit ratio falls.

   c.   reserve ratio rises.

   d.   inflation rate rises.

16.   The quantity equation of money describes the relationship between

   a.   money and nominal GDP.

   b.   money and real GDP.

   c.   unemployment and inflation.

   d.   the monetary base and the money supply.

17.   Suppose the currency to deposit ratio is 5 percent and the reserve ratio is 10 percent. What is the money multiplier?

   a. $\dfrac{1}{7}$.

   b. $\dfrac{3}{19}$.

   c. $6\dfrac{1}{3}$.

   d.   7.

Use the following table for questions 18 to 20. Consider an economy described by the following information:

Year	Money	Velocity	Real GDP	Price Level
2000	2,000	2.2		1.1
2100	2,500	2.42	5,000	

18. What is real GDP in the year 2000?
    a. 2,000
    b. 3,000
    c. 4,000
    d. 5,000
19. What is the price level in the year 2100?
    a. 1.0
    b. 1.1
    c. 1.11
    d. 1.21
20. The quantity equation of money describes the relationship between money and
    a. inflation.
    b. nominal GDP.
    c. velocity.
    d. real GDP.

ANSWERS TO THE REVIEW QUESTIONS

Fill-In Questions

1. Money

2. currency; deposits

3. medium of exchange; store of value; unit of account

4. barter system

5. coincidence of wants

6. gold standard

7. Federal Open Market Committee

8. reserves; loans; bonds

9. Banks

10. required reserve ratio

11. monetary base

12. money multiplier

13. Hyperinflation

14. currency deposit ratio

15. Velocity

True-False Questions

1. **True**. Money is only part of a person's wealth, that part that can be readily used for transactions.

2. **False**. Most money is held as deposits.

3. **True**. In a barter system, goods are exchanged directly for other goods.

4. **False**. Currency in the United States is not linked to any commodity.

5. **True**. Banks are required to hold a fraction of deposits as reserves at the Fed.

6. **False**. Because reserves do not pay interest, banks try to minimize their holdings of reserves.

7. **False**. The money multiplier describes by how much changes in the monetary base change the money supply.

8. **False**. In the long run, inflation is closely related to money growth.

9. **True**. In the long run, the unemployment rate equals its normal or natural level independent of the inflation rate.

10. **False**. Inflation in the United States during the late 1970s was about 10 percent per year. Hyperinflation consists of much higher rates.

11. **True**. Countries with high inflation have low growth, and countries with low inflation have high growth.

12. **False**. Inflation in the United States has been about 3 percent per year in the early 1990s.

13. **True**. If banks hold fewer reserves at the Fed, they buy more bonds and/or make more loans, increasing the money supply. This raises the money multiplier.

14. **True**. A fall in the currency to deposit ratio raises deposits. Banks buy bonds and make loans with most of these deposits, increasing the money multiplier and the money supply.

15. **False**. The quantity equation describes the relationship between money and nominal GDP.

Short-Answer Questions

1. Money is defined as currency plus deposits; the monetary base is currency plus reserves.

2. M1 is defined as currency plus checking deposits. M2 adds time and savings deposits.

3. A barter system requires a coincidence of wants in order for transactions to occur.

4. The United States was on the gold standard from 1879 until World War I.

5. The Federal Reserve System is the central bank of the United States.

6. The assets of commercial banks are reserves, loans, and bonds. Their liabilities are the deposits that individuals or firms have made.

7. The currency to deposit ratio is the amount of currency divided by the amount of deposits.

8. Along a long-run growth path, an increase in money growth will increase inflation by the same amount (in percentage points) unless there is a change in velocity growth.

9. The FOMC makes decisions regarding the supply of currency and deposits.

10. A financial intermediary is a firm that "intermediates" or channels funds from savers to investors. A bank is a financial intermediary.

11. The required reserve ratio is the fraction of deposits that banks are required to hold at the Fed.

12. The monetary base equals currency plus reserves.

13. The money multiplier describes how much a change in the monetary base changes the money supply. It is greater than one. Using the currency deposit ratio k and the reserve ratio rr, the expression for the money multiplier is $(k+1)/(k+rr)$.

14. According to the quantity equation, an increase in money growth will increase inflation by the same amount unless there is a change in velocity growth.

15. The velocity of money is the term by which money is multiplied to get nominal GDP.

16. Alan Greenspan is the Chairman of the Board of Governors of the Federal Reserve System. He is often considered to be the second most powerful person in America because of his influence over monetary policy.

SOLUTIONS TO THE PRACTICE PROBLEMS

1. a. The money multiplier is 3.25.

   b. The new money multiplier is 3.57.

2. a. The money multiplier is 4.60.

   b. The new money multiplier is 5.00.

3. a. In the year 2000, velocity $= 2.0$.

   b. Calculating growth rates:

Decade	Money	Velocity	Real GDP	Inflation
2000 to 2010	10%	0%	?	10%
2010 to 2020	20%	0%	?	20%

   Using the quantity equation, real GDP growth is zero for both decades.

4. a. In the year 2000, money $= 4,000$.

   b. Calculating growth rates:

Century	Money	Velocity	Real GDP	Inflation
2000 to 2100	50%	10%	30%	?
2100 to 2200	50%	20%	20%	?

   Using the quantity equation, inflation is 30 percent for the twenty-first century and 50 percent for the twenty-second century.

ANSWERS TO THE CHAPTER TEST

1. d

2. c

3. b

4. c

5. d

6. a

7. d
8. c
9. c
10. b
11. b
12. a
13. b
14. d
15. b
16. a
17. d
18. c
19. d
20. b

PART 2

Sample Test (Chapters 5–10): Principles of Macroeconomics

1. Real GDP is

   a. a measure of the economy's potential.
   b. the amount of all goods and services produced during a specific time period adjusted for the general increase in prices.
   c. another term for inflation.
   d. the total of all goods and services produced during a specific time period.

2. Economic fluctuations are also called

   a. business cycles.
   b. recessions.
   c. expansions.
   d. recoveries.

3. Which of the following groups of people are *not* considered part of the labor force?

   a. People who are unemployed
   b. People who are working part time
   c. People who are *not* working and are looking for work
   d. People who are *not* working and are *not* looking for work

4. Potential GDP is

   a. the same as real GDP.
   b. always above real GDP.
   c. the average or normal level of real GDP.
   d. the maximum attainable level of real GDP.

5. Which of the following would *not* be included in the measurement of GDP for the United States?

   a. Legal and health-care services
   b. Computer and software products
   c. New Ford Broncos produced in Germany
   d. New Honda Accords produced in the United States

6. The three ways to measure GDP are the

   a. spending, income, and consumption approaches.
   b. spending, income, and production approaches.
   c. spending, income, and government purchases approaches.
   d. spending, income, and net exports approaches.

7. For a hypothetical economy in a given year, consumption equaled $355, investment equaled $124, government spending equaled $175, exports equaled $65, and imports equaled $59. What was the value of GDP?

   a. $654
   b. $660
   c. $719
   d. $778

8. When a government's expenditures are less than the government's receipts from taxes,
   a. the government dissaves.
   b. there is a budget deficit.
   c. there is a budget surplus.
   d. there is a balanced budget.

9. If there is inflation,
   a. nominal GDP grows faster than real GDP.
   b. nominal GDP grows faster than the GDP deflator.
   c. real GDP grows faster than nominal GDP.
   d. nominal GDP and real GDP grow at the same rate.

10. The measure of the price level that measures the price of a fixed collection of consumer goods and services in a year compared to some base year is
    a. the GDP deflator.
    b. the chain-weight price index.
    c. the purchasing power parity exchange rate.
    d. the consumer price index.

11. Unemployment that occurs because people have insufficient skills is referred to as
    a. cyclical unemployment.
    b. frictional unemployment.
    c. natural unemployment.
    d. structural unemployment.

12. A 25-year-old woman who decides to stay home and take care of her family after unsuccessfully searching for a job for two years is considered
    a. a discouraged worker.
    b. unemployed.
    c. in the labor force.
    d. self-employed.

Use Figure 1 for questions 13 and 14.

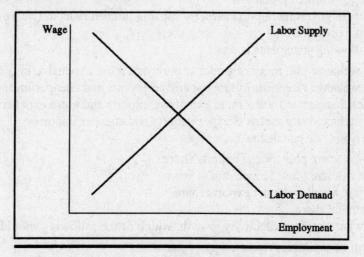

Figure 1

13. Using Figure 1, *ceteris paribus*, a leftward shift in the labor demand curve would cause
    a. both the real wage and the amount of labor employed to increase.
    b. both the real wage and the amount of labor employed to decrease.

    c.   the real wage to increase and the amount of labor employed to decrease.

    d.   the real wage to decrease and the amount of labor employed to increase.

14. Using Figure 1, *ceteris paribus*, a leftward shift in the labor supply curve would cause

    a.   both the real wage and the amount of labor employed to increase.

    b.   both the real wage and the amount of labor employed to decrease.

    c.   the real wage to increase and the amount of labor employed to decrease.

    d.   the real wage to decrease and the amount of labor employed to increase.

15. The natural unemployment rate occurs when the economy is in

    a.   normal times and real GDP is equal to potential GDP.

    b.   normal times and real GDP is greater than potential GDP.

    c.   normal times and real GDP is less than potential GDP.

    d.   recession.

16. The factories, equipment, and other productive resources used to produce goods and services by businesses is referred to as

    a.   net investment.

    b.   capital.

    c.   private sector expenditures.

    d.   public infrastructure investment.

17. Which of the following is the *least* sensitive to changes in the real interest rate?

    a.   The consumption share of GDP

    b.   The net exports share of GDP

    c.   The nongovernment share of GDP

    d.   The investment share of GDP

18. Which of the following *best* explains what is meant by the term *crowding out?*

    a.   An increase in consumption expenditures, by causing interest rates to rise, results in a decline in investment expenditures.

    b.   An increase in investment, by causing interest rates to rise, results in a decline in government purchases.

    c.   An increase in consumption expenditures, by causing interest rates to rise, results in a decline in government purchases.

    d.   An increase in government purchases, by causing interest rates to rise, results in a decline in investment expenditures.

19. Which of the following statements is *true?*

    a.   A higher exchange rate means cheaper exports and more expensive imports.

    b.   A higher exchange rate means more expensive exports and cheaper imports.

    c.   A higher exchange rate means more expensive exports and more expensive imports.

    d.   A higher exchange rate means cheaper exports and cheaper imports.

20. The national savings rate equals the

    a.   consumption share plus the net exports share.

    b.   consumption share plus the investment share.

    c.   investment share plus the net exports share.

    d.   nongovernment share.

21. To understand what causes productivity growth, which of the following should be focused on?

    a.   The growth of capital and technology

    b.   The growth of labor and technology

    c.   The growth of labor and capital

    d.   The growth of the labor force

22. The growth accounting formula

    a.   enables economists to estimate the relative contributions of labor and capital to economic growth.
    b.   enables economists to estimate the relative contributions of labor and technology to economic growth.
    c.   enables economists to estimate the relative contributions of capital and technology to economic growth.
    d.   enables economists to estimate the relative contributions of labor, capital and technology to economic growth.

23. The term that *best* describes what happens when fewer workers are needed to produce the same amount of output is

    a.   creative destruction.
    b.   diffusion.
    c.   capital-saving technological change.
    d.   labor-saving technological change.

24. Suppose that capital per hour of work grows by 2 percent and technology grows by 1 percent over a one-year interval. What is the growth rate of real GDP per hour of work?

    a.   0.67 percent
    b.   1.33 percent
    c.   1.67 percent
    d.   3.0 percent

25. Diminishing returns to labor occur when

    a.   each additional amount of capital results in a smaller addition to output.
    b.   each additional amount of capital results in a larger addition to output.
    c.   each additional amount of labor results in a smaller addition to output.
    d.   each additional amount of labor results in a larger addition to output.

26. M2 is

    a.   the narrowest measure of money.
    b.   currency plus checking deposits.
    c.   M1 plus deposits at the Fed.
    d.   M1 plus time and savings deposits.

Use Table 1 for question 27.

Assets		Liabilities	
Loans	375	Deposits	500
Bonds	100		
Reserves	25		

Table 1

27. Table 1 shows the balance sheet (in millions of dollars) for Bank Inf. Assuming that the bank's reserves are what is required by law, the required reserve ratio is

    a.   5 percent.
    b.   10 percent.
    c.   25 percent.
    d.   75 percent.

28. Suppose the amount of reserves in the banking system equals $60 billion, the amount of deposits equals $802 billion, and the amount of currency equals $321 billion. Under these circumstances, the money multiplier would equal

    a. 0.36.
    b. 1.80.
    c. 2.80.
    d. 2.95.

29. The quantity equation of money describes the relation between

    a. velocity and real GDP.
    b. velocity and nominal GDP.
    c. money and real GDP.
    d. money and nominal GDP.

30. Over the last 20 years, for the largest developed economies in the world, there has been

    a. no correlation between the rate of growth of money and the rate of inflation.
    b. a positive correlation between the rate of growth of money and the rate of inflation.
    c. a negative correlation between the rate of growth of money and the rate of inflation.
    d. both a positive and a negative correlation between the rate of growth of money and the rate of inflation.

ANSWERS TO THE SAMPLE TEST

1. b
2. a
3. d
4. c
5. c
6. b
7. b
8. c
9. a
10. d
11. d
12. a
13. b
14. c
15. a
16. b
17. a
18. d
19. b
20. c

21. a
22. c
23. d
24. c
25. c
26. d
27. a
28. d
29. d
30. b

PART 3

Ecomomic Fluctuations and Macroeconomic Policy

Understanding economic fluctuations, the ups and downs of the economy over the business cycle, is as important as understanding long term economic growth. Chapter 11 begins the study of economic fluctuations with an explanation of why shifts in aggregate demand may cause the economy fluctuate, and an introduction of forecasting GDP. Chapter 12 expands this discussion with the presentation of the economic fluctuations model, a graph consisting of an aggregate demand (AD) curve and inflation adjustment (IA) line, and an equilibrium at the intersection of the curve and the line. In chapter 13, the economic fluctuations model is used to determine the path an economy takes after a shift in aggregate demand due to changes in government purchases, monetary policy, or price shocks.

Chapters 14 and 15 present fiscal and monetary policy, including the federal government budget, impacts of the instruments of fiscal policy, and automatic and discretionary aspects of fiscal policy, as well as central banks, how money supply and money demand interest to determine the interest rate, and alternative monetary policy rules.

Chapter 16 examines the stock market and other financial markets with volatile prices, including the bond market and the foreign exchange market. The chapter defines the rate of return as a factor affecting stock, bond, and foreign exchange prices, and shows how it is calculated.

CHAPTER 11

The Nature and Causes of Economic Fluctuations

CHAPTER OVERVIEW

In the last few chapters, we have studied long-term economic growth. We examined the roles of labor, capital, and technology and looked at economic growth around the world. We now begin to study economic fluctuations, booms and recessions when real GDP departs from its long-run growth trend. In this chapter, we look at the initial movement of the economy as it enters a recession or boom. We consider why changes in aggregate demand first lead to changes in output and study the role of nominal rigidities. We learn about the marginal propensity to consume and the consumption function and see how to find real GDP when consumption and income move together. Finally, we see how the tools that we acquire in this chapter can be used to forecast real GDP. In subsequent chapters, we will study the size of the initial step, look at what makes the boom or recession mild or severe, and examine the process by which the economy returns, over time, to potential GDP.

CHAPTER REVIEW

1. *Economic fluctuations* are temporary departures of real GDP from its long-run growth trend. These departures include recessions, periods when real GDP falls below potential GDP, and booms, times when real GDP rises above potential GDP. Economic fluctuations are also called business cycles.

2. *Aggregate demand* is the total amount that consumers, businesses, government, and foreigners are willing to spend on all goods and services in the economy. Changes in aggregate demand occur when any or all of these groups expand or cut back their spending plans. These changes range from the government spending more on health care, to foreigners buying more American computers, to consumers feeling more optimistic about the future and buying more holiday presents.

3. What happens if an increase in aggregate demand occurs? Suppose that the economy is in "normal times," neither in a recession nor in a boom, so that real GDP equals potential GDP. In theory, firms could respond to the greater demand for their goods either by expanding output or by raising prices. In practice, firms do not raise prices in the short run. Instead, they expand output, and the economy enters a boom. But prices are not fixed forever. Over time, if demand stays high, firms raise their prices and the boom ends. If aggregate demand falls, the reverse occurs. In the short run, firms lower output instead of cutting prices, and the economy enters a recession. Over time, if demand stays low, prices fall and the economy recovers.

4. **Real business cycle theories** explain economic fluctuations by changes *in* potential GDP rather than by changes in aggregate demand that cause movements of real GDP *around* potential GDP. Although, in principle, short-run fluctuations in potential GDP are possible, the factors that underlie potential GDP growth—population, capital, and technology—do not seem to exhibit enough short-run variation to account for the magnitude of observed fluctuations in real GDP.

5. The **consumption function** describes how consumption depends on income. If you receive income, you can either consume or save. In its simplest form, the consumption function says that

when income increases—for an individual, the United States, or the whole world—consumption also increases. At low levels of income, individuals borrow—they consume more than their income. At higher income levels, they save—they consume less than their income.

6. The **marginal propensity to consume**, MPC for short, measures *how much* consumption changes for a given change in income. It is defined as the change in consumption divided by the change in income. The MPC is about 0.60 for the U.S. economy. Thus when income goes up by $1,000, consumption rises by about $600.

7. *Disposable income* is the income that households receive in wages, dividends, and interest payments plus transfers minus taxes. It is the preferred measure of income for use in the consumption function because it measures what households have available to spend. Another form of income used in the consumption function is *aggregate income*, which is also equal to real GDP. The simple consumption function ignores the effects of interest rates and wealth on consumption.

8. A *forecast* of real GDP is a prediction of its future level. A short-run forecast would be a prediction of real GDP one year ahead. Economic forecasters use the identity that real GDP is the sum of consumption, investment, government purchases, and net exports ($Y = C + I + G + X$ in symbols) to predict future real GDP based on their predictions of the four categories of spending. A *conditional forecast* is a prediction of what real GDP will be under alternative assumptions about future government purchases. This can be used to make predictions about the effects on the economy of proposed changes in government spending.

ZEROING IN

1. When demand for a firm's product rises, the firm can either raise prices and sell the same amount at a higher price or increase production and sell more at the original price. Why do firms first respond to increases in demand by adjusting output instead of by raising prices?

    In normal times, firms operate with excess capacity and underutilized equipment. Faced with an increase in demand, they will typically first respond by expanding production instead of by raising prices. The capacity utilization rate, the percent of firms' capacity used for production, is about 80 percent in normal times, falling to 70 percent or lower in recessions and rising to 90 percent or higher in booms.

2. How is income (GDP) determined?

    a. Income is determined when **spending balance** occurs. What is meant by spending balance? It means that two conditions hold simultaneously. These are the income-spending identity (Income = Consumption + Investment + Government purchases + Net exports, $Y = C + I + G + X$) and the consumption function relating consumption to income.

b.   The easiest way to understand the concept of spending balance is by using a graph. Figure
     11.1 puts spending on the vertical axis and income (real GDP) on the horizontal axis.
     Because income is always equal to spending, we draw a line, called the **45-degree line** that
     depicts this equality. If you remember geometry, it is called the 45-degree line because it
     bisects the 90-degree angle formed by the two axes. If you've forgotten all your geometry,
     just think of the 45-degree line as those points on the diagram where income and spending
     are equal.

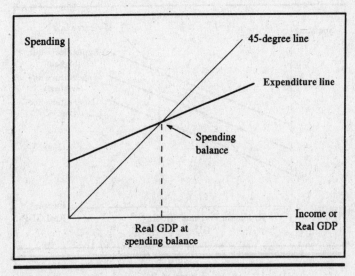

Figure 11.1

c.   The **expenditure line** is also depicted in Figure 11.1. The expenditure line is the sum of
     $C + I + G + X$. According to the simple consumption function, consumption depends only
     on income, and the slope of the consumption function is the marginal propensity to consume
     (MPC). Although we haven't said much about investment, government purchases, and net
     exports, assume, for the moment, that they are constant. (In particular, assume that they do
     not depend on income.) Then the expenditure line, the sum of the consumption function and
     three constants, has the same slope, the MPC, as the consumption function.

d.   Spending balance can now be defined as the intersection between the 45-degree line and the
     expenditure line. Along the 45-degree line, income equals spending. Along the expenditure
     line, consumption is determined by income according to the consumption function.
     Although either of these conditions can be satisfied by many values of real GDP, only one
     value, the point of spending balance, satisfies both.

3.   What causes income (GDP) to increase or decrease?

a.   We have shown how spending balance is determined by the intersection of the 45-degree
     line and the expenditure line. We now look at shifts of the expenditure line and show how
     they affect the point of spending balance and the level of real GDP.

b.   What shifts the expenditure line? Remember how the expenditure line was constructed.
     First, the consumption function was used to relate consumption to income. Then, investment
     I, government purchases G, and net exports X were added to the consumption function to
     determine the expenditure line. Changes in the same three variables cause the expenditure
     line to shift. Increases in I, G, and X shift the expenditure line upward, and decreases in I, G,
     and X shift the expenditure line downward.

c.   This can be seen in Figure 11.2, in which the initial point of spending balance is where real GDP equals potential GDP. If the expenditure line shifts up, spending balance occurs at a point where output exceeds potential, and the economy is in a boom. If the expenditure line shifts down, spending balance occurs at a point where output is less than potential, and the economy is in a recession. These movements of the point of spending balance are called the first steps toward a boom or recession because, as we shall see in the next few chapters, they are not the end of the story.

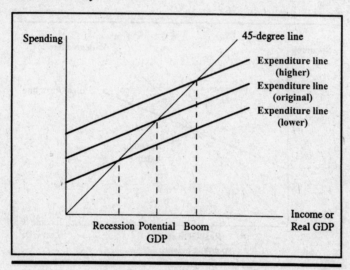

Figure 11.2

d.   The same diagram can also be used to illustrate shifts of the point of spending balance toward, instead of away from, potential GDP. Suppose that the initial point of spending balance in Figure 11.2 occurs during a recession, with output below potential. An increase in government spending would shift the expenditure line up, moving the point of spending balance toward potential GDP. Depending on the size of the increase in G, the expenditure line could move by enough to shift the point of spending balance so that real GDP equals, or even exceeds, potential GDP. Increases in I or X would have the same effect. On the other hand, a decline in G, I, or X would move the point of spending balance down, further reducing real GDP and causing a greater recession.

ACTIVE REVIEW

Fill-In Questions

1.   Economic _____ are temporary departures of real GDP from its long-run growth trend.

2.   _____ is the total amount consumers, businesses, government, and foreigners are willing to spend on all goods and services in the economy.

3.   The _____ is the percentage of firms' capacity used for production.

4.   Economists of the _____ school believe that economic fluctuations can be explained by movements in potential GDP.

5.   The response of consumption to income is described by the _____.

6.   The _____ measures how much consumption changes for a given change in income.

7. _____ income measures what households have available to spend.

8. _____ income is equal to real GDP.

9. A(n)_____ of real GDP is a prediction of its future level.

10. A(n) _____ is a prediction of what real GDP will be under alternative assumptions about future government purchases.

11. A short-run forecast is a prediction of real GDP _____ into the future.

12. _____ is determined when spending balance occurs.

13. The _____ depicts the equality between income and spending.

14. The _____ line is the sum of consumption + investment + government purchases + net exports.

15. _____ occurs at the intersection of the 45-degree line and the expenditure line.

True-False Questions

1. T F When the economy is in neither a recession nor a boom, real GDP equals potential GDP.

2. T F The economy is in a boom if real GDP is less than potential GDP.

3. T F Aggregate demand measures the amount of total consumer spending in an economy.

4. T F Booms and recessions are temporary.

5. T F Business cycles are easy to forecast because they are so regular.

6. T F Firms respond to an increase in demand by immediately raising prices.

7. T F Firms normally operate at 100 percent of capacity.

8. T F A forecast is a prediction of the future.

9. T F Conditional forecasts are always more accurate than unconditional forecasts.

10. T F At low levels of income, individuals consume more than their income.

11. T F The marginal propensity to consume is the change in consumption divided by the change in income.

12. T F Spending balance occurs when income equals consumption.

13. T F Spending balance occurs at the intersection of the 45-degree line and the expenditure line.

14. T F Spending balance can occur only at potential GDP.

15. T F The expenditure line shifts with changes in technology.

16. T F Economists on average greatly over-predicted economic growth in 2004. (Hint: See Economics in Action—The Blue Chip Consensus Forecast.)

Short-Answer Questions

1. What are the two types of economic fluctuations?

2. What is another name for economic fluctuations?

3. Are economic fluctuations permanent?

4.   What is real GDP in "normal times"?

5.   What is the first response by a firm to an increase in aggregate demand?

6.   How does a boom come to an end?

7.   What is the difference between a forecast and a conditional forecast of real GDP?

8.   How do economists who belong to the real business cycle school explain economic fluctuations?

9.   According to the simple consumption function, how is consumption determined?

10. What is measured by the marginal propensity to consume?

11. What does the simple consumption function ignore?

12. Which two conditions are satisfied at the point of spending balance?

13. Which two lines intersect at the point of spending balance?

14. What causes the expenditure line to shift?

15. What happens to the point of spending balance when the expenditure line shifts up?

16. Describe the economic impact of the terrorist attacks of September 11, 2001. (Hint: See Reading the News About – The Economic Impact of September 11).

17. Who was John Maynard Keynes, and why did he make *Time* magazine's list of the 100 most influential people in the twentieth century? (Hint: See Economics in Action – Making *Time's* Top 100).

WORKING IT OUT

1.   The first concept that we will illustrate is how, using graphs, to determine the level of income (GDP) at the point of spending balance. Then we will show what happens to income if a component of expenditure, in this case net exports, increases.

   a.   The first step is to draw a diagram, remembering to label the axes. In this case, illustrated in Figure 11.3, spending is on the vertical axis and income (real GDP) is on the horizontal axis.

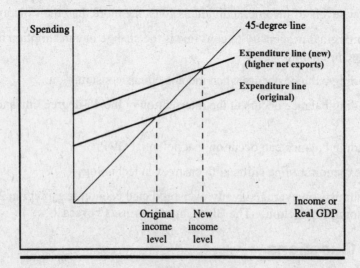

Figure 11.3

   b.   Spending balance occurs at the intersection of the 45-degree line and the expenditure line. As shown in Figure 11.3, the 45-degree line has a slope of 1, so that income equals spending. The expenditure line is also upward sloping, but it is flatter than the 45-degree line. Their intersection determines the point of spending balance.

   c.   Income will change if something occurs that shifts the expenditure line. In this case, the increase in net exports shifts the expenditure line upward from expenditure (original) to expenditure (new). This determines a new point of spending balance at a higher level of income. This is also shown in Figure 11.3.

2.   The point of spending balance can also be determined using tables. Suppose you are given the following information on the relation between income and consumption (in billions of dollars).

Income (Y)	Consumption (C)
0	500
1,000	1,000
2,000	1,500
3,000	2,000
4,000	2,500
5,000	3,000

Assume that investment I is $500 billion, government purchases G are $400 billion, and net exports X are $100 billion.

   a.   The first thing that you can determine is the marginal propensity to consume (MPC), which is the change in consumption divided by the change in income. Looking at the two columns of the table, you can see that whenever consumption increases by 500, income rises by $1,000. The MPC is the change in consumption, 500, divided by the change in income, 1,000, which is $500/1,000$, or 0.50.

   b.   You can also determine the level of income at the point of spending balance, which occurs when income $Y =$ consumption $C +$ investment $I +$ government purchases $G +$ net exports X. Subtracting C from both sides of the equation, this can be written as $Y - C = I + G + X$. Since $I + G + X = 500 + 400 + 100 = 1,000$, the point of spending balance is where $Y - C = 1,000$. When $Y = 3,000$, $C = 2,000$, and $3,000 - 2,000 = 1,000$. Thus income is $3,000 billion at the point of spending balance.

Worked Problems

1.   Draw a diagram with a 45-degree line and an expenditure line. What determines the point of spending balance? Assume that spending balance occurs when real GDP equals potential GDP. What happens to income if net exports decrease?

Answer

First, draw a diagram with spending on the vertical axis and income (real GDP) on the horizontal axis, as shown in Figure 11.4. The 45-degree line has a slope of 1, the expenditure line is upward sloping but flatter than the 45-degree line, and their intersection determines the point of spending balance. The problem assumes that this point occurs when real GDP equals potential GDP. If net exports decrease, the expenditure line shifts downward from expenditure (original) to expenditure (new). This causes a decrease in income. Since income decreases to below potential GDP, this is a recession.

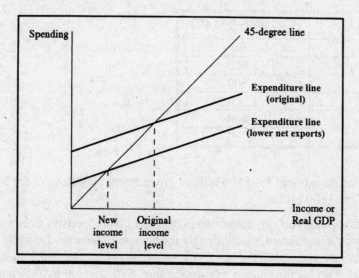

Figure 11.4

2. The following table shows the relationship between income and consumption (in billions of dollars).

Income (Y)	Consumption (C)
0	800
1,000	1,400
2,000	2,000
3,000	2,600
4,000	3,200
5,000	3,800

Assume that investment I is $400 billion, government purchases G are $300 billion, and net exports X are $100 billion.

a. What is the numerical value of the marginal propensity to consume?

b. What is the level of income at the point of spending balance?

Answer

c. The marginal propensity to consume (MPC) is the change in consumption divided by the change in income. Whenever consumption increases by 600, income rises by 1,000. The MPC is $600/1,000$, or 0.60.

d.   Spending balance occurs when income = consumption + investment + government purchases + net exports. Since $I + G + X + 800$, the point of spending balance is where $Y - C = 800$. When $Y = 4,000$, $C = 3,200$, and $4,000 - 3,200 = 800$. Thus income is $4,000 billion at the point of spending balance.

PRACTICE PROBLEMS

1.   Draw a diagram with a 45-degree line and an expenditure line. What determines the point of spending balance? Assume that spending balance occurs when real GDP equals potential GDP. What happens to income if government purchases decrease?

2.   Draw a diagram with a 45-degree line and an expenditure line. Assume that spending balance occurs when real GDP is below potential GDP. What happens to income if both investment and net exports increase?

3.   Draw a diagram with a 45-degree line and an expenditure line. Assume that spending balance occurs when real GDP equals potential GDP. What happens to income if government purchases increase and net exports decrease by exactly the same amount?

4.   The following table shows the relationship between income and consumption (in billions of dollars).

Income (Y)	Consumption (C)
0	500
1,000	1,000
2,000	1,500
3,000	2,000
4,000	2,500
5,000	3,000

Assume that investment I is $400 billion, government purchases G are $100 billion, and net exports X are $0 billion.

a.   What is the numerical value of the marginal propensity to consume?

b.   What is the level of income at the point of spending balance?

5.   The following table shows the relationship between income and consumption (in billions of dollars).

Income (Y)	Consumption (C)
0	600
1,000	1,300
2,000	2,000
3,000	2,700
4,000	3,400
5,000	4,100

Assume that investment I is $500 billion, government purchases G are $300 billion, and net exports X are $100 billion.

a.   What is the numerical value of the marginal propensity to consume?

b.   What is the level of income at the point of spending balance?

6.   The following table shows the relationship between income and consumption (in billions of dollars).

Income (Y)	Consumption (C)
0	400
1,000	1,200
2,000	2,000
3,000	2,800
4,000	3,600
5,000	4,400

Assume that investment I is $300 billion, government purchases G are $200 billion, and net exports X are – $100 billion.

a.   What is the numerical value of the marginal propensity to consume?

b.   What is the level of income at the point of spending balance?

CHAPTER TEST

1.   Economic fluctuations

    a.   never last more than two years.
    b.   are all alike.
    c.   are also called business cycles.
    d.   are permanent departures of real GDP from potential GDP.

2.   In "normal times," real GDP equals

    a.   consumption.
    b.   investment.
    c.   government purchases.
    d.   potential GDP.

3.   Firms respond to an increase in the demand for their goods in the short run by

    a.   expanding output.
    b.   raising prices.
    c.   reducing output.
    d.   cutting prices.

4.   In normal times, the capacity utilization rate is about

    a.   60 percent.
    b.   70 percent.
    c.   80 percent.
    d.   90 percent.

5.   Two examples of economic fluctuations are

    a.   consumption and investment.
    b.   booms and recessions.
    c.   disposable and aggregate.
    d.   government purchases and net exports..

6.   Prices

    a.   never change.
    b.   adjust immediately to changes in demand.

    c.   are fixed in the short run but adjust over time.

    d.   can go up, but they never come down.

7.   Economists who belong to the real business cycle school believe that economic fluctuations are caused by

    a.   fluctuations in potential GDP.

    b.   fluctuations in real GDP.

    c.   changes in aggregate demand.

    d.   changes in government purchases.

8.   The difference between a forecast and a conditional forecast of real GDP is that a

    a.   forecast is made under alternative assumptions about government purchases.

    b.   conditional forecast is made under alternative assumptions about government purchases.

    c.   forecast is made under alternative assumptions about net exports.

    d.   conditional forecast is made under alternative assumptions about net exports.

9.   The simple consumption function describes how

    a.   income depends on consumption.

    b.   income depends on interest rates.

    c.   consumption depends on income.

    d.   consumption depends on interest rates.

10.   Spending balance occurs when

    a. $Y - C = I + G + X$.

    b. $Y - I = C + G + X$.

    c. $Y - G = C + I + X$.

    d. $Y - X = C + I = G$.

11.   The 45-degree line depicts the equality of

    a.   consumption and income.

    b.   real GDP and potential GDP.

    c.   income and spending.

    d.   income and real GDP.

Questions 12 and 13 refer to the following table. (Income and consumption are in billions of dollars.)

Income (Y)	Consumption (C)
0	200
1,000	800
2,000	1,400
3,000	2,000
4,000	2,600
5,000	3,200

12.   Using the above table, the marginal propensity to consume is

    a.   0.3.

    b.   0.6.

    c.   0.8.

    d.   1.0.

13.   Suppose investment I is $300 billion, government purchases G are $200 billion, and net exports X are $100 billion. At what level of income does spending balance occur?

    a. $1,000 billion

    b. $2,000 billion

    c. $3,000 billion

    d. $4,000 billion

14. The expenditure line is the sum of

    a. $C + I + G$.

    b. $C + I + X$.

    c. $C + I + G + X$.

    d. $C + I + G + Y$.

15. The slope of the expenditure line is the marginal propensity to

    a.   consume.

    b.   invest.

    c.   export.

    d.   save.

16. Which of the following causes an upward shift in the expenditure line?

    a.   A decrease in investment

    b.   A decrease in government purchases

    c.   An increase in real GDP

    d.   An increase in net exports

Use Figure 11.5 for questions 17, 18, and 19.

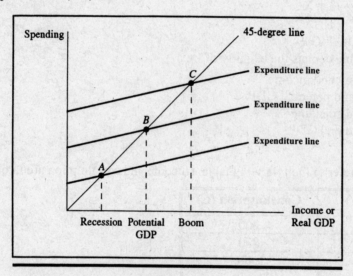

Figure 11.5

17. Starting from a point of spending balance with real GDP equal to potential GDP, a decrease in government purchases

    a.   shifts the expenditure line up from *A* to *B*.

    b.   shifts the expenditure line up from *B* to *C*.

    c.   shifts the expenditure line down from *B* to *A*.

    d.   leaves the expenditure line unchanged.

18. Starting from a point of spending balance with real GDP equal to potential GDP, an increase in net exports

    a.   shifts the expenditure line up from *A* to *C*.

    b.   shifts the expenditure line up from *B* to *C*.

    c.   shifts the expenditure line down from *C* to *A*.

    d.   leaves the expenditure line unchanged.

19. Starting from a point of spending balance with real GDP equal to potential GDP, an increase in investment matched by an equal decrease in net exports

    a.   shifts the expenditure line up from *A* to *B*.

    b.   shifts the expenditure line up from *B* to *C*.

    c.   shifts the expenditure line down from *C* to *A*.

    d.   leaves the expenditure line unchanged.

20. Starting from a point of spending balance with real GDP below potential GDP, an increase in government purchases

    a.   increases real GDP to equal potential GDP.

    b.   increases real GDP to above potential GDP.

    c.   increases real GDP, but to a point that is still below potential GDP.

    d.   increases real GDP, but we do not know whether a, b, or c is correct.

ANSWERS TO THE REVIEW QUESTIONS

Fill-In Questions

1.   fluctuations

2.   Aggregate demand

3.   capacity utilization rate

4.   real business cycle

5.   consumption function

6.   marginal propensity to consume

7.   Disposable

8.   Aggregate

9.   forecast

10. conditional forecast

11. one year

12. Income

13. 45-degree line

14. expenditure

15. Spending balance

True-False Questions

1.   **True**. Real GDP equals potential GDP in normal times.

2.   **False**. When real GDP is less than potential GDP, the economy is in a recession.

3.   **False**. Aggregate demand includes consumer spending and business, government, and foreign spending.

4.   **True**. Real GDP eventually returns to potential GDP.

5.   **False**. Business cycles are difficult to forecast because no two are alike.

6. **False**. In practice, firms do not raise prices in the short run.

7. **False**. In normal times, there is some unused capacity.

8. **True**. For example, a forecast of real GDP is a prediction of its future level.

9. **False**. The two types of forecasts cannot be compared in this manner.

10. **True**. At low levels of income, individuals borrow.

11. **True**. The MPC measures how much consumption changes when income changes.

12. **False**. Spending balance occurs when income equals spending and consumption is determined by income according to the consumption function.

13. **True**. Income equals spending along the 45-degree line, and the consumption function helps determine the expenditure line.

14. **False**. Spending balance can also occur during booms and recessions.

15. **False**. The expenditure line shifts with changes in government purchases, investment, taxes, and net exports.

16. **False**. Economic growth in 2004 was 4.4 percent. The consensus forecast, an average of economists surveyed in January 2004, was that economic growth would equal 4.6 percent, almost exactly on target.

Short-Answer Questions

1. Booms and recessions are the two types of economic fluctuations.

2. Another name for economic fluctuations is business cycles.

3. No, economic fluctuations are temporary. Real GDP returns over time to its long-run growth path.

4. In "normal times," real GDP equals potential GDP.

5. The first response by a firm to an increase in aggregate demand is to expand output.

6. Over time, firms raise their prices and the boom ends.

7. A forecast of real GDP is a prediction of its future level. A conditional forecast is a prediction of what real GDP will be under alternative assumptions about future government purchases.

8. Members of the real business cycle school believe that economic fluctuations are caused by fluctuations in potential GDP.

9. According to the simple consumption function, consumption is determined by income.

10. The marginal propensity to consume measures how much consumption changes for a given change in income.

11. The simple consumption function ignores the effects on consumption of forward-looking behavior, interest rates, and wealth.

12. The income-spending identity and the consumption function are satisfied at the point of spending balance.

13. The 45-degree line and the expenditure line intersect at the point of spending balance.

14. Changes in investment, government purchases, and net exports shift the expenditure line.

15. When the expenditure line shifts up, spending balance occurs at a higher level of income.

16. While certain sectors of the economy, such the airline industry, and certain areas of the country, primarily New York City, still feel the effects of the attacks, the overall economic impact of the tragic events of September 11 have not been as long-lasting as some people feared at the time.

17. John Maynard Keynes was a British economist who lived in the first half of the twentieth century. His ideas, including the marginal propensity to consume and the importance of aggregate demand, had an enormous influence on the development of macroeconomics.

SOLUTIONS TO THE PRACTICE PROBLEMS

1. The point of spending balance is always at the intersection of the 45-degree line and the expenditure line. A decrease in government purchases shifts the expenditure line down, reducing income and causing a recession.

2. Increases in investment and net exports shift the expenditure line up, increasing income. The initial point of spending balance occurred at a level of income below potential GDP, but we do not know whether the increase in income is sufficient to raise real GDP up to, or even beyond, potential GDP.

3. An increase in government purchases would shift the expenditure line up, and the decrease in net exports would shift it down. Since the increase in G is equal to the decrease in X, the two effects cancel each other out. The expenditure line does not move, and income remains at potential GDP.

4. a. The marginal propensity to consume (MPC) $= 500/1,000 = 0.50$.

    b. At the point of spending balance, income (Y) $= \$2,000$ billion .

5. a. The marginal propensity to consume (MPC) $= 700/1,000 = 0.70$.

    b. At the point of spending balance, income (Y) $= \$5,000$ billion .

6. a. The marginal propensity to consume (MPC) $= 800/1,000 = 0.80$.

    b. At the point of spending balance, income (Y) $= \$4,000$ billion .

ANSWERS TO THE CHAPTER TEST

1. c

2. d

3. a

4. c

5. b

6. c

7. a

8. b

9. c

10. a

11. c

12. b

13. b

14. c
15. a
16. d
17. c
18. b
19. d
20. d

APPENDIX TO CHAPTER 11

Deriving the Formulas for the Keynesian Multiplier and the Forward-Looking Consumption Model

OVERVIEW

The important concept introduced in this chapter is the multiplier, a number that determines by how much real GDP changes when government spending, investment, or net exports change. We study how to find the multiplier using both graphs and algebra and see that the size of the multiplier is uncertain. We then look at the multiplier when net exports depend on income and the multiplier for a tax change. Finally, we study the forward-looking consumption model and learn more about why the multiplier is uncertain.

REVIEW

1. The **multiplier** is a number that represents how much real GDP changes when expenditure changes. Algebraically, it is the change in real GDP divided by the change in expenditure, or the ratio of the two changes. The change in expenditure may be caused by a number of factors; changes in government purchases, taxes, investment, and net exports are the most important.

2. When expenditure increases, real GDP rises by more than the change in expenditure. Algebraically, the change in real GDP exceeds the change in expenditure, or the ratio of the two changes is greater than 1. The *size of the multiplier*, which is the ratio of the two changes, is greater than 1.

3. Why is the multiplier greater than 1? Suppose that the government increases spending so that NASA can build a space station. If this were the end of the story, the change in real GDP would equal the change in expenditure, and the multiplier would be 1. But there is more. In order to build the space station, NASA hires additional workers and outside suppliers, and they spend part of their wages and payments. This spending goes to more people (grocery store owners, etc.), who in turn spend part of their payments on other goods. Through these *rounds of spending*, the total change in real GDP exceeds the initial change in expenditure, and the multiplier is greater than 1. These rounds of spending occur quickly—the total change in real GDP is achieved in about a year.

4. The *marginal propensity to consume (MPC)* is the change in consumption divided by the change in income. In the above example, the additional workers that NASA hires will spend more of their wages if their MPC is higher than if their MPC is lower. More generally, each round of spending will be greater if the MPC is higher. The greater the spending, the larger the total effect on real GDP. Thus the multiplier, which measures by how much income increases when expenditure rises, will be larger if the MPC is higher. Uncertainty about the value of the MPC is an important cause of uncertainty about the value of the multiplier.

5. The *marginal propensity to import (MPI)* is the change in imports divided by the change in income. When U.S. income goes up, part of the increase is spent on foreign produced goods (automobiles, consumer electronics, etc.), and so the MPI is positive. Since most of the goods that

are consumed when income rises are produced in the United States (not imported), the MPI is smaller than the MPC.

6. *Net exports* are exports minus imports. Although imports, as explained above, are positively related to U.S. income, exports are not related to U.S. income. (Exports are positively related to foreign income, not U.S. income.) Net exports, exports minus imports, are negatively related to income because exports are unrelated to income and imports are positively related.

7. The value of the multiplier is negatively related to the value of the MPI. When the MPI is higher, a larger part of the rounds of spending goes to foreign-produced goods. Although this increases foreign income, it does not affect U.S. income, and so does not contribute to further rounds of spending.

8. The simple consumption function, with a constant marginal propensity to consume (MPC), does not provide a satisfactory theory of consumption. Instead of being constant, the MPC, and therefore the multiplier, seems to change in different situations. The **forward-looking consumption model**, although more complicated than the consumption function, provides a way to understand how the MPC changes.

9. The forward-looking consumption model has its origins in two models developed in the 1950s: Milton Friedman's **permanent income model** and Franco Modigliani's **life-cycle model**. The forward-looking model used in the 1990s, however, has been developed tremendously since that time.

10. The central idea of the forward-looking model is that most people engage in **consumption smoothing**. Instead of allowing their consumption to vary with their income, which would be implied by a constant MPC, they spend less than their income (and save) in good years and spend more than their income (and dissave) in bad years. Suppose you were to win $1 million in a lottery. If your MPC was 0.90, would you spend $900,000 in the year that you won and then return to your old lifestyle, or would you spread the winnings over time? A constant MPC implies the former; consumption smoothing implies the latter.

11. Consumption smoothing is not perfect. One reason is that some people are **liquidity constrained**: They cannot borrow enough to completely smooth their consumption. One example is (virtually) every reader of this study guide. As a student, if you go to your local bank and say, "I want a loan so that I can increase my consumption while I'm in school up to the level that I'll be able to afford after I graduate and get a high-paying job," don't expect the banker to reply, "That's fine, we always approve consumption smoothing loans."

12. A striking implication of the forward-looking model is that, because people attempt to smooth their consumption, the MPC is very small for temporary changes in income and very large for permanent changes in income. Thus the multiplier for a *temporary tax cut*, which produces only a temporary change in income, is smaller than the multiplier for a *permanent tax cut*, which produces a permanent change in income. This explains the contrast between the low MPC for the one-year tax rebate of 1975, which was explicitly temporary, and the high MPC for the tax cuts of the early 1980s, which were explicitly permanent.

13. A final implication of the forward-looking model is that *anticipated tax changes* will have effects before the tax changes are actually enacted. Suppose you expect a tax increase in the future. According to the forward-looking model, you will begin to reduce your consumption now in anticipation of your expected lower income in the future.

ZEROING IN

1. The important concept for you to understand in this advanced topic is that of the multiplier. Remember that the multiplier represents how much income changes when expenditure changes. In the review section, we explained the concept of the multiplier intuitively through rounds of spending. Here we will provide a graphical illustration.

    a. The first step in graphing the multiplier is to set up the diagram. In Figure 11A.1, with spending on the vertical axis and income (real GDP) on the horizontal axis, we draw the 45-degree line and the expenditure line. Note that the expenditure line slopes upward but is flatter than the 45-degree line.

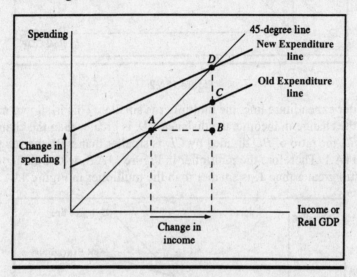

Figure 11A.1

    b. An increase in expenditure shifts the expenditure line up from the old expenditure line to the new expenditure line. The point of spending balance, the intersection of the 45-degree line and the expenditure line, shifts from point *A* to point *D*. Income (real GDP) increases.

    c. The change in spending (expenditure) is the vertical distance between the old and new expenditure lines. Since the two lines are parallel, this can be measured at any point on the lines and equals the distance *CD*. (By the distance *CD*, we mean the distance from the point *C* to the point *D*.) The change in income is the horizontal distance between the two dotted lines, or *AB*. (Since the two dotted lines are also parallel, this can also be measured at any point.)

    d. How much does income increase? Because *ABD* forms a right triangle, the distance *AB*, the change in income, equals the distance *BD*. Remember that the distance *CD* is the change in spending. Since the distance *BD* is greater than the distance *CD*, the change in income is greater than the change in spending. The multiplier, which is the change in income divided by the change in spending, is greater than 1.

2. What determines the value of the multiplier? We will show that a lower marginal propensity to consume (MPC) and/or a higher marginal propensity to import (MPI) will lower the multiplier.

    a. The MPC and the MPI determine the slope of the expenditure (expenditure) line. The smaller the MPC and the larger the MPI, the flatter the expenditure line. This is illustrated in Figure 11A.2.

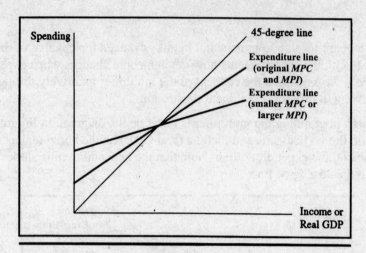

Figure 11A.2

b. With a flatter expenditure line, the multiplier is smaller. This is shown in Figure 11A.3. Although the change in income, the distance *BD*, is greater than the change in spending, the distance *CD*, the ratio of *BD* divided by *CD* is smaller than with the steeper expenditure line in Figure 11A.1. Therefore the multiplier in Figure 11A.3, with a flatter expenditure line, although still greater than 1, is smaller than the multiplier in Figure 11A.1.

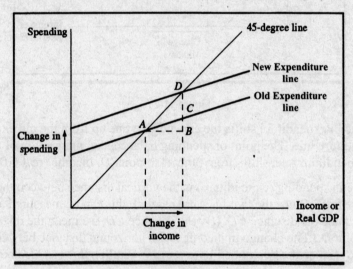

Figure 11A.3

ACTIVE REVIEW

Fill-In Questions

1. The _____ represents by how much real GDP changes when expenditure changes.

2. The multiplier is _____ than 1.

3. The _____ is the change in consumption divided by the change in income.

4. The _____ is the change in imports divided by the change in income.

5. _____ are exports minus imports.

6. The _____ consumption model allows the marginal propensity to consume to change.

7. The origins of the forward-looking consumption model are the _____ and _____ models.

8. _____ occurs when people try to keep their consumption steady over time.

9. When people cannot borrow enough to completely smooth their consumption, they are said to be _____.

True-False Questions

1.   T   F   The multiplier is the change in real GDP divided by the change in expenditure.

2.   T   F   When government purchases increase by $100 billion, real GDP increases by more than $100 billion.

3.   T   F   When government purchases increase by $100 billion, real GDP immediately increases by more than $100 billion.

4.   T   F   The total effect on real GDP of a change in net exports is achieved in about a decade.

5.   T   F   The marginal propensity to consume (MPC) and the multiplier are positively related.

6.   T   F   The marginal propensity to import is positive.

7.   T   F   Exports are positively related to U.S. income.

8.   T   F   The forward-looking consumption model assumes that the MPC is constant.

9.   T   F   Consumers are liquidity constrained if they cannot borrow all that they want.

10. T   F   According to the forward-looking model, the MPC is different for temporary and permanent changes in income.

11. T   F   According to the forward-looking model, people will spend a large proportion of a one-year tax rebate.

12. T   F   According to the consumption function, anticipated tax changes will have effects before the tax changes are enacted.

Short-Answer Questions

1. What factors cause expenditure to change?

2. How large is the multiplier?

3. Why is the multiplier greater than 1?

4. Why is the MPI smaller than the MPC?

5. What causes uncertainty about the value of the multiplier?

6. What is the central idea of the forward-looking consumption model?

7. What are the origins of the forward-looking consumption model?

8. According to the forward-looking model, how do the multipliers for temporary and permanent tax cuts differ?

9. According to the forward-looking model, why do anticipated tax cuts have effects before the tax cuts are actually enacted?

WORKING IT OUT

1. In Chapter 11, we used the 45-degree line and the consumption function to derive the point of spending balance. Here we will use the same concepts to derive the multiplier.

    a. Start with the identity that income equals spending,

    $$Y = C + I + G + X$$

    where Y is income, C is consumption, G is government purchases, and X is net exports. This is the algebraic version of the 45-degree line.

    b. The consumption function states that consumption consists of two parts. The first part, which we call c, does not depend on income. The second part consists of the marginal propensity to consume (MPC) times the level of income. Adding the two parts together,

    $$C = c + (MPC \times Y)$$

    The part of consumption that does not depend on income, c, is positive because at very low levels of income, people borrow rather than consume nothing.

    c. Assume (for the moment) that investment, government purchases, and net exports do not depend on income. Substitute the consumption function into the income = spending identity:

    $$Y = c + MPC \times Y + I + G + X$$

    Subtract $MPC \times Y$ from both sides of the equation:

    $$Y - MPC \times Y + c + I + G + X$$

    Gather terms involving Y:

    $$Y(1 - MPC) = c + I + G + X$$

    Divide both sides by $1 - MPC$ to get

    $$\Delta Y = \frac{1}{1 - MPC} (\Delta I + \Delta G + \Delta X)$$

    $$\frac{1}{1 - MPC + MPI} = \frac{1}{1 - 0.6 + 0.1} = \frac{1}{0.5} = 2$$

    $$Y = \frac{1}{1 - MPC} (c + I + G + X)$$

    d. To derive the multiplier, we need to write the above equation in terms of changes. Using the Greek letter Δ to denote the change in a variable,

    $$\Delta Y = \frac{1}{1 - MPC} (\Delta I + \Delta G + \Delta X)$$

    where $\Delta c = 0$ because c is a constant. The multiplier

    $$\frac{1}{1 - MPC}$$

    is the number that shows how much income changes when any of the categories of expenditure, I+G+X , change. Note that the multipliers for investment, government spending, and net exports are identical.

2. The multiplier can also be derived using specific numerical values for the variables and the MPC.

    a. As above, start with the identity that income equals spending,

    $$Y = C + I + G + X$$

    Suppose that the consumption function is

    $$C = c + 0.8Y$$

    where the $MPC = 0.8$.

    b. Substitute C (from the consumption function) into the identity:

    $$Y = c + 0.8Y + I + G + X$$

    Subtract $0.8Y$ from both sides

    $$Y - 0.8Y = c + I + G + X$$

    Gather terms involving Y:

    $$Y(1 - 0.8) = c + I + G + X$$

    $$Y(0.2) = c + I + G + X$$

    Divide both sides by 0.2 (or multiply both sides by 5):

    $$Y = 5(c + I + G + X)$$

    c. To complete the derivation, write the equation in terms of changes:

    $$\Delta Y = 5(\Delta I + \Delta G + \Delta X)$$

    The multiplier equals 5.

    d. You can also use the formula to find the multiplier. With the MPC = 0.8,

    $$\frac{1}{1 - MPC} = \frac{1}{1 - 0.8} = \frac{1}{0.2} = 5$$

    The multiplier again equals 5.

3. Another way to think about the multiplier is by starting with numbers instead of equations. In Chapter 10, we looked at this example to determine the point of spending balance.

Income (Y)	Consumption (C)
0	500
1,000	1,000
2,000	1,500
3,000	2,000
4,000	2,500
5,000	3,000

We will use the same values to derive the multiplier.

a. We first need to calculate the marginal propensity to consume. Remember that the MPC is the change in consumption divided by the change in income. In this example, $\Delta C / \Delta Y = 500/1,000 = 0.5$.

b. Now use the formula for the multiplier.

$$\frac{1}{1 - MPC} = \frac{1}{1 - 0.5} = \frac{1}{0.5} = 2$$

The multiplier equals 2.

Worked Problems

1. Suppose that the consumption function is

$$C = -c + 0.8Y$$

and the net export function is

$$X = x - 0.2Y,$$

where the MPC = 0.8 and the marginal propensity to import (MPI) = 0.2. What is the multiplier?

Answer

Substitute the consumption and net export functions into the income = spending identity:

$$Y = c + 0.8Y + I + G + x - 0.2Y.$$

Collecting and gathering terms,

$$Y - 0.8Y + 0.2Y = c + I + G + x$$

$$Y(1 - 0.8 + 0.2) = c + I + G + x$$

$$Y(0.4) = c + I + G + x.$$

Dividing both sides by 0.4 (multiplying by 2.5) and writing the result in change form, gives

$$Y = 2.5(c + I + G + x)$$

$$\Delta Y = 2.5(\Delta I + \Delta G)$$

The multiplier is 2.5. Because net exports depend on income, the formula $\dfrac{1}{1 - MPC}$, which is correct only if only consumption depends on income, is not applicable. The correct formula when both consumption and net exports depend on income is $\dfrac{1}{1 - MPC + MPI}$.

2. The following table shows the relationship among income, consumption, and net exports (in billions of dollars).

Income (Y)	Consumption (C)	Net Exports (X)
0	800	400
1,000	1,400	300
2,000	2,000	200
3,000	2,600	100
4,000	3,200	0
5,000	3,800	-100

What is the multiplier?

Answer

In order to calculate the multiplier, you first need to calculate the MPC and the MPI. The $MPC = \Delta C / \Delta Y = 600 / 1,000 = 0.6$. Calculating the MPI is more subtle. When income increases by 1,000, net exports decrease by 100. Since exports do not depend on income, this means that imports must increase by 100. Thus the $MPI = \Delta Imports / \Delta Y = 100 / 1,000 = 0.1$. The multiplier can now be calculated from the formula:

$$\frac{1}{1 - MPC + MPI} = \frac{1}{1 - 0.6 + 0.1} = \frac{1}{0.5} = 2$$

PRACTICE PROBLEMS

1. Suppose that the consumption function is

$$C = c + 0.9Y,$$

where the $MPC = 0.9$. What is the multiplier?

2. Suppose that the consumption function is

$$C = c + 0.9Y$$

and the net export function is

$$X = x - 0.3Y,$$

where the $MPC = 0.9$ and the $MPI = 0.3$. What is the multiplier?

3. The following table shows the relationship between income and consumption (in billions of dollars).

Income (Y)	Consumption (C)
0	800
1,000	1,500
2,000	2,200
3,000	2,900

Income (Y)	Consumption (C)
4,000	3,600
5,000	4,300

What are the MPC and the multiplier?

4. The following table shows the relationship between income, consumption, and net exports (in billions of dollars).

Income (Y)	Consumption (C)	Net Exports (X)
0	900	500
1,000	1,500	300
2,000	2,100	100
3,000	2,700	-100
4,000	3,300	-300
5,000	3,900	-500

What are the MPC, the MPI, and the multiplier?

ANSWERS TO THE REVIEW QUESTIONS

Fill-In Questions

1. multiplier
2. greater
3. marginal propensity to consume
4. marginal propensity to import
5. Net exports
6. forward-looking
7. permanent income; life cycle
8. Consumption smoothing
9. liquidity constrained

True-False Questions

1. **True**. The multiplier is the ratio of the two changes.
2. **True**. The multiplier is greater than 1.
3. **False**. The full multiplier effect on GDP is reached through rounds of spending.
4. **False**. The full multiplier effect is achieved in about a year.

5. **True**. The higher the MPC, the higher the multiplier.

6. **True**. When U.S. income goes up, part of the increase is spent on imported goods, and so the MPI is positive.

7. **False**. Exports are positively related to foreign income, not to U.S. income.

8. **False**. The forward-looking consumption model provides a way to understand how the MPC changes.

9. **False**. They are liquidity constrained if they cannot borrow enough to completely smooth their consumption.

10. **True**. Because people smooth their consumption, the MPC is much smaller for temporary than for permanent changes in income.

11. **False**. The MPC for a one-year tax rebate is very low.

12. **False**. This is an implication of the forward-looking model, not of the consumption function.

Short-Answer Questions

1. Changes in expenditure are caused by changes in government purchases, taxes, investment, and net exports.

2. Although the exact size of the multiplier depends on a number of factors, it is always greater than 1.

3. The multiplier is greater than 1 because the initial change in expenditure induces rounds of spending that cause the total change in real GDP to exceed the initial change in expenditure.

4. The MPI is smaller than the MPC because most of the goods that are consumed when income rises are produced in the United States.

5. Uncertainty about the value of the MPC causes uncertainty about the value of the multiplier.

6. The central idea of the forward-looking consumption model is that people attempt to smooth consumption over their lifetimes.

7. The permanent income and life cycle models of consumption are the origins of the forward-looking model.

8. The multiplier for temporary tax cuts is smaller than the multiplier for permanent tax cuts.

9. If you expect your taxes to be reduced in the future, you will increase your consumption now in anticipation of your expected higher future income.

SOLUTIONS TO THE PRACTICE PROBLEMS

1. The multiplier $= \dfrac{1}{1-MPC} = \dfrac{1}{1-0.1} = \dfrac{1}{0.9} = 10$.

2. The multiplier $= \dfrac{1}{1-MPC+MPI} = \dfrac{1}{1-0.9+0.3} = \dfrac{1}{0.4} = 2.5$.

3. The MPC=0.7 .

    The multiplier $= \dfrac{1}{1-MPC} = \dfrac{1}{1-0.7} = \dfrac{1}{0.3} = 3.33$.

4. The MPC=0.6 and the MPI=0.2 .

$$\text{The multiplier} = \frac{1}{1-\text{MPC}+\text{MPI}} = \frac{1}{1-0.6+0.2} = \frac{1}{0.6} = 1.67.$$

CHAPTER 12

The Economic Fluctuations Model

CHAPTER OVERVIEW

In our discussion of economic fluctuations, we first learned how the economy moves from potential GDP into a boom or recession. In this chapter, we construct the economic fluctuations model. We derive the aggregate demand (*AD*) curve and the inflation adjustment (*IA*) line, and see how the equilibrium level of real GDP and inflation is given by the intersection of the *AD* curve and the *IA* line. We learn what causes movements along the *AD* curve, how changes in government purchases or the central bank's inflation target cause the *AD* curve to shift, and how the *IA* line shifts in response to changes in expectations of inflation or changes in commodity prices. The *AD* curve and *IA* line will be used extensively in the rest of the text, so it is important that you learn to derive and manipulate them now.

CHAPTER REVIEW

1. The **aggregate demand (*AD*) curve** is an inverse (negative) relation between inflation and real GDP. It is derived using two concepts that we will explain below. First, the level of real GDP at the point of spending balance is negatively related to the interest rate. Second, the interest rate is positively related to the inflation rate because of the central bank's policy rule.

2. The inflation rate is the annual rate of change in the overall price level. It is important to remember the distinction between the inflation rate, which is expressed as a percent, and the price level, which is expressed as a number. When inflation is positive, prices are rising. When inflation is negative, prices are falling. If inflation is positive but decreasing, prices are still rising, but at a slower rate.

3. At the point of spending balance, real GDP depends on aggregate expenditure. *Real GDP depends negatively on interest rates* because three of the components of aggregate expenditure, investment, net exports, and consumption, depend negatively on interest rates.

4. The *real interest rate* is the nominal interest rate minus the expected rate of inflation. It is the correct measure of the effect of interest rates on investment, net exports, and consumption because it adjusts for inflation. If inflation is low and stable, as in the early 1990s, the real interest rate is not much different than the nominal interest rate.

5. The *central bank* is the part of the government that controls monetary policy. Examples are the U.S. Federal Reserve System, the German Bundesbank, and the Bank of Japan. Most central banks set goals for inflation, called **target inflation rates**, which they try to maintain on average over the long run. The target inflation rate for the Fed and the Bundesbank is about 2 percent.

6. A **monetary policy rule** is a systematic response by the central bank to economic events. A particular policy rule is that the central bank raises the real interest rate whenever inflation rises. Since the real interest rate is the nominal interest rate minus the expected rate of inflation, this means that the central bank must raise the nominal interest rate by more than the rise in inflation. This policy rule provides a good description of the actions of the Federal Reserve in the late 1980s and 1990s.

7. The central bank does not control interest rates directly. It buys and sells bonds so that through the forces of supply and demand, interest rates are affected. In the United States, the Federal Reserve focuses on the **federal funds rate**, a very short-term interest rate on overnight loans between banks.

8. The **inflation adjustment** *(IA)* line depicts the inflation rate in the economy at any point in time. Like the *AD* curve, it is drawn on a diagram with inflation on the vertical axis and real GDP on the horizontal axis. The inflation adjustment line has three important features:

    a. *The IA line is flat.* Firms and workers adjust their prices and wages so that inflation stays constant in the short run, even when real GDP changes.

    b. *The IA line moves over time when real GDP departs from potential GDP.* In normal times, when real GDP $=$ potential GDP, inflation does not change. Firms and workers continue the previous wage and price increases. The *IA* line does not shift. In a boom, real GDP $>$ potential GDP. Firms, seeing high demand for their products, raise their prices. Workers, seeing low unemployment, demand higher wages. Inflation increases. The *IA* line shifts up. In a recession, real GDP $<$ potential GDP. Firms, seeing low demand for their products, lower their prices to retain market share. Workers, seeing high unemployment, lower their wage demands. Inflation decreases. The *IA* line shifts down.

    c. *The IA line shifts with changes in expectations or commodity prices.* If firms and workers expect inflation to rise, they will raise their prices and wages to keep up with the expected inflation, causing the *IA* line to shift up. If inflation is expected to fall, the *IA* line will shift down. An increase in commodity prices, such as an oil price increase, will raise firms' costs of production. This will cause firms to charge higher prices, shifting the *IA* line up.

9. Expectations of continuing inflation are an important reason why the inflation adjustment (*IA*) line is flat. Suppose that wages and prices have been rising at 5 percent per year for a long time, so that both current and expected inflation is 5 percent. When workers negotiate new contracts, they believe that a 5 percent annual wage increase will both make them as well off as before, because prices are also rising by 5 percent, and not change their wages relative to those of other workers, whose wages are also rising by 5 percent. Firms face a similar calculation. Suppose they agree to the 5 percent wage increase and then raise the price of their goods by 5 percent. They remain as well off as before, both relative to their costs, because wages are rising by 5 percent and relative to their competitors, who are also raising prices by 5 percent.

10. Staggered price and wage setting is another reason why the inflation adjustment (*IA*) line is flat. Wages and prices are not all set at the same time. They are staggered over different months and, in the case of three-year union contracts, different years. Since firms and workers care about prices and wages in other firms (and even other industries), this imparts a backward-looking component to price and wage decisions. This backward-looking component means that wages and prices change slowly over time.

ZEROING IN

1. Why does real GDP depend negatively on the real interest rate? The answer comes from an understanding of how investment, net exports, and consumption, three of the components of aggregate expenditure, depend negatively on the real interest rate.

    a. Why is investment negatively related to the real interest rate? Recall that investment includes both the purchase of new equipment and factories by business firms and the purchase of new houses by households. Many of these purchases, both by firms and by households, are financed by borrowing, and higher real interest rates make borrowing more expensive. This raises the cost of investment. With higher real interest rates, firms and households are less likely to build new factories or buy new houses, and so investment is lower than it would have been with lower real interest rates.

b. Why are net exports negatively related to the real interest rate? If the U.S. real interest rate is high relative to foreign real interest rates, U.S. financial assets become more attractive than foreign assets, and the value of the domestic currency rises. When the value of the domestic currency is high, U.S. goods are expensive relative to foreign goods. This decreases U.S. exports and increases U.S. imports, both of which decrease U.S. net exports. Thus a high real interest rate causes net exports to decrease. Conversely, a low U.S. real interest rate causes the value of the domestic currency to fall. U.S. goods become relatively cheap, causing exports to rise, imports to fall, and thus net exports to rise.

c. Why is consumption negatively related to the real interest rate? Although most of consumption, such as food, is purchased out of current income, consumer durables such as automobiles are financed by borrowing. High real interest rates increase the cost of borrowing, lowering spending on those items.

d. These effects are illustrated in Figure 12.1. Recall that the expenditure line is constructed by adding up consumption, investment, net exports, and government spending. A lower real interest rate raises the first three components of aggregate expenditure, shifting the expenditure line up. A higher real interest rate lowers these three components, shifting the expenditure line down.

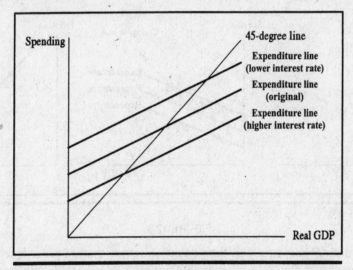

FIGURE 12.1

2. The monetary policy rule described above, that the central bank raises the real interest rate when inflation rises, is illustrated in Figure 12.2. At the inflation target of 2 percent, consistent with price stability, the real interest rate equals its target of 2 percent. When inflation exceeds 2 percent, the central bank raises the real interest rate above 2 percent. Note that the slope of the line depicting the monetary policy rule is positive and less than 1. This reflects the fact that the Federal Reserve needs to increase the nominal interest more than one-for-one with inflation in order to raise the real interest rate.

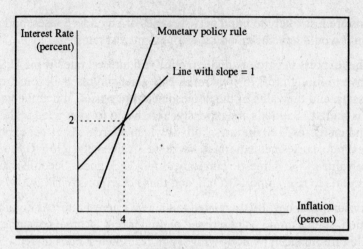

FIGURE 12.2

3.   We now combine two concepts: the monetary policy rule that links the real interest rate to inflation and the dependence of expenditure on the real interest rate, to derive the aggregate demand (*AD*) line. The derivation is illustrated in Figure 12.3. In order to learn this material, you should use pencil and paper to replicate the derivation.

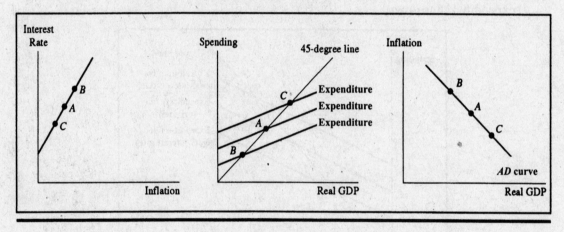

FIGURE 12.3

a.   To derive the *AD* line, first start with an inflation rate that, in accordance with the central bank's monetary policy rule, is consistent with the interest rate depicted by point *A* in the first panel. (The choice of how high or low the interest rate is at *A* is completely arbitrary.) The interest rate determined by the policy rule will produce values of consumption, investment, and net exports that define an expenditure line in the second panel. The expenditure line intersects the 45-degree line at the point of spending balance *A* to determine GDP. In the third panel, the inflation rate from the first panel and real GDP from the second panel are depicted by point *A*. Note that we have not yet defined a line, just a point.

b.   Suppose that inflation rises. In accordance with its policy rule, the Federal Reserve increases the real interest rate in the first panel to point *B*. This shifts the expenditure line down to intersect the 45-degree line at the point of spending balance *B* in the second panel. Through the multiplier effect, real GDP falls. The combination of higher inflation and lower real GDP defines point *B* in the third panel.

c.   Suppose that inflation falls. The central bank lowers the interest rate to point *C*. This raises consumption, investment, and net exports, shifting the expenditure line up to intersect the

45-degree line at point *C* and increasing real GDP. Lower inflation and higher real GDP are depicted by point *C* in the third panel.

d. Connect the dots. The line *BAC* defines an inverse (downward-sloping) relationship between inflation and real GDP called the aggregate demand (*AD*) curve. (Because the "curve" is a straight line, you really needed only two points.) Make sure you understand how the *AD* curve (third panel) is derived from the policy rule (first panel) and spending balance (second panel).

e. Changes in inflation cause movements along the *AD* curve. When inflation rises, the Federal Reserve raises the real interest rate, lowering real GDP and causing a movement up and to the left. When inflation falls, the Federal Reserve lowers the real interest rate, raising real GDP and causing a movement down and to the right.

f. What causes shifts in the *AD* curve? First, anything that shifts the expenditure line will shift the *AD* curve. This includes changes in government purchases, taxes, investment, and net exports. If the expenditure line shifts up, as with an increase in government purchases, the *AD* curve shifts out (to the right). If the expenditure line shifts down, as with an increase in taxes, the *AD* curve shifts in (to the left). Second, changes in the monetary policy rule will shift the *AD* curve. If the policy rule changes toward a higher inflation target, the *AD* curve shifts out. If the rule changes toward a lower inflation target, the *AD* curve shifts in.

4. The inflation adjustment (I*A*) line is another important concept introduced in this chapter. There are three things that you need to understand about the *IA* line:

a. The *IA* line is flat. In Figure 12.4 inflation is on the vertical axis and real GDP is on the horizontal axis. The *IA* line is a horizontal (flat) line depicting the inflation rate. In the short run, the inflation rate is constant. It does not depend on the level of real GDP.

Figure 12.4

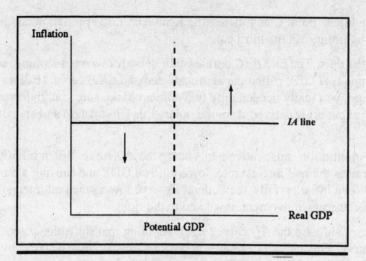

Figure 12.5

b.   The *IA* line moves over time when real GDP departs from potential GDP. This is illustrated
in Figure 12.5. When real GDP is greater than potential GDP, the *IA* line shifts up and
inflation rises. When real GDP is less than potential GDP, the *IA* line shifts down and
inflation falls. If real GDP equals potential GDP, the *IA* line stays in place and inflation is
unchanged.

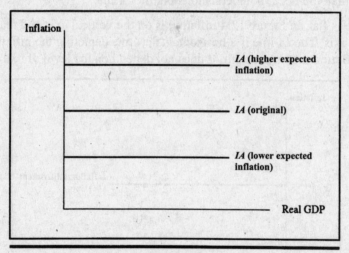

Figure 12.6

c.   Changes in expectations or commodity prices shift the *IA* line. Suppose that expected
inflation rises. Firms and workers, as discussed above, raise wages and prices, and actual
inflation rises. This is depicted as an upward shift of the *IA* line in Figure 12.6. Conversely,
suppose that expected inflation falls. This causes actual inflation to fall and is shown as a
downward shift of the *IA* line in Figure 12.6. Increases in the prices of commodities, such as
oil, raise inflation and shift the *IA* line up, whereas decreases in commodity prices lower
inflation and shift the *IA* line down.

5.   The intersection of the aggregate demand (*AD*) curve and the *IA* line gives an equilibrium level of real GDP and inflation. It is important to understand that this intersection does not have to be where real GDP equals potential GDP. As shown in Figure 12.7, the intersection can, in the short run, produce real GDP lower, above, or equal to potential GDP.

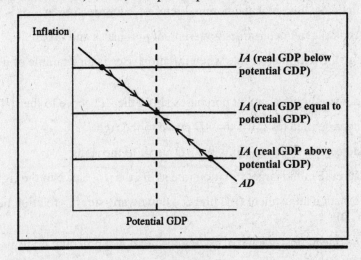

Figure 12.7

ACTIVE REVIEW

Fill-In Questions

1.   The _____ curve is an inverse relation between inflation and real GDP.

2.   The _____ is the annual rate of change in the overall price level.

3.   Real GDP depends _____ on interest rates.

4.   The _____ is the nominal interest rate minus the expected rate of inflation.

5.   The _____ is the part of the government that controls monetary policy.

6.   In the United States, the central bank is called the _____.

7.   Goals for inflation are called _____ inflation rates.

8.   A(n) _____ is a systematic response by the central bank to economic events.

9.   The interest rate on overnight loans between banks is called the _____.

10.   Consumption, investment, and net exports are _____ related to the real interest rate.

11.   Changes in government purchases cause _____ the *AD* curve.

12.   Changes in inflation cause _____ the *AD* curve.

13.   The _____ line depicts the inflation rate at any point in time.

14.   Inflation adjustment is influenced by _____ of future inflation.

15.   A reason for slow inflation adjustment is _____ price and wage setting.

True-False Questions

1. T F   The aggregate demand curve is downward-sloping.

2. T F   When inflation is decreasing, prices are falling.

3. T F   If inflation is low, real and nominal interest rates are similar.

4. T F   The central bank determines government purchases and taxes.

5. T F   Raising the real interest rate when inflation rises is an example of a monetary policy rule.

6. T F   An increase in government purchases shifts the *AD* curve to the right.

7. T F   An increase in taxes shifts the *AD* curve to the right.

8. T F   An increase in inflation shifts the *AD* curve to the right.

9. T F   An increase in the target inflation rate shifts the *AD* curve to the right.

10. T F   The inflation adjustment (*IA*) line is a downward-sloping relation between inflation and real GDP.

11. T F   The *IA* line moves when real GDP does not equal potential GDP.

12. T F   The *IA* line always moves over time.

13. T F   In the United States, wages in most industries are set at the same time.

14. T F   The setting of prices and wages by firms and workers is based only on expectations of future inflation.

15. T F   Potential GDP is determined by the intersection of the *AD* curve and the *IA* line.

Short-Answer Questions

1. What are the two concepts used to derive the *AD* curve?

2. Why does real GDP depend negatively on the real interest rate?

3. Why is the real interest rate, rather than the nominal interest rate, the correct measure of the effect of interest rates on aggregate expenditure?

4. Describe the policy rule that the Federal Reserve System has used during the late 1980s and 1990s.

5. In order to raise the real interest rate when inflation increases, how must the central bank change the nominal interest rate?

6. What is the relation between inflation and real GDP during a typical business cycle?

7. Why is the slope of the monetary policy rule greater than 1?

8. Why does the *AD* curve slope downward?

9. What causes shifts in the *AD* curve?

10. What is depicted by the inflation adjustment (*IA*) line?

11. Why is the *IA* line flat?

12. Describe the process of inflation adjustment in terms of the relation between inflation and real GDP.

13. How does the *IA* line move over time?

14. What causes the *IA* line to shift?

15. What is determined at the intersection of the aggregate demand (*AD*) curve and the *IA* line?

16. What did the Federal Open Market Committee (FOMC) do at its meeting of February 2, 2005? (Hint: See Reading the News About—Interest Rate Changes Made by the Federal Reserve.)

WORKING IT OUT

1. The most important tool for you to learn in this chapter is how changes in aggregate expenditure shift the *AD* curve. Let's examine a decrease in government purchases.

   a. The first step is to draw a diagram of the economy before the policy action occurs. The first panel of Figure 12.8 shows the expenditure line and the point of spending balance. The second panel shows the *AD* curve. Although the *AD* curve is drawn for a specific monetary policy rule, it is not necessary to diagram the rule because it will not change.

Figure 12.8

   b. The decrease in government purchases shifts the expenditure line down, moving the point of spending balance from *A* to *B*. This causes the *AD* curve to shift to the left. If inflation is unchanged, as it will be in the short run before prices have time to adjust, the point of spending balance shifts from *A* to *B*.

2. A change in the monetary policy rule also shifts the *AD* curve. We will consider a change toward a lower inflation target.

   a. The first step is again to diagram the economy before the policy change occurs. The three panels of Figure 12.9 depict the original policy rule, the expenditure line, and the *AD* curve.

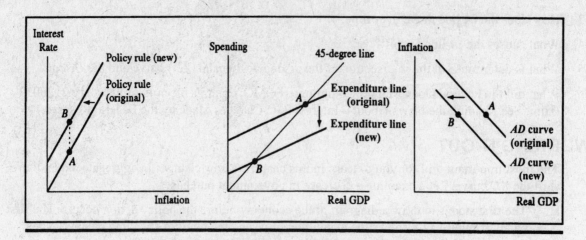

FIGURE 12.9

b.   A change in the monetary policy rule toward a lower inflation target shifts the policy rule to the left. In the short run, with inflation fixed, this raises the real interest rate. The higher real interest rate lowers aggregate expenditure, shifting the expenditure line in the second panel down and moving the point of spending balance from A to B. This causes the AD line in the third panel to shift to the left.

Worked Problems

1.   Suppose that taxes are cut. How will this affect the expenditure line and the AD curve?

Answer

According to the theory of consumption, the tax cut will raise current consumption. This will shift the expenditure curve up and shift the AD curve to the right.

2.   The following table shows two monetary policy rules.

Inflation	Real Interest Rate Policy Rule A	Real Interest Rate Policy Rule B
0	3	2
1	3.5	2.5
2	4	3
3	4.5	3.5
4	5	4

Suppose that the Federal Reserve changes its monetary policy rule from policy rule A to policy rule B. Is this a switch to a higher or a lower inflation target? How would this change affect the expenditure line and the AD curve?

Answer

To understand the switch in targets, start with equal real interest rates and examine the resultant inflation rates. Compared to policy rule A, policy rule B produces higher inflation at each interest rate, implying a higher inflation target. To understand the effect on the expenditure line, read across the columns. At each inflation rate, rule B has a lower real interest rate than rule A, so the change from rule A to rule B shifts the expenditure line up and shifts the AD curve to the right.

PRACTICE PROBLEMS

1. Suppose that the low U.S. exchange rate causes U.S. consumers to buy more American and fewer Japanese automobiles. How will this affect the expenditure line and the *AD* curve?

2. Suppose that U.S. business firms, worried about a possible recession in the next few years, build fewer factories. How will this affect the expenditure line and the *AD* curve?

3. Suppose that the price of imported oil increases, raising the U.S. inflation rate. How will this affect the expenditure line and the *AD* curve?

4. Suppose that the Federal Reserve changes its policy rule to a higher inflation target. How will this affect the expenditure line and the *AD* curve?

5. The following table shows two monetary policy rules.

Inflation	Real Interest Rate Policy Rule A	Real Interest Rate Policy Rule B
0	2	4
3	4	6
6	6	8
9	8	10
12	10	12

Suppose that the Federal Reserve changes its monetary policy rule from policy rule A to policy rule B. Is this a switch to a higher or to a lower inflation target? How would this change affect the *expenditure* line and the *AD* curve?

CHAPTER TEST

1. The *AD* curve illustrates the negative relation between
   a. inflation and unemployment.
   b. inflation and real GDP.
   c. interest rates and inflation.
   d. interest rates and real GDP.

2. If inflation is falling, then what is happening to prices?
   a. Prices are rising.
   b. Prices are falling.
   c. Prices are staying the same.
   d. There is not enough information to tell.

3. The components of aggregate expenditure that depend negatively on the real interest rate are
   a. consumption, investment, and government purchases.
   b. investment, government purchases, and net exports.
   c. consumption, investment, and net exports.
   d. consumption, taxes, and net exports.

4. The real interest rate is the nominal interest rate

    a. minus the expected rate of inflation.
    b. divided by the expected rate of inflation.
    c. minus the price level.
    d. divided by the price level.

5. The inflation adjustment (*IA*) line

    a. is downward-sloping.
    b. shifts with changes in expectations of the prices of commodities.
    c. depicts real GDP in the economy at any point in time.
    d. remains constant over time when real GDP departs from potential GDP.

6. Suppose wages and prices have been rising at 3 percent per year over a period of time. In light of this, workers negotiate 3 percent annual wage increases. If expected inflation falls to 2 percent but wage increases remain at 3 percent, then

    a. firms remain equally well off.
    b. workers are worse off.
    c. workers are better off.
    d. firms are better off.

7. The policy rule recently followed by the Federal Reserve involves raising the

    a. real interest rate when real GDP rises.
    b. real interest rate when inflation rises.
    c. real interest rate when the value of the domestic currency falls.
    d. nominal interest rate when the value of the domestic currency falls.

8. The equilibrium level of real GDP and inflation is given by the intersection of the

    a. aggregate demand curve and the potential GDP line.
    b. aggregate demand curve and the inflation adjustment line.
    c. aggregate demand curve and the zero inflation line.
    d. inflation adjustment line and the potential GDP line.

9. The federal funds rate is the interest rate on

    a. overnight loans between federal agencies.
    b. long-term loans between federal agencies.
    c. overnight loans between banks.
    d. long-term loans between banks.

10. In a typical business cycle, real GDP

    a. rises after inflation increases.
    b. falls after inflation increases.
    c. is unrelated to inflation.
    d. always equals potential GDP.

11. Higher inflation causes

    a. a positive departure of real GDP from potential GDP in the long run.
    b. a negative departure of real GDP from potential GDP in the long run.
    c. no departure of real GDP from potential GDP in the long run.
    d. the Federal Reserve Board (following its policy rule) to decrease interest rates.

12. Consumption is negatively related to real interest rates because

    a. most consumption is financed by borrowing.
    b. consumer durables, such as automobiles, are often financed by borrowing.
    c. new houses are usually financed by borrowing.
    d. changes in interest rates affect the value of the domestic currency.

13. Suppose that inflation rises from 2 percent to 4 percent. If the Federal Reserve follows a policy rule of raising the real interest rate when inflation increases, then the nominal interest rate would

    a. increase by less than 2 percent.
    b. increase by exactly 2 percent.
    c. increase by more than 2 percent.
    d. remain unchanged.

Use Figure 12.10 for questions 14–16.

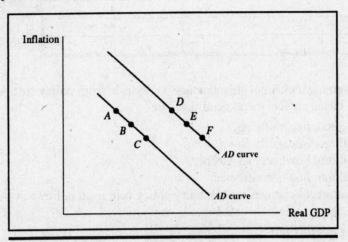

Figure 12.10

14. An increase in government purchases can be represented as a movement in the economy

    a. from *A* to *B*.
    b. from *C* to *B*.
    c. from *B* to *E*.
    d. from *E* to *B*.

15. An increase in taxes can be represented as a movement in the economy

    a. from *A* to *B*.
    b. from *C* to *B*.
    c. from *B* to *E*.
    d. from *E* to *B*.

16. An increase in inflation can be represented as a movement in the economy

    a. from *A* to *B*.
    b. from *C* to *B*.
    c. from *B* to *E*.
    d. from *C* to *D*.

17. An decrease in net exports causes a

    a. shift out of the *AD* curve.
    b. shift in of the *AD* curve.
    c. movement up the *AD* curve.
    d. movement down the *AD* curve.

18. A decrease in inflation causes a

    a. shift out of the *AD* curve.
    b. shift in of the *AD* curve.
    c. movement up the *AD* curve.
    d. movement down the *AD* curve.

Use the following table for questions 19 and 20.

Inflation	Real Interest Rate Policy Rule A	Real Interest Rate Policy Rule B
0	5	2
2	6	3
4	7	4
6	8	5
8	9	6

19. Suppose the government changes its monetary policy rule from policy rule A to policy rule B. How would this change affect the expenditure line?
    a. The expenditure line shifts up.
    b. The expenditure line shifts down.
    c. The expenditure line becomes steeper.
    d. The expenditure line is unaffected.
20. Suppose the government changes its monetary policy rule from policy rule A to policy rule B. How would this change affect the *AD* curve?
    a. The *AD* curve shifts left.
    b. The *AD* curve shifts right.
    c. The *AD* curve becomes steeper.
    d. The *AD* curve is unaffected.

ANSWERS TO THE REVIEW QUESTIONS

Fill-In Questions
1. aggregate demand
2. inflation rate
3. negatively
4. real interest rate
5. central bank
6. Federal Reserve System
7. target
8. monetary policy rule
9. federal funds rate
10. negatively
11. shifts in
12. movements along
13. inflation adjustment (*IA*)
14. expectations

15. staggered

True-False Questions

1. **True**. It depicts a negative relation between inflation and real GDP.

2. **False**. Inflation can decrease but still be positive, in which case prices are still rising.

3. **True**. The real interest rate equals the nominal interest rate minus the expected rate of inflation. If inflation is low, there is not much difference between the two interest rates.

4. **False**. The central bank determines monetary policy.

5. **True**. This is the rule followed by the Fed and other central banks.

6. **True**. An increase in government purchases shifts the expenditure line up and shifts the *AD* curve to the right.

7. **False**. An increase in taxes shifts the *AD* curve to the left.

8. **False**. An increase in inflation causes a movement along the *AD* curve.

9. **True**. An increase in the target inflation rate lowers the interest rate, shifting the *AD* curve out.

10. **False.** The *IA* line is flat.

11. **True.** The *IA* line shifts up when real GDP is greater than potential GDP and shifts down when real GDP is less than potential GDP.

12. **False.** When real GDP equals potential GDP, the *IA* line is fixed.

13. **False.** They are staggered over different months and years.

14. **False.** Staggered price and wage setting imparts a backward-looking component to price and wage decisions.

15. **False.** The *AD* curve and the *IA* line determine current real GDP, not potential GDP.

Short-Answer Questions

1. First, real GDP is negatively related to the interest rate at the point of spending balance. Second, because of the central bank's policy rule, the interest rate is positively related to the inflation rate.

2. Real GDP depends negatively on the real interest rate because investment, net exports, and consumption depend negatively on the real interest rate.

3. The real interest rate is the correct measure because it adjusts the nominal interest rate for the effects of inflation.

4. The Federal Reserve System has raised the real interest rate when inflation has increased.

5. In order to raise the real interest rate, the central bank must raise the nominal interest rate by more than the increase in inflation.

6. At the beginning of a cycle, the expansion of real GDP above potential GDP causes inflation. The Federal Reserve responds by raising interest rates, causing real GDP to fall.

7. The slope of the monetary policy rule is greater than 1 because, in order to raise the real interest rate, the Federal Reserve needs to increase the nominal interest rate more than one-for-one with inflation.

8. The *AD* curve slopes downward because higher inflation causes the Federal Reserve to raise interest rates, shifting the expenditure line down and lowering real GDP.

9. Changes in aggregate expenditure and changes in the money supply rule shift the *AD* curve.

10. The *IA* line depicts the inflation rate in the economy at any point in time.

11. The *IA* line is flat because the inflation rate is constant in the short run. In particular, it does not depend on the level of GDP.

12. If real GDP exceeds potential GDP, inflation rises. If real GDP is less than potential GDP, inflation falls. If real GDP equals potential GDP, inflation does not change.

13. If real GDP is greater (less) than potential GDP, inflation increases (decreases) and the *IA* line moves upward (downward).

14. Changes in expectations or commodity prices shift the *IA* line.

15. Inflation and real GDP are determined at the intersection of the *AD* curve and the *IA* line.

16. The FOMC raised its target level for the federal funds interest rate from 2.25 percent to 2.5 percent.

SOLUTIONS TO THE PRACTICE PROBLEMS

1. U.S. imports will decrease, raising net exports. This shifts the expenditure line up and shifts the *AD* curve to the right.

2. This will decrease investment, lowering the expenditure line and shifting the *AD* curve out.

3. The higher inflation rate will cause the Federal Reserve, acting in accordance with its policy rule, to raise interest rates. This shifts the expenditure line down. The higher inflation rate represents a movement up and to the left along the *AD* curve, not a shift of the curve.

4. A change in the monetary policy rule to a higher inflation target lowers the interest rate, shifting the *expenditure* line up and the *AD* curve to the right.

5. The change from policy rule A to policy rule B represents a switch to a lower inflation target. This raises the real interest rate at each inflation rate, shifting the expenditure line down and the *AD* curve to the left.

ANSWERS TO THE CHAPTER TEST

1. b
2. d
3. c
4. a
5. b
6. c
7. b
8. b
9. c
10. b
11. c
12. b
13. c

14. c
15. d
16. b
17. b
18. d
19. a
20. b

CHAPTER 13

Using the Economic Fluctuations Model

CHAPTER OVERVIEW

We have constructed the economic fluctuations model from the aggregate demand (*AD*) curve and the inflation adjustment (*IA*) line and shown how the equilibrium level of real GDP and inflation is given by the intersection of the *AD* curve and the *IA* line. In this chapter, we use the economic fluctuations model to study the effects, both in the short run and in the long run, of shocks to the economy, changes in aggregate expenditure, and changes in the monetary policy rule. The process of inflation adjustment is particularly important, for it allows us to understand the transition from short-run booms or recessions back to long-run potential GDP.

CHAPTER REVIEW

1. The *economic fluctuations model* is employed by academic, government, and private economists to study the effects of economic policy proposals such as changes in monetary policy rules and tax and spending changes. The economic fluctuations model, which was derived in Chapter 12, consists of three parts:

    a. The aggregate demand (*AD*) curve is a negative relation between inflation and real GDP.

    b. The inflation adjustment (*IA*) line depicts the inflation rate in the economy at any point in time.

    c. The equilibrium level of real GDP and inflation is given by the intersection of the *AD* curve and the *IA* line.

2. An important use of the economic fluctuations model is to analyze contemplated policy changes. The *baseline* is the path of an economic variable that would occur without the policy change under consideration. The model is used to compare the path of the economy with the policy change relative to the baseline.

3. The economy is never completely at rest. It is always subject to a number of shocks. **Demand shocks** are shifts in the *AD* curve, including changes in government purchases, investment, net exports, or the monetary policy rule. **Price shocks** are shifts in the *IA* line, such as changes in the price of oil or other commodities. *Supply shocks* are shifts in potential GDP, such as technological progress that causes an increase in productivity growth.

4. A *boom* occurs when real GDP exceeds potential GDP, and a *recession* is when real GDP falls below potential GDP. A *temporary growth slowdown* is a decrease in the rate of growth of real GDP that is not large enough to make real GDP growth negative. **Stagflation** occurs when real GDP falls and inflation rises simultaneously. A *boom-bust cycle* is a complete economic fluctuation that occurs when the central bank lowers the interest rate too much. This causes a boom and inflation, leading the central bank to raise interest rates and cause a recession.

5. Changes in the monetary policy rule are an important source of economic fluctuations. A common objective is to lower the rate of inflation. **Disinflation** is a reduction in the rate of inflation. Be sure that you understand the difference between disinflation and **deflation**, a negative inflation

rate, which is not a typical policy objective. **Reinflation**, the opposite of disinflation, is an increase in the inflation rate.

ZEROING IN

1. The *intersection* of the aggregate demand (*AD*) curve and the *IA* line determines real GDP and inflation. It is important to understand that this intersection does not have to be where real GDP equals potential GDP. As shown in Figure 13.1, the intersection can, in the short run, produce real GDP lower, above, or equal to potential GDP.

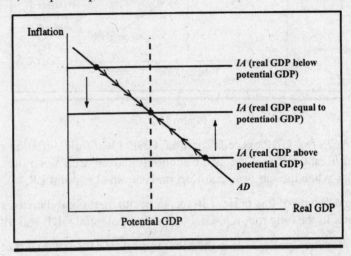

Figure 13.1

   a. Suppose that the intersection of the *AD* curve and the *IA* line produces real GDP that is less than potential GDP, causing inflation to fall. This is illustrated as a downward movement in the *IA* line in Figure 13.1. The economy moves down the *AD* curve, in the direction of the arrows, until the long-run equilibrium is reached where real GDP equals potential GDP. Once the economy attains its long-run equilibrium, inflation stops falling and real GDP stops rising.

   b. Suppose that the intersection of the *AD* curve and the *IA* line produces real GDP that is greater than potential GDP, causing inflation to rise. As shown in Figure 13.1, the *IA* line moves up, causing the economy to move up the *AD* curve until the long-run equilibrium is attained. At that point, inflation stops rising, real GDP stops falling, and real GDP equals potential GDP.

   c. Suppose that the *AD* curve intersects the *IA* line where real GDP equals potential GDP. End of story. The economy is in long-run equilibrium, and there is no reason for either inflation or real GDP to change.

2. *Changes in aggregate expenditure* are an important source of economic fluctuations. In Chapter 11, we saw how changes in expenditure shift the *AD* curve and cause short-run departures of real GDP from potential GDP. Now we complete the story. Suppose that, starting with real GDP equal to potential GDP, government purchases increase.

   a. In the short run, the *AD* curve shifts to the right and the *IA* line is fixed. As shown in Figure 13.2, the economy enters a boom at the point *SR* (short run), defined by the intersection of the *AD* curve and the *IA* line.

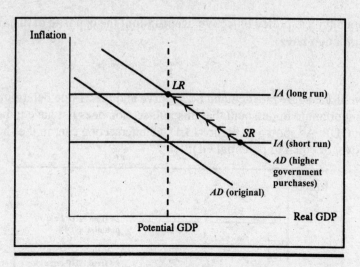

Figure 13.2

b. At the point *SR*, real GDP exceeds potential GDP. Over time, inflation rises, shifting the *IA* line upward. Real GDP declines as the economy moves back along the *AD* curve. The process stops when the long-run equilibrium is attained at point LR.

c. What is the outcome of this policy? In the short run, real GDP increases at a constant inflation rate. In the long run, real GDP returns to potential GDP and inflation is higher.

3. A *change in the monetary policy rule* is the other important cause of a shift of the *AD* curve. Suppose that, starting with real GDP equal to potential GDP, the monetary policy rule shifts to a lower inflation target.

a. In the short run, the *AD* curve shifts to the left and the *IA* line is fixed. As shown in Figure 13.3, the economy enters a recession at the point *SR*.

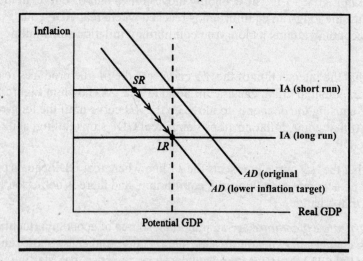

Figure 13.3

b. At the point *SR*, real GDP is below potential GDP. Over time, inflation falls, shifting the *IA* line downward. Real GDP recovers as the economy moves back along the *AD* curve. The process stops when the long-run equilibrium is attained at point LR.

c. What is the outcome of this policy? In the short run, real GDP decreases at a constant inflation rate. In the long run, real GDP returns to potential GDP and inflation is lower. The central bank has achieved its target (lower inflation), but at a cost (the recession until the equilibrium is attained).

4. *Price shocks* are the other cause of economic fluctuations. Suppose that an oil price increase occurs at a long-run equilibrium with real GDP equal to potential GDP. Remember that an oil price increase is an example of a price shock.

   a. In the short run, the oil price increase shifts the *IA* line upward. As shown in Figure 13.4, inflation rises and real GDP falls below potential, causing stagflation at point *SR*.

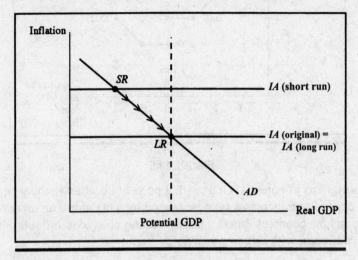

Figure 13.4

   b. With real GDP below potential GDP at the point *SR*, inflation begins to fall, shifting the *IA* line downward. Real GDP rises, and the economy returns, over time, to potential GDP. Long-run equilibrium is attained at point LR, with inflation at its original level and real GDP equal to potential GDP.

5. Although no two business cycles are identical, there is a pattern in the movements of real GDP and inflation that characterizes most economic fluctuations. It is this relation between real GDP and inflation that the aggregate demand (*AD*) curve and inflation adjustment (*IA*) line attempt to explain.

   a. A typical business cycle is illustrated in Figure 13.5. Although fictional, it illustrates many of the features of real-world economic fluctuations. The inflation rate (in percent) is on the vertical axis. The gap between real GDP and potential GDP (also in percent) is on the horizontal axis.

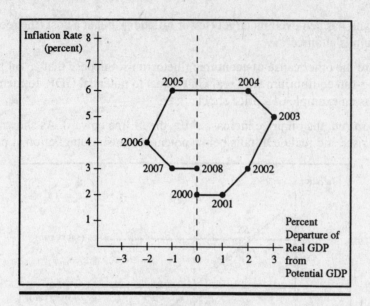

FIGURE 13.5

b. The economy starts at potential GDP with 2 percent inflation in the year 2010. In 2011, aggregate expenditure increases (maybe caused by a tax cut or an increase in government spending), and the economy enters a boom with no change in inflation. In 2012 and 2013, the boom continues, with inflation rising.

c. The higher inflation rate causes the Federal Reserve Board (following its policy rule) to raise interest rates, lowering real GDP in 2014 even though inflation continues to rise. Recession strikes in 2015, with GDP below potential as inflation stays high. Inflation falls in 2016 as the recession gets worse. Finally, in 2017, a recovery occurs, with inflation continuing to fall. The economy returns to potential GDP with a higher (3 percent) inflation rate in 2018.

d. The long-run impact of the change in policy is that real GDP returns to potential GDP. In other words, there is no long-run impact from inflation and the departures of real GDP from potential GDP. Although this example shows a slightly higher inflation rate at the end of the cycle than at the beginning, it could have been lower, the same, or even much higher, depending on the Fed's policy rule. In any case, real GDP would return to potential GDP.

ACTIVE REVIEW

Fill-In Questions

1. The _____ is used to study the effects of economic policy proposals.

2. The _____ is the path of an economic variable that would occur without the policy change under consideration.

3. _____ are shifts in the aggregate demand (*AD*) curve.

4. _____ are shifts in the inflation adjustment (*IA*) line.

5. _____ are shifts in potential GDP.

6. A(n) _____ is when real GDP falls below potential GDP.

7. A(n) _____ is when real GDP exceeds potential GDP.

8. A(n) _____ is a small decrease in the rate of growth of real GDP.

9. _____ occurs when real GDP falls and inflation rises simultaneously.

10. A(n) _____ is an economic fluctuation caused by the central bank.

11. _____ is a reduction in the rate of inflation.

12. _____ is a negative inflation rate.

13. An increase in the inflation rate is called _____.

14. In the _____, real GDP can be above, below, or equal to potential GDP.

15. A long-run _____ is reached when real GDP equals potential GDP.

True-False Questions

1. T F   The baseline is the predicted path of a variable following a policy change.

2. T F   A change in net exports is an example of a demand shock.

3. T F   A change in the monetary policy rule is an example of a price shock.

4. T F   Price shocks are shifts in potential GDP.

5. T F   Supply shocks are shifts in potential GDP.

6. T F   A temporary growth slowdown causes a recession.

7. T F   Stagflation occurs when real GDP and inflation fall simultaneously.

8. T F   Deflation is a decrease in the price level.

9. T F   Reinflation is the opposite of deflation.

10. T F   Changes in investment shift the *AD* curve.

11. T F   Movements in the exchange rate shift the *IA* line.

12. T F   Changes in the target inflation rate shift the *AD* curve.

13. T F   Oil price increases shift the *IA* line.

14. T F   Changes in expected inflation shift the *AD* curve.

15. T F   Changes in government purchases shift the *IA* line.

Short-Answer Questions

1. What is the economic fluctuations model used for?

2. What are demand shocks?

3. What are price shocks?

4. What are supply shocks?

5. When do booms and recessions occur?

6. What is a temporary growth slowdown?

7. When does stagflation occur?

8. When does a boom-bust cycle occur?

9. What is the difference between disinflation and deflation?

10. Which is the more typical policy objective, disinflation or deflation?

11. When is the economy in long-run equilibrium?

12. Describe the behavior of inflation when the economy is in long-run equilibrium.

13. Starting from a long-run equilibrium, describe the path of inflation and real GDP following a decrease in government purchases.

14. Starting from a long-run equilibrium, describe the path of inflation and real GDP following a shift by the Fed to a higher inflation target.

15. Starting from a long-run equilibrium, describe the path of inflation and real GDP following a decrease in the price of oil.

16. Which type of policy, monetary or fiscal, was the most important factor in the recovery from the Great Depression of the 1930s? (Hint: See Economics in Action—Explaining the Recovery from the Great Depression.)

WORKING IT OUT

1. The most important technique for you to learn in this chapter is how to work with the *AD-IA* diagram. In the "Zeroing In" section, we presented a purely graphical approach. Here, we will combine numbers and graphs.

   a. The *AD* curve is a downward-sloping relation between inflation and real GDP. Given a set of values for inflation and real GDP, you can graph the *AD* curve. The following values are graphed in Figure 13.6. The numbers for inflation represent the inflation rate (in percent), whereas those for real GDP represent billions of dollars.

	Inflation				
	9	7	5	3	1
Real GDP	5,800	5,900	6,000	6,100	6,200

   b. The *IA* line is a flat (horizontal) line depicting the current inflation rate. Potential GDP is a vertical line. In Figure 13.6, the *IA* and potential GDP lines are drawn for a current inflation rate of 7 percent and a value of $6,000 billion for potential GDP. The *IA* line is labeled *IA* (*SR*) to indicate that it depicts the short-run (current) inflation rate.

   c. In the short run, the economy is at the intersection of the *AD* curve and the *IA* (*SR*) line. This point, with 7 percent inflation and $5,900 billion real GDP, is labeled *SR* in Figure 13.6.

d.   At the point *SR*, real GDP is below potential GDP. Over time, the *IA* line moves downward, inflation falls, and the economy moves along the *AD* curve as depicted by the arrows in Figure 13.6. In the long run, the *IA* line shifts down far enough, to *IA* (LR), so that real GDP equals potential GDP. At the long-run equilibrium point LR, real GDP equals $6,000 billion and inflation is 5 percent.

Figure 13.6

2.   We have focused on movements of real GDP and inflation in the *AD-IA* diagram. By looking at the other two diagrams used to derive the *AD* curve, the policy rule and the AE line/45-degree line diagrams, we can trace out what happens to consumption, investment, and net exports during a cycle.

a.   Suppose that we start from real GDP equal to potential GDP, and study the short- and long-run effects of an increase in government purchases. In the short run, the AE line shifts upward and the *AD* curve shifts to the right. As shown by the points labeled *SR* in Figure 13.7, real GDP increases, but inflation and the real interest rate do not change.

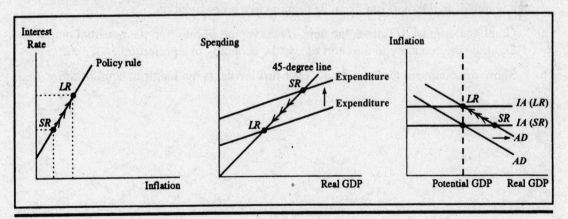

FIGURE 13.7

b.   At the point *SR*, real GDP exceeds potential GDP, so the *IA* line moves up and inflation rises. According to the policy rule, the central bank raises the real interest rate when inflation rises. The higher real interest rate shifts the AE line downward, lowering real GDP. In the long run, labeled LR in Figure 13.7, real GDP returns to potential GDP. This is depicted as both a movement along the *AD* curve and a downward shift of the AE line back to potential GDP. Inflation and the real interest rate are both higher.

c. We can now look at consumption, investment, and net exports. Remember that consumption depends positively on real GDP and negatively on the real interest rate, investment depends negatively on the real interest rate, and net exports depend negatively on both real GDP and the real interest rate. The key to tracing *C*, *I*, and *X* is to keep track of real GDP and the real interest rate. In the short run, real GDP increases and the real interest rate is unchanged. In the long run, the real interest rate increases and real GDP returns to potential.

d. What happens to consumption, investment, and net exports when government purchases increase? In the short run, the increase in real GDP raises consumption and lowers net exports. Investment is unchanged. In the long run, the higher real interest rate lowers consumption, investment, and net exports. These results are summarized in the table below.

	Y	*C*	*I*	*X*
SR			—	↓
LR	—	↓	↓	↓

Worked Problems

1. Consider an economy characterized by the following relation between inflation and real GDP:

	Inflation				
	9	7	5	3	1
Original real GDP	6,700	6,800	6,900	7,000	7,100
New real GDP	6,900	7,000	7,100	7,200	7,300

Current inflation is equal to 3 percent, and potential GDP is equal to 7,000. Suppose that the economy moves in the short run from the original to the new relation.

a. Graph the original *AD* curve, the new *AD* curve, the *IA* line, and the potential output line. Describe the economy in the short run. Is the economy in equilibrium?

b. Show what happens to the economy over time. What is the long-run equilibrium?

Answer

a.   The original and new *AD* curves are downward-sloping lines depicting the values of inflation and real GDP. The *IA* line is a horizontal line at 3 percent inflation, and the potential output line is a vertical line at 7,000 real GDP. The economy is originally in long-run equilibrium, with the intersection of the *AD* curve and the *IA* line where real GDP equals potential GDP. In the short run, the economy is at the intersection of the new *AD* curve and the IA line, with inflation at 3 percent and real GDP at 7,200. This is illustrated in Figure 13.8. Since real GDP exceeds potential GDP, the economy is not in long-run equilibrium.

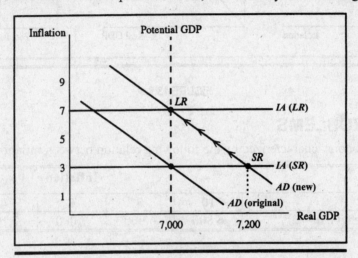

Figure 13.8

b.   In the short run, real GDP is greater than potential GDP, causing inflation. Over time, the *IA* line shifts up, inflation rises, and real GDP moves back toward potential. In the long-run equilibrium, real GDP is 7,000 and inflation is 7 percent. This is also shown in Figure 13.8.

2.   Starting from a long-run equilibrium with real GDP equal to potential GDP, suppose that a fall in oil prices causes a negative price shock. What are the effects, in both the short and the long run, on real GDP, inflation, consumption, investment, and net exports?

Answer

The negative price shock shifts the *IA* line downward, lowering inflation. The Fed, following its policy rule, lowers the real interest rate, shifting the *AE* curve up and raising real GDP above potential GDP. In the short run, consumption increases (real GDP rises), investment increases (the real interest rate falls), and net exports increase (the fall in the real interest rate dominates the rise in real GDP). Over time, the *IA* line moves up, inflation rises, and real GDP falls. In the long run, inflation, the real interest rate, and real GDP all return to their original levels, as do consumption, investment, and net exports. The effects are shown in Figure 13.9 and summarized in the table below.

	Y	*C*	*I*	*X*
SR				
LR	—	—	—	—

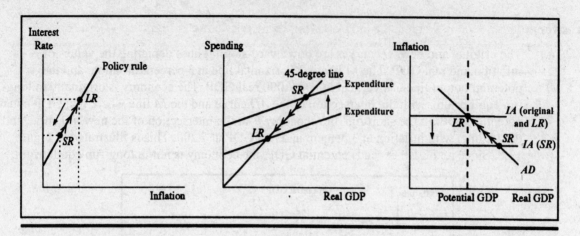

FIGURE 13.9

PRACTICE PROBLEMS

1. Consider an economy characterized by the following relation between inflation and real GDP:

	Inflation				
	10	8	6	4	2
Real GDP	6,800	6,900	7,000	7,100	7,200

Current inflation is equal to 4 percent, and potential GDP is equal to 7,100.

a. Graph the *AD* curve, the *IA* line, and the potential output line. Describe the economy in the short run. Is the economy in long-run equilibrium?

b. Show what happens to the economy over time. What is the long-run equilibrium?

2. Consider an economy characterized by the following relation between inflation and real GDP:

	Inflation				
	10	8	6	4	2
Original real GDP	5,700	5,800	5,900	6,000	6,100
New real GDP	5,400	5,500	5,600	5,700	5,800

Current inflation is equal to 8 percent, and potential GDP is equal to 5,800. Suppose that the economy moves in the short run from the original to the new relation.

a. Graph the original *AD* curve, the new *AD* curve, the *IA* line, and the potential output line. Describe the economy in the short run. Is the economy in long-run equilibrium?

b. Show what happens to the economy over time. What is the long-run equilibrium?

3. Consider an economy characterized by the following relation between inflation and real GDP:

	Inflation				
	9	7	5	3	1
Original real GDP	8,100	8,200	8,300	8,400	8,500
New real GDP	8,300	8,400	8,500	8,600	8,700

Current inflation is equal to 7 percent, and potential GDP is equal to 8,400. Suppose that the economy moves in the short run from the original to the new relation.

a. Graph the original *AD* curve, the new *AD* curve, the *IA* line, and the potential output line. Describe the economy in the short run. Is the economy in long-run equilibrium?

b. Show what happens to the economy over time. What is the long-run equilibrium?

4. Starting from a long-run equilibrium with real GDP equal to potential GDP, suppose that U.S. business firms purchase more computers. What are the effects, in both the short and the long run, on real GDP, inflation, consumption, investment, and net exports?

5. Starting from a long-run equilibrium with real GDP equal to potential GDP, suppose that the Fed changes its policy rule to a higher inflation target. What are the effects, in both the short and the long run, on real GDP, inflation, consumption, investment, and net exports?

6. Starting from a long-run equilibrium with real GDP equal to potential GDP, suppose that people expect higher inflation. What are the effects, in both the short and the long run, on real GDP, inflation, consumption, investment, and net exports?

CHAPTER TEST

1. The long run in the economic fluctuations model is determined by the intersection of the
    a. aggregate demand curve and the inflation adjustment line.
    b. aggregate demand curve, inflation adjustment line, and the potential GDP line.
    c. aggregate demand curve and the potential GDP line.
    d. inflation adjustment line and the potential GDP line.
2. The baseline is the path of an economic variable that would occur
    a. without an aggregate demand shock.
    b. after an aggregate demand shock.
    c. without the policy change under consideration.
    d. after the policy change under consideration.
3. In a boom, real GDP
    a. falls short of potential GDP, and inflation falls.
    b. falls short of potential GDP, and inflation rises.
    c. exceeds potential GDP, and inflation falls.
    d. exceeds potential GDP, and inflation rises.

4. A reduction in the rate of inflation is referred to as

   a. a temporary growth slowdown.
   b. deflation.
   c. disinflation.
   d. reinflation.

5. Demand shocks result from changes in

   a. government purchases, consumption, investment, or net exports.
   b. government purchases, investment, net exports, or the monetary policy rule.
   c. consumption, investment, net exports, or the monetary policy rule.
   d. government purchases, investment, net exports, or inflation.

6. Supply shocks are indicated by shifts in

   a. potential GDP.
   b. the inflation adjustment (*IA*) line.
   c. the aggregate demand (*AD*) curve.
   d. the aggregate expenditure (*AE*) line.

7. If a fall in GDP coincides with a rise in inflation, then the economy is experiencing

   a. a temporary growth slowdown.
   b. stagflation.
   c. a boom-bust cycle.
   d. disinflation.

8. If the central bank reduces the interest rate too much, then the economy experiences

   a. a supply shock.
   b. a temporary growth slowdown.
   c. stagflation.
   d. a boom-bust cycle.

9. When real GDP is less than potential GDP, the *IA* line

   a. shifts upward, and inflation falls.
   b. shifts upward, and inflation rises.
   c. shifts downward, and inflation falls.
   d. does *not* shift, and inflation remains unchanged.

10. If real GDP is less than potential GDP at the intersection of the *AD* curve and the *IA* line, then the economy is in

    a. a long-run equilibrium, and there is no reason for inflation or real GDP to change.
    b. a recession, causing inflation to fall and GDP to rise until long-run equilibrium occurs.
    c. a boom, causing inflation to fall and GDP to rise until long-run equilibrium occurs.
    d. a boom, causing inflation to rise and GDP to rise until long-run equilibrium occurs.

11. Suppose the economy is in long-run equilibrium and the government subsequently decides to decrease purchases. In the short run, the *AD* curve

    a. shifts left, and the *IA* line is fixed.
    b. shifts right, and the *IA* line is fixed.
    c. is fixed, and the *IA* line shifts upward.
    d. is fixed, and the *IA* line shifts downward.

12. Suppose the economy is in long-run equilibrium and the government subsequently decides to decrease purchases. In the long run, real GDP

    a. falls short of potential GDP, and inflation remains unchanged.
    b. equals potential GDP, and inflation remains unchanged.
    c. equals potential GDP, and inflation is higher.
    d. equals potential GDP, and inflation is lower.

13. If the central bank shifts to a monetary policy rule with a lower inflation target, then the
   a. *IA* line shifts upward.
   b. *IA* line shifts downward.
   c. *AD* curve shifts right.
   d. *AD* curve shifts left.
14. Suppose the economy is in long-run equilibrium and the central bank subsequently decides to change the monetary policy rule to a higher inflation target. In the short run, real GDP
   a. decreases, and the inflation rate remains constant.
   b. increases, and the inflation rate remains constant.
   c. decreases, and the inflation rate increases.
   d. increases, and the inflation rate decreases.

Use Figure 13.10 for question 15.

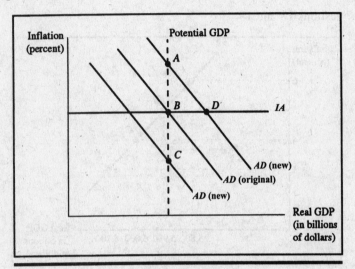

Figure 13.10

15. Initially the economy is in long-run equilibrium at point *B*. If the monetary policy rule changes to a higher inflation target, then which point in the above diagram represents long-run equilibrium?
   a. Point *A*
   b. Point *B*
   c. Point *C*
   d. Point *D*

16. Suppose the economy is initially in long-run equilibrium and subsequently the price of oil decreases. In the short run, the oil price decrease shifts the

    a. *AD* curve right.
    b. *AD* curve left.
    c. *IA* line upward.
    d. *IA* line downward.

17. Suppose the economy is in long-run equilibrium and subsequently the price of oil decreases. In the long run, real GDP

    a. exceeds potential GDP, and inflation is higher.
    b. equals potential GDP, and inflation returns to its original level.
    c. equals potential GDP, and inflation is higher.
    d. equals potential GDP, and inflation is lower.

Use Figure 13.11 for questions 18 and 19.

Figure 13.11

18. If the current inflation rate is 4 percent and the economy is in equilibrium, then potential GDP equals

    a. $5,800 billion.
    b. $5,900 billion.
    c. $6,000 billion.
    d. $6,100 billion.

19. If the economy is in long-run equilibrium at point *B*, movement from point *B* to point *A* represents

    a. a boom.
    b. a boom-bust cycle.
    c. stagflation.
    d. disinflation.

20. What are the short-run effects on real GDP, consumption, investment, and net exports when government purchases decrease?
    a. Real GDP, consumption, investment, and net exports fall.
    b. Real GDP, investment, and net exports fall, whereas consumption is unchanged.
    c. Real GDP, consumption, and investment fall, whereas net exports are unchanged.
    d. Real GDP, consumption, and net exports fall, whereas investment is unchanged.

ANSWERS TO THE REVIEW QUESTIONS

Fill-In Questions

1. economic fluctuations model
2. baseline
3. Demand shocks
4. Price shocks
5. Supply shocks
6. boom
7. recession
8. temporary growth slowdown
9. Stagflation
10. boom-bust cycle
11. Disinflation
12. Deflation
13. reinflation
14. short run
15. equilibrium

True-False Questions

1. **False**. The baseline is the path of an economic variable that would occur without the policy change under consideration.
2. **True**. Net exports, which shift the *AD* curve, are a type of demand shock.
3. **False**. A change in the monetary policy rule is an example of a price shock.
4. **False**. Price shocks are shifts in the *IA* line.
5. **True**. Supply shocks cause permanent changes in real GDP.
6. **False**. A temporary growth slowdown lowers the rate of growth of real GDP, but does not make it negative.
7. **False**. Stagflation occurs when real GDP falls and inflation rises simultaneously.
8. **True**. Deflation is a negative inflation rate, which decreases the price level.
9. **False**. Reinflation is the opposite of disinflation.

10. **True**. Changes in investment change aggregate expenditure, which shifts the *AD* curve.

11. **False**. Movements in the exchange rate affect net exports, changing aggregate expenditure and shifting the *AD* curve, not the *IA* line.

12. **True**. Changes in the target inflation rate are changes in the monetary policy rule, which shift the *AD* curve.

13. **True**. An oil price increase is an example of a price shock, which shifts the *IA* line.

14. **True**. Changes in expected inflation shift the *IA* line.

15. **False**. Changes in government purchases shift the *AD* curve.

Short-Answer Questions

1. The economic fluctuations model is used to study the effects of economic policy proposals such as changes in monetary policy rules and tax and spending changes.

2. Demand shocks are shifts in the *AD* curve, including changes in government purchases, investment, net exports, or the monetary policy rule.

3. Price shocks are shifts in the *IA* line, such as changes in the price of oil or other commodities.

4. Supply shocks are shifts in potential GDP, such as technological progress that causes an increase in productivity growth.

5. Booms occur when real GDP is greater than potential GDP. Recessions occur when real GDP is less than potential GDP.

6. A temporary growth slowdown is a decrease in the rate of growth of real GDP that is not large enough to make real GDP growth negative.

7. Stagflation occurs when real GDP falls and inflation rises simultaneously.

8. A boom-bust cycle occurs when the Fed lowers the interest rate too much, causing a boom and inflation. The Fed responds by raising interest rates, causing a recession.

9. Disinflation is a decrease in the inflation rate. Deflation is negative inflation.

10. Disinflation, a reduction in the rate of inflation, is a typical policy objective. Deflation, a negative inflation rate, is not.

11. The economy is in long-run equilibrium when real GDP equals potential GDP.

12. Inflation is constant when the economy is in equilibrium.

13. The decrease in government purchases shifts the *AD* curve to the left, lowering real GDP in the short run. Over time, inflation falls and the *IA* line moves downward. In the long run, real GDP equals potential GDP and inflation is lower.

14. The shift by the Fed to a higher inflation target shifts the *AD* curve to the right, raising real GDP in the short run. Over time, inflation rises and the *IA* line moves upward. In the long run, real GDP equals potential GDP and inflation is higher.

15. The oil price decrease is a price shock that shifts the *IA* line downward, lowering inflation and raising real GDP in the short run. Over time, inflation rises and the *IA* line shifts back. In the long run, real GDP equals potential GDP at the original inflation rate.

16. Monetary policy, not fiscal policy, was the most important factor in the recovery from the Great Depression. Interest rates fell in 1933 and remained low during most of the 1930s, while

government purchases and tax policy were basically unchanged until 1941, at which point real GDP was already close to potential GDP.

SOLUTIONS TO THE PRACTICE PROBLEMS

1. a. The answer is illustrated in Figure 13.12. The *AD* curve intersects the *IA* line at potential GDP. The economy is in equilibrium.

    b. Since the economy is in long-run equilibrium, nothing happens over time. The long run is the same as the short run.

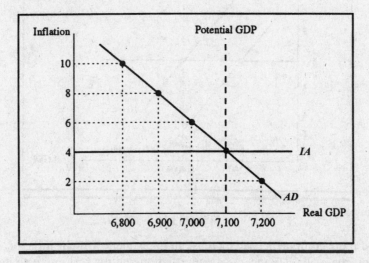

Figure 13.12

2. a. The answer is illustrated in Figure 13.13. The original *AD* curve intersects the *IA* line with real GDP equal to potential GDP. The new *AD* curve intersects the *IA* line with real GDP (5,500) below potential GDP (5,800). The economy is not in long-run equilibrium.

    b. With real GDP below potential GDP in the short run, inflation falls. The *IA* line shifts down, and GDP rises. In the long-run equilibrium, real GDP equals potential GDP at 2 percent inflation.

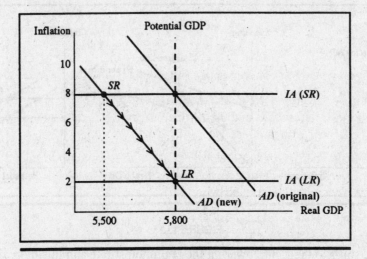

Figure 13.13

3. a. The answer is illustrated in Figure 13.14. The original *AD* curve intersects the *IA* line with real GDP (8,200) below potential GDP (8,400). The new *AD* curve intersects the *IA* line with real GDP equal to potential GDP. The economy is in long-run equilibrium.

    b. Since the economy is in long-run equilibrium, nothing happens over time. The long run is the same as the short run.

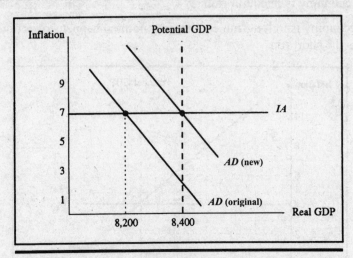

Figure 13.14

4. The purchase of more computers is an increase in investment, which shifts the *AD* curve to the right. In the short run, real GDP increases and inflation and the real interest rate are unchanged. In the long run, real GDP returns to potential GDP at higher inflation and a higher real interest rate. The results, summarized below and shown in Figure 13.15, are the same as those for an increase in government purchases except for investment, which is higher in both the short and the long run.

	Y	*C*	*I*	*X*
SR				↓
LR	—	↓		↓

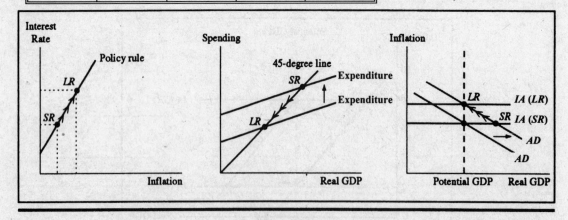

FIGURE 13.15

5. The policy rule shifts to the right, lowering the real interest rate and raising real GDP above potential GDP in the short run. Over time, inflation rises, causing the Fed to raise the real interest rate and real GDP to fall. In the long run, real GDP equals potential GDP at a higher inflation rate.

The real interest rate returns to its original level, but, because of the higher inflation, the stated interest rate is higher. The results are shown in Figure 13.16 and summarized below.

	Y	C	I	X
SR				
LR	—	—	—	—

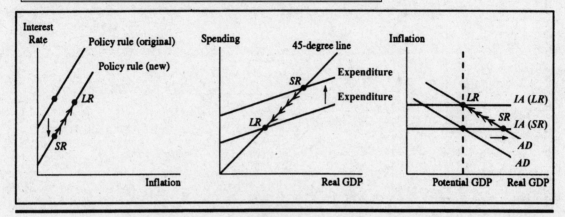

FIGURE 13.16

6. The expectations of higher inflation cause a positive price shock, increasing inflation, raising the real interest rate, and reducing GDP below potential GDP in the short run. Over time, inflation and the real interest rate fall. In the long run, real GDP returns to potential GDP at the original values of inflation and the real interest rate. The results are shown in Figure 13.17 and summarized below.

	Y	C	I	X
SR	↓	↓	↓	↓
LR	—	—	—	—

FIGURE 13.17

ANSWERS TO THE CHAPTER TEST

1. b

2. c

3. d

4.   c
5.   b
6.   a
7.   b
8.   d
9.   c
10. b
11. a
12. d
13. d
14. b
15. a
16. d
17. b
18. c
19. c
20. d

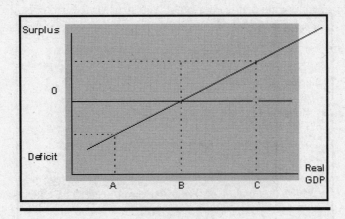

Figure 14.1

b. We are ready to look at the structural surplus, the budget surplus when real GDP equals potential GDP. Figure 14.2 includes the potential GDP line, which is at a value of real GDP that produces a structural surplus. Figure 14.2 also incorporates a value for actual real GDP. Since actual GDP is less than potential GDP, the actual surplus is less than the structural surplus, and so the cyclical surplus is negative.

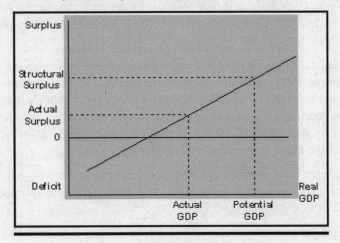

Figure 14.2

c. Another example is given in Figure 14.3, which also includes the potential GDP line at a value of real GDP that produces a structural surplus and incorporates a value for actual real GDP. Since actual GDP is greater than potential GDP, the actual surplus is greater than the structural surplus, and so the cyclical surplus is positive.

Figure 14.3

2. The federal budget for the United States was in deficit, with spending greater than taxes, for every year between 1970 and 1997, and the deficits were forecasted to continue indefinitely. To the surprise of the forecasters (and everyone else), the budget switched to a surplus in 1988. There were more surpluses in 1999 and additional surpluses were expected in the future. But the surprises did not end. In 2001, the budget went into deficit and budget projections switched again, this time from surpluses to deficits.

    a. Why did the federal budget suddenly switch from deficits to surpluses? As the economy expanded between 1995 and 1998, people's incomes grew very rapidly. Moreover, fueled by the stock market boom, income of the rich grew much more rapidly than income of everyone else. Since tax rates on the rich are higher than tax rates on everyone else, tax revenues increased. The spreading of the income distribution in a rapidly growing economy was the major cause of the move from deficits to surpluses.

    b. The surpluses were not caused by changes in fiscal policy. The last major change in tax rates occurred when they were increased in 1993, and there were no major spending cuts in the 1990s.

    c. Why did the federal budget switch back from surpluses to deficits? The major causes were the recession of 2001 and the tax cuts passed in June 2001. Other factors included higher government expenditures associated with September 11th and the military buildup in Afghanistan. Even though the economy has recovered from the recession of 2001, the budget is still in deficit.

ACTIVE REVIEW

Fill-In Questions

1. _____ is the government's plans for spending, taxes, and borrowing.

2. If spending by the government is greater than taxes, there is a budget _____.

3. If taxes exceed spending, there is a budget _____.

4. If taxes equal spending, the budget is _____.

5. The three major categories of spending by the government are _____, _____, and _____.

6. The two largest taxes are _____ and _____ taxes.

7. The _____ or _____ deficit is the budget deficit that would occur if real GDP equaled potential GDP.

8. The _____ deficit is the actual deficit minus the structural deficit.

9. The _____ is the total amount of outstanding loans that the federal government owes.

10. _____ fiscal policy attempts to offset the effects of demand shocks.

11. Changes in the instruments of fiscal policy that do not require legislative action are called _____ stabilizers.

12. Structural budget balance implies a(n) _____ structural surplus.

13. With a(n) _____, individual tax payments rise as a proportion of income as income increases.

14. When the actual budget surplus is less than the structural surplus, the cyclical surplus is _____.

15. _____ and _____ regarding the impact of policy make discretionary fiscal policymaking problematic.

True-False Questions

1. T   F   The largest item in the federal budget is national defense.

2. T   F   Corporate income taxes are the largest source of revenue in the United States.

3. T   F   The president determines the federal budget.

4. T   F   Even after the budget is passed, it is not final.

5. T   F   The United States' budget deficits are the largest of any industrialized nation.

6. T   F   State and local governments typically run large budget deficits.

7. T   F   Deficits and surpluses are changes in the federal debt.

8. T   F   Most economists believe that the deficit is the best measure of fiscal policy.

9. T   F   Discretionary fiscal policy always stabilizes economic fluctuations.

10. T   F   Unemployment insurance payments always stabilize economic fluctuations.

11. T   F   The structural budget surplus is zero when real GDP equals potential GDP.

12. T   F   The budget surplus is positively related to real GDP.

13. T   F   Fiscal policy rules that emphasize automatic stabilizers are considered desirable because of their stability and reliability.

14. T   F   Discretionary fiscal policy does not have a good track record in stabilizing the economy.

15. T   F   The economy would be stabilized if the budget was always in balance.

16. T   F   The federal budget deficit for the United States in 2004 was 3.5 percent of GDP, the largest amount since World War II. (Hint: See Reading the News About—Budget Deficits.)

Short-Answer Questions

1.   How is fiscal policy related to the budget deficit?

2.   List the four steps in the budget cycle process.

3.   Why do actual spending and taxes differ from the president's proposed budget?

4.   Why is the structural deficit a useful long-run measure of fiscal policy?

5.   What is the difference between the federal debt and the federal budget deficit?

6.   How does the government borrow?

7.   What are the instruments of fiscal policy?

8.   Give four examples of automatic stabilizers.

9.   What is the relation between the structural surplus, the actual surplus, and real GDP?

10.   Describe some differences between state and federal governments' budgets.

11.   Explain how the surplus rises as GDP rises.

12.   Give two reasons why actual taxes and spending might differ from the proposed budget.

13.   Between 1990 and 1997, was the federal budget for the United States usually in surplus or in deficit?

14.   Describe how the U.S. moved from a position of federal budget deficit to budget surplus in the late 1990s. (Hint: See Economics in Action—Why Did All the Deficits Go Away in the Late 1990s?)

15.   Why did projections for future federal budgets moved from surpluses to deficits in 2001?

WORKING IT OUT

1.   We start by reviewing the effects of changes in the instruments of fiscal policy—government purchases, transfers, and taxes—on the aggregate demand (*AD*) curve.

   a.   An increase in government purchases, as you should remember from Chapter 14, shifts the *AD* curve to the right, and a decrease in government purchases shifts the *AD* curve to the left. This is illustrated in Figure 14.4.

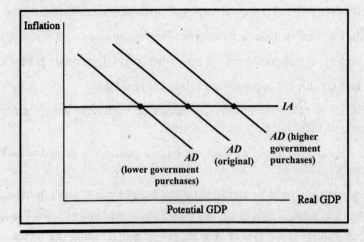

Figure 14.4

b. The same diagram can be used for transfer payments and taxes. An increase in transfer payments or a decrease in taxes shifts the *AD* curve to the right, whereas a decrease in transfer payments or an increase in taxes shifts the *AD* curve to the left.

c. Figure 14.4 does not include the potential GDP line. The reason for this omission is that the shifts in the *AD* curve are the same whether the change in fiscal policy occurs when real GDP is above, below, or equal to potential GDP. Depending on the situation, fiscal policy can either move real GDP closer to potential GDP or move real GDP further away from potential GDP.

2. Countercyclical fiscal policy attempts to use changes in taxes, transfers, and spending to "counter" or reduce the size of economic fluctuations caused by demand shocks. The successful use of discretionary fiscal policy to counter a demand shock is illustrated in Figure 14.5.

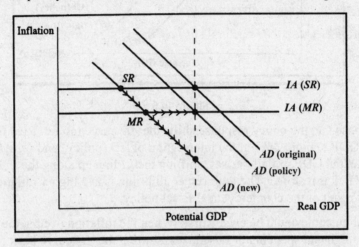

Figure 14.5

a. Suppose that the economy is in long-run equilibrium with real GDP equal to potential GDP when a negative demand shock, such as a decrease in investment, shifts the *AD* curve to the left. In the short run, real GDP is below potential GDP at unchanged inflation. This is shown by point *SR* at the intersection of *AD* (new) and *IA* (*SR*).

b. In the absence of a policy response, inflation will fall, the *IA* line will shift down, and the economy will eventually return to equilibrium at the intersection of *AD* (new) and the potential GDP line. The cost of not responding is a recession, which may last a number of years, as the economy moves along the *AD* curve.

c. A countercyclical fiscal policy response, such as an increase in unemployment benefits or a tax cut, would shift the *AD* curve back to *AD* (policy). Since there are lags in the discretionary policy process, the economy first shifts down the *AD* (new) curve to point *MR* (medium run), then shifts along the *IA* (*MR*) line. If the policy response exactly counters the shock, the economy moves to the intersection of the *AD* (policy) curve and the potential output line.

d. The major advantage of this policy is a shorter recession. Although you can't tell this by looking at the arrows in the diagram, the recovery along *IA* (*MR*) is much faster than the recovery along *AD* (new). Automatic stabilizers could be even more effective. If they are activated quickly enough, the economy could move back along (or close to) the *IA* (*SR*) line, providing an even faster recovery.

3. Countercyclical fiscal policy does not always work well. An example of unsuccessful policy is shown in Figure 14.6.

a.   Suppose that the economy starts in equilibrium and that the initial demand shock is the same as in Figure 14.5. In the short run, the *AD* curve shifts to the left, and the economy is at point *SR*. In the medium run, the *IA* curve shifts down to point *MR*.

Figure 14.6

b.   Now suppose that the policy response shifts the *AD* curve too far. Real GDP increases above potential GDP to point *MR1* at the intersection of *AD* (policy) and *IA* (*MR*). With real GDP above potential GDP, inflation rises, shifting the *IA* line up along the *AD* (policy) curve until potential GDP is restored. The long-run equilibrium is at a higher inflation rate, a completely unwanted result of the countercyclical fiscal policy.

c.   The actual outcome could be even worse. When the inflation occurs, the president and Congress might cut spending or raise taxes, shifting the *AD* curve back to the left. If the timing of this contractionary policy is no better than the timing of the expansionary policy, the economy could go into a recession.

Worked Problems

1.   Consider an economy with the following relation between budget surpluses and real GDP:

Surplus (millions of dollars)	180	190	200	210	220
Real GDP (billions of dollars)	5,800	5,900	6,000	6,100	6,200

Suppose that real GDP equals $6,100 billion and potential GDP equals $6,000 billion. What are the actual, structural, and cyclical surpluses? Draw a diagram, using the values for real and potential GDP, to illustrate this example.

Answer

The actual surplus is the surplus at the current value of real GDP, $210 million, whereas the structural surplus is the surplus at potential GDP, $200 million. The cyclical surplus is the actual surplus minus the structural surplus, $10 million. Figure 14.7 illustrates the example. The surplus is on the vertical axis, and real GDP is on the horizontal axis. The values of the surplus at actual and potential real GDP are plotted. The line is upward-sloping, indicating that the surplus falls when real GDP is higher.

Figure 14.7

2.   Consider an economy characterized by the following relation between inflation and real GDP:

		Inflation				
		10	**8**	**6**	**4**	**2**
Original	Real GDP	7,800	7,900	8,000	8,100	8,200
New	Real GDP	7,600	7,700	7,800	7,900	8,000
Policy	Real GDP	7,700	7,800	7,900	8,000	8,100

Current inflation is equal to 6 percent, and potential GDP is equal to 8,000.

a.   Suppose that the economy moves in the short run from the original to the new relation. Graph the original *AD* curve, the new *AD* curve, the *IA* line, and the potential output line. Describe the economy in the short run.

b.   Now suppose that inflation falls by 2 percent in the medium run. Show how the *IA* line shifts. Describe the economy in the medium run.

c.   Finally, suppose that countercyclical fiscal policy moves the economy from the new to the policy relation. Graph the *AD* curve under the new policy and describe the response of inflation and real GDP. Is the economy in equilibrium? If not, what will occur next?

Answer

a.   The original and new *AD* curves are downward-sloping lines depicting the values of inflation and real GDP. The *IA* line is a horizontal line at 6 percent inflation, and the potential output line is a vertical line at 8,000 real GDP. The economy is originally in equilibrium, with the intersection of the *AD* curve and the *IA* line where real GDP equals potential GDP. The short run is the intersection of the new *AD* curve and the *IA* line, with inflation at 6 percent and real GDP at 7,800. This is illustrated in Figure 14.8.

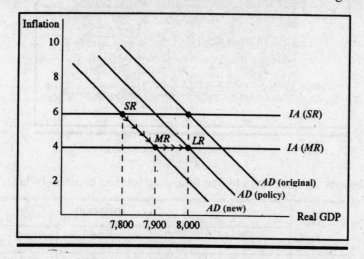

Figure 14.8

b.   *In* the short run, real GDP is less than potential GDP, so that, in the medium run, the *IA* line shifts down. The economy moves down the *AD* (new) curve. Inflation is at 4 percent and real GDP at 7,900.

c.   The countercyclical fiscal policy shifts the *AD* curve to the right, intersecting the *IA* (*MR*) line at inflation=4 percent and real GDP=8,000 . Real GDP = potential GDP , so the economy is in equilibrium.

PRACTICE PROBLEMS

1.   Consider an economy with the following relation between budget surpluses and real GDP:

Surplus (millions of dollars)	160	170	180	190	200
Real GDP (billions of dollars)	6,800	6,900	7,000	7,100	7,200

Suppose that real GDP equals $6,800 billion and potential GDP equals $7,000 billion. What are the actual, structural, and cyclical surpluses?

2.   Consider an economy with the following relation between budget surpluses and real GDP:

Surplus (millions of dollars)	0	15	30	45	60
Real GDP (billions of dollars)	5,100	5,200	5,300	5,400	5,500

Suppose that real GDP equals $5,500 billion and potential GDP equals $5,300 billion. What are the actual, structural, and cyclical surpluses?

3.   Consider an economy with the following relation between budget surpluses and real GDP:

Surplus (millions of dollars)	80	100	120	140	160
Real GDP (billions of dollars)	7,600	7,700	7,800	7,900	8,000

Suppose that real GDP equals $7,700 billion and potential GDP equals $7,700 billion. What are the actual, structural, and cyclical surpluses?

4.   Consider an economy characterized by the following relation between inflation and real GDP:

		Inflation				
		10	8	6	4	2
Original	Real GDP	6,500	6,600	6,700	6,800	6,900
New	Real GDP	6,700	6,800	6,900	7,000	7,100
Policy	Real GDP	6,600	6,700	6,800	6,900	7,000

Suppose that current inflation is equal to 4 percent and potential GDP is equal to 6,800. In the short run, the economy moves from the original to the new relation. In the medium run, inflation rises by 2 percent. Finally, a countercyclical policy response occurs. Using an *AD-IA* diagram, describe the response of inflation and real GDP. Is the economy in equilibrium? If not, what will occur next?

5.   Consider an economy characterized by the following relation between inflation and real GDP:

		Inflation				
		9	7	5	3	1
Original	Real GDP	4,900	5,000	5,100	5,200	5,300
New	Real GDP	4,700	4,800	4,900	5,000	5,100
Policy	Real GDP	5,000	5,100	5,200	5,300	5,400

Suppose that current inflation is equal to 7 percent and potential GDP is equal to 5,000. In the short run, the economy moves from the original to the new relation. In the medium run, inflation falls by 2 percent. Finally, a countercyclical policy response occurs. Using an *AD-IA* diagram, describe the response of inflation and real GDP. Is the economy in equilibrium? If not, what will occur next?

6.   Consider an economy characterized by the following relation between inflation and real GDP:

		Inflation				
		9	**7**	**5**	**3**	**1**
Original	Real GDP	6,600	6,800	7,000	7,200	7,400
New	Real GDP	6,200	6,400	6,600	6,800	7,000
Policy	Real GDP	6,300	6,500	6,700	6,900	7,100

Suppose that current inflation is equal to 5 percent and potential GDP is equal to 7,000. In the short run, the economy moves from the original to the new relation. In the medium run, inflation falls by 2 percent. Finally, a countercyclical policy response occurs. Using an *AD-IA* diagram, describe the response of inflation and real GDP. Is the economy in equilibrium? If not, what will occur next?

CHAPTER TEST

1.   If government spending is less than tax payments, then
   a.   there is a budget deficit.
   b.   there is a budget surplus.
   c.   the budget is balanced.
   d.   the government must borrow.
2.   Which of the following is *not* considered on the expenditure or spending side of the federal budget?
   a.   Purchases of goods and services
   b.   Transfer payments
   c.   Tax payments
   d.   Interest payments
3.   The federal budget for the United States
   a.   has been in a deficit for every year since 1970.
   b.   has been in a surplus for every year since 1970.
   c.   switched from deficits to surpluses in 1998, and back to deficits in 2001.
   d.   switched from surpluses to deficits in 1998, and back to surpluses in 2001.
4.   The total amount of outstanding loans that the government owes is the
   a.   federal debt.
   b.   structural deficit.
   c.   cyclical deficit.
   d.   federal budget deficit.
5.   The instruments of fiscal policy are
   a.   government purchases, transfer payments, and interest payments.
   b.   government purchases, interest payments, and taxes.
   c.   government purchases, transfer payments, and taxes.
   d.   transfer payments, interest payments, and taxes.
6.   A structural budget balance
   a.   requires a positive structural surplus.
   b.   requires a zero structural surplus.
   c.   is an unreasonable fiscal policy goal for the U.S. economy.

    d.   would decrease investment and economic growth in the long run.

7.   The major categories on the revenue side of the federal budget are

    a.   personal income taxes, payroll taxes, property taxes, and sales taxes.
    b.   personal income taxes, payroll taxes, property taxes, and corporate income taxes.
    c.   personal income taxes, payroll taxes, sales taxes, and corporate income taxes.
    d.   personal income taxes, property taxes, sales taxes, and corporate income taxes.

8.   The cyclical surplus is

    a.   the difference between the actual surplus and the structural surplus.
    b.   the difference between the federal debt and the structural surplus.
    c.   the budget surplus that occurs when real GDP equals potential GDP.
    d.   a measure of the surplus that is independent of the current state of the economy.

9.   Which of the following is *not* a major category of spending for state and local governments?

    a.   Education
    b.   Police
    c.   Defense
    d.   Prisons

10.   Changes in the instruments of fiscal policy that do *not* require legislative action are referred to as

    a.   supplementals.
    b.   discretionary.
    c.   automatic stabilizers.
    d.   proposals.

11.   When real GDP falls,

    a.   tax payments increase and transfer payments decrease, increasing the surplus.
    b.   tax payments increase and transfer payments increase, causing an indeterminate effect on the surplus.
    c.   tax payments decrease and transfer payments increase, decreasing the surplus.
    d.   tax payments decrease and transfer payments decrease, causing an indeterminate effect on the surplus.

12.   The budget surplus and real GDP are

    a.   negatively related.
    b.   positively related.
    c.   unrelated.
    d.   either positively or negatively related, depending on other factors.

13.   Which of the following is *not* an automatic fiscal policy instrument?

    a.   Government purchases
    b.   Progressive income taxes
    c.   Social security payments
    d.   Unemployment payments

14.   The major categories on the expenditure side of the federal budget are

    a.   government purchases, taxes, and transfer payments.
    b.   progressive taxes, interest on government debt, and transfer payments.
    c.   government purchases, transfer payments, and interest on government debt.
    d.   government purchases, investment, and transfer payments.

15.   Fiscal policy rules that emphasize automatic stabilizers are considered reliable because

    a.   implementation is inexpensive.
    b.   changing them is easy.
    c.   they are stable and reliable.
    d.   no legislative action is required.

16. Which of the following shifts the *AD* curve to the left?

    a.   An increase in transfer payments

    b.   An increase in taxes

    c.   An increase in government purchases

    d.   An increase in inflation

Use Figure 14.9 for questions 17 and 18.

Figure 14.9

17. The structural surplus is equal to

    a.   zero.
    b. $100 million.
    c. $200 million.
    d. $300 million.

18. The cyclical surplus is equal to

    a.   zero.
    b. $100 million.
    c. $200 million.
    d. $300 million.

Use Figure 14.10 for questions 19 and 20.

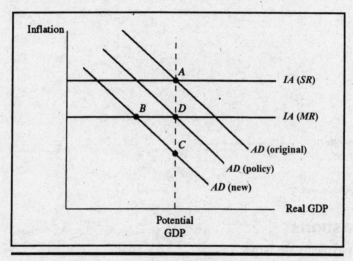

Figure 14.10

19. Suppose that the economy is in equilibrium at point *A* when a negative demand shock occurs, shifting the *AD* curve from *AD* (original) to *AD* (new). In the absence of a policy response, which point on the diagram represents long-run equilibrium for the economy?

    a.   Point *A*
    b.   Point *B*
    c.   Point *C*
    d.   Point *D*

20. Suppose that the economy is in equilibrium at point *A* when a negative demand shock occurs, shifting the *AD* curve from *AD* (original) to *AD* (new). If, after the *IA* curve shifts from *IA* (*SR*) to *IA* (*MR*), the government invokes a countercyclical fiscal policy response that exactly counters the shock, which point on the diagram represents long-run equilibrium for the economy?

    a.   Point *A*
    b.   Point *B*
    c.   Point *C*
    d.   Point D

ANSWERS TO THE REVIEW QUESTIONS

Fill-In Questions

1. Fiscal policy

2. deficit

3. surplus

4. balanced

5. purchases of goods and services; transfer payments; interest payments on the government debt

6. personal income; payroll

7. structural; full employment

8. cyclical

9. federal debt

10. Countercyclical

11. automatic

12. zero

13. progressive tax system

14. negative

15. Lags; uncertainty

True-False Questions

1. **False**. Transfer payments are larger.

2. **False**. Both personal income taxes and payroll taxes are larger.

3. **False**. The president submits a proposal to Congress, but it is always modified.

4. **True**. Changes in tax laws and spending programs, called supplementals, affect the budget in the current fiscal year.

5. **False**. They are not out of line with those in other industrialized countries when measured as a percentage of GDP.

6. **False**. State and local budgets are usually in surplus or in balance.

7. **True**. Deficits represent additions to the debt, and surpluses represent subtractions from the debt.

8. **False**. Many economists believe that change in the debt to GDP ratio is a better measure.

9. **False**. Because of lags and uncertainty, discretionary fiscal policy can magnify business cycles.

10. **True**. Unemployment insurance payments rise during recessions and fall during booms, stabilizing fluctuations.

11. **False** When real GDP equals potential GDP, there can be a structural surplus, deficit, or balance.

12. **True**. When real GDP increases, the surplus rises because of automatic stabilizers.

13. **True**. Fiscal policy certainty is enhanced with automatic stabilizers which alone tend to stabilize the fluctuations of real GDP.

14. **True**. Lags, uncertainty, and large deficits have made discretionary fiscal policymaking problematic.

15. **False**. With a balanced budget, automatic stabilizers would not be able to reduce the effects of demand shocks.

16. **False**. The federal budget deficit of 3.5 percent is below the amount for the United States in the late 1980s.

Short-Answer Questions

1. Fiscal policy is the government's plans for spending, taxes, and borrowing. If spending exceeds taxes, there is a budget deficit, and the government must borrow.

2. The budget cycle is the process in which the federal budget is proposed, modified, enacted, and implemented.

3. First, the actual budget also depends on Congress, which modifies the president's proposed budget. Second, unexpected events cause actual spending and taxes to differ from the enacted budget.

4. The structural deficit measures what the deficit would be if real GDP equaled potential GDP, and so is not affected by current economic fluctuations.

5. The federal debt is the total amount of outstanding loans that the federal government owes. The federal deficit is the change in the debt, the amount added to the debt each year.

6. The government borrows by selling government bonds.

7. The instruments of fiscal policy are government purchases, taxes, and transfers.

8. The progressive tax system, unemployment benefits, social security payments, and welfare payments are four examples of automatic stabilizers.

9. When real GDP exceeds potential GDP, the actual surplus is greater than the structural surplus. When real GDP is less than potential GDP, the actual surplus is less than the structural surplus. When real GDP equals potential GDP, the actual and structural surpluses are equal.

10. Most state and local budgets are in balance or surplus, and many are required to be so by law. Categories of spending include education and police; sales and property taxes, more than income taxes, are major sources of revenue.

11. The reason is automatic stabilizers. When real GDP rises, taxes increase and transfer payments fall, increasing the surplus. When real GDP falls, taxes decrease and transfer payments rise, lowering the surplus.

12. Congress modifies the president's budget. Unexpected changes in the economy (such as wars, floods, and recessions) cause actual taxes and spending to change.

13. The federal budget for the United States was in deficit for every year between 1970 and 1997.

14. As the economy grew in the late 1990s, incomes grew. The stock market boom caused the income of the rich to grow faster than income of others. Tax revenues increased. This spreading of the income distribution was the major cause of the move from deficits to surpluses.

15. The major causes are the recession of 2001 and the tax cuts passed in June 2001.

SOLUTIONS TO THE PRACTICE PROBLEMS

1. The actual surplus is $160 million, and the structural surplus is $180 million. The cyclical surplus is minus $20 million.

2. The actual surplus is $60 million, and the structural surplus is $30 million. The cyclical surplus is $30 million.

3. Since real GDP equals potential GDP, the actual surplus is the same as the structural surplus, or $100 million. The cyclical surplus is zero.

4. The answer is illustrated in Figure 14.11. In the short run, real GDP rises to 7,000 at unchanged inflation as the *AD* curve shifts to the right. In the medium run, the *IA* line shifts up, inflation rises to 6 percent, and real GDP falls to 6,900. The countercyclical policy response shifts the *AD* curve to the left; real GDP falls to 6,800, and inflation stays at 6 percent. This is an equilibrium because real GDP equals potential GDP.

Figure 14.11

5. The answer is illustrated in Figure 14.12. In the short run, real GDP falls to 4,800 at unchanged inflation as the *AD* curve shifts to the left. In the medium run, the *IA* line shifts down, inflation falls to 5 percent, and real GDP rises to 4,900. The countercyclical policy response shifts the *AD* curve to the right; real GDP rises to 5,200, and inflation stays at 5 percent. This is not an equilibrium because real GDP exceeds potential GDP. In the absence of another policy response, the *IA* line will shift up along the *AD* (policy) curve until potential GDP is reached at 9 percent inflation.

Figure 14.12

6. The answer is illustrated in Figure 14.13. In the short run, real GDP falls to 6,600 at unchanged inflation as the *AD* curve shifts to the left. In the medium run, the *IA* line shifts down, inflation falls to 3 percent, and real GDP rises to 6,800. The countercyclical policy response shifts the *AD*

curve to the right; real GDP rises to 6,900, and inflation stays at 3 percent. This is not an equilibrium because real GDP is less than potential GDP. In the absence of another policy response, the *IA* line will shift down along the *AD* (policy) curve until potential GDP is reached at 2 percent inflation.

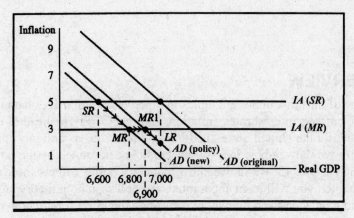

Figure 14.13

ANSWERS TO THE CHAPTER TEST

1. b
2. c
3. c
4. a
5. c
6. b
7. c
8. a
9. c
10. c
11. c
12. b
13. a
14. d
15. c
16. b
17. b
18. c
19. c
20. d

CHAPTER 15

Monetary Policy

CHAPTER OVERVIEW

Monetary policy is one of the most important topics in macroeconomics. By changing the money supply, the central bank affects interest rates, inflation, and real GDP. The head of the Federal Reserve System, the central bank for the United States, is often said to be the second most powerful person in America. In Chapter 10, we showed how long-run inflation is determined by the rate of growth of the money supply, while in Chapter 13, we showed how monetary policy affects short-run economic fluctuations. In this chapter, you will learn about monetary policy in both theory and practice. We see how money supply and money demand interact to determine the interest rate, how Fed policy actions work, and why independence of the central bank is desirable.

CHAPTER REVIEW

1. *Monetary policy* is the set of actions taken by the government that affect the money supply and thereby interest rates, exchange rates, inflation, unemployment, and real GDP. The *central bank—* the *Federal Reserve System (Fed)* in the United States, the *European Central Bank*, and the *Bank of Japan*—is responsible for monetary policy in most countries. The most important feature of a central bank is *central bank independence*, the degree of independence the law gives it from the government.

2. **Money demand** is defined as a relationship between the interest rate and the amount of money that people want to hold at that interest rate. Money is only part of most individuals' wealth. Currency pays no interest, while checking accounts pay relatively low interest. Alternatives, such as certificates of deposit and Treasury bills, pay higher interest rates. The *opportunity cost* of holding money is the interest rate on the alternatives minus the interest paid on checking accounts for deposits. When the interest rates on the alternatives to holding money rise, the opportunity cost increases and money demand falls. When the interest rates on the alternatives fall, the opportunity cost decreases and money demand rises.

3. The interest rate is determined by the demand for money and the supply of money. When the Fed wants to lower the interest rate, it buys bonds, increasing the money supply. When the Fed wants to raise the interest rate, it sells bonds, decreasing the money supply. The *federal funds rate* is the interest rate that the Fed looks at to make sure its actions have the intended effect. It is the short-term interest rate that banks charge one another on overnight loans. The federal funds rate is closely related to the longer-term interest rates on Treasury bills and certificates of deposit, which are relevant for money demand.

4. The **discount rate** is the rate that commercial banks are charged when they borrow from the Fed. The ability to borrow from the Fed increases people's confidence in the safety of their bank deposits, and the Fed is called the *lender of the last resort*. Changes in the discount rate always receive a lot of publicity, and the Fed sometimes changes the discount rate when it wants to bring public attention to its actions or provide a signal of its future intentions.

5. In Chapter 12, we studied a monetary policy rule in which the Fed increases the real interest rate when inflation rises and decreases the interest rate when inflation falls and used the rule to derive a downward-sloping aggregate demand (*AD*) curve. Including real GDP in the monetary policy

rule is a slight modification of this rule. Along with reacting to inflation, the Fed raises the interest rate when real GDP rises above potential GDP and lowers the interest rate when real GDP falls below potential GDP. When the economy enters a boom, so that real GDP exceeds potential GDP, the Fed raises the interest rate even if inflation has not yet started to increase. When the economy goes into a recession, so that real GDP falls below potential GDP, the Fed lowers interest rates, stimulating investment and net exports and leading to a quicker recovery. The Fed and other central banks respond to the *gap*, or the *difference*, between real GDP and potential GDP, as well as to inflation, in this way.

6.   A *constant money growth rule* is simply to keep the growth rate of the money supply fixed from year to year. Although this rule would keep inflation low in the long run, central banks and most economists feel that money demand moves around too much for such a rule to work well in practice.

7.   **Exchange market intervention** occurs when governments buy and sell currencies to prevent changes in the exchange rate. The world currency market is so large, however, that intervention does not affect exchange rates for long. Unless it is accompanied by changes in interest rates, exchange market intervention has only small effects.

8.   The ideal for monetary policy is to have inflation at the target inflation rate and real GDP equal to potential GDP. This is sometimes called the "Goldilocks Economy"—not too hot, not too cold, but just right.

ZEROING IN

1.   A unique aspect of monetary policy is that central banks have varying degrees of independence from the government. At first glance, **central bank independence** seems like a strange idea. Why shouldn't the president and Congress, who are elected by the public, have control over monetary policy? In fact, some degree of independence is the most important attribute for a central bank to have in order to run a good monetary policy.

   a.   There is a natural tendency toward higher inflation in the political system. We learned in Chapter 13 that, in the short run, a change in the monetary policy rule toward higher inflation would increase real GDP with little or no change in inflation, but in the long run, real GDP returns to potential at higher inflation. This is known as the "gain then pain scenario." Even though there is no long-run tradeoff between inflation and unemployment, there is a short-run gain from a higher inflation monetary policy.

   b.   Under the "gain then pain scenario," the government in power, looking toward the next election, would be tempted to raise the inflation target in order to make the economy look good at election time. If the government was reelected, the long-run inflation consequences could be dealt with later. If it was defeated, inflation would become the other party's problem. Countries in which the central bank has greater independence have lower long-run inflation than countries in which the central bank is more controlled by the government.

   c.   The **political business cycle** refers to the tendency of governments to regularly use economic policy, either fiscal or monetary, to influence elections. This involves creating a boom just before the election, then slowing down the economy afterward. Although such cycles are possible in theory, recent evidence for a political business cycle in the United States is not strong. The independence of the Fed is the most important reason for the absence of a political business cycle in the United States.

   d.   Not all arguments for central bank independence involve such a cynical view of the political process. **Time inconsistency** describes the tendency of governments, attempting to improve the welfare of their citizens, to announce a low inflation policy, but then stimulate the economy in order to reduce unemployment. Unfortunately, a central bank that adopts this type of policy will lose credibility over time as people learn what it is doing, and this loss of credibility is very costly. Think of a professor who announces a final exam in order to get the students to study, but then walks into the classroom on the day of the final and cancels the exam. It may work the first time, but how hard do you think students would study for the same professor's final the next semester?

2. The most basic issue for a country facing the world economy is what *exchange rate policy* to adopt. The choice is between a **fixed exchange rate policy**, where governments set, or fix, exchange rates between their currencies, and a **flexible exchange rate policy**, where governments do not try to set the value of their currencies. Both throughout history and at the present time, countries have made a number of different choices.

    a. The current flexible exchange rate system has been in place since 1973. Major countries such as the United States and Japan follow flexible exchange rate policies.

    b. The *Bretton Woods system* was the exchange rate system between the end of World War II and 1971. Under the Bretton Woods system, the United States bought and sold gold at a fixed price and the other countries fixed their exchange rates to the dollar.

    c. The *euro* is the single currency formed in 1999 by eleven European countries that permanently fixed their exchange rates by forming a monetary union. The euro fluctuates against the dollar and the yen.

3. Why are fixed exchange rate systems desirable? Why do they break down? The answers to these questions help us understand why some countries, such as the United States and Japan, let their exchange rate fluctuate, whereas others, such as France and Germany, have joined together to form a single currency.

    a. Suppose that the Fed and the Bank of Japan (BOJ) agreed to fix the dollar/yen exchange rate. This can be accomplished by equalizing interest rates between the United States and Japan. Now suppose that the Fed wants to raise interest rates, maybe to move to a lower inflation target. Investors, looking for higher yields, would switch from yen- to dollar-denominated assets, causing the dollar to appreciate relative to the yen. The only way to keep the exchange rate fixed is for the Fed to not raise interest rates in the first place, a loss of international monetary independence.

    b. The crisis in Europe during 1992 can be explained by the loss of independence. Germany, concerned with rising inflation, raised interest rates. The United Kingdom, in contrast, did not want to raise interest rates because of fears that higher interest rates would cause a recession. While it first attempted to keep its exchange rate with the deutsche mark stable by raising interest rates, eventually domestic economic considerations proved to be more important than fixing exchange rates. The United Kingdom lowered interest rates and gave up the fixed exchange rate.

    c. Why do countries form fixed exchange rate systems? One reason for fixed exchange rates, which was an important motivation in the establishment of the euro, is the belief that flexible exchange rates, by increasing uncertainty, can interfere with trade. Another reason is that countries with a history of poor monetary policies, such as Italy, can benefit from fixing their exchange rates and adopting the monetary policy of countries, such as Germany, with a history of good monetary policies.

    d. Argentina fixed the value of the peso to the dollar in 1991, giving up its independent monetary policy. This was beneficial when interest rates in the U.S. fell in the mid 1990s. When interest rates rose in the U.S. in 2000, Argentina was forced to raise their interest rate, causing a recession. The recession worsened in 2001, and Argentina abandoned the peg in December 2001.

ACTIVE REVIEW

Fill-In Questions

1. _____ is the set of actions taken by the government that affect the money supply and interest rate.

2. The central bank is called the _____ in the United States, the _____ in Europe, and the _____ in Japan.

3. The most important feature of a central bank is _____.

4. Money demand is a relationship between the _____ and the amount of money people want to hold.

5. The _____ of holding money is the interest rate on the alternatives minus the interest paid on checking accounts for deposits.

6. When the interest rates on the alternatives to holding money rise, the opportunity cost _____ and money demand falls.

7. The _____ is the interest rate that the Fed follows to make sure its actions have the intended effect.

8. The _____ is the rate that commercial banks are charged when they borrow from the Fed.

9. When real GDP falls below potential GDP, the Fed lowers interest rates, stimulating _____ and _____ and leading to a quicker recovery.

10. A(n) _____ is to keep the growth rate of the money supply fixed from year to year.

11. _____ occurs when governments buy and sell currencies to prevent changes in the exchange rate.

12. The ideal outcome for monetary policy is called the _____.

13. The _____ is the tendency of governments to regularly use economic policy to influence elections.

14. _____ describes the tendency of governments to announce a low inflation policy but then stimulate the economy in order to reduce unemployment.

15. Countries face a choice between a(n) _____ and a(n) _____ exchange rate policy.

True-False Questions

1. T F The actions of the Federal Reserve System are determined by the president and Congress.

2. T F The opportunity cost of holding currency is the rate of inflation.

3. T F The Fed exactly determines the money supply.

4. T F The federal funds rate is the interest rate on Treasury bills.

5. T F The discount rate is set by the Fed.

6. T F The Fed affects interest rates through the purchase and sale of government securities.

7. T F Intervention in the exchange rate market always has a large effect on exchange rates.

8. T F All major central banks are independent of their government.

9. T F There is a natural tendency toward higher inflation in the political system.

10. T F Central bank independence and inflation are unrelated.

11. T F In recent times, monetary policy has regularly been used to influence elections in the United States.

12. T F Loss of international monetary independence is the most important characteristic of any flexible exchange rate system.

13. T F If there is a fixed exchange rate between the United States and Japan and the Fed raised U.S. interest rates, the Bank of Japan would have to raise Japanese interest rates.

14. T F The central bank faces a long-run tradeoff between the level of inflation and the level of unemployment.

15. T F In practice, the Fed increases the interest rate only when inflation rises.

Short-Answer Questions

1. What is central bank independence?

2. How does the Fed affect interest rates?

3. Why is the Fed referred to as the "lender of last resort"?

4. Why do some economists criticize a constant money growth rule?

5. What is the ideal outcome for monetary policy?

6. What is meant by the "gain then pain scenario"?

7. What are the two advantages of credibility for the Fed?

8. What is the political business cycle?

9. What is time inconsistency?

10. What is the cost to a central bank of adopting time-inconsistent policies?

11. Why do countries form fixed exchange rate systems?

12. What are the two basic alternatives available to a country when it chooses an exchange rate system?

13. What is the loss of international monetary independence in a fixed exchange rate system?

14. What is the current exchange rate system in Europe?

15. What monetary policy rule do the Fed and other central banks follow?

16. Why did Argentina abandon its pegged exchange rate with the United States dollar in December 2001? (Hint: See Reading the News About—The Crisis in Argentina.)

WORKING IT OUT

1. We learned in Chapter 12 that a change in the monetary policy rule toward a higher inflation target would raise real GDP in the short run and increase inflation in the long run. Let's review that material.

    a. In Figure 15.1, inflation is on the vertical axis and real GDP is on the horizontal axis. The aggregate demand (*AD*) curve is downward-sloping, and the inflation adjustment (*IA*) line is horizontal. The *AD* (original) line is drawn to intersect the *IA* line at an equilibrium where real GDP equals potential GDP.

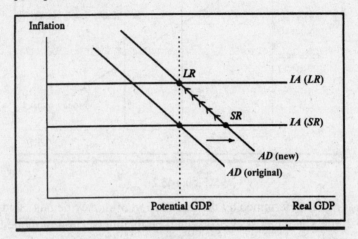

Figure 15.1

    b. A change in the monetary policy rule toward a higher inflation target shifts the *AD* curve to the right. In the short run, depicted by the intersection of *AD* (new) and *IA* (*SR*), real GDP rises with unchanged inflation. This is the "gain" part of the "gain then pain scenario."

    c. Over time, inflation rises and the *IA* line shifts up. The economy moves back toward potential GDP along the *AD* (new) curve. In the long run, at the intersection of *AD* (new) and *IA* (*LR*), inflation is higher and real GDP equals potential GDP. This is the "pain" part of the "gain then pain scenario."

2. A monetary policy rule that accurately describes central bank behavior can be depicted by the following equation (all variables in percent):

    Interest rate $= 1 + 1.5$(Inflation rate)$ + 0.5$(Gap between real GDP and potential GDP) .

    Suppose that the inflation rate equals its 2 percent target and real GDP equals potential GDP. Then the interest rate $= 1 + 1.5(2) + 0.5(0) = 1 + 3 = 4$ (percent).

    If the inflation rate is above target and/or real GDP is above potential GDP, the central bank raises the interest rate.

    If the inflation rate is below target and/or real GDP is below potential GDP, the central bank lowers the interest rate.

    This monetary policy rule shares an important property with the simpler monetary policy rule discussed in Chapter 12. When inflation rises, the central bank raises the nominal interest rate by more than one-for-one. (The coefficient on inflation is 1.5). This means that the central bank raises the real interest rate when inflation increases.

3. We have discussed how the interest rate is determined by the supply of money and the demand for money. Let's look at this graphically.

a. Figure 15.2 shows a graph with the interest rate on the vertical axis and money on the horizontal axis. Money demand is a downward-sloping line because the interest rate is the opportunity cost of holding money. When the interest rate is higher, money demand is lower because other financial assets, such as Treasury bills, pay higher rates. Money supply is vertical because it is controlled by the Fed and does not depend on the interest rate.

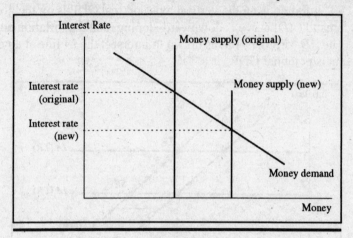

Figure 15.2

b. The interest rate is determined by the intersection of money demand and money supply. In Figure 15.2, this is at interest rate (original), at the intersection of money demand and money supply (original).

c. What happens if the Fed increases the money supply? The money supply line shifts to the right, lowering the interest rate from interest rate (original) to interest rate (new). This illustrates how the Fed lowers the interest rate by raising the money supply.

d. How does the Fed raise the interest rate? It lowers the money supply. Although this is not shown in Figure 15.2, you can see it for yourself. Draw a diagram like Figure 15.2 but instead of raising the money supply and shifting the money supply line to the right, lower the money supply and shift the money supply line to the left. The interest rate rises.

Worked Problems

1. Suppose that central bank behavior can be depicted by the following monetary policy rule (all variables in percent):

    Interest rate $= 1 + 1.5$(Inflation rate) $+ 0.5$(Gap between real GDP and potential GDP) .

    a. What is the interest rate if inflation is 4 percent and the gap is 2 percent?

    b. What is the interest rate if inflation is 2 percent and the gap is –2 percent?

Answer

a. Interest rate $= 1 + 1.5(4) + 0.5(2) = 1 + 6 + 1 = 8$ percent.

b. Interest rate $= 1 + 1.5(2) + 0.5(-2) = 1 + 3 - 1 = 3$ percent.

2.   Consider an economy characterized by the following money demand line:

	Interest Rate				
	10	**8**	**6**	**4**	**2**
Money	300	400	500	600	700

The money supply is equal to $500 billion.

a.   Draw the money demand and money supply lines. What is the interest rate?

b.   Suppose that the money supply falls to $400 billion. What is the new interest rate?

Answer

a.   Money demand is downward sloping and money supply is vertical, as shown in Figure 15.3. The interest rate, determined at the intersection of the two lines, is 6 percent.

Figure 15.3

b.   If the money supply falls to $400 billion, the money supply line shifts left and the interest rate rises to 8 percent.

PRACTICE PROBLEMS

1.   Suppose that central bank behavior can be depicted by the following monetary policy rule (all variables in percent):

Interest rate $= 1 + 1.5$(Inflation rate) $+ 0.5$(Gap between real GDP and potential GDP) .

a.   What is the interest rate if inflation is 8 percent and the gap is 0 percent?

b.   What is the interest rate if inflation is 6 percent and the gap is 2 percent?

2.   Suppose that central bank behavior can be depicted by the following monetary policy rule (all variables in percent):

Interest rate $= 1 + 1.5$(Inflation rate) $+ 0.5$(Gap between real GDP and potential GDP) .

a.   What is the interest rate if inflation is 0 percent and the gap is 0 percent?

b.   What is the interest rate if inflation is 4 percent and the gap is –2 percent?

3. Consider an economy characterized by the following money demand line:

	Interest Rate				
	6	**5**	**4**	**3**	**2**
Money	300	400	500	600	700

The money supply is equal to $400 billion. Draw the money demand and money supply lines. What is the interest rate? Suppose that the money supply rises to $600 billion. What is the new interest rate?

4. Consider an economy characterized by the following money demand line:

	Interest Rate				
	11	**9**	**7**	**5**	**3**
Money	500	600	700	800	900

The money supply is equal to $800 billion. Draw the money demand and money supply lines. What is the interest rate? Suppose that the money supply falls to $700 billion. What is the new interest rate?

CHAPTER TEST

1. The most important feature of a central bank is

   a. the discount rate.
   b. the monetary transmission channel.
   c. central bank independence.
   d. preemptive monetary strikes.

2. Who makes decisions regarding monetary policy in the United States?

   a. The president
   b. The Congress
   c. The European Central Bank
   d. The Federal Reserve System

3. When the interest rate on alternatives to holding money falls, the opportunity cost of holding money

   a. decreases and money demand rises.
   b. decreases and money demand falls.
   c. increases and money demand rises.
   d. increases and money demand falls.

4. When the Fed buys government bonds, it

   a. lowers reserves, decreasing the monetary base.
   b. lowers reserves, increasing the monetary base.
   c. raises reserves, decreasing the monetary base.
   d. raises reserves, increasing the monetary base.

5. In practice, the Fed affects the money supply by changing

   a. the required reserve ratio.
   b. the monetary base through open market operations.
   c. total government purchases.
   d. tax rates.

6.   When the Fed wants to lower the interest rate, it

   a.   buys bonds, increases the monetary base, and increases the money supply.
   b.   buys bonds, decreases the monetary base, and decreases the money supply.
   c.   sells bonds, increases the monetary base, and increases the money supply.
   d.   sells bonds, decreases the monetary base, and decreases the money supply.

7.   The discount rate is the

   a.   short-term interest rate on overnight loans between commercial banks.
   b.   long-term interest rate on loans between commercial banks.
   c.   rate that commercial banks are charged when they borrow from the Fed.
   d.   long-term interest rate on Treasury bills.

8.   When governments buy and sell currencies to prevent fluctuations in the exchange rate, this is called

   a.   exchange rate policy.
   b.   open market operations.
   c.   exchange market intervention.
   d.   currency fluctuations.

9.   The ideal outcome for monetary policy is to have

   a.   inflation low and real GDP equal to potential GDP.
   b.   inflation low and interest rates low.
   c.   inflation at the target inflation rate and real GDP equal to potential GDP.
   d.   a constant money supply.

10.   The constant money growth rule is to keep the growth rate of

   a.   the money supply fixed from year to year.
   b.   the money supply increasing from year to year.
   c.   money demand fixed from year to year.
   d.   money demand increasing from year to year.

11.   Time inconsistency describes the tendency of governments to announce a

   a.   low unemployment policy, but then stimulate the economy in order to reduce inflation.
   b.   high unemployment policy, but then stimulate the economy in order to reduce inflation.
   c.   low inflation policy, but then stimulate the economy in order to reduce unemployment.
   d.   high inflation policy, but then stimulate the economy in order to reduce unemployment.

12.   The political business cycle refers to the tendency of governments to use the following to influence elections:

   a.   the media.
   b.   fiscal or monetary policy.
   c.   open market operations.
   d.   exchange rate intervention.

13.   A political business cycle

   a.   is a common occurrence in the United States.
   b.   involves creating a boom just after an election.
   c.   is commonly observed in countries in which the central bank is highly independent of the government.
   d.   refers to the tendency of governments to regularly use economic policy to influence elections.

14.   Under the "gain then pain scenario," the government in power, looking toward the next election, would be tempted to

   a.   lower the unemployment target in order to make the economy look good at election time.
   b.   raise the unemployment target in order to make the economy look good at election time.
   c.   lower the inflation target in order to make the economy look good at election time.

d.   raise the inflation target in order to make the economy look good at election time.

15. Exchange market intervention

  a.   has a lasting effect on exchange rates in the world currency market.
  b.   occurs when governments buy and sell currencies to make changes in the exchange rates.
  c.   occurs when governments buy and sell currencies to prevent changes in the exchange rate.
  d.   accompanied by changes in interest rates has only small effects.

16. The major drawback of fixed exchange rate systems is

  a.   loss of international monetary independence.
  b.   increased exchange rate uncertainty.
  c.   lower trade.
  d.   poor monetary policies.

17. The crisis in Europe in 1992 can be explained by

  a.   time inconsistency.
  b.   loss of independence.
  c.   the political business cycle.
  d.   the constant money growth rule.

18. In practice, the Fed and other central banks increase the interest rate when

  a.   inflation rises and/or when real GDP falls below potential GDP.
  b.   inflation falls and/or when real GDP rises above potential GDP.
  c.   inflation rises and/or when real GDP rises above potential GDP.
  d.   inflation falls and/or when real GDP falls below potential GDP.

19. The Bretton Woods system

  a.   is the current flexible exchange rate system that has been in place since 1973.
  b.   is the single currency formed by eleven European countries.
  c.   was the exchange rate system until World War I.
  d.   was the exchange rate system between the end of World War II and 1971.

Use Figure 15.4 for question 20.

Figure 15.4

20. When the money supply equals $400 billion, what is the interest rate?

  a.   2 percent
  b.   3 percent
  c.   4 percent
  d.   5 percent

ANSWERS TO THE REVIEW QUESTIONS

Fill-In Questions

1.   Monetary policy

2.   Federal Reserve System; European Central Bank; Bank of Japan

3.   central bank independence

4.   interest rate

5.   opportunity cost

6.   increases

7.   federal funds rate

8.   discount rate

9.   investment; net exports

10. constant money growth rule

11. Exchange market intervention

12. Goldilocks Economy

13. political business cycle

14. Time inconsistency

15. fixed; flexible

True-False Questions

1.   **False**. The Federal Reserve System enjoys a degree of independence.

2.   **False**. The opportunity cost of holding currency is the interest rate on the alternatives.

3.   **False**. The Fed exactly determines the monetary base.

4.   **False**. The federal funds rate is the interest rate on overnight loans between banks.

5.   **True**. It is the rate that banks are charged when they borrow from the Fed.

6.   **True**. When the Fed sells (buys) securities is causes rates to rise (fall).

7.   **True**. The Fed raises the interest rate in anticipation of a rise in inflation.

8.   **False**. Some central banks are closely tied to the government.

9.   **True**. The temptation to make the economy look good at election time imparts an inflation bias to the political system.

10. **False**. Countries with more independent central banks have lower long-run inflation than countries with less independent central banks.

11. **False**. Recent evidence does not support a political business cycle for the United States.

12. **False.** Loss of international monetary independence is a characteristic of fixed exchange rate systems.

13. **True**. If the Bank of Japan did not act, the Japanese currency would fall or depreciate against the U. S. dollar.

14. **False**. There is no long-run tradeoff between inflation and unemployment.

15. **False**. The Fed also increases the interest rate when real GDP rises above potential GDP.

Short-Answer Questions

1. Central bank independence is the degree of independence the law gives the central bank from the government.

2. When the Fed wants to lower rates, it buys bonds, increasing the money supply. When the Fed wants to raise the interest rate, it sells bonds, decreasing the money supply.

3. The ability to borrow from the Fed increases people's confidence in the safety of their bank deposits.

4. Although this rule would keep inflation low in the long run, central banks and most economists feel that money demand moves around too much for such a rule to work well in practice.

5. It is to have inflation at the target inflation rate and real GDP equal to potential GDP.

6. Even though there is no long-run tradeoff between inflation and unemployment, there is a short-run gain from a higher inflation monetary policy.

7. With credibility, policy announcements by the Fed are more likely to be believed and inflation can be reduced with lower cost.

8. The political business cycle is the tendency of governments to regularly use economic policy in order to influence elections.

9. Time inconsistency is the tendency of governments to first announce a low inflation policy but later stimulate the economy to reduce unemployment.

10. The central bank will lose credibility if its policy is inconsistent.

11. One reason is the belief that flexible exchange rates, by increasing uncertainty, can interfere with trade. Another is that countries with a history of poor monetary policies can benefit from fixing their exchange rates and adopting the monetary policy of countries with a history of good monetary policies.

12. Countries are faced with a choice between a fixed and a flexible exchange rate system.

13. In a fixed exchange rate system, central banks cannot adjust interest rates to achieve domestic economic objectives, but only to set the exchange rate.

14. The *euro*, the single currency formed by eleven European countries that have permanently fixed their exchange rates by forming a monetary union, is the current exchange rate system in Europe.

15. The Fed and other central banks increase the interest rate when inflation rises and/or when real GDP rises above potential GDP and decrease the interest rate when inflation falls and/or when real GDP falls below potential GDP.

16. Interest rates rose in the United States in 2000. In order to maintain the pegged exchange rate between the Argentinean peso and the U.S. dollar, Argentina was forced to raise their interest rate, causing a recession. The high interest rate necessary to continue the peg caused the recession to worsen in 2001. During the second half of 2001, the economy contracted at an annual rate of 11 percent and unemployment was as high as 20 percent. The pegged exchange rate had become too costly, and Argentina abandoned the peg in December 2001.

SOLUTIONS TO THE PRACTICE PROBLEMS

1. a.   Interest rate $= 1 + 1.5(8) + 0.5(20) = 1 + 12 + 0 = 13$ percent.

    b.   Interest rate $= 1 + 1.5(6) + 0.5(2) = 1 + 9 + 1 = 11$ percent.

2. a.   Interest rate $= 1 + 1.5(0) + 0.5(0) = 1 + 0 + 0 = 1$ percent.

    b.   Interest rate $= 1 + 1.5(4) + 0.5(-2) = 1 + 6 - 1 = 6$ percent.

3.   When the money supply is \$400 billion, the interest rate is 5 percent. When the money supply rises to 600, the interest rate falls to 3 percent. This is illustrated in Figure 15.5.

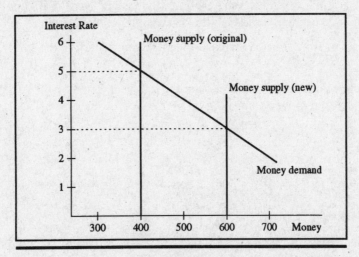

Figure 15.5

4.   When the money supply is \$800 billion, the interest rate is 5 percent. When the money supply falls to 700, the interest rate rises to 7 percent. This is illustrated in Figure 15.6.

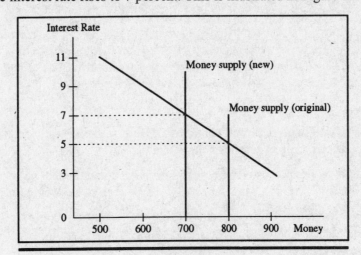

Figure 15.6

ANSWERS TO THE CHAPTER TEST

1.   c

2.   d

3.   a

4.   d

5.   b

6.   a

7.   c

8.   c

9.   c

10.   a

11.   c

12.   b

13.   d

14.   d

15.   c

16.   a

17.   b

18.   c

19.   d

20.   b

CHAPTER 16

Financial Markets

CHAPTER OVERVIEW

This chapter examines the microeconomic foundations of financial markets. The word *capital* can mean many things. First, there is physical capital. This refers to machines, factories, equipment, computers, and the like. Then, there is financial capital, mainly stocks, bonds, and other financial assets. Financial markets not only price assets, they also play a central role in the determination of interest rates. An issue related to financial capital is the construction of a financial portfolio. At the heart of portfolio management are the interrelated issues of risk, return, and diversification. Decisions concerning financial capital involve the payment and receipt of money at different points of time. Dollars to be received in the future must be converted into present dollars through the process of discounting. Finally, the foreign exchange market is discussed. Purchasing power parity (PPP) is used to show exchange rate determination over the long run.

CHAPTER REVIEW

1. **Financial capital** refers to funds that a business raises. Financial capital can be in the form of a **debt contract** like a bond or loan or in the form of an **equity contract** like a share of stock.

2. Discussions of financial capital usually center on stocks and bonds. The **return** from holding a stock is the *dividend,* or the amount the firm pays out to the owners of the stock each year, plus the **capital gain** or **capital loss**, the increase or decrease in the price of the stock during the year. The return and dividend can be expressed as a percent of the stock price. In this form they are referred to as the **rate of return** and the **dividend yield**. Stocks are often judged, in part, by their **price-earnings ratio,** the price of the stock divided by the annual earnings per share. (**Earnings** is another word for the accounting profits of the firm.)

    The issuer of bonds makes periodic payments of a fixed amount (the **coupon**) to the bondholders. At the **maturity date,** the **face value** of the bond is paid. It is important to note that there is an inverse relationship between a bond's price and its **yield**. Assume that you paid $100 for a bond that, after one year, will repay you the $100 plus $5 interest. Now assume that you had to pay only $95 for the same bond. Clearly the yield is greater. Not only do you get $5 interest, you also earn the $5 difference between the price you paid and the face value of the bond. The price of the bond went down and the yield went up.

    Decisions about purchasing either physical capital or financial capital involve comparing payments of money at different points in time. A problem is that future dollars are worth less than current dollars. Ask yourself, would you rather have a dollar today or a dollar next week or next year? Future dollars must be translated into current terms before a decision can be reached. The value of the future in the present is called the present discounted value.

3. The return on stocks and bonds is also dependent on their riskiness. Most individuals are risk averse. If offered the same return on two alternative investments with different risks, most people would select the less risky of the two. Stated another way, people need greater **expected returns**, or the returns with the different gains or losses weighted according to how probable they are, to take on more risk. This is shown by the **equilibrium risk-return relationship**.

A way of dealing with risk is through **portfolio diversification**. This reduces the risk associated with holding any one specific stock. *Index funds* are an example of extensive diversification. However, diversification does not remove **systematic risk**, which is due to the ups and downs in the economy.

Because stock markets have many participants and ease of entry and exit, many economists argue that stock prices adjust to new information so rapidly that profit opportunities are eliminated. This is the **efficient market hypothesis**.

4. The **exchange rate** is the price of one currency in terms of another in the **foreign exchange market**. The standard supply and demand model can be used for studying the determination of the exchange rate.

5. The *law of one price* is a theory that says that exchange rates are determined so that the price for the same good is about the same in different countries. This notion is called **purchasing power parity (PPP)**. PPP works well in the long run, but less so in the short run. Furthermore, it works better for *tradable goods*, where transport costs are low compared to the value of the good, than for nontradable goods, where transport costs are high.

6. In the short run, exchange rates often differ from what might be expected under purchasing power parity. The primary reason for these deviations is that the rate of return may vary in different countries. International investors are able to move money between financial assets in different countries.

ZEROING IN

1. Suppose that the market price of a one-year bond that pays $100 at maturity plus $5 interest is currently $90. The yield is $[(\$105 - \$90)/\$90] = 16.67$ percent. Now suppose that the demand for these bonds increases (the demand curve shifts to the right) because the Federal Reserve decided that this would be good for the economy and, as a result of this action, the price rises to $95. The yield from a purchase of a similar bond is now $[(\$105 - \$95)/\$95] = 10.53$ percent. Thus, when bond prices rise, the yield falls—an inverse relationship.

2. Many companies, at least in their early stages of existence, do not pay dividends. Young companies tend to reinvest the money that would have been used for dividends. If this is the case, why do investors buy their stock? Dividends are not the only component of the returns to holding stock. Investors who buy the stock of companies that do not pay dividends are expecting a return on the appreciation of the stock price. While some investors are only interested in dividend pay out, others are interested in stock appreciation.

3. Economists generally assume that most people are risk averse. This is to say, if faced with two alternatives that offer the same return but one has more risk than the other, a person will always select the less risky alternative. However, a risk-averse person will take on the risky alternative if they are offered more return. How much more? This is dependent on a person's relative subjective values attached to risk and return. Using the concepts from Chapter 5, risk provides disutility to an investor. Risk by itself makes a person worse off. Return offers positive utility. As such, return is needed to offset the disutility that additional risk would create.

4. The foreign exchange market is just like any other market that economists might study. There is a demand for a country's currency and there is a supply of a country's currency. The resulting market price is called the exchange rate. This price, or alternatively, the underlying demand and supply relationship, is largely affected by people's expectations concerning the rate of return from holding a country's currency and by the prices of goods and services in the trading countries.

ACTIVE REVIEW

Fill-In Questions

1. Machines, factories, and computers used in production are referred to as _____.

2. _____ may take the form of a debt contract or an equity contract.

3. The sum of the _____ and the _____ is the _____ from holding a share of stock.

4. The _____ of a company are the same as its accounting profits. Often, stock tables list the _____ as information.

5. The amount that an issuer of a bond agrees to pay the bondholder each year is the _____. These payments end and the principal is paid back on the _____. The amount of principal paid on this date is the _____.

6. The _____ is defined as the annual rate of return on a bond if the bond were held to maturity. There is a(n) _____ relationship between the yield and the price of a bond.

7. Many people are described as _____ because they do not like uncertainty.

8. The _____ on an investment weighs the different gains or losses according to their probability of occurrence.

9. There is a positive relationship between risk and return. This is captured by the _____.

10. Investors use _____ to minimize risk and maximize return. However, _____ cannot be removed by this form of portfolio management.

11. The _____ prices one currency in terms of another.

12. _____ is the theory of exchange rate determination that comes from the *law of one price*.

13. _____ and _____ are two things that often cause PPP to not explain exchange rate determination in the short run.

14. By using _____, investors are able to reduce the overall risk of their portfolios.

15. The _____ suggests that profit opportunities in financial markets from new information will not last for very long.

True-False Questions

1. T F   Financial capital, like stock for example, appreciates in value.

2. T F   Shares of stock are a form of debt contract.

3. T F   A bond is a form of debt contract.

4. T F   Stocks experience only capital gains.

5. T F   A stock's rate of return and its dividend yield are expressed as percents of the dividends paid.

6. T F   The coupon and the face value of a bond are the same thing.

7. T F There is an inverse relationship between a bond's yield and its price.

8. T F Portfolio diversification is a way to get rid of systematic risk.

9. T F The return on a portfolio is always guaranteed.

10. T F Some feel that the stock market adjusts to new information so fast that profit opportunities are eliminated.

11. T F The theory of purchasing power parity works very well in the short run.

12. T F Profit opportunities in financial markets that come from new information last for extended periods of time.

Short-Answer Questions

1. How are debt contracts and equity contracts similar and how are they different?

2. What is the return from holding a stock? Can this be expressed relative to the price of a share?

3. What is the purpose of the maturity date of a bond?

4. Is there a relationship between bond prices and bond yields?

5. What does it mean to be risk averse?

6. Why is expected return important in making investment decisions?

7. What is the purpose of portfolio diversification, and what does it do to systematic risk?

8. Briefly describe the efficient market hypothesis.

9. Explain the *law of one price* and how it relates to the theory of purchasing power parity?

10. What is the equilibrium risk-return relationship?

WORKING IT OUT

This chapter has brought out the role of uncertainty in decision making. Uncertainty is implicit in the idea of an expected return. Many financial choices have uncertain outcomes, and you, as an investor, need to get some handle on the meaning of these possibilities. Also, a better understanding of the underlying determinants of the exchange rate is very useful in understanding the role of the U.S. economy in a global market place.

Worked Problems

1. Assume that you have $10,000 you want to invest. Suppose your stockbroker tells you of a stock that pays a 20 percent dividend. There is a 40 percent chance that the share price will fall by 50 percent; on the other hand, there is a 60 percent chance that the share price will rise by 50 percent. What is the expected value?

Answer

First, calculate the outcome possibilities. In each case you will get a 20 percent dividend, so

$10,000 × 0.20 = $2,000

But in the first case, you lose half your original investment. Thus,

$10,000 × 0.50 = -$5,000

In the second case, however, the opposite will occur:

$10,000 \times 0.50 = \$5,000$

If the first case happens, you will have a net loss of $3,000. However, if the second case occurs, you will have a net gain of $7,000. Over many times, what will the outcome be on average?

$(-\$3,000 \times 0.40) + (\$7,000 \times 0.60) = \$3,000$

This is the expected value.

2.   Assume that a friend asks you to buy a bond that he or she just purchased. (Your friend just wrecked her car and needs some money fast!) The bond pays $1,000 a year from now with a $100 coupon, for a yield of 10 percent. Your friend is asking $975. What should you do?

Answer

First, calculate the bond price based on the information. (See Table 16.1 in the text for the formula.)

Bond price $= [(\$100)/(1+0.10)] + [\$1,000/(1+0.10)] = (\$90.90) + (\$909.09) = \$999.99$

At a 10 percent rate, the price of receiving $1,100 a year from now is $999.99. Your friend wants only $975. Buy! You can pay less than the calculated bond price, thereby earning a higher yield.

3.   Assume the United States (domestic) has a price level of 1 dollar and Japan (foreign) has a price level of 100 yen.

a.   What is the purchasing power exchange rate?

b.   What is the new purchasing power exchange rate if there is a 20 percent inflation in Japan?

Answer

a.   The purchasing power exchange rate is determined by the formula $E \times P = P^*$, where E is the exchange rate, P is the domestic price level, and P^* is the foreign price level. Substituting for P and P^*, and then solving for E, the purchasing power exchange rate is 100 yen per dollar.

b.   If the Japanese inflation rate is 20 percent, then P^* rises to 120. Again, using the formula in (a), the new purchasing power exchange rate is 120 yen per dollar.

PRACTICE PROBLEMS

1.   Assume that you have $5,000 to invest. A good friend tells you of a great investment opportunity in the stock market. The stock pays a 10 percent dividend, and there is a 30 percent chance that it will double in price. However, there is also a 70 percent chance that the stock price will fall by half. What is the expected value of this once-in-a-lifetime opportunity?

2.

a.   What will be the price of a $6,000 bond that has a coupon of $500 for two years? Assume an interest rate of 6 percent.

b.   What happens if the interest rate rises to 10 percent?

3.   Assume that the U.S. (domestic) price level is 100 dollars and the German (foreign) price level is 500 marks.

a.   What is the purchasing power exchange rate?

b.   Assume there is 25 percent inflation in the United States, *ceteris paribus*. What is the new purchasing power exchange rate?

CHAPTER TEST

1.   An example of an equity contract is

   a.   a bond.
   b.   a loan.
   c.   the depreciation of physical capital.
   d.   a share of stock.

2.   When owners of stock sell it for less than they paid for it,

   a.   they earn a capital gain.
   b.   they suffer a capital loss.
   c.   they increase their return.
   d.   they will still receive dividends.

3.   The dividend plus the capital gain is the _____ from holding a stock.

   a.   coupon
   b.   return
   c.   price-earnings ratio
   d.   dividend yield

4.   At the maturity date of a bond,

   a.   coupon payments stop and the principal is paid.
   b.   the principal is paid, but coupon payments continue.
   c.   the principal is paid, coupon payments stop, and a stock certificate is issued.
   d.   dividend payments stop and the principal is paid.

5.   There is _____ relationship between bond prices and bond yields.

   a.   an inverse
   b.   a positive
   c.   a proportional
   d.   no

6.   Discounting

   a.   converts present payments into future values.
   b.   converts future payments into present values.
   c.   is never used in investment decisions.
   d.   converts future payments into other future payments.

7.   A bungee jumper who ties two ropes to her legs before jumping off the tower is _____ compared to one who ties only one rope to his leg.

   a.   a risk lover
   b.   thinking less about risk
   c.   risk averse
   d.   discounting

8.   The expected return from an investment

   a.   accounts for the probabilities of alternative outcomes.
   b.   is always equal to an investor's opportunity cost.
   c.   is what an investor must earn to make a profit.
   d.   is an unnecessary calculation because investing is very certain.

9.   In equilibrium, we expect to see a _____ relationship between risk and return.

   a.   negative
   b.   positive
   c.   proportional
   d.   constant

10. Systematic risk is

    a. removed through portfolio diversification.
    b. due to the ups and downs in the economy and affects all stocks to some degree.
    c. what the first bungee jumper in question 7 is trying to avoid.
    d. never a factor in investing.

11. The efficient market hypothesis is

    a. based on asymmetric information.
    b. never observed because financial markets are known to work slowly.
    c. the idea that there is an elimination of profit opportunities in financial markets as prices adjust quickly to new information.
    d. held to be false by all economists.

12. Exchange rates are determined

    a. in the labor market.
    b. by the law of diminishing returns.
    c. in the foreign exchange market.
    d. by government decree.

13. Purchasing power parity suggests that, over the long run,

    a. nontradable goods will have the same price in different countries.
    b. tradable goods will have different prices in different countries.
    c. tradable goods will have the same price in different countries.
    d. nontradable goods eventually become tradable goods.

14. Due to risk aversion,

    a. investors need to be compensated to take on extra risk.
    b. investors will pay for extra risk.
    c. there is no relationship between risk and return.
    d. new risk guarantees more return.

15. With more inflation in Japan than in the United States, *ceteris paribus*,

    a. the yen will appreciate.
    b. the dollar will depreciate.
    c. the exchange rate will not change.
    d. the yen will depreciate.

ANSWERS TO THE REVIEW QUESTIONS

Fill-In Questions

1. physical capital

2. Financial capital

3. dividend; capital gain; return

4. earnings; price-earnings ratio

5. coupon; maturity date; face value

6. yield; inverse

7. risk averse

8. expected return

9. equilibrium risk-return relationship

10. portfolio diversification; systematic risk

11. foreign exchange market

12. Purchasing power parity (PPP)

13. Inflation rate; differences in rates of return

14. diversification

15. efficient market hypothesis

True-False Questions

1. **True**. A stock price can rise and thereby appreciate.

2. **False**. They are a form of equity contract.

3. **True**. A bond is an IOU and, therefore, a form of debt.

4. **False**. Capital losses can also occur if stock prices fall.

5. **False**. Both are expressed as percents of the price of a stock.

6. **False**. The coupon is the fixed payment for each period. The face value is the principal amount due at the maturity date.

7. **True**. When the price of a bond falls, the difference between the price and the face value increases, and so the yield increases.

8. **False**. Systematic risk is that component of risk that cannot be dealt with through diversification.

9. **False**. The return can only be estimated by the expected value.

10. **True**. This is a form of the efficient market hypothesis.

11. **False**. PPP works best in the long run. Inflation rates and differences in rates of return affect the short-run ability of PPP to work very well.

12. **False**. The efficient market hypothesis argues that this would not be the case. Financial markets process information rapidly as buyers and sellers try to exploit the profit opportunities. As a result, profit opportunities do not last very long.

Short-Answer Questions

1. Both debt contracts and equity contracts are tools for raising financial capital. With a debt contract, money is borrowed, interest is paid, and the principal is repaid at some future date. An equity contract is an exchange of ownership for funds. Equity holders receive profits through the payment of dividends.

2. The return from holding a stock is the dividend plus the capital gain or loss. The return is expressed relative to the price, which is the return divided by the price of a share.

3. The maturity date is the date on which the principal is repaid to the bondholder. The difference between the date of purchase of the bond and the maturity date is the period over which interest payments are received.

4. Yes. There is an inverse relationship. As bond prices fall, the yields rise.

5. Risk aversion means that people will choose the less risky of two alternatives offering the same return.

6. Often the return from an investment is uncertain. Several outcomes are possible, each with a different probability of occurring. The expected return is created by weighting the different outcomes according to their probabilities.

7. Portfolio diversification reduces the risk associated with holding any one stock. However, it does not remove systematic risk. This is the risk due to the ups and downs in the economy, which affect all stocks to some degree.

8. The efficient market hypothesis states that there is an elimination of profit opportunities in financial markets as prices quickly adjust to new information.

9. The same tradable commodity will sell for about the same price in different countries. PPP is a theory that exchange rates are determined in such a way that the prices of tradable goods in different countries are the same when measured in the same currency.

10. Because investors are risk averse, they need a higher expected return to induce the purchase of a financial investment with higher risk. Therefore, the equilibrium risk-return relationship reflects a positive relationship between expected return and risk.

SOLUTIONS TO THE PRACTICE PROBLEMS

1. If the first case occurs, you will gain a dividend of

$$\$500 = (\$5,000 \times 0.10)$$

and a capital gain of

$$\$5,000 = (\$5,000 \times 1.00)$$

for a total of $5,500. If the second case occurs, you still get the dividend of $500, but you will also suffer a loss of

$$-\$2,500 = (\$5,000 \times 0.50)$$

for a total of –$2,000.

The expected value of your opportunity is

$$(\$5,500 \times 0.30) + (-\$2,000 \times 0.70) = \$250.$$

2. a. Using the formula in Table 16.1 in the text,

$$\text{Bond price} = [(\$500/(1+0.06)] + [\$500/(1+0.06)^2] + [\$6,000/(1+0.06)^2]$$
$$= \$471.70 + \$445.00 + 5,339.98 = \$6,256.68.$$

   b. With an interest rate of 10 percent, the bond price will be $5,826.44. The price will fall.

3. a. The exchange rate is 5 marks per dollar.

   b. The new exchange rate is 4 marks per dollar.

ANSWERS TO THE CHAPTER TEST

1. d

2. b

3. b

4. a

5. a

6.   b

7.   c

8.   a

9.   b

10.   b

11.   c

12.   c

13.   c

14.   a

15.   d

APPENDIX TO CHAPTER 16

Present Discounted Value

OVERVIEW

One of the characteristics of investing in financial and physical capital, as well as many other economic decisions, is the fact that there is the anticipation of *future* returns in the form of revenue or benefits. Yet, most of the expenditures for such investments are made upfront or at the *present* time. A problem is that individuals prefer dollars received today over dollars that will be received tomorrow. So, how do you know to invest? The first step is to convert or discount *future dollars* into *present dollars*. The end result of this conversion is called the present discounted value.

ZEROING IN

1. The concept of discounting is based on the simple notion that a dollar in the future is worth less than a dollar today. Imagine the following situation. Your economics professor offers you (because you are the best student in the class) $100 today or $100 a year from now. With total honesty, which would you choose? People generally have what economists call a positive time preference—you will pick the $100 now. Instead of waiting, you could purchase things and derive utility from them now or you could invest the money and earn interest. But what if the offer is $100 now or $110 a year from now? Here, waiting provides a benefit of $10. You may still opt for the $100. However, if your professor continued to increase the future payoff, it would eventually reach a point where you would wait.

    This could be described another way. Suppose the offer was $90 now or $100 a year from now? Again there is a benefit from waiting. You may still feel that $90 today is worth more than the future payment of $100. But the present value could be lowered until you did not know which one to take—both would be equally desirable to you.

2. The formula for finding the present discounted value (*PDV*) of a future amount (*F*) received one year from now is $PDV = F/(1+r)$. This formula can be expanded to determine the present discounted value for future amounts received over many future years as well. Regardless of the length of the chain, it is important to see the role played by the interest rate or the discount rate (*r*) found in the denominator. What rate should you choose? Well, it depends on many things including what rate you could have made on your next best investment alternative—your opportunity cost. Furthermore, you should note that as the discount rate rises, the discounted present value falls. This is to say, as the interest rate rises, the value of the future falls.

ACTIVE REVIEW

Fill-In Questions

1. The process of converting a future payment into a present amount is called _____. The value in the present is called the _____. Discounting requires the use of a(n) _____.

2. As the interest rate rises, the discounted present value _____.

WORKED PROBLEM

1.

    a.   What is the present value of $5,000 three years from now at a discount rate of 10 percent?

    b.   What would be the present value of $5,000 in each of the next three years?

    c.   What would happen to the present value in 1a. if the interest rate fell to 5 percent?

Answer

1.

    a.   Using the formula in the Appendix to Chapter 16,

$$PDV = [\$5,000/(1+0.10)^3] = \$5,000/1.331 = \$3,756.57$$

    b. $$PDV = [\$5,000/(1+0.10)][\$5,000/(1+0.10)^2][\$5,000/(1+0.10)^3]$$

$$= \$4,545.45 + \$4,132.23 + \$3,756.57$$

$$= \$12,434.25 \,.$$

    c. $$PDV = [\$5,000/(1+0.05)3] = \$5,000/1.1576 = \$4,319.28$$

    The present value rises as the interest rate falls from 10 percent to 5 percent

PRACTICE PROBLEM

1.

    a.   What is the present value of $4,000 to be received two years from now? Assume an interest rate of 4 percent.

    b.   What is the present value of $4,000 to be received in each of the next three years? Again assume an interest rate of 4 percent.

    c.   What happens to the present value in 1a. if the interest rate rise to 8 percent?

ANSWERS TO THE REVIEW QUESTIONS

Fill-In Questions

1.   discounting; present discounted; discount rate

2.   falls

SOLUTIONS TO THE PRACTICE PROBLEM

1.   a.   Using the general formula in the Appendix to Chapter 16,

$$PDV = [\$4,000/(1+0.04)^2] = \$3,698.22$$

    b. $$PDV = [\$4,000/(1+0.04)] + [\$4,000/1+0.04)^2] + [\$4,000/1+0.04)^3]$$

$$= \$3,846.15 + \$3,698.22 + \$3,555.98$$

$$= \$11,100.35$$

    c. $$PDV = [\$4,000/(1+0.08)^2] = \$3,429.36 \,.$$ The present value falls as the interest rate rises from 4 percent to 8 percent.

PART 3

Sample Test (Chapters 11–16): Economic Fluctuations and Macroeconomic Policy

1. According to real business cycle theory, economic fluctuations are caused by fluctuations in
   a. the money supply.
   b. aggregate demand.
   c. real GDP.
   d. potential GDP.
2. According to the consumption function, as income increases,
   a. consumption increases by the same amount.
   b. consumption increases by a greater amount.
   c. consumption increases by a smaller amount.
   d. consumption decreases by a smaller amount.
3. An increase in the marginal propensity to consume results in the aggregate expenditure line
   a. getting steeper.
   b. shifting up in a parallel direction.
   c. getting flatter.
   d. shifting down in a parallel direction.
4. One-year-ahead forecasts for real GDP
   a. are usually equal to the current year's GDP.
   b. are usually equal to a weighted average of real GDP over the past five years.
   c. reflect what forecasters believe will happen to the different spending components of real GDP.
   d. reflect forecasters' beliefs about the determinants of potential GDP over the next year.

Use Table 1 for question 5.

Income (Y) (in billions of dollars)	Consumption (C) (in billions of dollars)
0	250
500	500
1,000	750
1,500	1,000
2,000	1,200
2,500	1,500

Table 1

5.   Suppose investment *I* is $400 billion, government purchases *G* are $200 billion, and net exports *X* are $200 billion. Using Table 1, at what level of income does spending balance occur?

   a. $1,000 billion
   b. $1,500 billion
   c. $2,000 billion
   d. $2,500 billion

6.   If the marginal propensity to consume is 0.75 and investment declines by $5 billion, then real GDP will decline by

   a. $3.75 billion.
   b. $5.00 billion.
   c. $6.67 billion.
   d. $20.0 billion.

7.   According to the aggregate demand (*AD*) curve, there is a

   a.   positive relation between inflation and real GDP.
   b.   negative relation between inflation and real GDP.
   c.   positive relation between consumption and real GDP.
   d.   negative relation between consumption and real GDP.

8.   An increase in the real interest rate leads to a(n)

   a.   increase in both exports and imports.
   b.   increase in exports and a decrease in imports.
   c.   decrease in exports and an increase in imports.
   d.   decrease in both exports and imports.

Use Table 2 for question 9.

Inflation	Real Interest Rate Policy Rule A	Real Interest Rate Policy Rule B
0	3	5
3	5	7
6	7	9
9	9	11
12	11	13

Table 2

9.   Suppose the government changes its monetary policy rule from policy rule A to policy rule B. How would this change affect the expenditure line and the *AD* curve?

   a.   The expenditure line shifts up, and the *AD* curve shifts to the right.
   b.   The expenditure line shifts down, and the *AD* curve shifts to the left.
   c.   The expenditure line shifts up, and the *AD* curve shifts to the left.
   d.   The expenditure line shifts down, and the *AD* curve shifts to the right.

10.   The expenditure line shifts *down* when

   a.   government purchases rise.
   b.   investment falls.
   c.   taxes are cut.
   d.   net exports rise.

11. The situation that occurs when inflation is up and real GDP is down is called
    a. disinflation.
    b. a supply shock.
    c. deflation.
    d. stagflation.

12. Which of the following is *not* one of the important features of the inflation adjustment (*IA*) line?
    a. The *IA* line is flat.
    b. The *IA* line moves over time when real GDP departs from potential GDP.
    c. The *IA* line is upward-sloping.
    d. The *IA* line shifts with changes in expectations or raw materials prices.

13. When real GDP falls and inflation rises simultaneously, it is called
    a. disinflation.
    b. a supply shock.
    c. deflation.
    d. stagflation.

14. The inflation adjustment (*IA*) line will move up if there is a(n)
    a. decrease in real GDP.
    b. increase in potential GDP.
    c. increase in expected inflation.
    d. decrease in expected inflation.

15. If real GDP stays below potential GDP,
    a. the *AD* curve will begin to shift to the right.
    b. the *AD* curve will begin to shift to the left.
    c. the *IA* line will shift up.
    d. the *IA* line will shift down.

Use Figure 1 for question 16.

Figure 1

16. Starting with real GDP equal to potential GDP, Figure 1 depicts the response of the economy to a(n)
    a. oil price shock.
    b. increase in government purchases.
    c. change in the monetary policy rule to a lower inflation target.

d.   increase in potential GDP.

Use Figure 2 for question 17.

Figure 2

17. Starting with real GDP equal to potential GDP, Figure 2 depicts the response of the economy to a(n)

    a.   oil price shock.
    b.   increase in government purchases.
    c.   change in the monetary policy rule to a lower inflation target.
    d.   increase in potential GDP.

18. When tax revenues are equal to spending, there is a

    a.   budget deficit.
    b.   budget surplus.
    c.   budget supplement.
    d.   balanced budget.

19. The budget deficit and real GDP are

    a.   positively related.
    b.   negatively related.
    c.   unrelated.
    d.   either positively or negatively related depending on other factors.

20. The instruments of fiscal policy are

    a.   government purchases, transfer payments, and interest payments.
    b.   government purchases, interest payments, and taxes.
    c.   government purchases, transfer payments, and taxes.
    d.   transfer payments, interest payments, and taxes.

Use Table 3 for questions 21 and 22.

Surplus (millions of dollars)	170	190	210	230	250
Real GDP (billions of dollars)	6,000	6,200	6,400	6,600	6,800

Table 3

21. What is the structural surplus in this economy when real GDP equals $6,400 billion and potential GDP equals $6,000 billion?

    a. $170 million
    b. $210 million
    c. $40 million
    d. $380 million

22. What is the cyclical surplus in this economy when real GDP equals $6,600 billion and potential GDP equals $6,200 billion?

    a. $190 million
    b. $230 million
    c. $40 million
    d. $420 million

23. The central bank of the United States is the

    a.   Unites States Treasury.
    b.   Bank of America.
    c.   Federal Reserve System.
    d.   International Monetary Fund.

24. The most important feature of a central bank is

    a.   the members of the Board of Governors.
    b.   central bank independence.
    c.   the ability to change the discount rate.
    d.   the ability to print money.

25. When the Fed wants to raise the interest rate,

    a.   it buys bonds.
    b.   it sells bonds.
    c.   it increases the money supply.
    d.   it increases the monetary base.

26. Changes in the instruments of fiscal policy that do not require legislative action are referred to as

    a.   automatic stabilizers.
    b.   discretionary.
    c.   supplementals.
    d.   proposals.

27. The constant money growth rule, advocated by monetarists, is to keep the growth rate of

    a.   the money supply fixed from year to year.
    b.   the money supply increasing from year to year.
    c.   money demand fixed from year to year.
    d.   money demand increasing from year to year.

28. Which of the following is an example of financial capital?

    a. Car
    b. Vault
    c. Cash
    d. Office building
    e. Computer

29. Systematic risk is

    a. risk that cannot be avoided by diversifying within the market.
    b. avoided by diversifying within the market.
    c. avoided by portfolio rearrangement.
    d. called market risk.

30. Economists believe that the price of a share of stock contains all the known current information about a firm because

    a. there are barriers to entry in the stock market.
    b. stockbrokers have secret information.
    c. the stock market is an efficient market.
    d. the costs of entering the marketplace are very high.
    e. the government regulates the stock market.

ANSWERS TO THE SAMPLE TEST

1. d
2. c
3. a
4. c
5. c
6. d
7. b
8. c
9. b
10. b
11. d
12. c
13. d
14. c
15. d
16. b
17. a
18. d
19. b

20. c
21. a
22. c
23. c
24. b
25. b
26. a
27. a
28. c
29. a
30. c

PART 4

Trade and Global Markets

Chapter 17 looks at economic growth around the world. Predictions of growth theory work better for industrialized countries than for developing countries, and this chapter considers developing countries in more detail, examining how their policy choices, both good and bad, have affected their growth rate. Chapter 18 examines the gains from international trade. Gains from trade are related to comparative advantage and economies of scale, and the chapter describes how the gains from international trade can be measured.

Chapter 19 covers international trade policy, including the effects of current and historical trade restrictions, the arguments in favor of trade restrictions, and policies to reduce trade barriers. Transition economies, including centrally planned economies, are the subject of chapter 20.

CHAPTER 17

Economic Growth Around the World

CHAPTER OVERVIEW

We have studied how labor, capital, and technology combine to produce economic growth. Now we turn our attention to economic growth around the world and see why some countries become rich while others remain poor. We start by looking at the predictions of growth theory and see that, while they hold for states of the United States and for industrialized countries, they do not work well for developing countries. We then consider developing countries in more detail and see how obstacles to the spread and adoption of new technology and obstacles to increases in capital per worker have hindered their growth. In this context, we look at issues ranging from restrictions on private enterprise and the importance of education to the role of international financial institutions. Finally, we study inward-looking versus outward-looking economic policies, and see that countries that have adopted outward-looking policies have experienced higher growth rates.

CHAPTER REVIEW

1. The *catch-up phenomenon* is that countries with low income (GDP) per capita will grow faster than, and therefore catch up to, countries with high income per capita. If technological advances can spread easily and if capital and labor have diminishing returns, then economic growth theory predicts catch-up.

2. **Economic development** attempts to explain why poor countries do not develop faster and to find policies to help them develop faster. There are large income disparities between relatively well-off countries, or *industrialized countries*, and the relatively poor countries, or **developing countries**. Developing countries are also called *less-developed countries*, or LDCs. *Newly industrialized countries*, such as Korea, are relatively poor countries that are growing rapidly whereas *countries in transition*, such as Poland, are relatively poor countries that are moving from central planning to market economies.

3. There are geographical patterns to economic development. The *North-South problem* describes the pattern that countries in the North are relatively rich and those in the South, with the exception of Australia and New Zealand, are relatively poor.

4. We learned in Chapter 9 that technological progress is necessary for sustained economic growth. In order to understand why some countries grow faster than others, it is natural to focus on the spread of technology.

    a. Why did the "miracle" of economic growth begin in Europe in the 1700s? The removal of restrictions on private enterprise seems to be the key. For the first time, entrepreneurs had the freedom to start businesses, hire workers, and ship products to market without political or religious restrictions.

    b. Why do poor countries remain poor? The most important reason seems to be restrictions on private enterprise. There is a tremendous amount of regulation in most developing countries. This regulation makes it so costly to start business enterprises that a huge **informal economy**, consisting of illegal businesses, has emerged. The centrally planned economies of the former Soviet Union, central Europe, and China also placed pervasive restrictions on entrepreneurs, which helps to explain both their large informal economies and their slow growth.

    c.   Development of human capital, better educated and more highly skilled workers, is another important facet of technology. The newly industrialized countries, the developing countries that have been catching up most rapidly, have strong educational systems.

5.   Increasing the amount of capital per worker, as we also learned in Chapter 9, is the second way to promote economic growth. Obstacles to increasing capital per worker can prevent developing countries from catching up to industrialized countries.

    a.   High population growth in many developing countries is an obstacle to increasing the amount of capital per worker. With high population growth rates, more investment is necessary to increase, or even to maintain, the level of capital per worker. Remember that national saving equals investment plus net exports. In most developing countries, national saving is low (less than investment) and thus net exports are negative.

    b.   When net exports are negative, foreign investment from abroad becomes the major source of capital formation. Foreign investment consists of **foreign direct investment**, when a foreign firm invests in more than 10 percent of the ownership of a business in another country; **portfolio investment**, when the ownership is less than 10 percent; and loans from banks and governments.

    c.   The **International Monetary Fund (IMF)** and the **World Bank** make loans to developing countries, and the IMF also makes loans to economies in transition. The IMF often tries to induce countries to make difficult economic reforms by making its loans dependent, or conditional, on the reforms; this is the idea of *conditionality*. There has been a lot of controversy in the past few years over whether the IMF goes too far with its conditions, especially during the financial crisis in East Asia. Most of the loans made by the World Bank are for specific projects.

ZEROING IN

1.   Understanding the catch-up phenomenon is the key to understanding the material in this chapter. We illustrate the catch-up phenomenon in Figure 17.1, where the *level* of income per capita is on the horizontal axis and the *growth rate* of income per capita is on the vertical axis. The **catch-up line** is a downward-sloping line that depicts the relation between the level and the growth rate of income per capita. A country on the upper left-hand part of the catch-up line, such as point *A*, is poor but growing rapidly. Although it has a relatively low level of income per capita, it has a relatively high growth rate of income per capita. A country on the lower right-hand part of the catch-up line, such as point *B*, is rich but growing more slowly. Although it has a relatively high level of income per capita, it has a relatively low growth rate of income per capita. The line is called the catch-up line because relatively poor countries are growing faster than, or catching up to, relatively well-off countries.

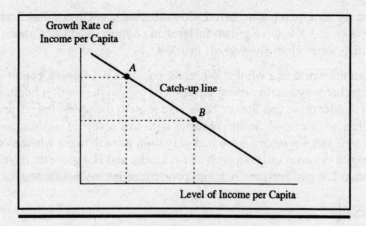

Figure 17.1

2. Why does economic growth theory predict that poor countries will grow faster than rich countries? There are two parts to the answer: diffusion of technology and diminishing returns to labor and capital.

    a. A major difference between rich and poor countries is that rich countries, with high productivity, utilize advanced technology, whereas poor countries, with low productivity, use more basic technology. If the spread of technology is not difficult, countries with low productivity will adopt the more advanced technology, thereby raising their productivity. As we know from the growth accounting formula, increasing technology would raise the growth rates of the poor countries, narrowing the gap between rich and poor. In other words, poor countries would catch up to rich countries.

    b. Think about a poor country with a low level of capital per worker. While this country exhibits diminishing returns to labor, it has so little capital that diminishing returns to capital have not set in. In the absence of obstacles, investment would be very profitable, and capital per worker would grow rapidly. According to the growth accounting formula, this would raise output per worker. In contrast, think about a rich country that has a high level of capital per worker and that exhibits diminishing returns to capital. This country would gain relatively little from investment that increases the amount of capital per worker. The flow of investment causes the poor country to grow faster than, or catch up to, the rich country.

    c. It is important to remember that growth theory does not predict catch-up under all circumstances. If there are obstacles to the spread of technology and/or obstacles to raising the level of capital per worker, the mechanism described above will not have the chance to operate and catch-up will not occur.

3. How does the catch-up prediction accord with the facts? We will look at three cases: states within the United States, industrialized countries, and the world as a whole.

    a. Suppose you think of the states within the United States as 50 different countries with a common language, a single currency, and free movement of capital and technology. Under these conditions, growth theory predicts catch-up, and that is exactly what has happened. Income per capita in states such as Florida and Texas, which were relatively poor in 1880, has grown quickly relative to income per capita in states such as California and Nevada, which were relatively well off in 1880.

    b. A similar picture emerges when we look at industrialized countries since 1960. Although capital and technology are not as mobile between industrialized countries as between states within the United States, there are relatively few obstacles to their diffusion. In accord with growth theory, catch-up has occurred. Countries such as Greece and Portugal, which were relatively poor in 1960, have grown faster than countries such as Canada and the United States, which were relatively well off in 1960.

c.   What about the world as a whole? When we consider developing countries, obstacles to the spread of technology and to raising the level of capital per worker become much more important. Under these conditions, economic growth theory no longer predicts catch-up, and, in fact, it has not occurred. Some countries with low levels of income per capita in 1960, such as Korea and Singapore, have had very high growth rates, whereas others with equally low per capita incomes in 1960, such as Sri Lanka and Bangladesh, have had very low growth rates. The gap between rich and poor countries has not closed.

ACTIVE REVIEW

Fill-In Questions

1.   The _____ phenomenon is that countries with low income per capita will grow faster than countries with high income per capita.

2.   _____ attempts to explain why poor countries do not develop faster.

3.   _____ countries are relatively well off.

4.   _____ countries are relatively poor.

5.   Developing countries are also called _____.

6.   _____ countries, such as Korea, are relatively poor countries that are growing rapidly.

7.   _____ are relatively poor countries that are moving from central planning to market economies.

8.   The _____ describes the pattern that most countries in the North are relatively rich and those in the South are relatively poor.

9.   The illegal sector is called the _____ economy.

10.   Foreign investment consists of _____, _____, and _____.

11.   The _____ makes loans to developing countries and to economies in transition.

12.   _____ is the idea that the International Monetary Fund often tries to induce countries to make difficult economic reforms by making its loans dependent on those reforms.

13.   Most of the loans made by the _____ are for specific projects.

14.   _____ is necessary for sustained economic growth.

15.   The _____ is a downward-sloping line that depicts the relation between the level and the growth rate of income per capita.

True-False Questions

1.   T   F   The catch-up phenomenon is that countries with low income per capita will grow faster than countries with high income per capita.

2.   T   F   The differences in income per capita between industrialized and developing countries are small.

3.   T   F   Newly industrialized countries are countries that are moving from central planning to market economies.

4.   T   F   All countries in the South are relatively poor.

5.   T   F   Obstacles to the spread of technology help explain why some countries grow faster than others.

6.   T   F   Centrally planned economies are characterized by large informal economies.

7.   T   F   Education is an important part of economic growth for developing countries.

8.   T   F   Obstacles to increasing capital per worker help explain why catch-up does not always occur.

9.   T   F   Portfolio investment occurs when a foreign firm invests in more than 10 percent of the ownership of a business in another country.

10. T   F   Both the International Monetary Fund and the World Bank make loans to developing countries.

11. T   F   The International Monetary Fund often tries to induce countries to make difficult economic reforms by making its loans dependent on the reforms.

12. T   F   Along the catch-up line, relatively poor countries are growing at the same rate as relatively well-off countries.

13. T   F   According to growth theory, catch-up will occur if there are no obstacles to the spread of technology.

14. T   F   Catch-up has occurred for industrialized countries since 1960.

15. T   F   Catch-up has occurred for the world as a whole since 1960.

Short-Answer Questions

1.   When does economic growth theory predict catch-up?

2.   What is the goal of economic development?

3.   What is the North-South problem?

4.   What appears to have been the key factor that caused economic growth to begin in Europe in the 1700s?

5.   What growth-limiting characteristic is shared by most developing and all centrally-planned economies?

6.   Why does a large informal economy exist in most developing countries?

7.   Why is development of human capital an important determinant of economic growth?

8.   Why is high population growth an obstacle to increasing the amount of capital per worker?

9.   Why do most developing countries need to look abroad for investment?

10. What is conditionality?

11. When will growth theory not predict catch-up?

12. What is the catch-up line?

13. Under what conditions does economic growth theory predict catch-up?

14. How are diminishing returns to capital related to the catch-up phenomenon?

15. Why does growth theory predict catch-up for states within the United States?

16. Why did national saving rates around the world decline from about 25 percent in the 1970s to about 23 percent in the 1990s at the same time that the average world interest rate rose? (Hint: See Economics in Action—Did World Saving Shift Down in the 1990s?)

WORKING IT OUT

1. The phenomenon of catch-up, that relatively poor countries grow faster than relatively well-off countries, is the central prediction of growth theory. We can use some algebra to test the catch-up prediction.

    a. We learned the formula for compound growth in the appendix to Chapter 4. It states that the rate of growth depends on the initial level of income and the level of income at the end of n years, as follows:

    Rate of growth = (Level of income at end of n years/Initial level of income)$^{1/n} - 1$

    Remember that you need a calculator with an exponent key to use this formula.

    b. Consider income (GDP) per capita for industrialized countries. The data begin in 1960 and end in 1990, so that $n = 30$. The level of income per capita in 1960 and the level of income per capita in 1990 for five countries are:

Country	Level of GDP per Capita (1985 U.S. dollars)	
	1960	1990
Canada	7,288	17,415
Greece	2,088	6,679
Portugal	1,869	6,525
Spain	3,196	9,663
United States	9,776	18,399

    c. Using the compound growth formula, you can calculate the annual rate of growth of income per capita. (Look at the Appendix to Chapter 11 of the *Study Guide* if you don't remember how.)

Country	Rate of Growth (percent)
Canada	2.95
Greece	3.95
Portugal	4.26
Spain	3.76
United States	2.13

d.   Using the compound growth formula, you can calculate the annual rate of growth of income per capita. (Look at the Appendix to Chapter 11 of the *Study Guide* if you don't remember how.)

Country	Rate of Growth (percent)
Canada	2.95
Greece	3.95
Portugal	4.26
Spain	3.76
United States	2.13

2.   The catch-up line plots the relation between the level and growth rate of income per capita. Another way of testing whether the catch-up prediction holds is to see how close groups of countries are to being on the catch-up line.

a.   We will again look at industrialized countries. Set up a diagram with the growth rate of GDP per capita on the vertical axis and the level of GDP per capita on the horizontal axis. Using the level of GDP per capita in 1960 and the growth rates calculated above, plot the points for the five countries and draw a line through the points.

b.   This is the catch-up line; it is illustrated in Figure 17.2. The catch-up line is downward sloping, indicating that those countries with relatively low incomes per capita in 1960 grew faster than those countries with relatively high incomes per capita in 1960. In other words, the catch-up prediction holds for the industrialized countries.

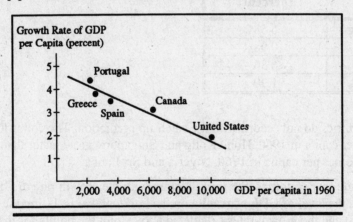

Figure 17.2

Worked Problems

1. Consider the following data on income (GDP) per capita for four developing countries. The data begin in 1960 and end in 1989, so that $n = 29$. The level of income per capita in 1960 and the level of income per capita in 1989 for the four countries are:

Country	Level of GDP per Capita (1985 U.S. dollars)	
	1960	**1989**
Hong Kong	2,210	14,035
Nigeria	560	742
Singapore	1,712	10,240
Sri Lanka	1,285	2,218

    a. Using the compound growth formula, calculate the annual rate of growth of per capita income for each country.

    b. Do these four countries accord with the catch-up prediction?

Answer

    a. Using the compound growth formula, the annual growth rates of income per capita are:

Country	Rate of Growth (percent)
Hong Kong	6.58
Nigeria	0.98
Singapore	6.36
Sri Lanka	1.90

    b. These countries do not accord with the catch-up prediction. The countries with the highest incomes per capita in 1960, Hong Kong and Singapore, grew faster than those with the lowest incomes per capita in 1960, Nigeria and Sri Lanka.

2. Consider the same four countries. Set up a diagram with the growth rate of GDP per capita on the vertical axis and the level of GDP per capita on the horizontal axis. Using the level of GDP per capita from 1960 and the growth rates calculated above, plot the points for the four countries and draw a line through the points. Does the catch-up prediction hold?

Answer

The answer is illustrated in Figure 17.3. There is no clear downward-sloping line through the four points, and so the catch-up prediction does not hold. This shows how the catch-up prediction does not hold for developing countries in general.

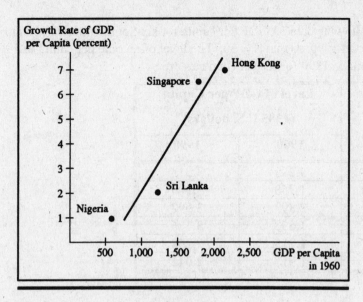

Figure 17.3

PRACTICE PROBLEMS

1. Consider the following data on GDP per capita for five European countries. The data begin in 1960 and end in 1990, so that $n = 30$. The level of income per capita in 1960 and the level of income per capita in 1990 for the five countries are:

	Level of GDP per Capita (1985 U.S. dollars)	
Country	1960	1990
Denmark	6,751	13,801
Germany	6,637	14,498
Netherlands	6,122	12,868
Sweden	7,492	14,495
Switzerland	9,639	17,007

a. Using the compound growth formula, calculate the annual rate of growth of income per capita for each country.

b. Do these five countries accord with the catch-up prediction?

2. Consider the following data on GDP per capita for six South American countries. The data begin in 1960 and end in 1990, so that $n = 30$. The level of income per capita in 1960 and the level of income per capita in 1990 for the six countries are:

Country	Level of GDP per Capita (1985 U.S. dollars) 1960	1990
Argentina	3,293	3,513
Brazil	1,758	3,906
Chile	2,893	3,992
Colombia	1,652	3,186
Paraguay	1,215	2,258
Peru	1,917	2,041

   a. Using the compound growth formula, calculate the annual rate of growth of income per capita for each country.

   b. Do these six countries accord with the catch-up prediction?

3. Consider the five countries in Practice Problem 1. Draw the catch-up line. Does the catch-up prediction hold?

4. Consider the six countries in Practice Problem 2. Draw the catch-up line. Does the catch-up prediction hold?

CHAPTER TEST

1. The phenomenon that countries with low income per capita will grow faster than countries with high income per capita is called the

   a. catch-up phenomenon.
   b. development phenomenon.
   c. transition phenomenon.
   d. industrialization phenomenon.

2. Which of the following countries is an example of a newly industrialized country?

   a. Germany
   b. Japan
   c. England
   d. Korea

3. The illegal sector is called the

   a. illegal economy.
   b. informal economy.
   c. unlawful economy.
   d. unauthorized economy.

4. Which of the following are also called less-developed countries?

   a. Industrialized countries
   b. Newly industrialized countries
   c. Developing countries
   d. Countries in transition

5.   Which of the following attempts to explain why poor countries do *not* develop faster?

    a.   Economic development
    b.   The catch-up phenomenon
    c.   Import substitution strategy
    d.   Export-led strategy

6.   Which of the following is the key factor that caused economic growth to begin in Europe in the 1700s?

    a.   Population growth
    b.   Removal of restrictions on private enterprise
    c.   Better industrial policies
    d.   The French Revolution

7.   Which of the following is *not* one of the main reasons for economic growth?

    a.   Increasing the amount of capital per worker
    b.   Development of human capital
    c.   Deregulating industries
    d.   High population growth

8.   Investment by a foreign firm in more than 10 percent of the ownership of a business in another country is called

    a.   portfolio investment.
    b.   foreign indirect investment.
    c.   foreign direct investment.
    d.   capital investment.

9.   Which of the following makes loans to countries in transition?

    a.   International Monetary Fund
    b.   World Bank
    c.   Federal Reserve Bank
    d.   Bank of America

10.   Which of the following is *not* one of the reasons why economic growth theory predicts catch-up?

    a.   Diffusion of technology
    b.   Diminishing returns to capital
    c.   Diminishing returns to labor
    d.   Innovation

11.   The catch-up line is

    a.   upward-sloping.
    b.   downward-sloping.
    c.   horizontal.
    d.   vertical.

12.   The catch-up line depicts the relationship between the level of

    a.   income and the growth rate of income.
    b.   the money supply and the growth rate of the money supply.
    c.   income per capita and the growth rate of income per capita.
    d.   investment and the growth rate of investment.

13.   Which of the following is *not* a true phenomenon for rich and poor countries?

    a.   Rich countries utilize advanced technology, and poor countries use more basic technology.
    b.   Rich countries have high productivity, and poor countries have low productivity.
    c.   Rich countries have a high level of capital per worker, and poor countries have a low level of capital per worker.
    d.   Rich countries do not exhibit diminishing returns, and poor countries exhibit diminishing returns.

14. The catch-up phenomenon will *not* occur if there are obstacles to
    a. the spread of technology.
    b. decreasing the level of capital per worker.
    c. increasing the money supply.
    d. raising the interest rate.
15. Which of the following countries has had very high growth rates since the 1960s?

    a. Sri Lanka
    b. Singapore
    c. Bangladesh
    d. Canada

Use the following table for questions 16 and 17.

Country	Level of GDP per Capita (1985 U.S. dollars)	
	1960	1990
Australia	7,879	14,300
Italy	4,638	12,557
Japan	3,032	14,839
United Kingdom	6,549	13,069

The data begin in 1960 and end in 1990, so that $n = 30$. Use the compound growth formula to answer question 16.

16. What is the annual rate of growth of GDP per capita for Australia, Italy, Japan, and the United Kingdom, respectively?
    a. 2.33, 5.44, 3.38, and 2.01 percent
    b. 2.33, 3.38, 5.44, and 2.01 percent
    c. 2.01, 5.44, 3.38, and 2.33 percent
    d. 2.01, 3.38, 5.44, and 2.33 percent
17. Do these four countries accord with the catch-up prediction?

    a. Yes, because the countries with the lowest incomes per capita in 1960, Italy and Japan, grew faster than those with the highest incomes per capita in 1960, Australia and the United Kingdom.
    b. Yes, because the countries with the lowest incomes per capita in 1960, Italy and Japan, grew slower than those with the highest incomes per capita in 1960, Australia and the United Kingdom.
    c. No, because the countries with the lowest incomes per capita in 1960, Italy and Japan, grew faster than those with the highest incomes per capita in 1960, Australia and the United Kingdom.
    d. No, because the countries with the lowest incomes per capita in 1960, Italy and Japan, grew slower than those with the highest incomes per capita in 1960, Australia and the United Kingdom.

Use Figure 17.4 for question 18.

Figure 17.4

18. Which of the figures appropriately represents the catch-up line?

    a.   Figure A
    b.   Figure B
    c.   Figure C
    d.   Figure D

Use Figure 17.5 for questions 19 and 20.

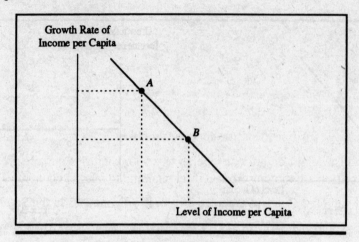

Figure 17.5

19. Country A, which is depicted by point *A*, is

    a.   poor and growing rapidly.
    b.   rich and growing rapidly.
    c.   poor and growing more slowly.
    d.   rich and growing more slowly.

20. Country B, which is depicted by point *B*, is

    a.   poor and growing rapidly.
    b.   rich and growing rapidly.
    c.   poor and growing more slowly.
    d.   rich and growing more slowly.

ANSWERS TO THE REVIEW QUESTIONS

Fill-In Questions

1. catch-up

2. Economic development

3. Industrialized

4. Developing

5. less-developed countries

6. Newly industrialized

7. Countries in transition

8. North-South problem

9. informal

10. foreign direct investment; portfolio investment; loans from banks and governments

11. International Monetary Fund

12. Conditionality

13. World Bank

14. Technological progress

15. catch-up line

True-False Questions

1. **True**. The catch-up phenomenon is that countries with low income per capita will grow faster than, and therefore catch up to, countries with high income per capita.

2. **False**. There are large income disparities between industrialized and developing countries.

3. **False**. Newly industrialized countries are relatively poor countries that are growing rapidly. Countries in transition are moving from central planning to market economies.

4. **False**. Australia and New Zealand are relatively well-off countries in the South.

5. **True**. Technological progress is necessary for sustained economic growth.

6. **True**. Centrally planned economies place pervasive restrictions on entrepreneurs, which cause the development of large informal economies.

7. **True**. The newly industrialized countries, the developing countries that have been catching up most rapidly, have strong educational systems.

8. **True**. Obstacles to increasing capital per worker can prevent developing countries from catching up to industrialized countries.

9. **False**. When the ownership is more than 10 percent, it is foreign direct investment.

10. **True**. The International Monetary Fund also makes loans to countries in transition.

11. **True**. This is the idea of conditionality.

12. **False**. Along the catch-up line, relatively poor countries are growing faster than, or catching up to, relatively well-off countries.

13. **True**. If the spread of technology is not difficult, countries with low productivity will adopt the more advanced technology, raising their growth rates and narrowing the gap between rich and poor.

14. **True**. Industrialized countries that were relatively poor in 1960 have grown faster than industrialized countries that were relatively well off in 1960.

15. **False**. Some countries with low levels of income per capita in 1960 have had very high growth rates, whereas others with equally low incomes per capita in 1960 have had very low growth rates.

Short-Answer Questions

1. Economic growth theory predicts catch-up if technological advances can spread easily and if capital and labor have diminishing returns.

2. Economic development attempts to explain why poor countries do not develop faster and to find policies to help them develop faster.

3. The North-South problem is that most countries in the North are relatively well off and most countries in the South are relatively poor.

4. The removal of restrictions on private enterprise seems to have been the most important factor.

5.   Most developing and all centrally planned economies place stringent restrictions on private enterprise, which helps to explain their slow growth.

6.   Regulation in most developing countries makes it costly to start legal business enterprises, causing a large informal economy to emerge.

7.   Human capital is an important facet of technology, which is a vital element of growth.

8.   With high population growth rates, more investment is necessary to increase, or even to maintain, the level of capital per worker.

9.   Investment equals national saving plus net exports. In most developing countries, national saving is low, and so they must look abroad for investment.

10.   Conditionality is the idea that the International Monetary Fund often tries to induce countries to make difficult economic reforms by making its loans dependent on those reforms.

11.   If there are obstacles to the spread of technology and/or obstacles to raising the level of capital per worker, catch-up may not occur.

12.   The catch-up line is a downward-sloping line that depicts the relation between the level and the growth rate of income per capita.

13.   Economic growth theory predicts catch-up if there are no obstacles to the spread of technology and no obstacles to raising the level of capital per worker.

14.   Investment would be very profitable in a poor country that has so little capital that diminishing returns to capital have not set in. Capital per worker, and therefore output per worker, would grow rapidly.

15.   States within the United States, with a common language, a single currency, and free movement of capital and technology, have no obstacles to catch-up.

16.   National saving rates around the world declined between the 1970s and the 1990s because of a shift of the world saving rate in the direction of lower world saving, which raised the equilibrium world interest rate. If the cause had been a shift of the world investment curve toward lower world investment, the equilibrium world interest rate would have fallen rather than risen.

SOLUTIONS TO THE PRACTICE PROBLEMS

1.   a.   The annual growth rates of GDP per capita are:

Country	Rate of Growth (percent)
Denmark	2.41
Germany	2.64
Netherlands	2.51
Sweden	2.22
Switzerland	1.91

   b.   These countries accord with the catch-up prediction. The countries with the lowest incomes per capita in 1960, the Netherlands and Germany, grew faster than those with the highest incomes per capita in 1960, Sweden and Switzerland.

2. a.   The annual growth rates of GDP per capita are:

Country	Rate of Growth (percent)
Argentina	0.22
Brazil	2.70
Chile	1.08
Colombia	2.21
Paraguay	2.09
Peru	0.21

   b.   These countries accord in part with the catch-up prediction. The countries with the lowest incomes per capita in 1960, Colombia and Paraguay, grew faster than those with the highest incomes per capita in 1960, Argentina and Chile. The two countries in the middle in 1960, Brazil and Peru, exhibited the fastest and slowest growth, respectively.

3. The answer is illustrated in Figure 17.6. There is a downward-sloping line through the five points, and so the catch-up prediction holds.

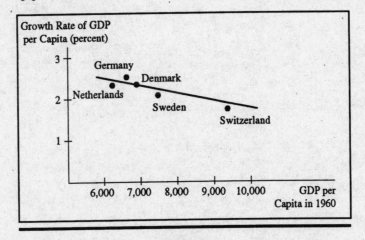

Figure 17.6

4. The answer is illustrated in Figure 17.7. There is a downward-sloping line through the six points, but the countries are not grouped as tightly as the industrialized countries. The catch-up prediction holds, but not as well as for the industrialized countries.

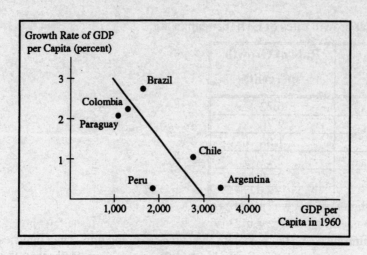

Figure 17.7

ANSWERS TO THE CHAPTER TEST

1. a

2. d

3. b

4. c

5. a

6. b

7. d

8. c

9. a

10. d

11. b

12. c

13. d

14. a

15. b

16. d

17. a

18. d

19. a

20. d

CHAPTER 18

The Gains from International Trade

CHAPTER OVERVIEW

It may be an old cliché, but the world does get smaller every day. This author's running shoes were made in Korea; his digital watch was assembled in Malaysia; he is looking forward to French wine with dinner, but not before calling his editor in Boston on a Japanese portable telephone. How international is your world at this moment?

International considerations permeate virtually every nook and cranny of the economy. This chapter begins to explore the role of international trade in the economy by examining the microeconomic foundations of why countries exchange goods and services. The theories of absolute and comparative advantage are presented. While you are just beginning to look at these things, economics has a rich history of interest in international trade, going back to Adam Smith and the *Wealth of Nations* (1776). By comparing and contrasting free trade with mercantilism, Smith showed how countries benefit from trade. The reasons for trade were more formally developed by David Ricardo in his theory of comparative advantage. The theory of comparative advantage stresses the importance of relative opportunity costs in determining what a country exports and what it imports. As a result of trade, the relative prices of products and of factors of production change. In fact, over time they tend to equalize between countries. This is shown using the already familiar production possibilities curve. Next, the Heckscher-Ohlin model is presented. This model addresses the determinants of comparative advantage. At its heart lie the abundance of factors of production and the intensity of their use.

Comparative advantage is not the only reason for trade. Economies of scale are also a reason to gain from trade. Here, complete specialization within a world market permits *ATC* to decline to a lower level than would have prevailed in a smaller market without trade. This is coupled with product differentiation to place the model of monopolistic competition into the world economy. Finally, the movement toward free trade and the costs associated with transition are discussed.

CHAPTER REVIEW

1. **International trade** offers many benefits to all countries. These can come in the form of increased specialization, a redistribution of existing supplies of goods, economies of scale in production, and increased competition. The importance of international trade in the world economy can be seen in the recent agreement between Mexico, Canada, and the United States to integrate their economies into a free trade area. In addition, there are many ongoing conversations among countries aimed at developing areas for expanded free trade. The **commerce clause** of the U.S. Constitution prohibits trade restraints between the states.

2. A basic foundation of international trade is the theory of comparative advantage. A country will export those goods in which it has a comparative advantage. Such an advantage exists when the opportunity cost of producing a good in a country is lower than the opportunity cost of producing the same good in another country. This is to say, a country that is relatively more efficient than another country in producing one good rather than another good has a comparative advantage in the production of that good. This is true even if one country has an **absolute advantage** in the production of both goods. If countries specialize in the goods in which they have a comparative advantage, the resulting trade flow will equate relative prices in each country. This can be shown

with a production possibilities curve. If opportunity costs do not increase, countries will specialize in the production of goods in which they have a comparative advantage, and the total amount of goods available for consumption will increase, leading to **gains from trade**. The relative price after trade, or the quantity of imported goods that a country can obtain in exchange for a unit of exported goods, is called the **terms of trade**.

3. The Heckscher-Ohlin model attempts to identify the determinants of a country's comparative advantage. According to the model, a country has a comparative advantage in those goods that are intensively produced with its most abundant factor of production—that is, a country that is relatively **capital abundant** has a comparative advantage in goods whose production is relatively **capital intensive**, and a country that is relatively **labor abundant** has a comparative advantage in goods whose production is relatively **labor intensive**. Using the Heckscher-Ohlin framework, it can be argued that **factor-price equalization** will occur.

4. Gains from trade are also due to economies of scale. By specializing within a larger market brought about by free trade, a firm can take advantage of larger-scale economies. As a result, *ATC* and price fall as quantity grows. Trade flows founded in economies of scale tend to be intraindustry in character, whereas trade flows based on comparative advantage tend to be interindustry.

5. As the number of firms in a market of a given size increases, *ATC* tends to rise, as each firm has a smaller market share. However, as markets grow in size through trade, the *ATC* of existing firms falls. Also, as new firms enter the market, competition and product variety increase and, as a result, price falls, so that only normal profits are earned over the long run.

ZEROING IN

1. One of the most important ideas in economics is that of comparative advantage. A specific example will be explored in "Working It Out." For now, one way to think about comparative advantage is by using opportunity costs, another important economic notion. *Absolute* productivity (or absolute advantage) really does not matter in the determination of what goods are traded. This is hard for many people to accept. If absolute productivity were the determinant of trade, the United States would export nearly everything it produces, since the United States has the most resources, the most physical capital, and many workers with large amounts of human capital. However, in comparative advantage, *relative* efficiency or productivity matters. This can be measured using opportunity cost, or what must be given up to produce another unit of some product. Given the fundamental problem of scarcity, the maximization of net benefits also includes the minimization of costs. Comparing opportunity costs across countries focuses trade on the most efficient producer. So absolute advantage does not necessarily matter.

2. The Heckscher-Ohlin model is one of the better-known theories that attempt to identify the determinants of comparative advantage. This explanation is based on two things. First, comparative advantage depends on the relative abundance of inputs within a country. For a given demand, inputs that are relatively abundant have lower prices than they would if they were less plentiful. The second consideration is the way resources are used within the production process— the intensity of their use. Therefore, goods that are produced with a lot (intensity) of the most plentiful (abundant) resource are goods that can be produced by giving up the least amount of other things. Stated another way, the Heckscher-Ohlin model also identifies the determinants of opportunity costs.

ACTIVE REVIEW

Fill-In Questions

1.   The movement of goods and services between countries is called _____.

2.   Although sovereign governments often restrict trade with other countries, the _____ of the U.S. Constitution prevents such restraint between states.

3.   Quotas and _____ are forms of _____ .

4.   _____ are taxes on imports.

5.   In the *Wealth of Nations*, _____ argued that _____ would create benefits for trading partners.

6.   Adam Smith argued that international trade increases the size of the market, which allows for a(n) _____ .

7.   The theory of comparative advantage was initially developed by _____.

8.   _____ can also be expressed in terms of opportunity costs.

9.   A person with a lower opportunity cost of producing a good than another person has a(n) _____ in that good.

10.   _____ efficiency is synonymous with comparative advantage.

11.   The price of one good in terms of another is called its _____ .

12.   With trade, the _____ of a good in different countries will converge to the same value.

13.   The after-trade relative price is called the _____ .

14.   A straight-line production possibilities curve will result in _____ within an economy after trade.

15.   _____ describes changes in comparative advantage over time.

16.   The _____ is used to describe an exception to the Heckscher-Ohlin model.

17.   One implication of the Heckscher-Ohlin model is that trade will bring about factor-price _____ in different countries.

18.   Not all gains from trade are based on _____; there are also gains based on _____ .

19.   The gains from trade that result from economies of scale are the _____ .

20.   Trade due to comparative advantage tends to be _____, whereas trade due to economies of scale tends to be _____ .

21.   There is a(n) _____ relationship between the number of firms and the *ATC* of each firm.

True-False Questions

1.   T   F   International trade creates gains only by exploiting a country's comparative advantage.

2.   T   F   Trade within the United States can be subject to tariffs levied by individual states.

3. T F   International trade has been growing rapidly as a result of declining costs of transportation and communication and the removal of restrictions on trade between countries.

4. T F   David Ricardo argued that trade was based on comparative advantage.

5. T F   International trade makes home markets more competitive.

6. T F   David Ricardo's concept of comparative advantage shows how a country can improve the incomes of its citizens by allowing them to trade with others.

7. T F   Absolute advantage can be expressed in terms of opportunity costs.

8. T F   Trade has very little effect on the prices of goods within a country.

9. T F   International trade allows countries to consume beyond their domestic (before trade) production possibilities curves.

10. T F   Increasing opportunity costs produce complete specialization within a country in a free trade environment.

11. T F   A straight-line production possibilities curve reflects constant opportunity costs.

12. T F   A country's comparative advantage remains constant over time.

13. T F   The Heckscher-Ohlin model is based, in part, on a country's factor supplies.

14. T F   The Heckscher-Ohlin model implies factor-price equalization.

15. T F   Trade that is a result of economies of scale tends to be interindustry in nature.

16. T F   As the number of firms in a market of a given size grows, the *ATC* falls.

17. T F   The movement toward free trade has no costs.

Short-Answer Questions

1. Give two reasons why international trade is beneficial.

2. How did mercantilism promote the wealth of nations?

3. "The tailor does not attempt to make his own shoes, but buys them from the shoemaker." Explain.

4. Briefly explain David Ricardo's theory of comparative advantage.

5. Why do prices change with trade?

6. What are the terms of trade?

7. What does trade do to a country's production possibilities curve?

8. Is comparative advantage dynamic?

9. What is the purpose of the Heckscher-Ohlin model?

10. Is the Heckscher-Ohlin model always correct in predicting the nature of trade?

11. What is factor-price equalization?

12. Why does *ATC* tend to fall for a given number of firms as the market grows?

WORKING IT OUT

Because of the importance of the theory of comparative advantage, it is worthwhile to try to identify the comparative advantage in a specific example. There are several ways to determine comparative advantage. One way is to look at the relative productivity per worker in each country. Another way is to look at the opportunity cost of moving workers from one type of production to another.

Suppose that both wool yarn and beef are produced in both Australia and Argentina. Assume that both goods are made with only labor, and that the following relationships hold:

- In Australia, 3 units of labor produce 105 pounds of beef, and 1 unit of labor produces 40 spools of wool yarn.

- In Argentina, 2 units of labor produce 60 pounds of beef, and 2 units of labor produce 30 spools of wool yarn.

Furthermore, Australia has 600 units of labor and Argentina has 200 units of labor.

1. Figure 18.1 shows the production possibilities curves for Australia and Argentina. The production information may be used to determine the end points for each curve. For example, Australia can produce 21,000 pounds of beef $[(600/3) \times 105]$ or 24,000 spools of wool yarn $[(600/1) \times 40]$.

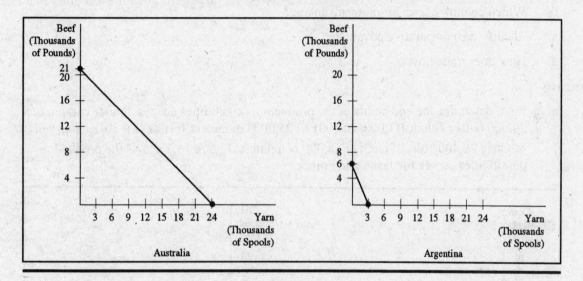

Figure 18.1

2. First, look at the absolute advantage in each good. Australia has an absolute advantage in the production of both beef and wool yarn. One Australian worker can produce more of both yarn and beef.

3. To describe the comparative advantage, let's look first at the relative productivity per worker in each country. In Australia, 1 worker produces 35 pounds of beef (105/3) or 40 spools of yarn (40/1). In Argentina, 1 worker produces 30 pounds of beef (60/2) or 15 spools of yarn (30/2). Thus, workers are relatively more productive in beef production in Argentina and in yarn production in Australia. Alternatively, to produce an additional 1,000 pounds of beef, it takes 28.6 workers in Australia (1,000/35), whereas it takes 33.33 workers (1,000/30) in Argentina. If those workers were moved into beef production from yarn production, Australia would lose 1,144 spools of yarn (28.6 × 40) and Argentina would lose approximately 500 spools of yarn. Obviously, beef is more expensive in terms of yarn in Australia than it is in Argentina. Thus, Australia has a comparative advantage in wool production and Argentina has a comparative advantage in the production of beef.

4. What happens to the price of the imported good in each country? Australia imports beef from Argentina. The supply curve for beef in Australia shifts to the right as a result of the imports. Assuming that demand is constant, the price of beef in Australia will fall. Argentina imports yarn

from Australia. The supply curve of yarn shifts to the right, and the price of yarn in Argentina falls, *ceteris paribus*.

Worked Problems

1. Assume that both Japan and France produce both cloth and computers. Assume that they are produced with only labor according to the following schedule:

    *   In France, 5 units of labor produce 100 bolts of cloth and 2 units of labor produce 50 computers.

    *   In Japan, 6 units of labor produce 132 bolts of cloth and 3 units of labor produce 45 computers.

    France has 1,000 units of labor and Japan has 1,200 units of labor.

    a.   Construct the production possibilities curves.

    b.   Which country has an absolute advantage?

    c.   Identify the comparative advantage.

    d.   How does trade flow?

Answer

a.   First, determine the end points of the production possibilities curves. France can produce 20,000 bolts of cloth $[(1,000/5)\times100]$ or 25,000 computers $[(1,000/2)\times50]$. Japan can produce 26,400 bolts of cloth or 18,000 computers. Figure 18.2 shows the production possibilities curves for Japan and France.

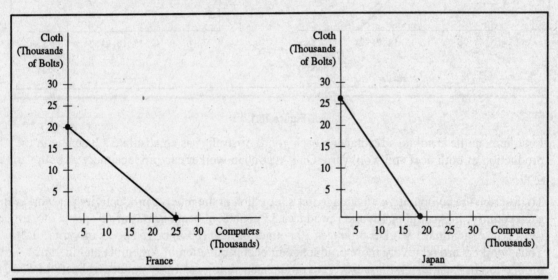

Figure 18.2

b.   France has an absolute advantage in the production of computers, and Japan has an absolute advantage in the production of cloth.

c.   In France, 1 worker can produce 20 bolts of cloth or 25 computers. In Japan, 1 worker can produce 22 bolts of cloth or 15 computers. Thus, workers in Japan are relatively more efficient in cloth production than are French workers. Alternatively, to produce 100 additional bolts of cloth France must give up 125 computers $[(100/20) \times 25]$, and Japan must give up 68 computers $[(100/22) \times 15]$]. Thus, the opportunity cost of cloth in terms of computers is lower in Japan. Japan has a comparative advantage in cloth production, whereas France has a comparative advantage in the production of computers.

d.   Computers flow from France to Japan, and cloth flows from Japan to France. The price of computers will fall in Japan, and the price of cloth will fall in France.

2.   Whenever possible, it is helpful to present a new concept using the familiar tool of supply and demand analysis. Here we will look at the Heckscher-Ohlin model from a market perspective.

It was shown in "Working It Out" that Australia has a comparative advantage in wool production and Argentina has a comparative advantage in beef production. Assume that two kinds of labor, skilled and unskilled, are used to produce both wool and beef in both countries. Furthermore, assume that Argentina's comparative advantage is based on the fact that it has a very large number of unskilled workers and that they are employed intensively in beef production. Will the wage level of unskilled workers in Australia fall to that of unskilled workers in Argentina? Use the Heckscher-Ohlin model to support your answer.

Answer

Trade causes a reallocation of existing supplies of beef and wool between Argentina and Australia. It also causes a movement in each country toward specialization in the good in which that country has *a* comparative advantage. This movement causes shifts in the demand for skilled and unskilled workers. Assume that the supply curve of unskilled workers is upward-sloping (and not backward- bending). With trade, beef production in Australia falls. This results in a decline in the demand for unskilled workers in Australia, and their wages will fall. At the same time, the demand for unskilled workers in Argentina rises as the production of beef increases. As a result, their wages rise. In a perfect Heckscher-Ohlin model, factor prices will tend to equalize between the two beginning wages, not necessarily at the lowest one.

PRACTICE PROBLEMS

1.   Assume that Japan and France initially trade cloth and computers as described in Worked Problem 1. However, assume that the Japanese government subsidizes computer research so that 3 units of labor now produce 90 computers. Also, because of a unique environmental problem, Japanese cloth producers have had to cut back to 120 bolts per 6 workers.

a.   Identify the comparative advantage.

b.   Briefly discuss the trade flows.

2.   Assume that the comparative advantage for Japan in Worked Problem 1 was due to an intensive use of abundant unskilled workers.

a.   What will happen to these workers' wages?

b.   What will happen to their wages based on the events in Practice Problem 1?

3.   Using Figure 18.2, what happened to price, ATC, and the number of firms when trade is allowed?

4.   What happens to Figure 18.2 when a new technological discovery lowers the ATC for all firms?

5.   Compare your answers in problems 3 and 4.

CHAPTER TEST

1.   David Ricardo based his ideas concerning international trade on

a.   comparative advantage.

    b.   absolute advantage.

    c.   the commerce clause of the Constitution.

    d.   the use of effective tariffs.

2.   Individual states in the United States are prohibited from restricting the free flow of goods by the

    a.   Federal Reserve Act of 1914.

    b.   Fair Labor Standards Act.

    c.   Declaration of Independence.

    d.   commerce clause of the U.S. Constitution.

3.   Constant opportunity costs lead to

    a.   absolute advantage.

    b.   total specialization.

    c.   no trade at all.

    d.   incomplete specialization.

4.   Factor-price equalization

    a.   is a foundation of absolute advantage.

    b.   tends to promote intraindustry trade.

    c.   suggests that the price of inputs in different countries will tend to equalize with trade.

    d.   will prevent trade from occurring.

5.   The benefits of free trade come from

    a.   a redistribution of existing supplies of goods.

    b.   a movement toward specialization.

    c.   increased competition.

    d.   All of the above.

6.   Free trade increases the size of markets. As a result, firms

    a.   can take advantage of economies of scale.

    b.   can strengthen their monopoly positions.

    c.   can maximize *ATC*.

    d.   are guaranteed profits.

7.   David Ricardo's theory of _____ advantage shows how a country benefits from trading with others.

    a.   absolute

    b.   constant

    c.   comparative

    d.   proportion

8.   Economists often use the concept of opportunity costs to explain

    a.   demand.

    b.   comparative advantage.

    c.   monopoly.

    d.   gravity.

9.   With trade, relative prices within a country

    a.   only rise.

    b.   change.

    c.   only fall.

    d.   are unaffected.

10.   Trade causes a country's production possibilities curve to

    a.   change slope.

    b.   shift inward in a parallel manner.

    c.   shift outward in a parallel manner.

    d.   remain constant.

11. If there are increasing opportunity costs, trade results in
    a. complete specialization.
    b. constant specialization.
    c. partial specialization.
    d. no specialization.

12. A major attempt at explaining the determinants of comparative advantage is found in
    a. the model of consumer behavior.
    b. diminishing returns to variable factors of production.
    c. the Taylor model.
    d. the Heckscher-Ohlin model.

13. According to the Heckscher-Ohlin model, a country will export goods
    a. produced intensively with its least abundant resource.
    b. not produced with its most abundant resource.
    c. produced intensively with no more than 10 percent of its most abundant resource.
    d. produced intensively with its most abundant resource.

14. If Sri Lanka exports products produced intensively with labor, its most abundant resource, then
    a. wages will fall relative to the prices of other resources.
    b. wages will remain unchanged.
    c. there is a Leontief paradox present.
    d. wages will rise relative to the prices of other resources.

15. Intraindustry trade refers to
    a. trade between different industries.
    b. trade within the same industry.
    c. trade within a country's own borders.
    d. trade determined by tariffs.

16. Interindustry trade refers to
    a. trade between different industries.
    b. trade within the same industry.
    c. trade within a country's own borders.
    d. trade determined by tariffs.

17. In a given market, as the number of firms increases,
    a. *ATC* falls.
    b. *MC* falls.
    c. *ATC* rises.
    d. *ATC* remains constant.

18. For a given number of firms, as the market grows,
    a. *ATC* rises.
    b. *AFC* rises.
    c. *ATC* remains unchanged.
    d. *ATC* falls.

19. When free trade occurs between countries,
    a. the number that benefit is equal to the number that do not benefit.
    b. there will be no impact on the price of factors of production in the countries involved.
    c. quotas and tariffs will be used to enhance the benefits for every country.
    d. all parties involved will benefit.

ANSWERS TO THE REVIEW QUESTIONS

Fill-In Questions

1. international trade
2. commerce clause
3. quotas; trade restrictions
4. Tariffs
5. Adam Smith; free trade
6. greater division of labor
7. David Ricardo
8. Comparative advantage
9. comparative advantage
10. Relative
11. relative price
12. relative price; converge
13. terms of trade
14. complete specialization
15. Dynamic comparative advantage
16. Leontief paradox
17. equalization
18. comparative advantage; economies of scale
19. reduction in costs per unit
20. interindustry; intraindustry
21. positive

True-False Questions

1. **False**. Gains from trade also result from economies of scale.
2. **False**. The commerce clause of the U.S. Constitution prohibits the restriction of trade between the states.
3. **True**. Recently, the United States, Canada, and Mexico formed a free trade area.
4. **True**. Ricardo's ideas of free trade were based on absolute advantage.
5. **True**. International trade increases the number of suppliers in a country. When there are more sellers, the market power of each is reduced.
6. **True**. Ricardo used the theory of comparative advantage and not absolute advantage. The benefits from trade between countries are based on the relative advantage of each country.
7. **False**. Opportunity costs are a way to define comparative advantage and not absolute advantage.

8. **False**. International trade is the movement of supplies of goods between countries. By changing the location of supplies, international trade does affect the prices of goods. In fact, trade flows will quickly eliminate price differences.

9. **True**. This is one way to show the gains from trade.

10. **False**. Under increasing opportunity costs, as more and more of a good is produced, the opportunity cost changes. These changes can reduce the gains from trade to the point where further specialization is no longer beneficial.

11. **True**. The tradeoff between the goods remains the same over the entire curve. Increasing opportunity costs are reflected by a production possibilities curve that bows outward.

12. **False**. Comparative advantage is a dynamic concept, especially if a country invests in human and physical capital and in technology.

13. **True**. According to the Heckscher-Ohlin model, a country will export those goods that are produced intensively with the country's most abundant resource.

14. **True**. Not only does trade change the location of the supplies of products, it also changes the demand for factors of production. Over time, shifts in demand and supply in product and input markets (in trading countries) will tend to equalize prices.

15. **False**. It tends to be intraindustry. Trade based on comparative advantage tends to be interindustry.

16. **False**. As the number of firms in a market of a given size rises, the market share of each falls. Thus, ATC will rise.

17. **False**. Often trade barriers need to be phased out over an extended period of time. Trade adjustment assistance programs may be necessary to help workers who are adversely affected by the movement toward free trade.

Short-Answer Questions

1. First, firms are able to reduce costs through economies of scale because trade makes markets larger. Second, trade allows countries to specialize in producing those goods in which they are relatively efficient.

2. According to mercantilist theory, a country would become wealthy through the accumulation of gold and silver. This was accomplished by maximizing exports while minimizing imports, or maximizing net exports. Government regulation of trade through tariffs and quotas is required for this to happen.

3. This is from the *Wealth of Nations*. In this passage, Adam Smith is arguing that trade is based on absolute advantage.

4. The theory of comparative advantage explains how a country can gain from trading with others. A country exports those products in which it has a comparative advantage. Simply stated, country A has a comparative advantage in a good relative to country B if the opportunity cost of producing that good in country A is less than it is in country B.

5. Trade reallocates the supplies of products. Assuming competition and negligible transportation costs, trade moves goods to the place (country) where they command the highest price. As a result, the price falls in one country and rises in the other.

6. Simply stated, the terms of trade for a country are given by the quantity of imported goods that it can obtain per unit of exported goods.

7. Trade causes the production possibilities curve to rotate out along the axis of the good that is imported. The change in the slope of the curve reflects the change in relative prices caused by trade.

8. Yes, comparative advantage can change. This can occur through investment in physical and human capital and in technology.

9. The Heckscher-Ohlin model attempts to explain the determinants of comparative advantage. The model argues that comparative advantage is based on the relative abundance of resource supplies and the relative intensity with which those supplies are used in production.

10. Not necessarily. The Leontief paradox describes a situation in which trade does not clearly reflect relative factor intensities.

11. Factor-price equalization is the tendency of the prices of factors of production to equalize across countries. As countries trade and specialize in production, the demand for inputs also changes. This causes the prices of factors of production to change. The wages of unskilled labor will fall in countries that import goods made with unskilled labor, whereas the wages of unskilled workers in countries that export these goods will rise as production expands.

12. As markets grow, the amount produced by each firm increases. This allows firms to take advantage of economies of scale, and, as a result, *ATC* falls.

SOLUTIONS TO THE PRACTICE PROBLEMS

1. a. In France, 1 worker still produces 20 bolts of cloth or 25 computers. In Japan, however, 1 worker now produces 20 bolts of cloth or 30 computers. Therefore, as a result of the research, Japan is now (relative to France) more productive in computer production than in cloth production—to get 100 more computers, Japan must give up 67 bolts of cloth $[(100/30) \times 20]$, whereas France must give up 80 $[(100/25) \times 20]$.

    b. Comparative advantage has shifted, and the flow of trade reverses.

2. a. As cloth production increases, the demand for unskilled workers in Japan will rise. This will cause the wages of the unskilled workers to rise, *ceteris paribus*.

    b. Comparative advantage has shifted. The demand for unskilled workers in Japan will fall, and their wages will fall.

1. NAFTA made the area of free trade larger. Thus, each firm had a larger market. As a result, firms should have become larger, and *ATC* should have fallen. This results in a rightward shift in F to F_1.

2. This will shift F to the right, indicating a lower *ATC* for a given number of firms in a market of a given size.

3. The results are essentially the same. Expanding free trade is like discovering a new technique of production.

ANSWERS TO THE CHAPTER TEST

1. a

2. d

3. b

4. c

5. d

6.　a

7.　c

8.　b

9.　b

10.　a

11.　c

12.　d

13.　d

14.　d

15.　b

16.　a

17.　c

18.　d

19.　d

CHAPTER 19

International Trade Policy

CHAPTER OVERVIEW

In the previous chapter, we explored the case for free trade. By exploiting comparative advantage and economies of scale, the citizens of a country (large or small) benefit from the free exchange of goods with other countries. However, free trade is not widely observed. For many reasons, governments restrict trade through tariffs, quotas, and other barriers. This chapter examines the consequences of these actions, looks at reasons supporting the use of trade restrictions, and presents ways of moving toward an environment of free trade. First, tariffs, quotas, and various nontariff trade barriers are examined, using the supply and demand model. Then a history of trade restrictions in the United States is presented. The discussion ranges from the tariff of abominations and Smoot-Hawley to GATT, the Uruguay Round, and the WTO. Next, many arguments supporting the use of trade barriers are discussed. These include strategic trade policy, infant industries, national security, and simple retaliation. Finally, the chapter ends with an examination of alternative policies to reduce trade barriers, including unilateral disarmament, bilateral and multilateral negotiations, customs unions, and free trade areas.

CHAPTER REVIEW

1. The United States is a relatively open economy. But this is a minority position in the world. Virtually all countries have protectionist policies; they impose **tariffs** (**ad valorem** and **specific**) and **quotas** on imported goods. Tariffs shift the **export supply curve** up by the dollar amount of the tariff, so that it intersects the **import demand curve** at a lower quantity. Tariffs generate duties or revenues for the government. Quotas can be analyzed in a similar fashion. Quotas, however, generate revenues for the individuals who hold the quota—those having the right to import the specific good.

2. In recent years, new alternatives to tariffs and quotas have been observed. One of these is the **voluntary restraint agreement** (**VRA**). Under a VRA, a government asks another country to "voluntarily" reduce its exports. This has market effects similar to those of a quota, except that the revenues go to the foreign producer. Other trade barriers include quality and performance standards, labor and environmental standards, and national defense.

3. The U.S. economy has not always been a relatively free trade environment. The use of **revenue tariffs** can be traced back to before 1800. Some of the more infamous and disruptive tariffs include the "tariff of abominations" of 1828 and the **Smoot-Hawley tariff** of 1930, which led to a **trade war** as each country tried to beat the others with higher tariffs. In 1934 the **Reciprocal Trade Agreement Act** was passed, allowing President Roosevelt to reduce tariffs if other countries reciprocated. This process was made permanent in 1947 with the passage of the **General Agreement on Trade and Tariffs** (**GATT**). Another form of trade restriction is **antidumping duties**, which address the problem of a foreign firm selling below its average cost or below the price in the home country (**dumping**). Other **nontariff barriers** to trade include the Multifiber Agreement (MFA).

4. Even though estimates suggest that removing trade restrictions from the economy would produce an annual gain of as much as $60 billion, arguments for the continuation of trade restrictions are

many. One such argument is that trade restrictions create benefits if the output of a monopoly can be reduced. Another argument suggests that tariffs and the like should be used to protect industries that are necessary for the national defense. Then there is the **infant industry argument**—trade restrictions should be imposed to give firms time to get established and become competitive. Finally, it is argued, if others restrict trade, why should we not also restrict trade? All of these arguments have weak points and disadvantages. It is also the case that there are alternatives to trade restrictions that are less harmful to the economy but that achieve the same ends.

5.   There is a growing movement toward expanding free trade. There are five approaches to doing this. One approach is simply unilateral disarmament; this is difficult to achieve today. An alternative is **multilateral negotiation**, which allows opposing political interests to cancel each other out. An example is the recent **Uruguay Round** of GATT negotiations and the creation of the **World Trade Organization** (**WTO**). Multilateral negotiations are almost always conducted on a **most-favored nation** (**MFN**) basis. Creating regional trading areas is another approach. With this approach, it is hoped that the increase in trade that results, or **trade creation**, will outweigh the replacement of low-cost firms from outside the area with high-cost firms within it, or **trade diversion**. There are two types of regional trading areas: **free trade areas** and **customs unions**. NAFTA is a recent example of a free trade area (FTA) involving the United States, Mexico, and Canada. With a free trade area, **domestic content restrictions** are needed to prevent external tariff avoidance.

ZEROING IN

The model of supply and demand was used to examine the effects of tariffs and quotas. Practicing with supply and demand will reaffirm your developing knowledge of this essential economic paradigm.

1.   Figure 19.1 shows the market for some imported good. D_1 is the import demand curve, and S_1 is the export supply curve before any trade restrictions are instituted. Thus, P_1 and Q_1 are the equilibrium price and quantity.

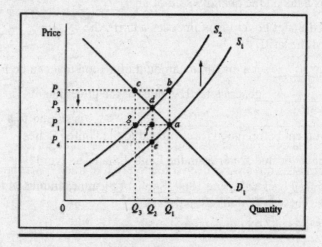

Figure 19.1

Assume that a tariff of amount ab is levied. As described in the text, this shifts the export supply curve up to S_2, where the vertical distance between S_1 and S_2 is equal to ab. Consumers must now pay P_1 plus the tariff, or P_2 ($P_2 = P_1 + ab$). At this point, however, there is a surplus on the market of cb. As a result, the price falls to P_3 with equilibrium quantity Q_2. Consumers now pay P_3 instead of P_1, and consumer surplus has fallen by the area P_1P_3da. However, although buyers pay P_3, foreign sellers get only P_4, where the difference de is the tariff collected by the government. Like consumer surplus, producer surplus has declined by the area P_1P_4ea. The tariff has made both domestic consumers and foreign producers worse off. The government, however, collects tariff revenue equal to the tariff per unit multiplied by the number of units subject to the tariff. In Figure 19.1 this is shown by the area P_3P_4ed. As you can see, the government is capturing some of the surplus lost by consumers and producers. The triangle *dea* is that part of the reduction in consumer and producer surplus that no one gets; this is the deadweight loss. So, a tariff is like a black hole in space—it makes some consumer and producer surplus disappear!

2. Figure 19.1 may also be used to review the effects of a quota. Assume that the free trade equilibrium is shown by P_1 and Q_1. One way a quota works is for the government to give someone an importing license. This allows this person to be the only importer of a product, making it easy for the government to keep track of imports to be sure the quota limit is not being violated. In terms of Figure 19.1, suppose that the license agreement says that no more than Q_2 may be imported. The quota holder now buys this amount from foreign suppliers for P_4 and sells it to domestic buyers for P_3. The area P_3P_4ed is the revenue earned by the quota holder. Also, there is still the deadweight loss of *dea*.

3. A VRA works like a quota, but we do away with the quota holder. The government sends an official representative to the foreign country and asks that country to export only Q_2. Alternatively, the official asks the country to hold Q_1Q_2 off the market. The foreign supplier now sells Q_2 at price P_3, and the area P_3P_4ed comes to the foreign firm as extra revenue. Also, like a tariff or quota, the VRA results in a deadweight loss of *dea*.

ACTIVE REVIEW

Fill-In Questions

1. A(n) _____ is a tax equal to a certain percentage of the value of an imported good.

2. A specific tax is a tax on the quantity sold of an _____.

3. When the United States government imposes a tariff, the _____ shifts by the dollar amount of the tariff.

4. _____ set a maximum amount of a good that can be imported.

5. _____ generate tax revenue for the government.

6. A(n) _____ or _____ is similar to a quota, but it is imposed by a foreign government before goods are shipped to the United States.

7. Foreign firms have located factories in the United States to avoid _____.

8. _____ and _____ are examples of trade barriers related to domestic issues. These are often referred to as _____.

9. In general, over time, tariffs in the United States have _____.

10. The _____ was levied during the Depression of the 1930s and may have, in fact, increased its duration and depth.

11. The _____ allowed President Roosevelt to lower tariffs if certain conditions were met in other countries. This approach was made permanent in 1947 with the creation of the _____.

12. Dumping occurs when a foreign firm sells a product at a price below _____ or the price in the home country. This has promoted the creation of _____.

13. Trade restrictions designed to permit firms to achieve economies of scale are referred to as _____.

14. Alexander Hamilton favored tariffs based on a(n) _____ argument.

15. The repeal of the Corn Laws in England is an example of the _____ approach to reducing trade barriers.

16. If a country is not granted _____, _____ are imposed on the imports of that country.

17. The _____ limited the amount of limited the imports into England during Adam Smith's time.

True-False Questions

1. T F A tariff shifts the export demand curve upward.

2. T F Tariffs create revenue for the government.

3. T F A VRA and a quota are both imposed by the importing country.

4. T F Fuel economy standards for cars sold in the United States are a form of trade restriction.

5. T F Tariffs are a new and growing method used by the U.S. government to raise revenues for domestic transfer payments.

6. T F The Smoot-Hawley tariffs of 1930 helped create a worldwide trade war.

7. T F Dumping is not permitted in the United States.

8. T F Tariffs are mutually beneficial.

9. T F National security has been used as a rationale for trade restrictions.

10. T F Unilateral disarmament is a more popular way of reducing trade barriers than multilateral negotiations.

11. T F A VRA is a way to manage trade.

12. T F NAFTA created a common currency in Canada, Mexico, and the United States.

Short-Answer Questions

1. What are some differences between a tariff and a quota?

2. Is the effect of a VRA similar to that of a quota?

3. What is a transplant?

4. What is a nontariff trade barrier?

5. What is the Reciprocal Trade Agreement Act, and how is it related to GATT?

6. Why is it difficult to identify dumping?

7. What is the infant industry argument?

8. Describe the Uruguay Round.

9. Differentiate between free trade areas (FTAs) and customs unions.

10. What is MFN?

WORKING IT OUT

International trade has linked markets in different countries and, as a result, has changed the prices of products and of factors of production. These linkages created net benefits for all the economies involved. In this chapter, we have examined the impact of blockages or restrictions to these connections. It is always useful to practice analysis with the supply and demand model. Let us look once again at the similar effects of tariffs, quotas, and VRAs on supply and demand.

In the competitive supply and demand model, tariffs, quotas, and VRAs are best modeled by shifting the supply of the imported product. Please refer to Figure 19.1. Assume that the beginning equilibrium price is P_1 and the equilibrium quantity is Q_1. In the case of tariffs, the supply curve shifts back by the amount ab. Under a quota, the domestic government limits imports to quantity $0Q_3$. This has the effect of shifting the supply curve back as well. Under a VRA, the foreign government tells its producers to only export the quantity $0Q_3$ to the importing country, and the effect is the same as the quota. The source of the limitation is different. In each instance, however, the final equilibrium price is P_3. In the case of the tariff, this price was reached from the excess supply of cd. The quota and the VRA initially created excess demand of ga. All three policies have a deadweight loss of dea.

Worked Problems

1.   Show the effects of a tariff on a market, assuming that demand is perfectly inelastic. How does your answer change if demand is less than perfectly inelastic?

Answer

Figure 19.2 shows the effects of a tariff and the role of differing elasticities.

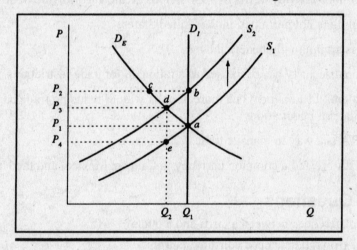

Figure 19.2

Assume that the pretariff supply curve is S_1. Two demand curves are indicated, D_I and D_E. For convenience, they both cross the supply curve at point a, making P_1 the pretariff equilibrium market price. As in previous examples, a tariff shifts the export supply curve up to S_2, where the distance ab is the amount of the tariff. If demand is perfectly inelastic (D_I), the effect of the tariff is to raise the market price to P_2. Here, quantity demanded is unaffected. Tariff revenue is shown by the area P_2P_1ab. Also, there is no deadweight loss. However, if the demand is relatively more elastic (D_E), the tariff raises the price only to P_3—because demand has a negative slope (not vertical), at P_2 there is a surplus of cb, and quantity falls to Q_2. Tariff revenue is now P_3P_4ed, which is less than the revenue generated when demand was vertical. Also, a deadweight loss exists equal to the area dea. When demand is perfectly inelastic, more revenue is generated and the deadweight loss is minimized.

2.   Using Figure 19.2, tell who bears the burden of the tariff.

Answer

When demand is D_I, price increases by the full amount of the tariff $(P_2P_1 = ba)$; therefore, domestic consumers bear the burden. However, if demand is D_E, the price increases only to P_3. Thus, domestic consumers pay P_3P_1 of the tariff, while foreign producers pay the portion P_1P_4. From this it appears that consumers bear more of the burden the greater the inelasticity of demand.

PRACTICE PROBLEMS

1.

    a.   Draw a market in such a way as to make foreign sellers pay all of a tariff.

    b.   From whom does the government collect revenue?

2.   Would a quota holder rather have a license for an imported product that had a relatively inelastic (not perfectly inelastic) demand or a relatively elastic demand? Draw a market diagram to support your answer.

CHAPTER TEST

1.   Policies that restrict trade are called
    a.   protectionist policies.
    b.   GATT agreements.
    c.   reciprocal trade agreements.
    d.   free trade zones.
2.   A tax equal to a certain percentage of the value of an imported good is a(n)
    a.   specific tariff.
    b.   ad valorem tariff.
    c.   quota.
    d.   nontariff trade.
3.   Tariffs
    a.   move the export supply curve right.
    b.   move the import demand curve left.
    c.   move the export supply curve left.
    d.   do not generate revenue for the government.
4.   The increased revenues that result from a quota are collected by
    a.   the government.
    b.   consumers through enhanced consumer surplus.
    c.   foreign monopolies.
    d.   the quota holder.
5.   Protectionist policies include the use of
    a.   VRAs.
    b.   quotas.
    c.   tariffs.
    d.   any of the above; they are all tools of managed trade.
6.   The revenue collected under a VRA goes to
    a.   the government.
    b.   the quota holder.
    c.   the foreign producer.
    d.   consumers as part of reduced consumer surplus.

7. Fuel economy standards for all cars (foreign and domestic) sold in the United States may be considered a form of

    a.   nontariff trade barrier.
    b.   quota.
    c.   tariff.
    d.   government labor standards.

8. Possibly the worst U.S. tariff policy

    a.   was that under Smoot-Hawley.
    b.   came from GATT.
    c.   was started under the Reciprocal Trade Agreement Act of 1934.
    d.   was passed in 1826 and was called the tariff of abominations.

9. Dumping is the selling of a product by a foreign company at a price below

    a.   the level of a tariff.
    b.   average costs.
    c.   average fixed costs.
    d.   marginal cost.

10. The deadweight loss from a VRA is

    a.   equal to the revenue collected by the government.
    b.   equal to the revenue collected by the quota holder.
    c.   the difference between the reduction in consumer surplus and the increase in producer surplus.
    d.   the extra taxes paid by firms as a result of their higher profits.

11. Arguments in favor of trade restrictions include

    a.   strategic trade policies.
    b.   national defense considerations.
    c.   infant industry arguments.
    d.   all of the above.

12. To encourage the development of new firms in a particular country is an example of the

    a.   infant industry argument.
    b.   retaliation argument.
    c.   environmental standards argument.
    d.   labor standards argument.

13. The stockpiling of strategic materials is an alternative to

    a.   tariffs.
    b.   antidumping rules.
    c.   infant industry arguments for restricting trade.
    d.   national security arguments for restricting trade.

14. According to a story written by Frédéric Bastiat,

    a.   French candle makers wanted trade protection from the sun.
    b.   infant industries need protection.
    c.   quotas are better than tariffs in generating revenue for the government.
    d.   it rains in Spain, but mainly on the plain.

15. GATT is an example of

    a.   how nontariff trade barriers are formed.
    b.   unilateral disarmament.
    c.   multilateral negotiations.
    d.   a customs union.

16. Recently, China

    a. signed VRA agreements with the United States.

    b. increased its quotas.

    c. was granted MFN status.

    d. was fined under its GATT status.

17. A disadvantage of a regional trading area is

    a. the lack of a common currency.

    b. trade diversion.

    c. the tendency to have trade wars within the area.

    d. that there are fewer countries involved than in multilateral negotiations.

18. If tariffs are increased, the export supply curve

    a. does not shift.

    b. decreases (shifts upward).

    c. increases (shifts downward).

    d. becomes perfectly inelastic.

19. Quotas

    a. cause the price of imports to fall.

    b. reduce the quantity of imports.

    c. raise revenue for the government.

    d. cause all of the above to happen.

20. If import demand is perfectly inelastic and a tariff is levied,

    a. foreign suppliers will pay all of the tariff.

    b. the government will collect no revenue.

    c. quotas are needed to shift export supply downward.

    d. consumers will pay all of the tariff.

ANSWERS TO THE REVIEW QUESTIONS

Fill-in Questions

1. ad valorem tariff

2. imported good

3. export supply curve

4. Quotas

5. Tariffs

6. voluntary restraint agreement (VRA); voluntary export restraint (VER)

7. voluntary restraint agreements (VRAs)

8. Environmental; labor standards; nontariff trade barriers

9. fallen

10. Smoot-Hawley tariff

11. Reciprocal Trade Agreement Act of 1934; General Agreement on Trade and Tariffs (GATT)

12. average costs; antidumping duties

13. strategic trade policy

14. infant industry

15. unilateral disarmament

16. most-favored nation status (MFN); Smoot-Hawley tariffs

17. Corn Laws

True-False Questions

1. **False**. It shifts the export supply curve upward.

2. **True**. Tariffs create revenues for the government and are called duties.

3. **False**. A quota is imposed by the importing country. With a VRA, the foreign government (in the exporting country) agrees to limit exports. Quotas and VRAs have similar market effects.

4. **True**. This is an example of a nontariff trade barrier.

5. **False**. Tariffs have a long history in the United States. However, tariffs are a declining source of revenue for the government. This has been especially true since 1910.

6. **True**. In fact, the Smoot-Hawley tariffs have been cited as one reason for the length and depth of the Great Depression of the 1930s.

7. **True**. Dumping occurs when a foreign producer sells in a foreign country at a price below average cost or below the price in the home country. There is antidumping legislation in the United States.

8. **False**. Tariffs possibly benefit one country at the expense of another. Thus, such actions cannot be mutually beneficial.

9. **True**. This argument claims that certain things need to be produced during times of war. Depending on foreign suppliers might be dangerous. Thus, domestic producers need to exist.

10. **False**. Some areas of the economy are hurt by unilateral disarmament. With multilateral negotiations, there is a simultaneous tariff reduction among many countries.

11. **True**. A VRA is a voluntary restraint agreement. It is one method that governments use to manage trade.

12. **False**. NAFTA only removed tariffs and quotas that existed between the three countries.

Short-Answer Questions

1. Tariffs are essentially taxes that are levied on an imported product. They generate duties, or tax revenue, for the government. Quotas simply limit the amount of a product that can be imported. Quotas generate revenue for the quota holder.

2. Yes. A VRA is a voluntary restraint agreement—for example, the U.S. government asks another government to voluntarily restrict exports to the United States. Thus, VRAs act like quotas. Foreign suppliers experience increases in profits.

3. Often, foreign companies try to avoid VRAs by building factories in the restricted country. The products of these factories are called transplants.

4. A nontariff trade barrier is anything that limits trade that is not a tariff or a quota. Examples include quality and performance standards, government procurement rules, regulatory rules and standards, and minimum content or fiber requirements.

5. The Reciprocal Trade Agreement Act of 1934 gave President Roosevelt the authority to cut tariffs if other countries cut their own tariffs. This legislation successfully reduced tariffs from the levels

imposed under Smoot-Hawley. This process of tariff reduction was so successful that it was made permanent by GATT in 1947.

6. Dumping is a form of predatory pricing, and it is difficult to differentiate between predatory pricing (discussed in Chapter 17) and aggressive pricing that results from active competition.

7. This is an argument used in favor of tariffs to protect an industry that is just getting started. Once the industry is established, the tariff on imports can be removed and competition proceeds. A problem with this argument is that infant industries never seem to grow up.

8. The Uruguay Round is the latest round of multilateral trade negotiations under GATT. This was a meeting (a round) of countries that tried to come to an agreement on a list of tariff reductions and the removal of other trade restrictions. The Uruguay Round included a reform of GATT. It created the World Trade Organization (WTO) to deal with trade disputes between countries.

9. Both are special trading areas within which barriers to trade between countries in the area are removed. However, external tariffs are the same for all countries in a customs union but may differ in a free trade area. Both forms may result in trade diversion.

10. MFN stands for most-favored nation status. When tariffs are reduced under GATT, they are reduced for all countries with MFN status.

SOLUTIONS TO THE PRACTICE PROBLEMS

1. a. Figure 19.3 shows a tariff that is paid completely by foreign suppliers.

Figure 19.3

Assume that the pretariff export supply curve is S_1 and the pretariff demand curve is D. Note that demand is perfectly elastic at the free trade equilibrium price P_1. A tariff of amount ab shifts the export supply curve up to S_2. Given the perfectly elastic demand curve, the market price remains at P_1 even though the quantity supplied falls from Q_1 to Q_2. Domestic consumers pay the same price as before the tariff. However, foreign producers get only P_2. The distance P_1P_4 is equal to the tariff ab. Thus foreign producers pay all of the tariff.

b. Because of the perfect elasticity of the demand curve, the domestic price stays at P_1. The before and after tariff price is the same. However, after the tariff foreign producers get only P_2 for their production. Thus, the government collects tariff revenue from foreign producers.

2. Figure 19.4 can be used to communicate the value of a quota based on differing elasticities.

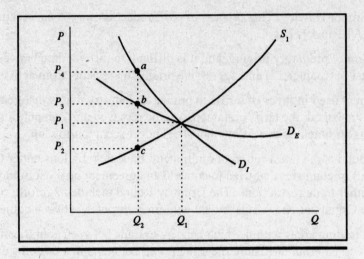

Figure 19.4

Assume that the export supply curve is S_1. Import demand curve D_E is relatively more elastic than import demand curve D_I. Further, assume that free trade equilibrium is at P_1 and Q_1. If the quota allows imports of only Q_2, the quota holder will purchase this quantity from foreign suppliers for P_2. The price at which the quota holder sells the imports to domestic consumers depends on the slope of the demand curve. Clearly, the quota holder can get a higher price if market demand is D_I. The revenue earned by the quota in this case is shown by area P_4P_2ca, as opposed to P_3P_2cb, when demand is based on D_E. Thus, quota holders would like to face relatively inelastic import demand functions.

ANSWERS TO THE CHAPTER TEST

1. a

2. b

3. c

4. d

5. d

6. c

7. a

8. d

9. b

10. c

11. d

12. a

13. d

14. a

15. c

16. c

17. b

18. b
19. b
20. d

CHAPTER 20

Transition Economies

CHAPTER OVERVIEW

The demise of communism, exemplified by the tearing down of the Berlin Wall, the reunification of Germany, and the breakup of the Soviet Union, is one of the major events of the twentieth century. The emergence of market economies in China, Eastern Europe, and the former Soviet Union is of similar importance. In this chapter, we study these countries, called transition economies. We first learn about how centrally planned economies operate. We then study different paths that countries can follow as they make the transition to a market economy and see how economic reform has actually worked in practice. The success of these transition economies is perhaps the most important economic issue facing the world today, not only for themselves but also for the United States, Europe, and Japan.

CHAPTER REVIEW

1. *Transition economies* are those countries that are making the transition from central planning or tight government control to an economy based much more on markets and freely determined prices. These include China, Eastern Europe, and the republics of the former Soviet Union.

2. In a market economy, also called **capitalism**, individuals own the capital—factories, farms, and machines—and decisions about production and employment are decentralized. In contrast, **socialism** is an economic system in which the government owns the capital and decisions regarding the economy are made by those who run the government as part of a central plan. **Communism** is a situation in which all the people of the country *collectively* own the capital without direct government ownership. While the former Soviet Union was called a communist country, its economic system was socialism.

3. The former Soviet Union operated under a system of central planning, through which government commands determined what was produced. Private firms were taken over by the government, in a process called **nationalization**. The state planning commission, called **Gosplan**, established **five-year plans** that stipulated **production targets** for the economy. Production of most industrial and agricultural goods took place at **state enterprises** and **collectivized farms**, business firms and farms that were owned and controlled by the government. Prices for individual goods were also controlled by the government. These were rarely set at levels that would equate the quantity supplied with the quantity demanded, with resultant shortages and surpluses. Central planning in China followed a similar pattern.

4. Reform of the central planning system in the Soviet Union began in 1985, when Mikhail Gorbachev became the leader of the Communist party. The process of reform began with **perestroika**, which translates as "restructuring." For example, enterprise managers were to be more accountable for their actions through worker and public criticism. Following the resignation of Gorbachev and the breakup of the Soviet Union in 1991, Boris Yeltsin, the President of Russia, disbanded central planning and began to enact more comprehensive reforms.

5. The goals of economic reform are simply the essential ingredients of a market economy. Prices must be freed and determined by competitive markets. A legal system must be established to specify property rights and enforce contracts. Freedom to trade at home and abroad is needed to

realize economic efficiencies. A monetary system and a system of tax collections must be put into place.

6. How a centrally planned economy should make the transition to a market economy is more controversial than the ultimate goals of economic reform. A major question is how fast the transition should be. The alternatives are **shock therapy**, in which all the elements of the market economy are put in place at once, and **gradualism**, in which the reforms are phased in slowly.

7. **Privatization** is the process by which existing state enterprises are sold by the government, or privatized, and new private firms are allowed to start up. This process is necessary in order for a market economy to succeed.

ZEROING IN

1. How has economic reform worked in practice? For the countries of Eastern Europe and the republics of the former Soviet Union, the transition was initially difficult. Most countries had deep recession, and for some the decline in real GDP was comparable to that of the United States during the Great Depression.

2. Following the initial transition, many of these countries have seen improved economic performance, but their experiences have not been monolithic. While the countries of Eastern Europe have performed better than Russia and the republics of the former Soviet Union, even the latter have grown on average by about 4 percent per year over the last decade.

3. Poland was the first country in Eastern Europe to attempt a transition to a market economy, with a reform program underway at the beginning of 1990. It is interesting to look at the Polish experience in more detail, for it may serve as a guide to the future prospects of other countries.

    a. The Polish stabilization program has several aspects. The government budget deficit was reduced sharply and most prices were deregulated. These reforms were instituted quickly, making Poland an example of the shock therapy approach to economic reform. Another important aspect of the Polish stabilization program involves the privatization of state enterprises. This part of the Polish reform program was instituted gradually.

    b. The most dramatic effect of the stabilization program was on inflation, which declined from an average of 420 percent in 1989 and 1990 to 25 percent in 1992. The cost of bringing down inflation can be seen by the decline in real GDP, which fell by 12 percent in 1990 and 7 percent in 1991. By 1992, however, real GDP had stopped falling. Economic growth was 6 percent by 1994, and remained strong, with a minor slowdown in 2001-2002, through 2004.

4. China has been a remarkable success story, averaging 8.3 percent growth per year over the last decade. Market reform in China began in 1978, much earlier than in the former Soviet Union. In the agricultural sector, where the reforms occurred first, the growth rate of production has doubled since 1978. In the mid-1980s, reform spread to the industrial sector, and GDP growth increased rapidly. China has also reduced restrictions on foreign trade.

ACTIVE REVIEW

Fill-In Questions

1. _____ are those countries that are making the transition from central planning or tight government control to a market-based economy.

2. A market economy is also called _____.

3. _____ is an economic system in which the government owns the capital.

4. _____ is an economic system in which all the people of the country own the capital.

5. Under a system of _____, the government determines what is produced.

6. The state planning commission of the former Soviet Union was called _____.

7. In the former Soviet Union, Gosplan established _____.

8. Five-year plans in the former Soviet Union stipulated _____ for the economy.

9. Production of most industrial goods in the former Soviet Union took place at _____.

10. Production of most agricultural goods in the former Soviet Union took place at _____.

11. The process of reform in the former Soviet Union began with _____, which translates as "restructuring."

12. The goals of economic reform are to establish the essential ingredients of a(n) _____ economy.

13. Two alternative paths for making the transition to a market economy are _____ and _____.

14. _____ is the process by which existing state enterprises are sold by the government.

15. _____ was the first country in Eastern Europe to attempt a transition to a market economy.

True-False Questions

1. T F Transition economies are those countries that are adopting central planning.

2. T F Russia is an example of a transition economy.

3. T F Poland is an example of a transition economy.

4. T F Socialism is an economic system in which the government owns the capital.

5. T F Capitalism is an economic system in which the government owns the capital.

6. T F The economic system of the former Soviet Union was communism.

7. T F In the former Soviet Union, government commands determined what was produced.

8. T F Central planning in the Soviet Union was disbanded in 1985.

9. T F The ultimate goals of economic reform are not a matter of much controversy.

10. T F In order for a centrally planned economy to make the transition to a market economy, the reforms need to be phased in slowly.

11. T F Economic reform can succeed without privatization.

12. T F Economic reform in the countries of Eastern Europe and the former Soviet Union has been relatively painless.

13. T F Countries of Eastern Europe have grown faster during the last decade than Russia and the republics of the former Soviet Union.

14. T F Market reform in China began later than in the former Soviet Union.

15. T   F   Economic growth in China has been slow during the last decade.

Short-Answer Questions

1. What are transition economies?

2. Which countries are classified as transition economies?

3. What is socialism?

4. Where did production of most goods in the former Soviet Union take place?

5. Why were there often shortages and surpluses of goods in the former Soviet Union?

6. How were production targets set for the economy in the former Soviet Union?

7. What was perestroika?

8. What are the goals of economic reform?

9. What are the alternative paths that a centrally planned economy can follow in order to make the transition to a market economy?

10. What is privatization?

11. What aspects of the Polish stabilization program were instituted quickly?

12. What aspect of the Polish stabilization program was instituted more gradually?

13. What happened to inflation during the Polish stabilization program?

14. What happened to real GDP during the Polish stabilization program?

15. What happened to economic growth in China following market reform?

16. Whose writings contributed to the rejection of capitalism in Russia, China, and Eastern Europe in the twentieth century? (Hint: See Economics in Action—Starting a Revolution.)

WORKING IT OUT

1. Analyzing economic performance during a transition from central planning is in some ways different from and in some ways the same as evaluating the performance of a market economy.

    a. A key element in macroeconomic analysis for the United States is the monetary policy rule that the Fed increases the interest rate when inflation rises. For the countries of Eastern Europe and the former Soviet Union, the policy rule is very different. During the past few years, government budget deficits have been very large. These deficits have been too large to finance through borrowing, and central banks have been forced to accelerate money growth in order to finance the deficits. With prices freed from central control, inflation has skyrocketed. The link between government budget deficits and inflation is much tighter for these countries than for the United States.

    b. The magnitude of the inflation and recession experienced by the countries of Eastern Europe and the former Soviet Union dwarfs the problems faced by the United States. When we discussed the rise of inflation in the United States in the 1970s and its fall in the 1980s, we were talking about an increase from 3 percent to 10 percent, with a subsequent fall back to 3 percent. For Russia and Ukraine, the two largest former republics of the Soviet Union, inflation was over 1,000 percent in 1992. In addition, the decline in real GDP in some of these countries has been nearly as large as the decline in real GDP in the United States during the Great Depression.

2.   The issue of credibility, which we have discussed in the context of the cost of lowering government budget deficits and reducing inflation for the United States, is even more important for countries making a transition from central planning to a market economy.

a.   An important element in our macroeconomic analysis has been the assumption that prices are sticky. For the countries of Eastern Europe and the former Soviet Union, prices, which were suddenly freed from decades of government control, have fluctuated dramatically. If the government's anti-inflation policy is credible, it is possible, at least in theory, for inflation to be brought down at relatively low cost. This appears to be what has occurred in Poland. If the anti-inflation policy is not credible, a large recession will be needed to reduce inflation. While it is too early to evaluate most of the reform programs, this may characterize most of the countries of the former Soviet Union.

b.   Achieving credibility is one argument for a shock therapy program. When all of the elements of a market economy are put in place at once, there is no doubt about the government's commitment to reform. With a gradualist approach, where the reforms are phased in slowly, you are never sure if the next step toward reform will actually occur.

Worked Problems

1.   Consider two transition economies characterized by the following data:

	Country A		Country B	
Year	Real GDP Growth	Inflation	Real GDP Growth	Inflation
2001	0	100	0	100
2002	−20	90	−5	95
2003	−15	20	−7	90
2004	−1	10	−9	85
2005	1	10	−7	80

Both real GDP growth and inflation are measured in percent per year. Which of these countries is characterized by a policy of shock therapy, and which is an example of a policy of gradualism?

Answer

Country A is characterized by a policy of shock therapy. There is a very large recession, but inflation is brought down relatively quickly. Country B is an example of a policy of gradualism. The recession is smaller, but inflation is brought down only very slowly.

2.   Consider two transition economies characterized by the following data:

	Country A		Country B	
Year	Real GDP Growth	Inflation	Real GDP Growth	Inflation
2001	0	100	0	100
2002	−30	90	−15	90
2003	−25	20	−10	20
2004	−5	10	0	10
2005	0	10	1	10

Both real GDP growth and inflation are measured in percent per year. Both countries have instituted shock therapy reform programs. Which government has greater credibility?

Answer

With credibility, inflation can be brought down at lower cost. Inflation falls at the same rate in the two countries, but the recession is more severe in country A than in country B. Therefore, the government of country B has greater credibility.

PRACTICE PROBLEMS

1. Consider two transition economies characterized by the following data:

Year	Country A		Country B	
	Real GDP Growth	Inflation	Real GDP Growth	Inflation
2001	0	100	0	100
2002	−10	90	−25	95
2003	−15	87	−30	90
2004	−15	83	−9	20
2005	−12	80	−2	10

Both real GDP growth and inflation are measured in percent per year. Which of these countries is characterized by a policy of shock therapy, and which is an example of a policy of gradualism?

2. Consider two transition economies characterized by the following data:

Year	Country A		Country B	
	Real GDP Growth	Inflation	Real GDP Growth	Inflation
2001	0	100	0	100
2002	−40	90	−35	95
2003	−10	15	−30	90
2004	0	5	−5	15
2005	2	5	−1	15

Both real GDP growth and inflation are measured in percent per year. Are these two countries characterized by policies of shock therapy or by policies of gradualism?

3. Consider two transition economies characterized by the following data:

Year	Country A		Country B	
	Real GDP Growth	Inflation	Real GDP Growth	Inflation
2001	0	100	0	100
2002	−20	95	−35	95
2003	−15	30	−30	30
2004	−2	10	−20	10
2005	−1	10	−10	10

Both real GDP growth and inflation are measured in percent per year. Both countries have instituted shock therapy reform programs. Which government has greater credibility?

4. Consider two transition economies characterized by the following data:

Year	Country A		Country B	
	Real GDP Growth	**Inflation**	**Real GDP Growth**	**Inflation**
2001	0	100	0	100
2002	–4	95	–6	95
2003	–6	90	–8	90
2004	–4	85	–6	85
2005	–3	80	–5	80

Both real GDP growth and inflation are measured in percent per year. Both countries have instituted gradualist reform programs. Which government has greater credibility?

CHAPTER TEST

1.   A market economy in which decisions about production and employment are decentralized and individuals own the factories, farms, and machines is called

   a.   socialism.
   b.   capitalism.
   c.   communism.
   d.   central planning.

2.   Which of the following countries is *not* classified as a transition economy?

   a.   Hungary
   b.   Romania
   c.   Germany
   d.   Bulgaria

3.   An economic system in which the government owns the capital and decisions regarding the economy are made as part of a central plan is called

   a.   socialism.
   b.   capitalism.
   c.   communism.
   d.   a market economy.

4.   An economic system in which all the people of the country own the capital is called

   a.   socialism.
   b.   capitalism.
   c.   communism.
   d.   a market economy.

5.   Which of the following is *not* one of the essential ingredients of a market economy?

   a.   Prices must be freed and determined by competitive markets.
   b.   A legal system must be established to specify property rights and enforce contracts.
   c.   A monetary system and a system of tax collections must be put in place.
   d.   Protectionist trade policies should be followed.

6.   The state planning commission of the former Soviet Union was called

   a.   Gosplan.
   b.   central planning.
   c.   perestroika.
   d.   Gorbachev.

7. The process by which existing state enterprises are sold by the government and new private firms are allowed to start up is called
   a. gradualism.
   b. shock therapy.
   c. privatization.
   d. restructuring.

8. The process of reform in the former Soviet Union began with
   a. Gosplan.
   b. central planning.
   c. privatization.
   d. perestroika.

9. A transition to a market economy, when the reforms are phased in slowly, is called
   a. gradualism.
   b. shock therapy.
   c. Gosplan.
   d. perestroika.

10. Which of the following countries was the first in Eastern Europe to attempt a transition to a market economy?
    a. Hungary
    b. Poland
    c. Romania
    d. Bulgaria

11. What happened to real GDP during the Polish stabilization program in 1994?
    a. Real GDP rose by 6 percent.
    b. Real GDP rose by 12 percent.
    c. Real GDP declined by 7 percent.
    d. Real GDP did not change.

12. What happened to inflation in Poland between 1990 and 1992?
    a. Inflation declined from 42 percent to 25 percent.
    b. Inflation rose from 25 percent to 42 percent.
    c. Inflation declined from 420 percent to 25 percent.
    d. Inflation was unchanged.

13. Which of the following was *not* one of the aspects of the Polish stabilization program?
    a. The government budget deficit was reduced sharply.
    b. State enterprises were privatized.
    c. The government budget deficit was financed through borrowing.
    d. Most prices were deregulated.

14. Which of the following does *not* characterize market reform in China?
    a. Reform in China first occurred in the agricultural sector.
    b. Reform in China began after reform in the former Soviet Union.
    c. Restrictions on foreign trade have been reduced.
    d. Inflation has been a problem.

15. Following market reform in China, GDP growth
    a. increased rapidly.
    b. increased slowly.

c. decreased rapidly.

d. decreased slowly.

16. Which of the following was *not* one of the difficulties that the countries of Eastern Europe and the republics of the former Soviet Union experienced during the transition?

a. High inflation

b. Deep recession

c. Rising government budget deficits

d. Deflation

17. For the countries of Eastern Europe and the former Soviet Union, central banks have financed government budget deficits by

a. borrowing.

b. accelerating money growth.

c. increasing the interest rate.

d. spending more.

18. In Russia, in 1992, inflation was over

a. 5 percent.

b. 50 percent.

c. 1,000 percent.

d. 500 percent.

Use the following table for questions 19 and 20.

Year	Country A		Country B	
	Real GDP Growth	Inflation	Real GDP Growth	Inflation
2001	0	100	0	100
2002	−25	95	−6	95
2003	−20	25	−8	90
2004	−4	8	−6	85
2005	2	8	−5	80

19. Which of these countries is (are) characterized by a policy of gradualism?

a. Country A

b. Country B

c. Neither country A nor country B

d. Both country A and country B

20. Which of these countries experienced the largest recession?

a. Country A

b. Country B

c. The recessions were equally severe.

d. Not enough information to tell

ANSWERS TO THE REVIEW QUESTIONS

Fill-In Questions

1. Transition economies

2. capitalism

3. Socialism

4. Communism

5. central planning

6. Gosplan

7. five-year plans

8. production targets

9. state enterprises

10. collectivized farms

11. perestroika

12. market

13. shock therapy; gradualism

14. Privatization

15. Poland

True-False Questions

1. **False**. Transition economies are those countries that are making the transition from central planning to an economy based much more on markets.

2. **True**. Russia is one of the republics of the former Soviet Union.

3. **True**. Poland is a formally centrally planned economy in Eastern Europe.

4. **True**. Under socialism, the government owns the capital and decisions regarding the economy are made by those who run the government as part of a central plan.

5. **False**. Under capitalism, individuals own the capital.

6. **False**. Although the former Soviet Union was called a communist country, its economic system was socialism.

7. **True**. The former Soviet Union operated under a system of central planning.

8. **False**. Although economic reform began in 1985, central planning was not disbanded until after the breakup of the Soviet Union in 1991.

9. **True**. The goals of economic reform, the essential ingredients of a market economy, are widely agreed upon.

10. **False**. An alternative is to put all of the elements of a market economy in place at once.

11. **False**. Privatization is necessary if a market economy is to succeed.

12. **False**. The transition has been difficult. Most countries initially experienced high inflation and deep recession.

13. **True**. Countries such as Hungary and Poland have grown faster than the countries that comprised the former Soviet Union.

14. **False**. Market reform in China began in 1978, much earlier than in the former Soviet Union.

15. **False**. Economic growth in China has been very rapid in the last decade.

Short-Answer Questions

1. Transition economies are those countries that are making the transition from central planning or tight government control to an economy based much more on markets and freely determined prices.

2. Transition economies include China, Eastern Europe, and the republics of the former Soviet Union.

3. Socialism is an economic system in which the government owns the capital and decisions regarding the economy are made as part of a central plan.

4. Production of most goods took place at state enterprises and collectivized farms.

5. Prices for individual goods, which were controlled by the government, were rarely set at levels that would equate the quantity supplied with the quantity demanded.

6. Gosplan, the state planning commission, established five-year plans that stipulated production targets for the economy.

7. Perestroika, which translates as "restructuring," was the beginning of the process of reform in the former Soviet Union.

8. The goals of economic reform are freely determined prices, property rights and incentives, competitive markets, freedom to trade at home and abroad, a role for government in establishing monetary and fiscal policy, and a role for nongovernment organizations.

9. The alternative paths are shock therapy, in which all the elements of the market economy are put in place at once, and gradualism, in which the reforms are phased in slowly.

10. Privatization is the process by which existing state enterprises are sold by the government and new private firms are allowed to start up.

11. The government budget deficit was reduced sharply and most prices were deregulated quickly.

12. Privatization of state enterprises is the aspect of the Polish stabilization program that was instituted more slowly.

13. Inflation fell dramatically in Poland between 1990 and 1992.

14. Real GDP in Poland declined sharply in 1990 and 1991, but rose since 1994.

15. China has been a remarkable success story, experiencing very rapid economic growth.

16. The writings of Karl Marx, an economist and social philosopher, played a key role in the rejection of markets in favor of socialism in Russia, China, and Eastern Europe.

SOLUTIONS TO THE PRACTICE PROBLEMS

1. Country A is an example of gradualism, whereas country B is characterized by shock therapy.

2. Both country A and country B are examples of shock therapy.

3. The government of country A has greater credibility.

4. The government of country A has greater credibility.

ANSWERS TO THE CHAPTER TEST

1. b

2.   c
3.   a
4.   c
5.   d
6.   a
7.   c
8.   d
9.   a
10. b
11. a
12. c
13. c
14. b
15. a
16. d
17. b
18. c
19. b
20. a

PART 4

Sample Test (Chapters 17–20): Trade and Global Markets

1. If the spread of technology is not difficult, then economic growth theory predicts
   a. that only countries with low levels of income per capita will grow.
   b. that only countries with high levels of income per capita will grow.
   c. that countries with high levels of income per capital will grow faster than countries with low levels of income per capita.
   d. that countries with high levels of income per capital will grow more slowly than countries with low levels of income per capita.

   Use Figure 1 for question 2.

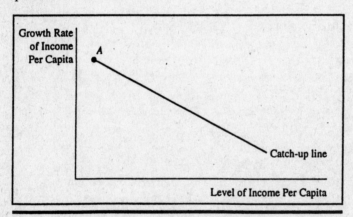

Figure 1

2. A country located at point A on the catch-up line in Figure 1 is a
   a. rich country enjoying rapid growth.
   b. rich country experiencing a slow rate of growth.
   c. poor country enjoying rapid growth.
   d. poor country experiencing a slow rate of growth.

3. The emergence of informal sectors in developing countries is due to
   a. the low income of the population.
   b. the lack of industrial base.
   c. the emergence of a service economy.
   d. heavy restrictions on business.

4. If a U.S. firm invests in a 15 percent ownership of a firm in France, the investment is referred to as
   a. foreign direct investment.
   b. foreign indirect investment.
   c. portfolio investment.
   d. capital investment.

5. The catch-up phenomenon will not occur if there are obstacles to

   a. increasing the money supply and raising the level of capital per worker.
   b. the spread of technology and raising the level of capital per worker.
   c. increasing the money supply and lowering the level of capital per worker.
   d. the spread of technology and lowering the level of capital per worker.

6. Trade between countries can be explained by

   a. absolute advantage only.
   b. the Heckscher-Ohlin model only.
   c. Arrow's impossibility theorem.
   d. comparative advantage.
   e. tides.

7. According to the Heckscher-Ohlin model, a country will export those goods that are

   a. produced most intensively with its least abundant resource.
   b. produced most intensively with its most abundant resource.
   c. capital-intensive.
   d. produced the least intensively with its most abundant resource.
   e. produced the least intensively with its least abundant resource.

8. Interindustry trade is defined as

   a. trade limited to a small group of trading partners.
   b. trade without any trade restrictions.
   c. trade between countries in goods from different industries.
   d. trade between countries in goods from the same or similar industries.
   e. trade primarily due to economies of scale.

9. International trade based on comparative advantage achieved through differences in capital per worker will tend to

   a. equalize wages in different countries.
   b. widen the wage gap in different countries.
   c. lower wages for technological jobs in high-productivity countries.
   d. cancel out any equalizing trends in different countries.

10. Even though transition to free trade is beneficial in the long run, it can cause problems in the short run, unless phase out of restrictions is

    a. immediate.
    b. tempered by the placement of new restrictions.
    c. slow.
    d. limited to nonmanufacturing industries.

11. The use of tariffs to give domestic industries time to develop is

    a. the national security argument for trade barriers.
    b. the infant industry argument for trade barriers.
    c. required for product differentiation to occur.
    d. supported under the Heckscher-Ohlin model.
    e. strategic trade policy.

12. Governments attempt to influence trade with

    a. tariffs.
    b. quotas.
    c. procurement regulations.
    d. VRAs.
    e. All of the above.

13. We can measure the impact of trade restrictions on an economy by the deadweight

    a. loss caused by the increase in quantity.

    b.   gain caused by the reduction in quantity.

    c.   loss caused by the reduction in quantity.

    d.   gain caused by the increase in quantity.

14.   Those who benefit from protection

    a.   lobby their governmental representatives heavily.

    b.   do not lobby their governmental representatives.

    c.   are indifferent toward their governmental representatives.

    d.   are more diffuse and have less power.

15.   A possible reason for a government to deviate from free trade is

    a.   to promote a strategic trade policy when domestic firms have a monopoly or considerable market power.

    b.   to retaliate against another country's trade restrictions.

    c.   to encourage development of an infant industry by protecting it from imports.

    d.   national security.

    e.   All of the above.

16.   Transition economies are countries making the transition from

    a.   central planning or tight government control to an economy based much more on markets and freely determined prices.

    b.   markets and freely determined prices to an economy based much more on central planning or tight government control.

    c.   free trade to managed trade.

    d.   managed trade to free trade.

17.   Which of the following is *not* one of the goals of economic reform?

    a.   Prices must be freed and determined by competitive markets.

    b.   A legal system must be established to specify property rights and enforce contracts.

    c.   Decisions about production and employment must be centralized.

    d.   A monetary system and a system of tax collections must be put into place.

18.   An economic system in which the government owns the capital and decisions regarding the economy are made as part of a central plan is called

    a.   socialism.

    b.   capitalism.

    c.   communism.

    d.   a market economy.

19.   A communist system is *best* described as an economic system where

    a.   the government owns the land and the capital and makes decisions about production and employment.

    b.   the government is involved in the economy because of market failures.

    c.   the people of a country collectively own the land and capital and make decisions about production and employment.

    d.   prices are determined in a decentralized fashion.

20.   Perestroika was a(n)

    a.   attempt by the Soviet Union to establish free trade.

    b.   attempt by the Soviet Union to reform centralized planning.

    c.   attempt by the Soviet Union to make its economic system more centralized.

    d.   plan for dismembering the Soviet Union.

ANSWERS TO THE SAMPLE TEST

1. d
2. c
3. d
4. a
5. b
6. d
7. b
8. c
9. a
10. c
11. b
12. e
13. c
14. a
15. e
16. a
17. c
18. a
19. c
20. b